Her Neighbor's Wife

POLITICS AND CULTURE IN MODERN AMERICA

Series Editors:
Margot Canaday, Glenda Gilmore, Matthew Lassiter, Stephen Pitti, Thomas J. Sugrue

Volumes in the series narrate and analyze political and social change in the broadest dimensions from 1865 to the present, including ideas about the ways people have sought and wielded power in the public sphere and the language and institutions of politics at all levels—local, national, and transnational. The series is motivated by a desire to reverse the fragmentation of modern U.S. history and to encourage synthetic perspectives on social movements and the state, on gender, race, and labor, and on intellectual history and popular culture.

Her Neighbor's Wife

A HISTORY OF LESBIAN
DESIRE WITHIN MARRIAGE

Lauren Jae Gutterman

PENN

UNIVERSITY OF PENNSYLVANIA PRESS

PHILADELPHIA

Published by
University of Pennsylvania Press
Philadelphia, Pennsylvania 19104-4112
www.upenn.edu/pennpress

Printed in the United States of America
on acid-free paper

10 9 8 7 6 5 4 3 2 1

A Cataloging-in-Publication record is available from the Library of Congress
ISBN 978-0-8122-5174-6

CONTENTS

Introduction

IT WAS HALLOWEEN NIGHT, 1961, in college-town Champaign, Illinois, but Mrs. Alma Routsong was not carving pumpkins. With her four daughters momentarily out of the way, likely out trick-or-treating with their father, Alma was sitting down to write at a small card table in the bedroom of her lover, Betty Deran. Alma was beginning a secret diary. An established novelist and an avid diarist, Alma wrote nearly every day in her journals, but some things were too private even to be recorded there: namely, her love affair with Betty. "I switch to this book so I can say what I want to," Alma began. "Betty says she will get me a lockbox to keep it in, because she too wants me to write about us, and has many times, she says, in reading an entry for some special day been disappointed by the flatness of it, the non-mention of the specialness, so we are prepared for the risks and delights of this record." By October, Alma's affair with Betty was roughly four months old, and their relationship had grown more serious and more consuming than either woman could have expected. Alma's secret diary provided her with a venue in which she could, like a schoolgirl, gush over Betty's intelligence, her dark hair, and her ease with people. It also allowed Alma to describe and revel in their striking physical passion.[1]

Yet despite Alma's reference to "risks," and the significant measures she took to protect her diary, Alma's affair with Betty was not exactly a secret. The women's lives were remarkably intertwined, and their relationship had unfolded within plain sight of their friends and family. Betty, an economist, and Alma's husband, Bruce, a veterinary science professor, both worked for the University of Illinois. The women met, not at a lesbian bar in a big city, but at their local Unitarian Church. In fact, a mutual friend introduced Alma and Betty at coffee hour one Sunday in the summer of 1961. "I just know you two ladies are going to love each other!" she declared.[2] Alma and Betty had more in common than their friend suspected; each had long recognized and struggled with her enduring sexual attraction to other women. The women quickly became friends and, despite Betty's reluctance to become involved in a lesbian relationship, they soon fell in love. Sometime afterward, Alma informed Bruce about her affair, but it likely came as little surprise. Alma had been open with her husband about her feelings for women throughout their marriage, and Bruce was remarkably accepting of her relationship with Betty. Perhaps he felt relieved that Betty had finally been able to pull Alma out of years of depression, or perhaps he was just thankful that their affair had made it easier for him to pursue his own extramarital romance.[3]

Alma initially planned to balance her marriage and her lesbian relationship until her youngest daughter reached eighteen, and if Betty had been willing to remain in Illinois that may well have happened.[4] Instead, as it turned out, Betty accepted a job at the US Treasury Department, forcing Alma to make a choice. Confronted with the possibility of resuming her previous, unhappy existence, Alma decided to divorce, to move with Betty to Washington, DC, and—despite the pain it caused her—to leave her four daughters behind (Figure 1). Alma and Betty's new life together was not easy. Because of her homosexuality, Betty was denied security clearance by the Federal Bureau of Investigation, she lost her position, and the couple moved yet again, this time to New York City's Greenwich Village.[5] There Alma wrote her third and most famous novel, *A Place for Us* (1969), which she published under the pseudonym Isabel Miller. *A Place for Us*, later retitled *Patience and Sarah*, tells the story of two women in nineteenth-century New England who fall in love and leave their families to begin a new life together. Alma could not have known it at the time, but scholars would one day point to her novel as marking a transformation in popular representations of lesbian life, the beginning of a new, affirming lesbian literature.[6]

This book traces the stories of women like Alma from the post–World War II period through the 1980s. Many—if not most—women who experienced same-sex desires during these years were married to men at some point, yet this significant population has been neglected in histories of gay and lesbian life, as well as in histories of marriage and the family. Just as Alma's relationship with Betty was not truly a secret, the history of wives who desired women has never been entirely hidden: letters, diaries, divorce records, and oral history interviews have long documented the experiences of wives who desired women. But contemporary political concerns have

Figure 1. Alma Routsong and her family in a press photo for her novel *Round Shape,* 1959. Curt Beamer for the *News-Gazette.* From the Isabel Miller Papers, Sophia Smith Collection, Smith College Libraries.

profoundly shaped the telling and recording of LGBT (lesbian, gay, bisexual, and transgender) history. Historians of homosexuality have been most concerned with describing the lives of those who identified publicly as gay or lesbian, with documenting urban gay and lesbian cultures, and with tracing the roots of the modern LGBT movement. So, while many scholars have recognized the great number of women who divorced and built new lesbian lives in the 1970s, the ways in which these same women were able to act on their same-sex desires *within* marriage have attracted much less attention.[7]

By drawing on a variety of different sources, I have gathered a group of more than three hundred wives who desired women. One-third of these women's stories come from the correspondence files of Del Martin and Phyllis Lyon, longtime lesbian activists who helped to found the Daughters of Bilitis (DOB), the nation's first lesbian rights group, in San Francisco in 1955. Dating from the 1950s through the 1980s, these letters provide an uneven source base. Some married women corresponded with Martin and Lyon for years and wrote lengthy letters describing their lives in great detail. Others dashed off brief one-time notes—confirming their membership or terminating their subscription to the DOB's magazine—that convey little specific personal information, but nonetheless tell us something about how wives navigated their desires for other women. In addition to this correspondence, I use letters that married women wrote to other gay, lesbian, and bisexual groups and leaders, legal records from divorce and child custody cases, as well as the personal papers and diaries of a few established writers.

Oral history interviews complement these archival sources. Between 2010 and 2016, I conducted twenty-nine oral history interviews with once or currently married women, their children, or their lovers.[8] I use sixty additional interviews that other researchers conducted between the 1970s and the early 2000s.[9] Oral history interviews provide a vital resource for LGBT history which is often inaccessible within traditional archival collections. Yet oral histories, like all historical sources, do not provide a simple window into the past.[10] Many oral history interviews with lesbian and bisexual women conform closely to a standard coming out narrative.[11] Oral history narrators typically describe overcoming ignorance and adversity to find solace, community, and an awakened consciousness. In the accounts of once-married lesbian-identified oral history narrators, in particular, the decisions to divorce and identify publicly as lesbian often appear as foregone conclusions.[12] In analyzing these sources, then, I try to remain attuned to the ways that hindsight and the coming out narrative affect such women's stories, shutting down other ways they might have understood their sexuality or their life choices at the time.

Although basic demographic information is not available for all the women who appear in this book, it is possible to draw a rough biographical sketch of this group. Of those women who stated or gave clues as to their age, the majority—68 percent—were born between 1925 and 1946; less than a third were born between 1946 and 1964. *Her Neighbor's Wife* is thus primarily a story about the women who created the baby boom, women who married and started families in the late 1940s, 1950s, and early 1960s. It is also, to a lesser extent, a story about their daughters, the baby boomers themselves, particularly those who were born in the first half of their generational cohort. This is a geographically diverse group: 27 percent of the wives I have identified lived in New England and the mid-Atlantic states; 26 percent lived in the West and Northwest; 25 percent lived in the Midwest; and 17 percent lived in the South and Southwest. While some of these women lived in or near major cities such as New York or San Francisco, they were more likely to be found in smaller cities, towns, suburbs, and, to a limited extent, rural areas across the nation.

Race and class are somewhat harder to identify. Most women did not specify their race or ethnicity in letters they wrote to lesbian leaders or organizations. Nonetheless, of those women whose race is clear, 81 percent were white, a statistic which reflects both the whiteness of the earliest gay and lesbian activist groups and the whiteness of most LGBT oral history collections. Throughout this book, I pay attention to the ways that racial privilege structured the experiences of these white women, but the story recounted here is not theirs alone. There are at least sixteen African American women, five Latina women, two Asian women, one woman of Middle Eastern descent, and three multiracial women. Their stories, though limited in number, allow me to point to commonalities and differences among wives of different races. Identifying women's class status is also challenging. Letters often fail to provide clues about their authors' income or education, while oral history interviews demonstrate how dramatically many women's class status changed over time. Nevertheless, few of the women here either enjoyed exceptional affluence or endured lifelong poverty. Most would probably have labeled themselves "middle class," but this broad and ambiguous category included women with a wide range of educational experiences, income levels, and employment histories. Many of the women described here worked in female-dominated professions such as nursing and teaching, but there are also small-business owners, professors, waitresses, industrial workers, and, of course, housewives.

These wives differ in terms of their sexual experiences and their life paths. Because lesbian oral history projects privilege the stories of those women who eventually divorced and began new lives, such stories dominate this book. Yet some women remained married for good, and in many cases it is simply impossible to know what paths these women's lives took. Some wives likely never had a sexual relationship with another woman, while others had many. Some were able to combine marriage and same-sex affairs for years, while others had only brief relationships. Still, despite their differences, each of the women described here chose to act on her desire for women in some way: by confessing an attraction to a fellow neighborhood mom, writing a letter to the DOB, visiting a lesbian bar, or carrying on an "open" marriage with her husband. As the lesbian poet and theorist Adrienne Rich—herself a once-married woman and mother of three—noted in her pathbreaking article "Compulsory Heterosexuality and Lesbian Existence," "We may have faithfully or ambivalently obeyed the institution [of marriage], but our feelings—and our sensuality—have not been tamed or contained within it."[13] They may have felt quite alone, but the women in this study were knitted together in a shared attempt to reconcile their marriages with their emotional and erotic attraction to women.

This book focuses on the years between 1945 and 1989 to chart the ways the gay liberation and lesbian feminist movements and the "no-fault" divorce revolution of the late 1960s and 1970s transformed the lives of wives who desired women. It is important to acknowledge, however, that this time line is somewhat artificial. The history of wives who desired women has no clear beginning or end. Alma Routsong's letters and diaries, in fact, place her in a lineage of wives who desired women that stretches both backward and forward in time. Beginning in high school, Alma began a decades-long correspondence with the acclaimed novelist Dorothy Baker, born in 1907. As Alma would discover, Dorothy, a wife and mother of two, carried on a relationship with another woman for more than thirty years until her death in the late 1960s. When Alma divorced and moved to DC with Betty, Dorothy understood Alma's decision, but she denied that such a choice was possible for herself.[14] Decades later, in 1991, Alma's eldest daughter, Natalie, left her husband for her lover, Sue. Though Alma supported Natalie in doing so, she was also frustrated that her daughter seemed to be reliving her life story. "I'd worked in gay liberation to make it easier on my kids," Alma wrote in her diary that year, "so they wouldn't have to duplicate my life. Why did Nat have to wait till she had kids to do this?"[15] As Alma's diary entry suggests, there were similarities between Natalie's life and her own. But the social and cultural changes of the 1970s did alter the ways in which wives who desired women made sense of their sexuality and organized their intimate relationships. In the early 1990s, Natalie debated whether or not she *should* leave her marriage, but she never doubted that she *could*.

Her Neighbor's Wife opens at the end of World War II, when urban gay and lesbian communities were growing, government policing of homosexuals was becoming more intense, and the pressure to marry was pervasive. In the two decades that followed, the wives in this study were entering marriages and starting families, despite any consciousness they may have had of feelings for other women. While we might assume that these women became trapped in unhappy marriages, unable to act on their feelings for women and cut off from the broader gay and lesbian world, this was not the case. One of this book's central goals is to reveal the surprising extent to which wives at midcentury were able to engage in sexual relationships with other women, to balance those relationships with marriage, and to participate, if only remotely, in an emerging gay and lesbian movement. Doing so requires that we shift our gaze away from urban gay and lesbian communities toward women's homes and the geography of their everyday lives: the workplace, the church, and the local neighborhood.[16] As we will see, while some wives engaged in sexual relationships with unmarried, lesbian-identified women, most wives' affairs tended to evolve from close friendships with other wives and mothers who were well integrated into their family lives. Such wives' experiences call into question the assumed straightness of the nuclear family home, while broadening the imagined boundaries of the gay and lesbian world far beyond urban centers.[17]

In the 1950s and 1960s, wives who engaged in lesbian relationships close to home, within the context of their local communities, experienced a type of constrained freedom. Certainly, many of these women lived in fear that their husbands would discover and become angry about their relationships with other women, and some men did. Some threatened their wives with divorce or responded with violence. Yet far more often, the husbands in this study chose to turn a blind eye to their wives' affairs and waited for them to end. A few men—like Alma's husband, Bruce—even consciously made space for their wives' lesbian relationships within their marriages. Understanding why husbands tended to respond in this way requires a closer look at the culture of postwar marriage. At this moment, marital experts urged husbands and wives *not* to confide in each other emotionally or share their darkest secrets, but rather to avoid marital conflict at all costs and "adjust" to their social roles. Before the late 1960s, when the laws and attitudes governing divorce began to change, divorce was costly, legally challenging, and socially stigmatizing. Many wives *and* their husbands, then, shared a common interest in avoiding a split and making their marriages work.

In the 1970s, wives who desired women became much less likely to balance marriage and lesbian relationships indefinitely as women had in the past. We tend to imagine the gay and lesbian movement as freeing those who privately experienced same-sex desires; and in some ways, this assumption holds true for the many wives who chose to divorce and begin new lesbian lives in this era. But the changes of the 1970s also brought new pressure to bear on wives who desired women. In the postwar period, gay and lesbian activists did not demand that wives choose between marriage and the lesbian community. The leaders of the DOB, for example, invited married women to correspond with them, become members, attend events, and participate in their cause. In the 1970s, however, many lesbian feminists came to see marriage as a central mechanism of women's and homosexuals' oppression, a repressive structure that could be overturned only if women refused to continue building their lives around men. These activists redefined lesbian identity as antithetical to marriage and made separating from husbands and male lovers a precondition of joining the lesbian community. Some wives who desired women happily embraced this ideology and divorced. Yet others now confronted a choice—between marriage and lesbianism—that they did not necessarily have to make before.

Transformations in marriage and divorce in the 1970s also influenced the ways in which wives negotiated their marriages and their same-sex desires. The emergence of no-fault divorce law in 1969, the increasing rate of divorce, and the growing social acceptance of it, made ending marriage an option for women who had never considered it before. At the same time, many husbands and wives began to expect a much greater degree of emotional connection within marriage. Honesty and communication, particularly around matters of sexuality, were now widely considered integral to a "healthy" marital relationship. These changing understandings of marriage, combined with gay and lesbian activists' new political emphasis on "coming out," disrupted the sense of discretion that had enabled many wives and their husbands to avoid divorce. Indeed, even the women in this study who embraced the fads of open, bisexual, and group marriage, which made it possible to balance marriage and same-sex relationships publicly, found that these marital "experiments" tended to remain just that.

It was not until the women in this study arrived in divorce court in significant numbers in the 1970s and 1980s that they began to experience the most intense state repression. To be sure, the limited number of wives who divorced in the postwar era did risk losing child custody and financial support in divorces in which they were proven to be "at fault" for the marriage's end. But some legal and cultural factors worked to the benefit of wives at midcentury, namely the legal preference for placing young children with their mothers and the reluctance of many husbands, lawyers, and judges to discuss homosexuality openly in court. Wives who divorced in the 1970s and 1980s encountered an entirely different legal environment. Fathers' rights activists had challenged the presumption that children should be placed with their mothers; legal reformers had decreased divorced women's chances of receiving alimony or child support; and judges and lawyers had replaced an earlier sense of discretion around homosexuality with a new obsession with the details of lesbian sex. In custody battles of this era, judges went further than they had before in their efforts to limit lesbian mothers' rights, by preventing mothers from participating in gay and lesbian activism or living with their lovers as conditions of receiving custody or visitation rights.

The fact that most wives did not face the full force of the state's ability to punish their homosexuality until the 1970s challenges the accepted trajectory of gay and lesbian history, which portrays the postwar era as the height of antigay government policing. Many historians have shown how state repression created a "closet" after World War II, forcing into hiding the vibrant gay world that had developed in the early twentieth century and expanded during wartime. In doing so, scholars have examined, for example, the police crackdown on gay bars and cruising areas, the Immigration and Naturalization Service's rejection of homosexual immigrants, and the federal government's expulsion of gays and lesbians from the armed forces and the Department of Defense.[18] Yet even in the postwar period women were rarely the focus of this government persecution.[19] "Such tools were deployed against women," as historian Margot Canaday has written, "only as they were more fully incorporated into the arena of first-class citizenship—most visibly, when they were permanently integrated into the military during the early years of the cold war. As women were more completely drawn into citizenship, then, state officials became more focused on lesbianism."[20] That women in the armed forces appeared to have chosen military careers in lieu of marriage only made them more suspicious to military officials, and thus more vulnerable to homophobic attack.

If women were able to avoid the brunt of antigay policing in the public sphere, within the private sphere of marriage and the family women's homosexuality was of greater concern to the state. As historian Alison Lefkovitz has shown, husbands who accused their wives of homosexuality were, in fact, *more* successful in securing fault-based divorces and favorable financial settlements in the postwar period than wives who accused their husbands of the same.[21] A postwar panic around the figure of the menacing lesbian wife within popular culture reflected this gendering of the homosexual threat by portraying lesbians as posing the greatest danger to the nation from within the home and the family. Yet so long as women tended to combine lesbian relationships with marriage in ways that did not disrupt men's access to their sexual, reproductive, or domestic labor, their husbands and the state remained largely unconcerned with their homosexual behavior.

Only after lesbianism had become a viable alternative to marriage did wives' same-sex relationships begin to pose a more significant social threat and warrant a more dramatic state response.[22] Ironically, then, by making lesbianism more visible and more sustainable as a way of life, lesbian feminism exposed wives who desired women to greater state regulation. Gay fathers, like lesbian mothers, also faced significant discrimination in divorce and custody battles of the 1970s and 1980s. But lesbian mothers who dared to divorce and raise children in families without men threatened the gender order in ways that gay fathers did not, by rejecting their subordination within the nuclear family and by denying men access to their bodies. Lesbian mothers and gay fathers, then, were not policed equivalently. While precise numbers are hard to pin down, by all accounts, custody cases involving lesbian mothers significantly outnumbered those of gay men at this time, and lesbian mothers encountered exceptionally intense scrutiny of their sexual behavior in court.[23] In other words, in the 1970s and 1980s family court functioned as a more critical site for the exercise of state power over lesbians than it did for gay men.

Centering on the experiences of wives who desired women thus highlights the ways in which the history of homosexuality has differed for men and women. Histories of homosexuality that focus on men have long overshadowed those about women. While some historians have resisted drawing generalizations about the history of homosexuality from men's lives, too often the history of male homosexuality has come to stand in for the whole. Indeed, in much the same way the category "lesbian" has been subsumed by "gay" or even "queer," women have often been subsumed within a history of male homosexuality. As literary scholar Terry Castle has argued, the lesbian has taken on an "apparitional" cultural and historical presence, and "seldom seemed as accessible, for instance, as her ingratiating twin brother, the male homosexual."[24] As much as I share Castle's sentiment, gay men and lesbians have never been twins. The gender hierarchy has structured men's and women's sexuality differently; homosexual cultures and communities have thus taken disparate—though often overlapping—forms among men and women. As long as gay men's lives and communities continue to serve as the model, we will remain blind to the specific ways that homosexuality's history has unfolded for women.[25]

There is also good reason to suspect that an understanding of lesbian history in the second half of the twentieth century that is drawn from married women's lives is more representative than one drawn from unmarried women's experiences. Many women who came of age in the postwar period believed that becoming a wife and mother was their natural destiny, the key to their personal fulfillment, and their most important responsibility as citizens. Economic inequality also pushed women into marriage, and those without the benefit of a male wage typically struggled to support themselves and their children. Women who escaped these cultural, political, and economic pressures to marry men and raise families were somewhat exceptional. Indeed, in an oral history interview conducted in the 1980s, Alma Routsong's lover, Betty, recalled being one of the few never-married women in their lesbian circle of friends in New York during the 1960s. As she told an interviewer decades later, "lesbians usually have a history of being straight."[26] Moving wives who desired women to the center of our analysis, then, can help us to see how women have negotiated space for same-sex relationships while reckoning directly with the single institution—marriage—that has historically shaped female sexuality the most.

Wives who desired women challenge not only our understanding of the history of homosexuality, but also our conception of marriage, particularly in the postwar period. At the ground level, marriage has always been more diverse than the law would seem to allow. Individual men and women have neither universally accepted nor wholly conformed to the roles that marriage has set out for them at any one time.[27] In the postwar period, historians have documented "cover" marriages between gay men and lesbians and noted the significant numbers of married men who engaged in homosexual sex. Yet despite our awareness of these phenomena, we have not adequately revised our conception of the institution as a whole. It is important to remember here that marriage operated quite differently from other state institutions that explicitly rejected homosexuals at midcentury. For although the postwar state prevented homosexual individuals from legally marrying their same-sex lovers, it did nothing to prevent them from marrying someone of the opposite sex. At a moment when the state inquired about the sexual behavior of men and women applying for citizenship, military service, or federal government employment, civil servants did not press individuals about their sexual desires and experiences when they applied for a marriage license.[28] Though couples applying for marriage licenses in many states after the war had to complete blood tests and identify their ages and racial statuses, no cursory psychological sexual examination or even fill-in-the-blank sexual self-identification was required.

Furthermore, once couples had married, their continued homosexual behavior did not *automatically* invalidate their union. Even in cases in which a married man's or woman's homosexuality came to the state's attention—through an arrest for public indecency or a federal government clearance check, for example—his or her marriage remained binding, unless a spouse took the initiative to secure a divorce, which very few spouses chose to do before the 1970s. It could have been otherwise. Until 1967, sixteen states refused to recognize interracial marriages, and to this day states consider marriages in which spouses are too closely related or still married to another living person to be null and void.[29] It was, then, not that the state lacked the legal infrastructure to invalidate marriages in which one or both partners were caught engaging in homosexual activity; rather, it lacked the political will to do so.

The postwar state's seeming reluctance to police homosexuality *within* marriage may seem inconsistent with its aggressive repression of homosexuality more broadly, but in fact the state's willingness to usher those with same-sex desires or experiences into marriage was compatible with—and perhaps even essential to—the goal of removing homosexuality from public view. For many gays and lesbians, the experience of being arrested in a gay-bar raid or subject to military investigations, contributed to the decision to get married. Some did so strategically, in an attempt to pass as heterosexual, while others did so sincerely, in an attempt to overcome their same-sex desires. In either case, the different arms of the state helped to push into marriage individuals who had recognized their same-sex desires, engaged in homosexual relationships, participated in gay and lesbian communities, or identified as gay or lesbian. Clearly, marriage could not prevent men and women from acting on their same-sex desires, but it could help to ensure that their sexuality would be subsumed, at least outwardly, by their identities as husbands and wives. Keeping marriage open to those with same-sex desires or experiences allowed the state to restrict homosexuality's public presence, which posed a far greater threat to the gender and sexual order than homosexual sex itself did.[30]

Postwar marriage, then, was "queer" in several senses of the word. In comparison with other state institutions that established elaborate mechanisms to exclude or weed out homosexuals, marriage was *strange* or *odd*. It was also *suspicious* or *questionable*: at the surface level, marriage organized men and women into seemingly heterosexual family units, but the laws governing marriage and divorce did not go very far at all to ensure husbands' and wives' heterosexuality. Finally, marriage was "queer" to the extent that it permitted space for *nonnormative* gender and sexual behavior. Marriage's ability to incorporate and withstand wives' lesbian relationships was emblematic of marriage's queerness in this sense. And while we might assume that these women were exclusively feminine, this was not the case. Some of the wives described here were quite masculine in their physical appearance and behavior; some identified explicitly as butch; and some—lacking the contemporary term "transgender"—even questioned whether or not they had been born in the "wrong" body.[31] What is more, the marriages discussed in this book include nearly as wide a range of sexual expression on the part of husbands as they do on the part of wives. Some of the husbands included here engaged in sexual relationships with men; some were very feminine; some were attracted to very masculine women; and others had no interest in sex at all. To call any of these marriages "straight" is historically misleading.

Recognizing postwar marriage's queerness allows us to see how marriage has maintained its ongoing power through both its legal rigidity and its flexibility as a lived relationship. When women combined marriage and same-sex relationships in ways that did not threaten their sexual and caretaking responsibilities as wives, mothers, and homemakers, marriage provided women with some protection from the social stigma and state policing of homosexuality. But when those same women chose to leave their marriages, and their sexual and emotional relationships with other women became exclusive, marriage law worked to punish them. We can then see marriage's queerness—the constrained freedoms of gender and sexual expression it offered, combined with the social and legal protections it provided—as one of the institution's many rewards for married people. While marriage continues to connote respectability, maturity, and morality, in fact, it has historically provided married couples with greater freedom to engage in unconventional, even socially unacceptable gender and sexual behavior while helping to insulate them from risk—so long, that is, as they remained within the institution.[32]

A history of wives who desired women, by definition, foregrounds the ways individuals' sexual identities often fail to match up with their sexual activities, much less their sexual desires. In the late nineteenth century, a "modern" system of sexuality emerged in the West within which sexual acts and desires were understood to be expressions of an inner sexual identity, the most fundamental truth of ourselves.[33] But many historians have demonstrated the limits of this sexual regime by showing how, even in the very recent past, people have engaged in same-sex acts without necessarily thinking of themselves as homosexual. "Throughout the twentieth century," historian John Howard has argued, "queer sexuality continued to be understood as both acts *and* identities, behaviors *and* beings."[34] Many of the wives in this study engaged in sexual relationships with other women without considering themselves to be "different" at the time. One woman, for example, recalled her same-sex affair in the 1970s in terms that would have resonated with many others: "It was just this relationship. *I* was not a lesbian."[35] At the time, this woman was not interested in leaving her marriage, and she did not identify with lesbians who seemed to have very little in common with herself: a mother of five, married for more than fifteen years.

At the same time, most of the women in this study did *eventually* come to identify as lesbian. This is a result, in part, of the sources I have used to craft this study. My major dependence on letters that women wrote to the DOB and interviews for lesbian oral history projects has produced a sample group of wives who were particularly likely to identify as lesbian. Yet not all the women described here understood or experienced their sexuality in the same way. Some of the women in this study experienced their sexual desires as having changed, as having moved from men to women.[36] Others conceived of themselves as having always been sexually drawn to both women and men, and as capable of pleasurable sexual relations with both. Yet others resisted categorizing their sexual identities at all, believing that any and all labels denied the irreducible complexity of their sexual desires and experiences.[37] This study demonstrates the many ways women have made sense of their sexual experiences and the extent to which women's sexual identities can shift over a lifetime.

Over the course of the decades examined here, the discursive tools—the words and concepts—with which wives could make sense of the complexity of their sexual desires and experiences changed dramatically. In the 1950s and 1960s, many married women who wrote to the DOB about their same-sex desires believed that "lesbian" was something one could be *by degrees*. They used phrases common to psychoanalytic writing at the time, such as "lesbian tendencies" or "lesbian inclinations," to describe their persisting erotic attraction to other women, regardless of whether or not they had acted on those feelings. Such women thus used the word "lesbian" as an adjective rather than a noun, to describe a part but not the whole of their sexuality.[38] These phrases, and the conception of partial or incremental lesbianism that they reflected and enabled, went out of favor in the 1970s, as gay and lesbian activists framed homosexuality as an all-or-nothing affair: either you were gay or you were not. By fully claiming homosexuality as an identity, gay and lesbian activists powerfully challenged its stigmatization, but they also compelled those who had engaged in homosexual sex without thinking of themselves as *wholly* gay or lesbian to claim those identities thoroughly and absolutely.

By narrowing the definition of "lesbian," these changes indirectly helped to make "bisexual" a more recognizable sexual identity label for women. In the postwar period, psychiatrists viewed bisexuality as a counterfeit identity, which individuals used in an attempt to deny their "true" homosexuality.[39] Very few women in the first part of this study claimed the label "bisexual" or even seemed to consider it an option. This changed in the 1970s, when describing oneself as bisexual became a marker of hipness or sophistication in some circles, and mainstream news publications heralded a new moment of "bisexual chic."[40] Yet bisexuality was also a politically controversial identity among gay and lesbian activists. Many lesbian feminists were particularly hostile, accusing bisexual women—whether married or not—of enjoying the benefits of lesbian sex and relationships while holding on to their heterosexual privilege, and giving their time and energy to male oppressors. By the 1980s, whether individual wives who desired women were best categorized as "bisexual" or "lesbian" was a concern not only of lesbian feminists, but also of journalists, filmmakers, novelists, and researchers more broadly. By highlighting the inadequacy of language to capture married women's sexual desires and experiences, this ultimately irresolvable question helped to lay the groundwork for contemporary understandings of female sexual "fluidity" that emerged at the turn of the twenty-first century.

My word choice when referring to women's sexuality within this book reflects my attempt to convey the complexity of these women's sexual desires and identities. While some scholars might describe them as "queer,"

I avoid using this term to refer to wives who desired women, because it would be inaccurate to portray them as anti-normative. In fact, it is precisely their normativity, in many respects, that I hope to emphasize here. I describe women's desires for and relationships with one another as "lesbian" or "same-sex," but I refrain from imposing an identity category on anyone. I only use terms such as "gay," "lesbian," "homosexual," and "bisexual" to describe women's identities when they themselves have done so. Even in these cases, I refrain from applying an identity label that a woman came to claim later in her life to her earlier self. I refer to the women in this study as a whole as wives who *desired* women, because I want to make room for the many different women included here, and to draw attention to their rich emotional lives. I am also uninterested in "proving" whether or not these women engaged in genital sex, a preoccupation that has plagued lesbian history.[41] Certainly, some readers will find the variety of terms I use to refer to these women frustrating or confusing. I can say only that I hope the messiness of the terminology in this book conveys something of the messiness of the desires and identities of the women described here, the frustration they likely experienced when trying to fit themselves into a limited social and sexual schema, and the slippery elusiveness and changeability of sexuality itself.

For similar reasons, I resist describing wives who desired women as "closeted" or as leading "double lives." To describe someone as closeted is to portray that person as either cowardly or sexually repressed. Furthermore, in describing someone as closeted, the speaker demonstrates and affirms her own political, emotional, and/or social superiority—that is, her own ability to perceive the "truth" of another person's sexuality. I avoid the phrase "the double life" as well, even though it—unlike the term "closeted"—was one that married women sometimes used to describe themselves. It too, though, implies personal cowardice or political backwardness. Within the historical literature specifically, the phrase "the double life" has worked to uphold a binary and to affirm a geographic separation between hetero- and homosexual worlds that this project seeks to undermine. Perhaps most importantly, both the phrase "the double life" and the word "closeted" suggest that there are and have been only two social possibilities for men and women who experience same-sex desire. Many of the women described here attempted to resist this very polarization, to find practical ways in their daily lives of maintaining and combining marriage and sexual relationships with other women.

In the broadest strokes, *Her Neighbor's Wife* demonstrates that we can no longer tell the histories of marriage and homosexuality in modern America as if they were two discrete entities with two discrete populations. In doing so, we have made marriage appear straighter in retrospect than it actually was. Postwar marriage did "contain" the changes in gender roles and sexual norms that the Great Depression and World War II wrought by disrupting marital patterns and bringing women into well-paid industrial jobs en masse.[42] Yet despite the very real limitations marriage brought, these wives were able—to varying degrees—to take advantage of the flexibility within it.[43] Social norms and economic pressures pushed the women described here into marriage. But just as marriage exerted pressure on these wives, they too exerted pressure on marriage by carving out time and space to act upon their feelings for other women. Despite the newness of legally recognized same-sex marriage, homosexuality has long been a part of the institution. The lives of wives who desired women suggest that it may have been precisely when American marriages were the strongest that homosexuality was most pervasive within them.

PART I

Elastic Institutions and Illicit Affairs,
1945–1969

CHAPTER 1

A "Normal" Life

IN THE WINTER OF 1950, Adrienne Rich pondered the question of women's role in society. Then a junior at Radcliffe College, Adrienne aspired to be a poet, but her greatest desire was to marry and start a family. "The women who demand 'equality' of the sexes . . . are an unhappy lot," she wrote in her journal. "What a woman most deeply wants is simply to subordinate herself to some man that she can stand in awe of, laugh at, comfort, and adore."[1] Soon Adrienne met and fell in love with a man she considered worthy of such devotion: Alfred Haskell Conrad, an economist and teacher at Harvard University who was several years her senior. By the time she began a relationship with Alfred, she had already embarked on a promising career. The famed poet W. H. Auden had selected her poetry for the Yale Series of Younger Poets and had written the introduction for her collection, *A Change of World*, published in 1951. Then, in 1952, Adrienne won a Guggenheim Fellowship to fund a year of study at Oxford University. Despite these accomplishments and her intention to continue her career after marriage, she continued to believe that her happiness depended on subordinating herself within the private sphere to "a strong and sensitive man."[2]

Marriage promised Adrienne, as it did so many other women at this time, a path to adulthood, a home of her own, and fulfillment as a woman through the roles of wife and mother. These were things a lesbian relationship could not offer, and Adrienne never considered the possibility. She did, however, privately acknowledge that her feelings for one female friend had an erotic component. Over and over again in letters to her family, she gushed about her friend Eleanor, whom she met at Radcliffe. "Eleanor is *intensely* stimulating, and we are equals in emotional *and* intellectual things," she wrote in one letter.[3] The pair debated philosophical questions for hours and ran into each other's rooms in the middle of the night with passages for the other to read.[4] Their relationship continued for years, but it fell apart in early 1952. It was then that Adrienne admitted their friendship had bordered on something more. Referencing the infamous line from the 1894 poem of Oscar Wilde's lover, Lord Alfred Douglas, she wrote in her journal, "I loved my friend with a deeper intensity than I knew while still we were friends; only now, only admitting the end, I know what gave the anger its edge was the frustrated and despairing love that could never rightly be told—never so as to reach its object."[5] Adrienne believed there could be no future in her unspeakable love for Eleanor, and she did not mention it in her journal again. She and Alfred married the following year.

Despite her elite education, early recognition as an artist, and exceedingly high hopes for married life, Adrienne typifies the women in this study who married and started families in the 1940s, 1950s, and 1960s. These women came of age at a moment when Americans were building nuclear families as never before, and they faced intense pressure to marry and devote themselves to caring for their husbands and children full-time. After World War II, the median age for women at the time of their first marriage fell from age twenty-two earlier in the century to a low of 20.1 in 1956.[6] Between 1940 and 1960, the birth rate for third children doubled, while the rate for fourth children tripled.[7] One 1961 survey of young women found that the vast majority expected to be married by age twenty-two, and most wanted to have four children.[8] Women who were still unmarried by their mid-twenties were typically blamed for their own misfortune, as it was their responsibility to "catch" a man. One 1948 advice book, *Win Your Man and Keep Him*, informed single women in their thirties that all hope was not lost, so long as they strictly adhered to the advice laid out in the text. "Don't resign yourself to spinsterhood," the authors reassured their readers. "It is more likely you, rather than men in general, who are at fault."[9] Psychiatrists and the mass media meanwhile painted women who rejected or resisted their "natural" roles as wives and mothers as psychologically maladjusted, or "sterile," in a young Adrienne Rich's words.[10] While *Playboy* magazine glamorized the life of the urban bachelor beginning in 1953, women who remained unmarried past their early twenties were the objects of pity rather than envy.[11]

Economic as well as cultural forces propelled women to marry. While single men earned a "family wage," whether supporting a dependent wife and children or not, unmarried women were at a distinct economic disadvantage. World War II brought more women than ever before into well-paid, unionized, industrial jobs, and even drew some attention to sexual discrimination in the workplace, but these gains were short-lived. After the war was over, wartime employers fired women workers—often terminating older women and African American women first—to create jobs for male veterans. Public sentiment turned against employed mothers of young children. Though rates of women's labor force participation remained higher than prewar levels through the 1960s, employers relegated female workers into "pink-collar" jobs, part-time or poorly paid positions with little opportunity for upward advancement. Growing needs for clerical and service sector employees, for example, provided women with roughly three million new jobs between 1950 and 1960.[12] In 1956, fully employed women earned just 63 percent of what men did, and this disparity only widened over time: by 1970, women's earnings had fallen to 59 percent of men's.[13]

Women who came of age in the postwar era also encountered a world in which homosexuality was simultaneously becoming more visible and more stigmatized. According to one historian, World War II served as "something of a nationwide coming-out experience" as many young people began to recognize their same-sex desires and to encounter a broader gay and lesbian community while serving in the armed forces or participating in wartime industries.[14] Following the war, gay and lesbian communities in coastal cities such as San Francisco and New York increased in size and visibility as young people choose to build new lives rather than return to the families and communities in which they had been raised. But as gay and lesbian communities grew after World War II, so too did the discrimination that they encountered. While officials in the armed forces had been willing to overlook homosexual sex among men and women for much of the war when the need for soldiers was high, by the end of the war, the army and navy had given an "undesirable discharge" to approximately nine thousand men and women because of their sexuality, thereby depriving them of the educational, mortgage, and health-care benefits the GI Bill promised.[15] And in 1950, the Senate issued a report titled *Employment of Homosexuals and Other Sex Perverts in Government*, alleging that homosexuals lacked "emotional stability" and "moral fiber," and could, like communists, contaminate a government office.[16] Following the federal government's lead, state and local governments, as well as private companies, began to investigate the sexual behavior of their employees and fire suspected homosexuals.[17]

At an historical moment when marriage seemed inescapable and building a life with a woman nearly impossible, the fact that the women I describe in this work married men tells us very little about their sexuality.[18] Only a few of the women discussed in this chapter considered themselves to be homosexual before they married. Many, like Adrienne, had some awareness of being attracted to women. Still others had engaged in same-sex sexual relationships. Such experiences can, in hindsight, take on great importance as early signs of a coherent, internal lesbian sexuality that would inevitably emerge.[19] And for most of the women described here, their desires for women *did* come to define a fundamental—if not *the* fundamental—truth of their deepest selves. Yet it is important to remember that this was not the case throughout the entire course of their lives. In their youth, when the expectation that they would marry was so powerful and the likelihood of their taking any other life course was so small, a kiss with a childhood friend or even a same-sex affair in adolescence could seem relatively insignificant, easily written off as a phase, an experiment, or an expression of female friendship in no way indicative of fundamental sexual difference. In fact, it was not until well into adulthood that most of these women gave significant thought to their sexual "identities" at all.

Taking marriage as evidence of women's heterosexuality not only erases the wide range of sexual desires and experiences married women had, it also makes women's sexual desires *for men* seem more important to marriage than they actually were. While popular culture depicted getting married as the culmination of mutual romantic and passionate love, in reality it often fell far short of this ideal. "I didn't know him that well. . . . It was just one of those things that happened. Don't ask me how," one woman recalled of her decision to marry after becoming pregnant at age seventeen in 1959.[20] Such an account of getting married, rather than those depicted in television shows or movies of this era, comes much closer to the experiences of the women described here. For most of these women, feelings of sexual desire for and emotional intimacy with their husbands did not play a significant part in either their decisions to marry or their later married lives. Even as marriage was a prerequisite of sexual and social normality at midcentury, it did not necessarily reflect women's attraction to men.

A Sexual Education

Many wives who desired women received little to no information about homosexuality while growing up. One woman who was raised by a single mother in a working-class Norwegian community in Minnesota recalled that, before marrying at age twenty in 1957, she was not "conscious of the possibility of lesbianism" and had not "heard the word."[21] While it may seem unlikely that a young woman could have so little awareness of homosexuality, many girls likely had little concrete information about sexuality at all. One 1960 study of working-class couples in Cincinnati and Chicago in the late 1940s and 1950s found that many women knew very little about contraception or even the process of reproduction itself when they married. What they did know about sex they learned *after* marrying, from their husbands and female relatives.[22] Likewise, in her more recent study of high school sex-education programs at midcentury, historian Susan Freeman found that classroom discussions "hardly invoked sexual intercourse at all" and focused instead on dating, getting married, and becoming parents. Only "occasionally" were topics such as single motherhood or homosexuality discussed.[23]

The taboo around homosexuality may have made it particularly difficult for parents to discuss this issue openly with their children. Parents who did attempt to communicate with their daughters about homosexuality often had trouble doing so clearly, sometimes with humorous results. Sandy Warshaw, who grew up in a Jewish family in a wealthy suburb of New York City, recalled that when she went to a girls' summer camp in the 1940s, her mother warned her to "be careful of those lesbians." But Sandy did not understand what "lesbian" meant, and she did not hear the word again. When she received a report at the end of the summer complimenting her on her performance in the camp's musical production and on becoming a "wonderful thespian," she fearfully recalled her mother's admonishment.[24] The warnings Marjory Nelson's mother provided her in the late 1940s in New Jersey were only slightly less opaque. When Marjory reached her teens, her mom warned that if she hung around with other girls too much, she could "get queer."[25] Although her mother failed to define the meaning of "queer," Marjory understood, unlike Sandy, that she needed to spend more of her time and energy on boys.

The ambiguous warnings or even stark silence most girls received about lesbianism while growing up may have been due to the fact that postwar anxieties about homosexuality among children focused primarily on boys. In the midst of the Cold War, maintaining the masculinity, physical strength, and sexual virility of American men was a cause for national concern. During these decades, a range of cultural commentators stoked fears that overbearing mothers were emasculating their sons, perverting their sexual development, and thereby weakening the nation in the face of the communist threat. The most famous of these commentators was Philip Wylie, who coined the term "momism" in 1942 to describe what he considered to be the smothering behavior of an entire generation of American mothers.[26] Yet it was not only misogynistic thinkers eager to delimit women's power within the household who propagated these ideas. Feminists who believed women should be able to balance motherhood with careers outside the home deployed arguments about the harmful impact unfulfilled housewives could have on their sons as well.[27] In her 1963 best seller, *The Feminine Mystique*, for example, Betty Friedan linked the apparent increase in homosexuality among American men to "excessive mother-son love."[28]

Girls were not entirely insulated from postwar concerns about homosexuality, but the fact that they were not the focus of the same anxiety that beset their male peers may have allowed girls more room to engage in same-sex sexual contact. According to Alfred Kinsey's groundbreaking 1953 study, *Sexual Behavior in the Human Female*, preadolescent "homosexual play" was quite common among girls, and by age thirteen more than 30 percent of the women in his study recalled having engaged in homosexual "play."[29] The experiences of wives who desired women echo Kinsey's findings. Around the age of ten, for instance, Ruth Debra, who grew up in a middle-class Jewish family in Long Island in the 1950s, had a group of female friends who would regularly meet at each other's homes, head down to the basement, and undress. According to Ruth, she had sexual experiences with these girls beginning at the age of ten. "I was pretty much the star of this group because I was more developed physically. And I had my period."[30] Other girls engaged in sexual contact with female friends as a type of practice for heterosexuality. "I *loved* those practice sessions," recalled one white woman of making out with her girl friends in high school in Oklahoma in the 1940s.[31]

Even girls who had more exclusive sexual relationships with their peers in adolescence insisted that they did not consider themselves "different" or their behavior "wrong" at the time. As lesbian feminist author Jill Johnston later noted of herself and girls like her who grew up in conventional, middle-class homes in the 1950s: "We were all heterosexually identified and that's the way we thought of ourselves, even of course when doing otherwise."[32] One woman who was raised in a strict Italian Catholic home in the 1950s, remembered that she had "a summer sort of affair" with a female friend when she was fifteen or sixteen, but she did not consider their behavior homosexual. "I never labeled it as anything," she later explained. "I mean I don't think I heard the word lesbian in Rhode Island in my background."[33] While historians have argued that a modern conception of homosexuality was firmly established by the postwar period, such comments demonstrate that this understanding of sexuality was neither ubiquitous nor complete.

In their 1993 oral history of the lesbian community in Buffalo, New York, between the 1930s and the 1950s, historians Madeline Davis and Elizabeth Kennedy found that many women, in particular those raised in Catholic homes, recalled receiving warnings only about having sex with men. They also found that Italian American girls experienced less guilt about same-sex sexual experiences than others.[34] The stories gathered in this chapter, however, suggest that such experiences—and girls' lack of concern about them—were not limited to any one religious or ethnic group. Long after the fact, some women continued to believe that same-sex sexual activity had been common, even normal, among their peers in adolescence. Growing up in a middle-class Lebanese Canadian family just outside of Detroit in the 1950s, Linda, for example, had relationships with girls in high school and grade school that involved kissing and petting. But this didn't make her "feel any different" from her friends. "It was just a normal thing," as she later described it. "I think we all experimented. I don't think it was just myself alone. . . . We knew you were not supposed to have sex with boys, but nobody said you couldn't have sex with your girlfriends. So we did!"[35]

As Linda's comment implies, anxiety about girls' sexual development at midcentury focused primarily on *heterosexual* sex and the risk of illegitimate pregnancy. Though rates of premarital sexual intercourse remained stable from the 1920s to the 1960s, concerns about female "promiscuity" grew during the war, often focusing on the threat such women posed to male soldiers by exposing them to venereal disease.[36] When World War II began, many commentators correctly predicted that it would bring an increase in the number of illegitimate births. Of particular concern to social workers was the apparent increase in illegitimacy among white, middle-class girls and women. In response to this change, social workers adjusted their understandings of the causes of premarital pregnancy. While social workers considered black unwed mothers innately immoral and incapable of reformation, they diagnosed white, middle-class, unmarried mothers as suffering from treatable psychological problems or "neuroses." These racially divergent understandings of unwed motherhood laid the ground-work for later policymakers and politicians who viciously blamed unmar-ried black mothers for urban crime, unemployment, and the rising cost of welfare.[37]

The tremendous stigma of premarital pregnancy and parental warnings about heterosexual sex may have convinced some girls that engaging in sexual activity with a female friend was a more acceptable alternative. In fact, some sex experts were concerned about precisely this possibility. These experts even encouraged parents to be less strident in their condemnation of premarital heterosexual sex, for fear that parents might indirectly foster their daughters' sexual activity with other girls.[38] Such concerns do seem to have had some basis in reality. Several wives who desired women recalled that sexual contact with other girls in their youth did not "count" in their minds as sex at all. While growing up in Washington State in the early 1940s, Shirley Maser, for example, experienced her first kiss with another girl while in reform school. Shirley, a white, working-class woman, later explained that she did not understand her behavior as sexual at the time. "You know, when you had girlfriends then it wasn't anything to do with sex. It was just someone that you liked a lot and you'd kiss each other."[39] Because the taboo on premarital intercourse at midcentury was so uncom-promising, many girls similarly considered a range of heterosexual behav-iors, including manual and oral sex, to be socially acceptable because they did not qualify as "real" sex.[40] It is thus possible to see girls' homosexual activities in much the same way as necking and petting with boys: as tactics girls employed in fulfilling their sexual desires without defying social prescriptions.

Girls' sexual relationships at midcentury were both similar to and differ-ent from the emotionally and erotically intense crushes common among girls at boarding schools and colleges in the nineteenth century. So frequent were such crushes in England and the United States that slang terms—"raves" and "smashes"—evolved to describe them.[41] Although some girls at midcentury continued to describe their same-sex relationships in romantic terms as they had in the past, others downplayed the emotional aspects of their same-sex sexual experiences, categorizing them as incidents of sexual exploration, experimentation, or practice for "real" sex with boys.[42] This suggests that some girls may have considered romantic ties to be *more* devi-ant than sexual encounters or "experiments" with other girls. Indeed, for a young Alma Routsong growing up in Michigan in the early 1940s, it was the intensity of her emotional attachment to her high school English teacher, Helen, which suggested to her she might be "different" in some way. "Maybe I'm a fairy and am in love with Helen. . . . I can't imagine it's normal to cry because a mere female friend has gone away," she wrote in her diary.[43] That Alma used vocabulary typically applied to homosexual men to describe her feelings for Helen demonstrates the difficulty some girls experienced in trying to find the words to express love and desire between women.

Girls and young women did continue to find space to explore their same-sex desires while growing up at midcentury, but such relationships typically continued only so long as they remained hidden from adults. Growing up in Houston, Texas, the black lesbian feminist poet Pat Parker carried on a sexual relationship with her best friend and next-door neighbor, Joyce, for years. During the summer of 1960, when Pat was sixteen years old, Pat's father discovered the girls together. Though Pat feared her father would hit her, he sent Joyce home and said nothing. The next morning, Pat's parents took her to a doctor who visually examined her body and reported that she was physically normal. "You're not funny, so I don't ever expect you to do what I saw you and Joyce doing again," Pat's father informed her.[44] The following day, Pat was forced to accompany her father as he told their neighbors what she and Joyce had been up to. In doing so, Pat's father both publicly humiliated her and enlisted their community in monitoring her sexuality without explicitly labeling Pat's activity as "homosexual." Despite her father's prodigious efforts, Pat continued her sexual relationship with Joyce until she left for college, but going forward the girls were more careful to keep their activities a secret.

Other parents took even more drastic action to end their daughters' same-sex relationships by seeking psychiatric treatment for them.[45] After Sally Duplaix was caught in a "sexually compromised position" with her roommate during her sophomore year at Smith College, the school's administrators informed her parents that she was having a mental breakdown.[46] Sally's parents first sent her to a psychoanalyst in Manhattan, and then to a residential facility for therapy, but Sally refused to renounce her homosexuality. "We're back to 1956," Sally told an interviewer decades later, "and I'm going around telling people how proud I am, and happy I am. . . . Well, back then that was considered 'crazy,'" she explained.[47] Sally's parents sent her to a private mental hospital, Elmcrest Psychiatric Institute in Portland, Connecticut. For five months, she was subjected to electric shock therapy in the morning and insulin shock therapy in the afternoon. One night, Sally attempted to escape, and she ran to a café where she hoped to call her parents. Instead, Elmcrest attendants found her and returned her to the facility. To deter Sally from running away again, the staff at Elmcrest permitted her to wear only a nightgown, bathrobe, and slippers.[48]

Not all girls' encounters with the mental health establishment were so traumatic. As a white, working-class high school student in Kalamazoo, Michigan, in the mid-1950s, P. J. Fagan had a girlfriend and was beginning to connect with an older group of lesbians through a basketball team at the local YWCA. After her parents found out about her new social circle, they sent P. J. to a Catholic-run mental hospital. When the doctor asked her if she knew why she was there, P. J. responded, "Because I am a lesbian."[49] P. J. met with a psychiatrist and remained in the hospital for a month, but she considered herself lucky because she was neither medicated nor forced to undergo shock treatment. At the end of her stay, her relatively sympathetic psychiatrist said that she had "chosen a very difficult lifestyle" and invited her to come back and talk with him if she wanted to.[50] When P. J. returned home, her parents seemed to admit that they could not change her. P. J.'s mother told her she could do as she pleased as long as she kept her curfew and obeyed one major rule: "I don't want to know who you see or what you do."[51] But in her early contact with a lesbian community and her unshakable sense of her own sexual difference, P. J. was exceptional among the women in this study, most of whom were not nearly so defiant.[52]

Peer pressure could be even more effective than psychiatric treatment in deterring girls from homosexuality. At age thirteen, Gini Morton (Figure 2), an African American woman who grew up during the 1940s in a family she described as "dirt poor" in Detroit, developed a sexual relationship with a female friend.[53] The girls' relationship continued for a time until Gini's mother realized what was going on and refused to let Gini see her friend. Still, Gini's mother did not explain her actions, and Gini did not realize why she was being punished. It was not until a group of teenaged boys called Gini "queer" that she began to understand the significance of her actions. Gini knew that the term meant "something really bad," but she still did not understand why the boys were directing the word at her until a friend explained that it was because she was "always hiding in bedrooms and under the steps with girls and you girls are doing it."[54] Gini decided then that she would stop being "strange" and would start focusing more of her attention on boys.[55]

Figure 2. Gini Morton, age twenty-three, with her children in St. Louis, Missouri, ca. 1955. From the Old Lesbian Oral Herstory Project, Sophia Smith Collection, Smith College Libraries. Printed by permission of Virginia "Gini" Morton.

Other women recalled encountering homosexuality's negative meaning through books. While in her early twenties, Deedy Breed, a white woman from Connecticut, took an engineering job at United Aircraft during World War II. There she met and had an affair with a woman who had been in the Women's Army Corps. Deedy did not know the word "lesbian," but she looked up "homosexual" in the dictionary and "found out it was this horrible thing."[56] Desperate for information, she came across Radclyffe Hall's tragic 1928 lesbian novel, *The Well of Loneliness*, which convinced her to renounce the relationship. "I thought, well, even in fiction they can't make it any better, so I thought who wants this? Not me."[57] A few years later Deedy began a relationship with another coworker, this time a man, and they married. Reflecting the ways the imperative to "be happy" directs men and women to follow very particular life paths, Deedy, like so many of her peers, believed that in choosing marriage over a lesbian relationship she was choosing a "normal" life and a better, happier future.[58]

Getting Married

Historians have argued that Americans' expectations for married life rose higher than ever at midcentury. By the 1950s, not only were husbands and wives supposed to depend on each other, above all others, for support and understanding, but sex was considered imperative to marital success.[59] As young, middle-class couples moved further away from extended family members, often into private, suburban homes, they expected nuclear family life to meet their needs for security, fun, and personal fulfillment as well. This belief was best summed up by the concept of "togetherness." Celebrating this new domestic ideal, the editor of *McCall's* magazine wrote in 1954 that Americans reaching adulthood at midcentury were "together" creating a "new and warmer way of life not as women *alone* or men *alone* . . . but as a *family* sharing a common experience."[60] Advertisements for new domestic gadgets depicting family members spending time together in front of the TV set or grilling in the backyard, provided powerful depictions of this ideal, which continued to shape many men's and women's expectations until well after the 1950s.

Some young women, like Adrienne Rich, did hold high hopes for the pleasure and meaning marriage would bring to their lives, but more often they recalled marrying with a sense of resignation rather than excitement. Several wives who desired women later explained that they did not make a conscious decision to marry because they had always taken for granted the fact that they would. One woman who married at age twenty-one in 1963 said, "Marriage was just assumed. It goes beyond even being a value. It was just so implicit in everything."[61] Another woman who married around the same time explained simply, "My God, what else was there to do?"[62] For young, middle-class, white women like these, the possibility of choosing a different life path did not become apparent until much later. Such women's attitudes toward marriage may be due in part to the benefits of hindsight; knowing how their marriages turned out, in retrospect these women may have forgotten the anticipation they had once had for married life. But we should not entirely discount such women's statements either, which suggest that even before marrying they were quite capable of seeing through the rosy portrait of family life that often appeared in popular culture.

Though some of these women had not experienced same-sex desires or relationships by the time they married, even those who were conscious of their sexual desires for women felt they had no choice but to marry men. In the late 1940s, Bea Howard, a Jewish New Yorker, knew that she was attracted to women. Then in her late teens, Bea made her way from the Bronx to Greenwich Village because she understood that was "where the lesbians were." She succeeded in locating a lesbian bar and was about to enter it when two women emerged from the bar fighting. Put off by the women's hostility, she decided a lesbian life was not what she wanted, and she made up her mind to get married. Though marriage was not all that appealing either, Bea felt there was no real alternative.[63]

Other women met their husbands while in the midst of same-sex relationships. Long before she became a leader in the black feminist and gay rights movements, Achebe Betty Powell, then known as Betty Jean, had an affair with her roommate while in graduate school in New York City in the early 1960s. The women loved each other and declared that they "belonged" to one another, but they never labeled their relationship as "lesbian," and they fully expected that they would marry men. Once they met their future husbands, Betty and her lover decided their relationship "would get in the way of us really being free for our marriages," and they ended their affair.[64] No matter how passionate such women's same-sex relationships were, they could not confer the economic stability, social recognition, and personal fulfillment through the roles of wife and mother that marriage seemed to offer. Beyond economic uncertainty, cultural stigma, and social isolation, lesbianism could not, it seemed at the time, ensure any future at all.

Yet other women became convinced that marriage was their only option after facing more severe social discrimination. Maureen, who was Mormon, met her first female lover when she joined the US Air Force in the early 1950s. Unfortunately, Maureen and her lover formed a relationship at the very moment when the military began actively discharging lesbians.[65] While the specific details of Maureen's investigation are unclear, we know that officers with the US Army's Criminal Investigation Division searched through the personal belongings—from letters to boxes of Tampax—of other women caught up in this postwar witch hunt. They picked up female soldiers in the middle of the night for questioning, held them under guard without explanation, questioned them about sexual acts they engaged in, and teased them for missing out on sex with men. So humiliating were such interrogations that historians have described them as psychological rape.[66] What is more, this ordeal could continue for months. While we do not know exactly what happened to Maureen, the air force ultimately discharged her, and she came to believe that her "involvement with women could only lead to unhappiness."[67] Afterward, she moved to Los Angeles and lived with her mother for three years before marrying a male coworker at Western Union in the late 1950s.[68]

Like Maureen, many women recalled feeling significant pressure from their families to marry. Such familial coercion ranged from subtle to extreme. During her second year of college in the late 1940s in Texas, Ann Allen's parents simply stopped providing her with financial support. "My mother said I had to get married. So they cut my money off!" she recalled indignantly. Despite her plans of becoming a doctor and her conscious attraction to women, Ann had no choice but to marry a man who could support her economically.[69] In an even more dramatic example of parental manipulation, Larraine Townend's mother threatened to commit suicide in an effort to terminate Larraine's two-year relationship with another woman in Ohio. Rather than dare her mother to make good on her threat, Larraine married a man soon after in the mid-1960s.[70]

Other women's families pressured them to marry after they became pregnant. Gini Morton's mother tried to force her to marry when she was only sixteen years old, in 1949. Though Gini's young age seems striking in retrospect, teenage marriage was not uncommon among girls of color at midcentury, and her mother's strategy of "righting" her out-of-wedlock pregnancy through early marriage was centuries old.[71] Ironically, Gini had become pregnant as part of a conscious effort to become straight. Not long after learning about the stigma of homosexuality from her peers and deciding she wanted to change, Gini agreed to have sex with a boy in exchange for fifty cents and a pair of roller skates. When Gini found out she was pregnant, her mother was horrified. Gini's mother—whom Gini later described as "in the civil rights movement long before it started"—had been adamant that her children would not have to clean white people's houses as she had, and she held high hopes for Gini's career, which her pregnancy derailed.[72] Gini's mother wanted Gini to marry the baby's father, but he denied responsibility for the pregnancy, and Gini refused to marry him. Within two years, though, Gini had married someone else.

Gini's story suggests some of the particular meanings that marriage had for black women, and some of the special pressures to marry that they faced. As Gini's mother recognized, marrying could be a means of contesting stereotypes of black sexual deviance, of asserting claims to respectability, and thus challenging racial oppression.[73] At midcentury, civil rights leaders began to replace an earlier tolerance for sexual diversity within working-class black culture with a new emphasis on sexual conformity. While queer preachers, singers, and drag performers were celebrated within working-class black culture in the early twentieth century, in the 1950s these celebrities began to encounter severe public criticism.[74] Blues singer Gladys Bentley's changing self-presentation reflected this shift. While Bentley had dressed in tuxedos and even married a white woman in a public ceremony in Harlem in the 1920s, in 1952 she proclaimed in *Ebony* magazine that she had married a man and "become a woman again" with the help of hormonal treatments.[75] This political and cultural transformation had repercussions for ordinary African Americans, and by the late 1950s there were apparently few openly gay black women in Detroit. According to one black woman who came of age in Detroit at the same time Gini did, "I'd say ninety percent of [black lesbians] was in the closet. We had special places that we met and partied, though immediately after that it was back to the closet."[76] Despite being conscious of her same-sex desires, this young woman, like Gini, chose to marry.

Marriage could function as a means of achieving financial stability, as well as respectability. Compounding the pressure to marry she experienced within her family, Gini found that racial discrimination made supporting a young child on her own even harder. After the birth of her son, racial discrimination prevented Gini from securing a well-paid job. Gini tried to qualify for public assistance so that she could return to high school, but the public was beginning to demonize young, black, unmarried mothers like Gini in the late 1950s. Hateful rhetoric motivated widespread legislative efforts to reduce the numbers of women receiving payment through Aid to Dependent Children, the federal welfare program for single mothers created in 1935 as part of the Social Security Act and renamed Aid to Families with Dependent Children in 1962.[77] Unsurprisingly, Gini's local welfare office denied her request. Forced into extremely low-wage work doing chores for her neighbors and flipping hamburgers at a local restaurant, Gini struggled to provide for herself and her child. Confronting both economic hardship and her mother's deep disappointment, at age eighteen Gini relented and married a man more than a decade her senior, "because that was all that was left for you, really, back then if you were straight. . . . Even if you weren't straight, you got married to shut people up."[78] In marrying, Gini finally achieved the respectability her family wanted and the financial security she needed, but her desires for other women continued.

While some wives who desired women married to please their families, others married to escape them. For many young women, marriage offered what seemed to be the only way of becoming an adult and separating emotionally and physically from the family in which they had been raised. Susie, for example, grew up in a small town near Kansas, Missouri. After her father passed away when she was thirteen, Susie's mother supported her and her three siblings by cleaning doctors' offices. Susie had long been aware of her feelings for girls, and she had a relationship with a female classmate in junior high. Even so, she sensed that a relationship with another woman would not allow her to escape her unhappy family life and the community in which she "didn't belong."[79] In 1956, when Susie was seventeen years old, she met a sailor in the navy stationed in Oklahoma and jumped at the opportunity: "I guess you might say it was kind of a way of getting out of the rut. I was married for 17 years. Got myself into another rut."[80] While Susie did not define exactly what "the rut" meant, it seems that life in her home town offered few opportunities or surprises. Marriage provided her a way out, but it proved no more exciting or fulfilling than life in Missouri had been.

Marriage also promised a different kind of escape, a "cure" for what some young women perceived as their sexual "deviance." Such a belief was not remarkable at midcentury when many psychiatrists insisted that homosexuality could be overcome. It was not until 1973 that the American Psychiatric Association removed homosexuality from its list of mental disorders. Before then, many mental health practitioners saw heterosexual marriage as the sign of success culminating a homosexual patient's treatment. Pat Gandy, a white, middle-class woman from Texas, married in the mid-1950s when she was twenty-five years old. Pat had "no interest in guys" and had long suspected that she was gay, but when she began researching homosexuality, all the texts she encountered stated that homosexuals were "sick." "I thought that's not me, that can't be me . . . I'll just try to forget all this stuff." By that time, her friends were all getting married, and so Pat decided that she would get married as well. She met a man who already had three children—two older sons and a young daughter whom Pat believed needed a mother. "I felt . . . this is an opportunity to have a child and raise somebody. Be normal," she remembered. Though Pat married with the expectation that doing so would allow her to overcome her same-sex desires, she never did.[81]

Despite the growing radicalism of the gay movement in the late 1960s, understandings of homosexuality as sin or sickness persisted and continued to influence women's decisions to marry. In 1966, while in college, Martha of Biloxi, Mississippi, began a two-year affair with another woman. When the woman's mother found out about the relationship, she threatened to kill Martha and attempted to physically assault her. Though the women's relationship continued, Martha began to have serious doubts. Considering her age and location on a college campus—the site of so much activism in the late 1960s—we might expect that Martha would have joined a feminist or homophile group and perhaps found support in her struggle. Instead, Martha became involved in a religious organization on campus and converted, as she put it, "to a fundamental faith."[82] She became convinced that homosexuality was wrong, ended the affair, and attempted to renounce her same-sex desires. As Martha later explained, "I had convinced myself that if I could be religious enough and dedicated to a personal commitment to God, I would not be bothered by those damnable lesbian feelings."[83] Soon after graduating, Martha began dating a man she met through her religious activities, and they married after only three months together.

Though conceptions of homosexuality as a spiritual ailment or psychological illness were pervasive in the postwar era, they were not universal, and several women married men who seemed to understand or accept their wives' lesbianism. Some of these sympathetic men understood that their marriages would be purely or primarily platonic. Despite cultural understandings of marriage in this period as based on romantic love and sexual attraction, these couples founded their marriages instead on mutual concern and understanding. In 1956, Suzanne Reed, an upper-middle-class white woman, married Howard, a man she had dated as a high school student in New Jersey. While away at college at the University of Massachusetts, and before any thought of marrying Howard, Suzanne began a relationship with a fellow student, Julie, that continued for two years. Their relationship ended tragically when Julie was killed in a boating accident, and Suzanne felt responsible for Julie's death. In the months that followed, Howard reappeared in Suzanne's life. He visited her at school and attempted to rekindle their high school relationship. After Suzanne graduated, they married. "I really liked him, I was very fond of him. And he was aware of my sexual orientation, but it didn't bother him."[84] Howard and Suzanne had what she called a "quasi-sexual" relationship, but essentially, during their seventeen-month marriage, they were "just kind of living together like brother and sister."[85]

Howard was not gay, but other women married men who were. Despite their shared histories of same-sex relationships, these couples often expected to have conventional or "straight" marriages.[86] In the late 1960s, one white woman, Grace, married a gay man ten years her senior in northern California when she was only in her late teens. Grace had engaged in at least one homosexual relationship before she married, as had her future husband, but both wanted to have children and live what she called a "normal" middle-class, suburban, family life. This young woman had a troubled early life. Her parents were alcoholic, violent, and often strapped for cash. She suffered from depression, ran away from home several times, and was briefly institutionalized in a mental health facility after a traumatic LSD trip. Marriage seemed to offer a path out of her troubles. "Life was too hard," she decided, and playing the part of the middle-class housewife seemed an appealing type of nonexistence: "I was gonna go watch TV, and run the vacuum cleaner," she recalled.[87] Grace later cast her decision to marry as a type of suicide. "My intention in marrying him was to go to the suburbs and die," she later reflected, thus linking marriage and suburban life with the end of her social self.[88]

While most wives who desired women did not enter marriage with this fatalistic attitude, neither did they hold lofty expectations about what married life would bring. They approached marriage functionally, rather than romantically or idealistically. The biggest choice they faced as young people was not whether to get married or not, but *whom* to marry and *when*. Typically these women selected as husbands men they liked and had fun with, men who seemed capable of being good providers, and men who came from "nice" families. To some extent such women's decision making echoed the very practical advice dispensed by marital educators like sociologist Ernest Burgess. In the late 1930s, Burgess brought a new scientific rigor to the study of marriage and family life. He downplayed the importance of romantic love as a predictor of marital "adjustment" and placed greater emphasis on an individual's "socialization"—that is, his or her participation and accomplishments in the realm of family, school, and church.[89]

Several wives who desired women reflected this sort of functional thinking when choosing a spouse. Of her reasoning when deciding to marry her husband in upstate New York in the early 1950s, Deedy Breed later reflected, "I thought, well, he comes from good stock. He comes from Maine. . . . His father is a Professor of Civil Engineering at M.I.T. He was schooled at Deerfield and M.I.T. I really enjoyed his family, and I liked his sister and of course I liked him but, I don't think it was a great all-consuming love affair."[90] New Yorker Connie Kurtz, who married in the late 1950s, recalled that she simply did not know her future husband, Bernie, well enough to feel very deeply about him. Rather, she married Bernie because he fit her basic requirements: he was Jewish, employed, and went to synagogue. Bernie was also "nice," and Connie "felt nice" with him. These warm but passionless feelings were perfectly in keeping with what Connie had been led to expect of marriage. "I mean, who knew the word passion? Who knew the word lust? . . . I had no, no idea what those words were. And they were never even presented to me."[91] Connie's comments may seem surprising, considering the extent to which popular songs and Hollywood films of the 1950s regularly idealized heterosexual romance, but her expectations of a passionless marriage were hardly exceptional. Indeed, another Jewish New Yorker who married at the same time Connie did later explained that her husband's lack of interest in sex was part of what she found most appealing about him as a potential spouse.[92]

Timing rather than passion, it seems, was the single most important factor in determining whom these women married. When women reached their early twenties and saw their peers getting married, the pressure to find a spouse grew more intense. Dorothy Hoffman, a white woman who grew up in Philadelphia in a well-off family hit hard by the Depression, had long known she "preferred women." Before meeting her future husband in New Jersey in the early 1940s, Dorothy engaged in a passionate affair with a fellow student at nurse training school—for which she was nearly expelled. Although Dorothy did recall being "attracted" to her husband when they met, she did not describe being in love with him.[93] More importantly, the time was right: she had finished nursing school and started working, and he seemed to fit certain criteria she was looking for in a spouse. "He was in the Signal Corp, Fort Thomas, and he was from Wisconsin. I just figured he was the man I wanted to marry, 'cause everybody got married. Even though I [was] very much attracted to this one gal who was the best maid at my wedding."[94]

In an even more dramatic example, the aforementioned Sandy War-shaw, an upper-class Jewish woman from Scarsdale, New York, agreed to marry a man on their first date. Then twenty-one years old, Sandy was nearly the last among her group of Vassar College friends to get married, and her mother had made it clear that she needed to do so soon. Even more concerning to Sandy than ending up an "old maid," though, was the fact that she could not move out of her parents' home without marrying. So, when a Jewish man from a "good family" proposed to her on their very first date together in the mid-1950s, she said yes. Three months later they were wed.[95]

Married Life

Even though they entered marriage without expectations of lifelong passion and romance, many of these women ultimately found married life disappointing. Wives who desired women were unexceptional in this way. Many scholars have found that unhappiness was common among married women at this time. One 1964 sociological study of more than fifty working-class couples found that "slightly less than one-third [were] happily or very happily married."[96] The following year, Betty Friedan published her book *The Feminine Mystique*, widely credited at the time with breaking the silence surrounding many middle-class women's dissatisfaction with their roles as wives and mothers. Through surveys and interviews with hundreds of women Friedan documented what she termed "the problem that has no name," the feelings of depression and worthlessness that plagued wives whose household labor failed to provide them with a sense of purpose or personal fulfillment.[97] Even before *The Feminine Mystique* was published, though, women's magazines produced a "discourse of discontent" by regularly publishing articles and marital advice columns documenting wives' unhappiness.[98]

Most of the problems that wives who desired women encountered with their husbands were not unique: a lack of emotional connection, financial problems, alcoholism, and physical abuse.[99] Even sexual incompatibility, a major complaint among the wives in this book, was by no means limited to this particular group of married women. While the 1964 study of working-class couples mentioned earlier found that most wives believed they should find sex pleasurable, these women also agreed that wives did have to "submit to intercourse" from time to time, regardless of their own feelings.[100] What is more, only 30 percent of these same respondents "express[ed] high satisfaction with their sexual relations."[101] Similarly, in a 1955 survey of three hundred white, middle-class, married couples, 84 percent of wives said that marital sex was "pleasant"; but at the same time, one-third of respondents said that they rarely or never achieved orgasm.[102] Midcentury marital advisors did not lead women to expect much more. Though most argued that an active sex life was integral to building a happy marriage, they continued to place far greater importance on husbands' rather than on wives' sexual pleasure. Indeed, as historian Carolyn Herbst Lewis has noted, while physicians considered male orgasm essential to the sexual health of a married couple, "female orgasm was a *goal* but certainly not a *necessity*."[103]

Although some wives felt ashamed about not enjoying sex with their husbands, many took for granted that marital sex was primarily about men's pleasure and never considered their lack of enjoyment a problem. One woman recalled being unsurprised to find that marital sex was not that exciting. Because she had heard enough negative things about sex from older women while growing up, she anticipated it was not "all going to be bells and whistles and what-have-you."[104] Julia of Fort Madison, Iowa, voiced even more extreme ideas about the need to sexually submit to her husband. Divorced with two young children by the time she was eighteen in 1962, Julia described marital sex as "just something a husband had a right to."[105] Other wives did not realize until they became sexually active with other women later in their lives how unfulfilling marital sex had been. As one woman recalled, quite typically, it was not until she first had sex with a woman that she realized she had never had an orgasm during her eighteen years of marriage.[106]

Yet other wives were dissatisfied because their marriages, both sexually and emotionally, fell so far short of their earlier relationships with women. It was not uncommon for these wives to continue fantasizing about their same-sex affairs from many years before. One white woman, Stella, continued to long for her first lover, Amy, for years after marrying. Amy and Stella were lovers in college, but in 1965, not long after graduating, Amy renounced their relationship and married. Stella was so distraught at the end of this affair that she felt as if she had died and "literally had to will

[her]self to breathe."[107] The following year, Stella rushed into a marriage of her own. Stella's husband was kind and devoted to her, but her feelings for him never came close to those she held for Amy. Stella ended up living in a suburban township in Michigan not far from her former lover, but Amy clearly wanted to put the relationship behind her and did not speak to Stella. Stella never gave up hope, though. Every weekday morning for years, Stella would stand at her kitchen window and watch Amy drive by on her way to work as teacher. Each day, Stella would pray that Amy would get a flat tire or her car would break down, so they would have a reason to talk again, but they never did.[108]

Stella never expected that marriage would "cure" her, but those women who had married in hopes of overcoming their same-sex desires were disappointed when marriage did not foreclose their same-sex desires.[109] Even women who discussed their same-sex desires with their husbands before marrying often found that their marriages did not work out as they had expected. In 1960, Shaba Barnes, a black Muslim woman from Brooklyn, married a fellow congregant who suspected her hidden attraction to women. "I had tried to bury my feelings for women so deep that it was burdensome," Shaba recalled; so when this man confronted her about her sexuality, she was both "shocked and relieved."[110] Shaba's friend suggested that they marry, since he knew her secret, and that way people would stop hounding them to get married. Eventually Shaba agreed. By that time, Shaba was a single mother with a young son. She wanted another child, and she believed that this man would be a good husband and father. Soon after they married, Shaba's husband announced that they had an opportunity to move to Cuba where he would join Fidel Castro's army. Shaba refused to go, but her husband left, and when he returned to the United States shortly before their daughter was born, Shaba found that the love she once felt for him had disappeared. Shaba did not believe in divorce, and she did not want to disappoint her family, but the marriage fell apart even so. Shaba's husband adhered more strictly to religious doctrine than she had expected, which became a source of conflict in their marriage, and he began to mistreat her. When he slapped her once during an argument, it was the final straw. Shaba responded by pushing him down the stairs, and soon after she moved out.

Many women who married gay men similarly found that their unconventional marriages fell far short of their expectations. In knowing that their wives wanted to hide or reject their lesbianism, gay husbands gained a measure of power over their spouses, which some attempted to exploit. Though it is possible that some wives attempted to exploit this same power over their gay husbands—perhaps by threatening to publicly expose or divorce their husbands if they did not behave as desired—my sources, documenting only the wives' side of the story, do not reflect this dynamic. Marilyn, for example, who married her gay male friend in San Francisco in the 1950s, felt isolated after they subsequently moved to San Jose together. While her husband led a vibrant gay social life, she knew no one in their new community in San Jose. And although they had agreed to lead an outwardly conventional existence, their home became a hub for her husband's group of gay friends who emptied the fridge filled with food she had paid for and often simply ignored her presence. "I felt really used," she remembered. A few months after she had married, Marilyn moved out in the middle of the night.[111]

In some ways, gay men simply took advantage of the power over their wives that marriage itself bestowed. Kiki Santikos, a Greek woman from a middle-class family in Mississippi, married a gay male friend, also Greek, in the early 1960s in Texas. At first, although Kiki and her husband never lived together, marriage provided them with a cover for their separate gay lives. Eventually, though, Kiki discovered that her husband had mortgaged her home and car to fund his travel. Marital property laws in Texas, as they pertained to women, were undergoing significant reform in the 1960s, but Kiki's husband was nonetheless able to mortgage everything she owned without her knowledge or consent. She filed for divorce soon after.[112]

Marriage to gay men, like marriage to heterosexual men, could bring physical as well as financial abuse. In the 1950s, Marion Coleman, a white working-class woman who began to identify as a lesbian in her teens, married a friend of a friend, a gay sailor who had been caught engaging in homosexual sex and who—she was told—would be sent to military prison without her help. So Marion married the man and he moved to Cape Cod to live with her. The marriage worked for a while until one night Marion's husband came home drunk and "beat the holy devil out of [her]." After he passed out, she was barely able to crawl out of her house before collapsing. Luckily someone found Marion on the street, and she and her husband divorced.[113]

Disastrous marriages like these, however, seem to have been the exception, rather than the norm, among wives who experienced same-sex desires. At best, these women married kind men and had loving—although often sexually unfulfilling—relationships. At worst, they found themselves stuck in dysfunctional marriages with men who emotionally or physically abused them. Yet most of these wives' marriages, like those of other women, fell somewhere in between these extremes. Reflecting on her marriage during the 1960s, one woman described it in a way that probably would have resonated with many others: "It wasn't fantastic . . . but it certainly wasn't bad."[114] Many married women at midcentury may not have felt entitled to much more.

On the daily level, the stresses of caring for children, managing a household, and holding down jobs often kept couples apart, which made persisting in a less than fulfilling marriage easier. Discussing how she was able to stay married to a physically abusive man for so long, Edith Daly stated, "The way that I was able to stay was because he was gone for twelve hours of the day. And basically it was like being a single mom."[115] Ruth Silver, a Jewish woman who married in the 1950s in New York after leading an active lesbian life, recalled, "My husband and I lived almost separate lives. We would go to the theatre together, do various and sundry things, but we had no sexual relationship. We were like siblings in the household."[116] Ruth knew that she would eventually have to end the marriage, but she was wary of the stigma of divorce and had young children to consider. Moreover, her relationship with her husband was easy to manage, and together they were able to create a comfortable and stable home for their kids. In such marriages, as in many others forged in this era, husbands' and wives' relationships with their children took precedence over their relationships with each other.[117]

Women's expectations and experiences of motherhood differed widely. For many of the women described here, children were not only the major factor keeping them within marriage, but also the most rewarding part of their married lives. In this respect, wives who desired women fulfilled the idea—apparent in the pages of women's magazines, marital advice books, and Hollywood films—that motherhood provided the key to women's happiness.[118] But while some women had always dreamed of becoming mothers and had married almost entirely because they wanted to have children, others experienced the social pressure to bear children as oppressive. Connie Kurtz later recalled that she had children because she wanted to be accepted in her community and to prove to herself and others that she was a "real" woman. "I didn't want a child. I wanted all this proof," she later explained, "so I could feel whole and complete. I could feel identified. I could feel part of [the] community."[119] Having a child failed to provide Connie with the sense of truly being a woman, as she had hoped. Instead, it thrust her into a deep depression.

Whether or not they had truly wanted to become parents, many women found motherhood more difficult and less fulfilling than they had anticipated. In general, these women did not have a great deal of social support in the trying early years of parenthood. Most did not recall receiving significant help from either members of their extended family or paid child-care providers. Even though social expectations of fathers increased in the postwar period, the responsibilities of caring for young children still lay heavily on women.[120] The experience of parenting young children, in other words, was deeply isolating. "Got my children, yes, and there I was stuck at home with them. Three of them under the age of five. Thinking to myself, is this all there is?" recalled one suburban housewife from Connecticut.[121] In some cases, such women's deep unhappiness and frustration was manifested in violence toward their children.[122] Others enacted violence upon themselves. Phoenix Wheeler, a white woman who grew up in a very poor family in Alabama and married in the late 1950s, became deeply depressed after the birth of her third child and attempted suicide. "I collected sleeping pills. I had several different varieties and I took them all. Didn't leave a note."[123] Such desperate actions may have been uncommon, but the feelings of hopelessness and powerlessness they expressed were widespread among mothers with young children in the postwar era.

While most challenges of parenting were not particular to wives who desired women, some women found that their same-sex desires made having children even more complicated. In particular, some wives feared their own homosexuality would cause their children to become gay as well. When Ruth Silver sought help from a therapist in the 1950s to discuss her continuing desires for other women, her therapist warned her that she needed to "resolve" her homosexuality and put her lesbian life behind her or it would be lived out in her daughter.[124] This advice was well in line with mainstream medical opinion at the time, which blamed an individual's homosexuality in large part on his or her parents.[125] Such ideas had a powerful impact on Ruth, who diligently fought her attraction to women for thirty-eight years of marriage. When her daughter *did* come out to her as a lesbian at age twenty, Ruth was distraught. Initially she thought, "I was indeed a bad person. I hadn't done my work of totally ridding myself of my true nature and of my love for women—and here was the result!"[126]

Alma Routsong also feared that her same-sex desires would have a detrimental effect on her daughters. In the early 1960s, as she considered whether or not to leave her marriage, she worried that she had developed an unhealthy erotic attachment to her children, particularly her youngest daughter, then three years old. In her secret diary, she cited the work of Swiss psychoanalyst Carl Jung, who warned that fathers could unconsciously turn their sexual attention to their daughters if their marital relationships became strained. "The only reason Jung didn't apply the same statement to mothers and daughters," she wrote, "is that it is not taken for granted that the mother is a lesbian."[127] At a moment when homosexual men, and to some extent women, were widely imagined as pedophiles and sexual predators, such fears were not as surprising as they may seem.[128] When Alma did leave her marriage, it was in part for this reason that she gave her husband full custody of their children. In her diary, she wrote of her daughters shortly before the divorce, "I damage them no matter what I do."[129] That women like Alma could see perversion in the love and affection they felt for their children demonstrates the profound emotional impact of lesbianism's social stigmatization.

◆ ◆

The stories captured in this chapter demonstrate women's desire, not for men, but for *normality*. Over and over again, when later explaining why they had married and describing what they had wanted from married life, the women in this study used the word "normal." "He provided me with the chance to become 'normal,'" one woman wrote of the man she married, despite her same-sex desires, in 1966.[130] Said another woman of her decision to marry while in the midst of a same-sex affair, "I wanted to do the normal thing an elementary school teacher does . . . get married and have children."[131]

But what precisely did being "normal" mean to these women? Certainly, in striving for normality, they disavowed sexual difference. "Normal" and "queer" were the two terms Americans used most frequently at midcentury to refer to sexual-identity categories, yet "normality" in these women's accounts seems somewhat different from, or rather broader than, "heterosexuality."[132] Indeed, for the women described here, normality was defined less by an inner essence than by one's life choices—namely, the decision to marry and publicly take on the morally "right," statistically average, and psychologically appropriate roles of wife and mother. Normality, in other words, was a social accomplishment, or even a type of public performance, insofar as it was achieved primarily through the perceptions of others.[133] Some women did hold out hope that marriage would transform their sexuality—that is, that marriage would "cure" them or help them "overcome" an attraction to women. But most women did not, both because they did not think of themselves as sexually different to begin with and because what they *did* publicly mattered far more than how they *felt* privately.

The condition of being normal that these women hoped to achieve also carried particular racial meanings. By the middle of the twentieth century, "normality" had come to represent a very specific notion of reproductive, emotionally intimate, monogamous marriage between gender-polarized, implicitly white men and women. So profound was the racial specificity of this discourse that it did not need to be stated explicitly, and thus it gave the appearance of a racially neutral ideal open to any and all. As a requirement of full citizenship at midcentury, normality also worked to justify the exclusion of racial and sexual others who, seemingly by their own fault, could not meet its standards.[134] White women were not the only ones who aspired to sexual normality, but in doing so these women in particular sought to achieve a position of power and privilege in society to which they felt entitled and which, regardless of their class status, seemed to be within their grasp. The few women of color mentioned in this chapter may have shared these goals, but they did not use this same language to describe them, and the possibility of their ever being considered truly "normal" full citizens likely seemed more remote.

Regardless of their race or economic status, though, in many ways "normal" or rather "average" lives were precisely what the women discussed here achieved. If sex was unsatisfying and an emotional connection with their husbands lacking, if marriage failed to provide economic security or introduced violence and abuse into their lives, if parenting turned out to be more difficult and less fulfilling than they had expected, these women were in good company. For most of them, married life was not abominable. Many of them married kind men with whom they had warm and supportive relationships; most enjoyed parenting and the rhythms of everyday family life. Yet even those women with the best marriages on this continuum discovered, in time, that normalcy did not necessarily bring happiness. Being normal, as it turned out, was not nearly enough.

Many scholars have acknowledged women's pervasive unhappiness within marriage during this period, but they have typically understood it to be a result of women's frustration with their subordination within marriage, as well as their unmet desires for achievement and self-expression beyond the household.[135] As this chapter demonstrates, there was more than just one "problem that ha[d] no name." For many white, middle-class wives, abandoned careers and forfeited educations produced depression and dissatisfaction. For others, both within and beyond this demographic group, it was the memories of female lovers they had knowingly given up, the nagging suspicion that their sexual and romantic lives with their husbands fell short of what they might have had with women, the fear that—despite their best efforts—marriage would not allow them to "overcome" their attraction to women as they had hoped, or the concern that their hidden homosexual urges would somehow detrimentally affect their children.

Such feelings were perhaps even harder to voice than those scholars more commonly cite as the reasons for married women's unhappiness at midcentury. In 1976, after her marriage had ended and she had begun a relationship with her long-term female lover, Adrienne Rich attempted to convey this failure of language in her essay "It Is the Lesbian in Us. . . ." Calling to mind the diary entry she had penned years before about her love for Eleanor, Adrienne wrote, "Whatever is buried in the memory by the collapse of meaning under an inadequate or lying language—this will become, not merely unspoken, but *unspeakable*."[136] Adrienne's description of love between women as "unspeakable" would likely have resonated powerfully with the many other women like her who married and had children in the postwar era despite their same-sex desires. Yet to see this silence as *only* oppressive would be a mistake. Silence can be productive as well as repressive, chosen as well as imposed, strategic as well as negligent.[137] As we will see, while wives struggled to create space for their lesbian desires within the context of their ongoing marriages, some quite skillfully turned the namelessness of their feelings for women to their advantage.

CHAPTER 2

Caution and Discretion

AFTER ENDURING YEARS OF sadness and frustration over her continuing desire for women, Lucy, a wife and mother of two from New Orleans, had reached what she considered to be an enlightened perspective on the issue. "The key to being able to live both ways comes under two simple words: Caution and Discretion," she wrote in the fall of 1960 in a letter to the Daughters of Bilitis (DOB), the national lesbian rights group.[1] Lucy went on to argue that wives like her could pursue sexual and emotional relationships with women as long as they hid their affairs from their spouses. "Why provide someone close with knowledge that could be upsetting and emotionally damaging to the point of wrecking many lives?" she reasoned.[2] Lucy's lover had recently ended their relationship, but Lucy was still looking for a female "counterpart" and exhorted other married women to do the same: "Let us not deny ourselves the right to seek happiness where we may—so long as we can strive to be discreet and cautious in our actions."[3]

Lucy was not alone. "Contained" within their marriages by fault-based divorce laws, limited employment opportunities, concern for their children, and the social stigma facing lesbians and divorcees, some wives nonetheless found that same-sex affairs were surprisingly compatible with "normal" married life.[4] While most historians have emphasized the ways that postwar marriage was oppressive for women, in some ways marriage's defining features in this period—specifically the overwhelming pressure to marry and the stigmatization of divorce, the emphasis on rigid gender roles, the expectation that married couples would establish a single-family household, and the privileging of domestic tranquility rather than open communication—*enabled* married women's same-sex relationships. Women's same-sex affairs did not fundamentally change postwar marriage, or alter the gendered division of power within it, but within these constraints some wives found they were able to adjust their relationships to their needs and desires.

Between the late 1940s and the end of the 1960s, few wives participated in "out" lesbian communities by visiting urban lesbian bars. Most found lovers among female friends they met within the context of their "straight" lives. While some exceptional women talked openly about their lesbian desires with their husbands, most wives, whatever their race or class status, found that caution and discretion were critical in balancing marriage and same-sex affairs.[5] Their affairs—which sometimes continued for years at a time—typically unfolded in and around the nuclear-family household while their husbands were at work. As long as they concealed their affairs and fulfilled their marital duties, such wives believed that they were entitled to seek emotional and sexual satisfaction with other women. Their husbands may not have agreed, but in most cases they chose, at least for a time, not to risk losing a functional marriage by asking too many questions.

Wives who secretly engaged in affairs with women were hardly the only ones to utilize such discretionary strategies during the 1950s and 1960s. Scholars have documented how many married men participated in gay subcultures during this period and how, often, they were caught up in police raids of gay bars and sweeps of public places where homosexual sex was known to occur. Married men were, in fact, critical to the development of postwar gay bars, since the numbers of unmarried "out" gay patrons were comparatively limited.[6] At a moment when suspected homosexuals could be arrested, fired, deported, and denied welfare benefits, even many unmarried gays and lesbians were compelled to lead outwardly heterosexual lives. Nor were wives whose families or communities feigned ignorance of their homosexuality entirely unique. Scholars have shown that gays and lesbians and their parents utilized similar discretionary tactics during this period, and southern and rural communities had, by the postwar period, long created space for queer men and women by avoiding explicit discussion of their sexual difference.[7]

But married women who quietly engaged in same-sex affairs were not only using the tactics of the closet; their silence was also an outgrowth of gendered marital roles. In a survey of several hundred white, middle-class, married couples conducted in the 1950s, many wives rated their marriages as successful despite major discontentment. Keeping silent about their unhappiness when communicating might cause tension or conflict was one way these women held their marriages together.[8] One woman who often disagreed with her husband took this method to the extreme: "So long as we maintain a state of breakdown in communication," she wrote, "we get along fine."[9] In fact, silence could pave the way for purposeful, if well-meaning, deception. Letting one's husband win at cards so he could feel skilled, creating problems around the house so that he could feel needed, feigning sexual enjoyment so he could feel satisfied—these were the secret maneuvers that kept many marriages going.

Wives did not come to this marital strategy on their own. In the 1950s and early 1960s, marital counselors, magazine columnists, religious leaders, and psychiatrists placed the responsibility for holding a marriage together largely on the woman's shoulders. Advice columns such as Can This Marriage Be Saved? in the *Ladies' Home Journal* taught women that any marriage—even one scarred by infidelity, abuse, or alcoholism—could survive if only they tried hard enough. When it came to dispensing advice for wives and mothers, "acceptance," "adjustment," and "adaptation" were the watchwords of the day.[10] Marital experts instructed women to accept their biologically determined roles, adjust themselves to marriage, and adapt to their husbands' needs, desires, and even neuroses. "Women of today have to make more of the adjustments in marriage than do men," one postwar marital advice book noted. "They adjust themselves, their personalities, and their interest to the life of the man primarily, rather than the man adjusting himself to the woman's life." While the authors of this book conceded that this discrepancy was not fair, they stated it was unlikely to change and informed women that they would do best to accept it.[11] Such understandings of marriage were influenced, in part, by the renowned Harvard sociologist Talcott Parsons, who argued in the late 1940s that in complex industrial societies the family was defined by specialized roles: the husband played the "instrumental" role of wage earner, while the wife played the "expressive" role of caretaker, emotionally supporting her husband and children.[12]

This idealized division of labor left little room for women's needs. The author of one 1961 article in the *Atlantic Monthly* titled "The Captivity of Marriage" demonstrated as much when she informed her female readers that the myriad problems they encountered in their daily lives must be dealt with silently and alone. "It can be painful to find oneself isolated, in marriage, with problems that have always been shared with mother or girl friends and to realize that there are some things that even one's husband cannot be told. *This is the hard lesson of discretion.*[13] To confront a husband with one's troubles, the author stated in no uncertain terms, was to risk the destruction of a marriage. Other experts warned that women who did not maintain a tranquil home threatened their husbands' careers and health, their children's futures and well-being. Faced with such messages, many wives hid their true feelings and disguised their inner lives. Their silence was a requirement of a successful marriage and family life. Married women who discretely engaged in same-sex affairs, then, were far more conventional wives than they may at first seem. Like so many married women during this period, they veiled their most intimate desires for the good of their families.

The Geography of Wives' Lesbian Lives

In the 1950s and 1960s, locating and participating in lesbian communities was difficult, even for many unmarried women. Bars were the most visible gay community spaces at midcentury, but they were typically located in red-light districts and associated with criminality. As many state liquor authorities considered the presence of homosexuals to be evidence of "disorderly conduct," owners often resorted to extralegal means to keep their bars open. Many gay and lesbian bars became havens for a range of illegal activities, from gambling to prostitution. Even when bar owners bribed police officers, the possibility of being arrested in a bar raid and having one's name and address printed in the morning paper was a constant threat; and bar patrons had to contend with harassment and abuse not only from police, but also from straight voyeurs. While men of all classes frequented gay bars, the women who visited lesbian bars were more likely to be working-class. Wary of socializing in public, middle-class lesbians tended to do so privately. Many middle- and upper-class lesbians also disapproved of working-class lesbians' butch and femme, or masculine and feminine, self-presentation.[14] Furthermore, bars had historically been men's spaces; women who frequented bars unescorted by male companions during the early twentieth century were often assumed to be prostitutes. As late as World War II, several cities even passed laws prohibiting women unaccompanied by men from sitting or standing at a bar in an effort to prevent the spread of venereal disease.[15] Wives who desired women may, therefore, have been disinclined to visit any bars at all.

Despite these obstacles, some wives did frequent gay bars, just as their single counterparts did. Reba Hudson, a lesbian who visited gay bars in San Francisco in the mid- to late 1940s, later recalled that married women had been a recognizable part of that world: "Of course, there were bisexual women downtown that were very well dressed. They were married to attorneys and bankers and . . . were having little affairs on the side."[16] Similarly, novelist Marijane Meaker, who wrote several journalistic paperbacks about the lesbian community in New York City in the 1950s, reflected years later, "We were all used to the occasional married woman who came to the bar late at night while her husband was away and her children were being babysat."[17] Married women in smaller cities also visited lesbian bars. In their oral history interviews with women of the lesbian community in Buffalo, Elizabeth Kennedy and Madeline Davis found that several married women participated in the gay bar scene there. Reggie, for example, a white, butch-identified woman, was married and raised two children during the 1940s but met multiple female lovers at Buffalo's lesbian bars during the course of her marriage.[18]

Wives of color were less inclined to visit predominantly white lesbian bars. While lesbian and gay bars in Buffalo were largely desegregated by mid-century, black women continued to face discrimination at lesbian bars in other cities. Feminist theorist Audre Lorde recalled the tenuous acceptance that black women found at Bagatelle, the most popular mid-fifties lesbian bar in New York City's Greenwich Village. There, the inner door was guarded by a male bouncer who kept out male interlopers as well as "undesirable" women. According to Lorde, "All too frequently, undesirable meant Black."[19] Yvonne Flowers, who was also among the few black women who visited lesbian bars in Greenwich Village at midcentury, recalled that one night a white lesbian, offended by Yvonne's and her friends' lack of attention, simply ordered the bouncer at Bagatelle kick them out.[20] While such bars may have been technically "racially integrated," they were, in practice, white spaces.

Partly in response to white lesbians' racism, black lesbians created their own community centers by holding parties in their homes. Though scholars typically assume that bars were at the center of postwar lesbian communities, this was not necessarily true for black lesbians. In Detroit between the 1940s and the 1970s, as in other cities, black lesbian life revolved around "semipublic" house parties.[21] Ruth Ellis, an unmarried African American lesbian who moved to Detroit to work as a domestic in the 1940s, remembered that she met lesbians—both married and single—at house parties, rather than in bars. Many of her friends gathered at the home of one married woman in particular. "One of the girls were married but the husband didn't care, and we went to her house," she explained. Later, in the 1950s, Ruth's own house became known as "a home where queers go." Some of the women who visited her house were church ladies who had been or were currently married. "They weren't supposed to be gay," Ruth noted, "so you can't always tell."[22] Black wives who used their homes as lesbian spaces, then, were not simply rejecting working-class lesbian culture in the way middle-class white women tended to do, but also responding to the racism of the white gay and lesbian community and participating in a cultural tradition specific to black lesbian life more broadly.

In addition to visiting lesbian bars and house parties, wives participated in lesbian communities by joining women's sports teams. Beverly Dale, a white, unmarried lesbian in Detroit, carried on an affair with a married woman named Donna in the 1950s, whom she met through a group of women who played on a softball and bowling team together. Beverly first noticed Donna—who was friends with the women on the team—sitting in the stands at all their games, and eventually the two women developed a sexual relationship that lasted for more than five years. Beverly later recalled that theirs was the first relationship which both she and her lover consciously labeled as gay.[23] What is more, Beverly soon discovered that many of the women on her team were in relationships with each other as well, and that many were married. The team, in fact, served as a convenient cover for the women's affairs. Sometimes when the couples wanted to get away together, they would tell their husbands or boyfriends that they were going to a bowling tournament and rent a motel room out of town. For married women who were wary of the bar scene, joining a women's sports team that had a significant lesbian presence but wasn't explicitly labeled as lesbian may have been a more appealing way to meet potential lesbian lovers and friends.

Most wives, however, typically engaged in affairs with women they met within the context of their daily lives. For married women tied to their homes by the responsibilities of child and home care, the physical proximity of their lovers was critical. Furthermore, wives' lesbian relationships were not usually brief sexual encounters but tended to grow out of close friendships with other neighborhood wives and mothers, with whom they had a great deal in common. Charlotte, of St. Joseph, Michigan, for example, was barely conscious of her attraction to women in the mid-1960s when, as she put it, "quite by accident, I met and fell in love with another suburban 'wife' and mother."[24] Such anecdotes suggest that desire between women abounded and was generated in seemingly heterosexual, suburban spaces.

Organizations and institutions where wives and mothers congregated, like the local parent-teacher association (PTA), could also become grounds for romantic and sexual relationships. After being elected president of the PTA in Norwalk, California, in the 1950s, Barbara Kalish went to San Francisco for a training conference. There she met Pearl, another PTA president, who also had two children and happened to live only a few blocks away from her. To Barbara's eyes, Pearl was "the most gorgeous woman in the world." Although she had not been conscious of her attraction to women before, Barbara "fell madly in love."[25] In an oral history interview recorded many years later, Barbara could not recall exactly how it happened, but somehow she was able to tell Pearl that she loved her and they began an affair that continued for twelve years. Significantly, it was not only suburban mothers who found potential lovers through PTA networks. Though Sandy Warshaw lived in New York City with her husband and two children, she was worlds away from the gay and lesbian communities of Greenwich Village and Fire Island, New York, where she vacationed with her family. When Sandy finally acted on her attraction to women in the late 1960s, she did not venture downtown to a lesbian bar but reached out to a friend and fellow PTA mother who, incidentally, rejected Sandy's overture—not because she found the idea unappealing, but because she had "been there, done that" and did not want to jeopardize her marriage again.[26]

Despite widespread religious condemnation of homosexuality, a number of wives found female lovers through their churches or other religious groups. Participating in church committees and special activities provided wives with a rare chance to spend time with other women without their husbands and children in tow. Marge Frantz, a white wife and mother of three, joined a Unitarian fellowship in Berkeley, California, in the early 1950s and, through her participation in the women's auxiliary committee, met Eleanor, who would become her lover and later life partner.[27] Similarly, in the late 1960s, Julia, a divorced mother of two, fell in love with Mindy, a married minister, while training to be a Salvation Army officer in Iowa. The women became friends and carried on an affair for two years, even planning to establish a household together once Mindy's children were grown. "Always there in the future beckoning to us was our 'Someday.' A time for us when the children were older," Julia recalled. Unfortunately, though, Mindy ended their affair when, as Julia put it, "I made the mistake of putting a label on what we were."[28] Confronted with the term "lesbian," Mindy refused to continue the relationship. Though Mindy's reaction to the word "lesbian" was dramatic, her aversion was not uncommon. For many married women, the labels "lesbian," "gay," and "homosexual" were more emotionally distressing than the behavior itself.

Religious retreats in particular provided wives with opportunities to meet women they might not have encountered otherwise. Pamela and Liz, each a wife and mother, "found each other" at a church retreat in 1960.[29] Although Pamela lived in Florida and Liz in Tennessee, the women's families became friends, and they were able to spend a few days alone together periodically, sustaining their affair for at least twelve years. Religious retreats could bring women together across racial as well as geographic distances. Margaret Killough, a black nurse, wife, and mother of three from Detroit, met her lover on a Catholic weekend retreat in the late 1960s. Margaret had initially resisted going because, as she put it, she did not want to spend a weekend "with a bunch of old white women talking religion to me."[30] Nevertheless, Margaret did attend the retreat and there met Eva, an Italian American former nun, and the first woman to whom Margaret had ever been attracted. Recalling the event decades later in an oral history interview, Margaret struggled to find the words to capture the powerful, soulful experience she had that weekend: "And I met this woman [Eva] there. . . . [W]e spoke together and we talked together and it was just wonderful. The most wonderful thing you could do. Met these women. These women were nice women. We just had a wonderful—. I don't know what—, how much Catholic it was, but it was a wonderful, spiritual weekend. Anyway, I met this woman, this one good-looking woman. And that was the first."[31] Though intended to help women foster a deeper relationship with God, in some cases such retreats fostered women's intimate relationships with each other.

Like church, the workplace served as an important space for meeting lovers, revealing how much lesbian desire was part of married women's routine daily lives. Amara, a multiracial Cuban woman who had immigrated with her husband to Ohio, began a relationship with a fellow secretary in the early 1960s. In Amara's case, acting on her feelings for other women was a way of remaining true to herself despite her roles as wife and mother, while also resisting her husband's attempts to control her. Amara first had an affair with another woman in Cuba. After her lover ended their relationship and got married, Amara, heartbroken, did the same. Several years later, after moving to the United States, Amara had yet another lesbian affair with her brother-in-law's girlfriend. She attempted to escape her marriage by running away, but her husband found her and forced her to return home. Soon after, Amara's husband secured a position for her answering phones at his company so that he could keep an eye on her, but Amara was persistent and met her third female lover at work. "We both guessed about each other," she later wrote, "and eventually I knew that I was in love with her and that she loved me too."[32] Unable to socialize in openly lesbian spaces, Amara had likely become skilled in reading the coded signs of homosexual desire: lingering glances and touches, and perhaps linguistic cues. In beginning yet another lesbian affair directly under her husband's nose, Amara both evaded her husband's control and defied his authority.[33]

Wives like Amara were resourceful in navigating space as they combined marriage and lesbian relationships. Some upper-class wives at midcentury were able to maintain sexual relationships with other women by spending part of the year with their husbands and the other part with their lesbian friends and lovers. After World War II, Fire Island grew into a major gay and lesbian vacation spot, and a group of wealthy white women, many of whom were married or divorced, claimed the Cherry Grove part of the island for themselves. Some of the married women in this community, like Kay, had reached a tacit understanding with their husbands. During the summer, Kay carried on an active lesbian life at her vacation home in Cherry Grove, while her husband lived at his golf club. Kay's husband was more of a friend than a lover; he knew about Kay's affairs with women and was uninterested in a sexual relationship with her. On Fire Island, Kay had a group of similarly wealthy lesbian friends, some married, and others divorced. Kay did not discuss her husband when she was on the island, and she did not talk about her lesbian relationships or friends with her husband during the rest of the year in Manhattan.[34] By midcentury, it was common for wealthy New York City wives to leave their husbands and take their children outside of the city during the summer. Such women's class status thus allowed them to maintain a greater degree of separation between their lesbian and heterosexual worlds than most middle- and working-class married women at midcentury could afford.

Wives who did not have the resources to maintain a lesbian life for part of the year found different ways of managing. Ken Sofronski, a white gay man born in 1938, recalled the complex arrangement by which his mother, Della Sofronski, maintained her marriage and a sexual relationship with her widowed neighbor Violet, a mother of four. Ken's mother and father, a landlord, began living apart when he was five years old. His father stayed in Philadelphia, while he, his mother, and two older siblings lived in Wagontown and then Coatesville, Pennsylvania. Such an arrangement would not have been all that unusual during World War II, when many families endured long separations as men and women went to war or migrated to participate in wartime industries. Ken's parents also maintained the appearance of a conventional marriage. His father visited them on holidays, and every weekend Ken's mother would drive to the city, pick up a check from her husband, and disappear with him to the bedroom, during which time Ken came to believe his father would claim his "conjugal rights." Instead of staying with her husband, though, Della would spend the rest of the weekend at her friend Violet's nearby home. Ken always knew that his mother and Violet were close, but the extent of their relationship did not become clear to him until he was around fourteen years old and accidentally walked in on the women in his mother's bedroom, kissing and naked from the waist up. Ken's mother was thus financially dependent on her husband and was compelled to provide him with a degree of companionship, but she was also able to achieve some independence and continue her relationship with Violet until her death in 1957.[35]

Historians have tended to conceptualize men and women like Della, who publicly "passed" as heterosexual while also engaging in gay or lesbian relationships, as leading "double lives." This metaphor may aptly describe the experiences of married men who engaged in sex with men far from home, but it is misleading when applied to the lives of women like Della, whose married and lesbian lives were so thoroughly intertwined. Two photographs of Della demonstrate this point. In the first (Figure 3), snapped on a family vacation in the mid-1940s, Della stands outdoors with her husband and children. The children are laughing and smiling in their swimming suits, but Della, squinting into the sun, appears more serious. She is touching her family members, yet nonetheless seems disconnected from them and somewhat out of place. In the second photograph (Figure 4), taken a few years later, Della wears a man's collared shirt, jacket, tie, and hat. Allowing a somewhat tentative smile, she looks away from the camera. Posing alone, she looks not like a working-class wife and mother, but like a butch on her way to snag a femme at a lesbian bar.

Figure 3. Della Sofronski and her family on vacation, ca. 1944. Printed by permission of Kenneth "Ken" Sofronski.

Figure 4. Della Sofronski dressed for a neighborhood Halloween party, which she and her female lover attended in costume as bride and groom, ca. 1950. Printed by permission of Kenneth "Ken" Sofronski.

While it is tempting to see these photographs as evidence of a separation between Della's straight and lesbian lives, the family vacation captured in the first photograph was less conventional than the photo conveys. Della insisted on bringing her lover, Violet, and two of Violet's children along, and even rented a cabin for them next to her own. And in the second photograph, Della was not dressed to go to a lesbian bar, but to a neighborhood Halloween party, which she and Violet boldly attended in costume as bride and groom. What is more, according to Della's son, Violet most likely took both of these photographs, reflecting the extent to which Della's lover was an inextricable part of her family life. (In fact, Violet was so much a part of Della's family that, after Della's death, Violet married Della's brother and continued to serve as a mother figure to Ken and his siblings). These photographs demonstrate how easily our understanding of the familial, domestic sphere as distinct from queer relationships and communities can distort our understanding of the past.

As wives like Della found, keeping a love affair secret was not easy, or even necessarily possible. Some wives socialized with their lovers and husbands together, hiding, as it were, in plain sight. Beverly Dale, for example, recalled that she and Donna often spent time together with Donna's husband. In fact, Donna's husband was around so often that it behooved Beverly to have a boyfriend. "It was just easier to have a guy around 'cause her husband's around. Let the two guys do something so we can be together," she explained. Beverly and Donna were not the only ones who balanced their straight and lesbian relationships in this way. Boyfriends and husbands often accompanied Beverly's teammates to bars and parties and on ski trips and bowling tournaments. As Beverly recalled with a touch of irritation, "They [the men] were with us a lot." So, the women developed a complicated routine that allowed them to manage their relationships with both men and women within the same spaces. "What you'd do is," Beverly informed an interviewer years later, "at these parties you'd be with your husband or your boyfriend and you'd kiss him a few times and dance with him a few times, but then in between you'd go dance with your girlfriend."[36] That both married and unmarried women deployed this technique suggests how common it was to balance relationships with both men and women in this period.

Though Beverly and Donna's affair played out in bars, bowling alleys, and baseball fields, more often the private and presumptively heterosexual spaces of family life served as the backdrop for married women's lesbian relationships. In the early 1960s, Carmen, a Puerto Rican wife and mother of two in her early twenties, took advantage of her husband's absences from the home to begin an affair with Kathy Martinez, the nineteen-year-old daughter of her close friend. Carmen lived in the same public housing project in Queens as Kathy, and their families often socialized together. One evening after a family picnic, Carmen began playing footsie with Kathy and invited her to spend the night on their couch. When they got home that evening, Carmen made her intentions clear. She sent her husband out on an errand, disappeared into her bedroom, and then reemerged in a peignoir set. Years later, Kathy was still amazed. "I just didn't know what was going down," she recalled.[37] That night, the women only kissed; but after Carmen's husband left for work the next day, they slept together, and their relationship continued for the next two years. Even in New York City, then, the nuclear-family household provided a valuable lesbian space for married women who could not get away from home or did not want to risk being publicly identified as homosexual.

Alma Routsong's evocative journal entries demonstrate how married women's intimacy could transform the spaces of everyday life. In 1953, Alma, then a mother of two living in rural Delton, Michigan, fell in love with another local mom, Maxine. After Maxine's death in the early 1960s, Alma revisited their relationship in her diary. A novelist, Alma spared no dramatic flair in her description of her encounters with Maxine. Of the first time they kissed, Alma recalled: "She sent me to the bedroom to look at a picture on the wall and came in and stretched out voluptuously on the bed. I asked if it was alright that I loved her and she said yes, of course." After they kissed passionately, Maxine responded as if in a movie, "That's powerful stuff, kid." On another occasion, the women kissed in the car at night, despite Maxine's initial protestations. As Alma remembered it years later, their conversation could have been ripped from the pages of a novel:

Maxine: What if we get to like that [kissing] pretty well?
Alma: I like it pretty well already.
Maxine: I did too, you know I did.
Alma: Yes.
Maxine: There was power behind those kisses.
Alma: There was love.
Maxine: Either way I lose you?
Alma: Yes.
Maxine: Then kiss me!

Alma and Maxine would never have dared set foot in some big-city lesbian bar in the 1950s, even if they could have. But being cut off from the places we consider central to midcentury lesbian life did not prevent Alma and Maxine from enacting their own lesbian soap opera.[38] Their setting—a family car more often associated with carpools and camping trips—may be surprising, but their script was all too familiar.

Using the nuclear-family household as a setting for lesbian love did not always turn out well, and married women were not necessarily safer at home than at a lesbian bar.[39] Yet despite its limitations, the nuclear-family home was often the only space in which many married women could engage in lesbian affairs, and they made use of the time when their husbands were at work. In some ways, in fact, the strength of the male-breadwinner family model after World War II facilitated married women's lesbian relationships. Shielded from the eyes of prying neighbors and extended family members, wives found ample opportunity to engage in sexual relationships with other women in their own homes while their husbands were at work. Some wives' unmarried lovers even came over first thing in the morning. A nurse who fell in love with a married patient in Pittsburgh in the 1950s later explained, "I worked the nightshift and after she was discharged I used to go to her house in the morning. Her husband was gone for the day and we'd spend the whole day together with those two little kids running around."[40] Similarly, one Texan wife and mother of eight who eventually left her husband for a "lady wrestler" in Houston put it, "You'd be surprised at what goes on in the neighborhood after the men go to work."[41]

Married women also took advantage of their husbands' work-related travel. Historian Nicholas Syrett has argued that the more extensive travel demanded by many midcentury businesses—undergirded by the growth of highways and car ownership—allowed married men to engage in same-sex affairs in the course of work-related trips.[42] By the same token, husbands' extended absences from the home allowed at least some wives to engage in same-sex relationships of their own. During her husband's frequent work trips, for instance, one Pennsylvania housewife and mother of two, identified by her divorce records only as "CD," developed a relationship with the athletic director of a local school. One winter day in 1949, her husband —who, quite fittingly, worked for the Pennsylvania Department of Highways—returned home early to find CD and her lover in bed together. When he demanded that the athletic director leave, to his surprise, his wife up and left with her. Even then, CD's husband expected that she would return home to beg his forgiveness, but she never did. Instead, the women carried on their relationship openly and set up house together in a nearby cottage belonging to CD's mother.[43]

Military wives, in particular, could easily engage in affairs while their husbands were deployed. Some military wives even developed a specific term to describe such women's behavior: "queering around." In the 1960s in Oklahoma, Barbara, a wife and mother who had long been conscious of her same-sex desires, had a sexual encounter with Susan, whom her friends told her "queered around" with women. Susan's husband was in the air force, Barbara's husband was in Officer Candidate School, and the husbands of most of Barbara's friends' were in the service as well. Despite the negative connotation of the term "queer," Barbara later recalled that her friends had not used this phrase in a derogatory manner. "No one cared one way or the other," she later recalled.[44] In fact, Barbara's friends seemed to condone the behavior, if not engage in it themselves. After an evening of drinking, Barbara, Susan, and two other friends all ended up in bed together. Barbara later claimed she could not remember much of what occurred that night, but she did recall how Susan had initiated sexual contact by touching and whispering to her, and how her friends had laughed amusedly at her shock before going off together and leaving her with Susan in bed. While it is unlikely that the term "queering around" was ever very widespread, sleeping with women while one's husband was gone was common enough among Barbara's friends to warrant its own terminology.

Still, scheduling time together around a husband's work schedule was not always easy for married women and their lovers, who were often the ones to make compromises. Mary Crawford, for example, went to great lengths to make herself available when it was convenient for her married lover, Muriel, during their more-than-decade-long affair in Manhattan in the 1940s and 1950s. Initially, the two white women were able to spend time together at the radio station where they worked, but eventually both quit. Muriel could afford not to work, and Mary secured work she could do from home so that she could be with Muriel during the daytime. This was no small sacrifice on Mary's part. Referring to Muriel and her husband, Robert, Mary explained, "I worked my life out around them . . . working from home."[45] Nearly every day after Robert left for work in the morning, Muriel would head to Mary's apartment in Greenwich Village. Most nights Muriel would leave in time to have dinner with her husband back home, but once or twice a week, when Robert was playing cards, Muriel would stay the night. Muriel did not hide Mary's existence from Robert entirely, however. The three of them got along well, and Mary often went out together with Muriel, Robert, and their friends. "This is the way relationships had to work . . . in the gay life, very often," Mary explained in an interview decades later.[46]

Making Marriage Work

It is unclear precisely how much Robert knew about his wife's relationship with Mary. Years later, when an interviewer asked Mary if Robert was aware that she had been sleeping with his wife, Mary was still unsure. "He was pretty suspicious," she recalled.[47] Robert may well have been suspicious, but he seems to have been unthreatened by the women's relationship, and he was surprisingly willing to tolerate Muriel's frequent absences at night. Mary even wondered if Robert turned a blind eye to her affair with Muriel because he was having an extramarital affair of his own. Nonetheless, Muriel and her husband continued to sleep together and eventually had a son. Muriel's relationship with Robert was, as Mary labeled it, a "working marriage," and their marriage worked in several ways.[48] Outwardly, they fulfilled all expectations of heterosexual normality, which concealed Muriel's homosexual inclinations and perhaps Robert's as well. The marriage also "worked" in the sense that Muriel and Robert shared an understanding of marriage that was not set along conventional gender roles. For a time, at least, Muriel and Robert both worked outside the home and shared domestic chores. Finally, the marriage "worked" because Muriel and her husband respected and permitted each other independence and privacy; Robert could do what he pleased on his card-playing nights, and Muriel could as well. Neither spouse pushed for details or expected to know everything about the other's life.

Robert's reticence was typical of husbands across different racial and economic groups, and men's silence may have signaled their tacit understanding.[49] When asked years later if any of her teammates' husbands ever found out about the lesbian relationships taking place around them in Detroit, Beverly Dale at first replied no but then clarified her response: "If they did, they never discussed it."[50] Similarly, Kathy Martinez, who engaged in her two-year affair with Carmen in New York City in the early 1960s, later recalled, "I'm sure my mother knew, I'm sure that Carmen's husband knew, but no one ever made it difficult for us."[51] Around the same time in St. Louis, Gini Morton, mentioned in Chapter 1, would have her husband drop her off at gay bars where she went to meet women, but they did not discuss what she was doing. "I think he knew," Gini remarked mildly decades after the fact. "He knew I was queer from the beginning."[52] Of course, some husbands and family members knew more than they let on. Believing their wives' same-sex relationships would pass, these men may have felt that silence was the best option.[53] Discretion thus worked in two ways: while most wives did not tell their husbands explicitly about their affairs, neither did their husbands demand to know. Discretion allowed wives to preserve their marriages while engaging in sexual relationships with women who seemed to be merely friends, and it allowed husbands to avoid (or put off) the pain, embarrassment, or disruption that confronting their wives could bring.

Some women and their husbands, however, were surprisingly forthright. "I don't care what you do with women, but don't do anything with men," one white, working-class woman's husband told her after she began frequenting lesbian bars at mid-century in Buffalo, New York.[54] In fact, this woman's husband had first introduced her to the gay and lesbian bar scene in Buffalo, and the couple sometimes engaged in threesomes with other women. Because he saw lesbianism as titillating, ephemeral, or inconsequential, this husband considered his wife's same-sex relationships less threatening than a heterosexual affair would have been. Surely he was not alone. But it would be a mistake to believe that such husbands' tolerance for their wives' same-sex relationships was based solely on their fetishization of lesbian sex, or even on their own desires for outside sexual relationships.

At the most fundamental level, husbands tolerated their wives' lesbian relationships because they wanted to remain married. Novelist Dorothy Baker's husband, Howard, made time for her to visit her lover because he did not want to divorce and was concerned for his wife's happiness. In California in 1945, after fifteen years of marriage and the births of their two daughters, Dorothy informed Howard about her persistent attraction to women and the true nature of her relationship with Mildred Stewart, her "dear friend and more than friend."[55] Years later Dorothy recalled the event in her journal, describing her lesbianism as a shameful affliction that she could not shake. Dorothy assumed that after telling Howard about her homosexuality they would have to divorce, but Howard insisted this was unnecessary. They loved each other and could find a way to accommodate her homosexuality. According to Dorothy's recollection of their conversation, Howard said that she should "be allowed [her] deviation from the norm . . . but in an *orderly* and controlled way." The pair then agreed that Dorothy would be allowed four separate weeks of vacation every year without Howard or the children when she could visit Mildred, whom Howard knew well and approved of as Dorothy's lover. Overall, the arrangement was successful. In fact, Dorothy called it her "salvation" and believed that it had only brought her and Howard closer together. Thirteen years after making their plan together, Dorothy wrote, "The Arrangement has had the effect of making me truly love Howard, the only person in the world I believe at once unconventional enough, to allow the one he loves (me, I guess) to be what I am. In an orderly way, of course."[56] In fact, Dorothy continued both her marriage and her relationship with Mildred Stewart for more than thirty years, until she passed away.

One husband, seemingly even more tolerant than Howard, allowed his wife's female lovers to live in their family's home. As a young, white butch in New Orleans in the early 1950s, Doris "Blue" Lunden lived with her married lover, Virginia, on and off for over a year. Blue was not the first of Virginia's lovers to live with her. Lila, Blue's friend and Virginia's former girlfriend, had also lived in her home. Blue first met Virginia at a lesbian bar called the Goldenrod in the French Quarter. After being arrested in a highly publicized police raid there, Blue had a falling-out with her father and left home for good.[57] With nowhere else to turn, she called up Virginia who did not hesitate to help: "Take a cab and come over," Blue remembered her saying.[58] Virginia lived with her spouse and four children, but she and her husband had negotiated an arrangement that allowed her some freedom. "She had her room and he had his room and she had to visit him once a week," Blue recalled. "But she was otherwise free to pursue her own interests as long as she took care of the house, and he would go to work and bring the money in."[59] During the time that she lived there, Blue stayed in Virginia's room in "*his* house," as she put it, succinctly capturing the economic ideology that underlay the household.[60]

Within the context of New Orleans's working-class lesbian community, Virginia's marital arrangement was rather unremarkable. In Blue's world, it was not merely common but nearly essential for lesbians to engage in sex with men in order to support themselves and their lovers.[61] Blue later explained that "the thing for butches was to have a girlfriend who supported you," typically though stripping, prostitution, or "somethin' like that."[62] Blue—and Virginia herself—may well have understood Virginia's marriage as a type of necessary sexual exchange akin to prostitution. Tellingly, Blue described Virginia's requisite visits to her husband's bedroom as "services."[63]

Blue avoided sex work until she became tired of depending on Virginia and her husband for support. Desperate for cash, one night she turned a trick and promptly became pregnant. She married a gay male friend so that her child would not be illegitimate, but the marriage provided Blue no economic security and she continued living with Virginia. Now Blue *and* her daughter were dependent on Virginia's husband, and he demanded that Blue begin visiting his bedroom too. "I had to," Blue explained. "I mean obviously I'd had a child so I'd been doin' it with somebody else, so I was fair game then."[64] Though other husbands appear to have welcomed their wives' lovers into their homes without making such sexual demands of them, Virginia's marriage provides an example of how easily men could turn their wives' lesbian relationships to their advantage.

In order to avoid divorce, maintain a household, and care for their large family, Virginia and her husband created room for her lesbian desires in their marriage. They created time for Virginia to frequent lesbian bars and sustain lesbian relationships, and they created space, quite literally, for Virginia to maintain some privacy and to shelter her lovers in their home. But their marriage, it should be noted, was in other ways exceedingly normal, if not entirely respectable. In exchange for her husband's financial support, Virginia was responsible for keeping up the home, tending to the children, and providing her husband with regular sexual release. (As a quasi second wife, Blue soon had to provide these same services.) From the outside, theirs was a successful marriage that met both spouses' needs while fulfilling the male-breadwinner ideal. The fact that Virginia found intimacy and sexual pleasure with women did not threaten the gendered structure of their relationship. Virginia's husband retained authority when it came to sex and money. Even Blue conceded that the marriage made sense for Virginia's husband: "I mean in a lotta ways . . . it was a wise decision on his part 'cause he wanted his kids, he wanted a home you know, and he couldn't afford to do that by himself."[65] In the language of the era's marital experts, Virginia and her husband *adapted*. They adapted *themselves* to fit marriage—both spouses fulfilled their formal, structural roles—and they adapted *marriage* to fit their needs.[66]

The Limits of Adaptation

Arrangements like this one were rare, though, and most wives who desired women found that they were either willing or able to stretch their marriages only so far. In some cases, husbands compelled their wives to choose between marriage and lesbian relationships. Muriel Crisara, a white, working-class woman from outside of Chicago, thought her husband was so unaware of her relationships with women that she asked her girlfriend to serve as maid of honor at their wedding in the early 1950s. Muriel's husband, in fact, knew more than he let on. At one point he discovered love letters between Muriel and another woman, but he was convinced that he could "change" her, and so chose to ignore them. After a few years of marriage, however, it became clear to Muriel's husband that her homosexuality was no passing phase. Aware that he could use evidence of her same-sex affair to secure a divorce, avoid alimony payments, or penalize her in their division of assets, Muriel's husband employed a detective to follow her on a trip to Detroit to visit her lesbian friends. When Muriel returned, her husband told her he knew where she had been, and she decided she was uninterested in continuing their marriage. The couple had no children, which made the divorce less traumatic, but even so, it was not easy. After-ward, Muriel felt she had no choice but to leave Illinois and move to Michi-gan, since her husband was "well known" in their community and, as she explained, "I couldn't go through the town without people knowing what was going on."[67] Though Muriel certainly sacrificed a degree of economic security in getting divorced, she had experience working in a factory and was able to find a well-paying union job in Detroit after her marriage ended.

Husbands like Muriel's, who accused their wives of homosexuality in court, were quite successful in securing fault-based divorces in the 1950s and 1960s.[68] But this success is striking, considering that lesbian sex did not clearly constitute adultery in a legal sense. Indeed, as late as 1962, most states continued to define adultery in gender-specific ways that did not include sex acts between women.[69] Perhaps because of this, in several cases judges and lawyers argued that wives' same-sex affairs constituted evidence of "extreme cruelty" rather than, or in addition, to adultery.[70] In the 1950 Pennsylvania case involving CD mentioned earlier, a judge noted that it was not the wife's homosexual affair itself that justified the divorce, but "the estrangement and disdain," or utter lack of respect she showed for her husband.[71] By carrying on her lesbian relationship openly after leaving her husband, CD became a "subject of gossip throughout the community."[72] It was this gossip that the judge found most "humiliating and degrading" to the husband in this case.[73] In this judge's eyes, the public embarrassment CD caused her husband was a more grievous error than her decision to engage in homosexual sex.

So hostile were judges to wives accused of lesbianism that they were willing to overlook a great deal of wrongdoing on husbands' part. In California in 1955, though Dixie Gilmore accused her husband, Don, of physical abuse, desertion, and at least six different acts of adultery, an appellate court believed Don's misdeeds were "trivial" when compared with Dixie's alcoholism, verbal and physical abuse, refusal to engage in marital sex, and "disregard of accepted standards of sexual behavior."[74] This latter offense referred not only to Dixie's withholding of sex from her husband, but also to Dixie's participation in sex acts with him and another woman who testified against her. Don, though part of this threesome, conveniently claimed that he was nothing more than a "glorified observer."[75] Don thus seemed to suggest that his presence was merely a cover for the women's true desire for each other, and the appellate court denied Dixie alimony. Similarly, in a later case in Pennsylvania, a superior court judge upheld a lower court's ruling granting a divorce to Walter Benkowski, whose wife, Sylvia, had, among other misdeeds, engaged in homosexual acts "in public view, to his great embarrassment and distress."[76] Though Sylvia accused her husband of abandoning and physically abusing her, the judge considered her charges unreliable and the acts of abuse she alleged to be "isolated and provoked."[77] Though the judge in this case did not consider Walter "completely without fault," to his mind Sylvia's was the greater wrong, and he ruled in Walter's favor.[78]

Husbands could also use evidence of their wives' lesbianism to deprive them of child custody. In 1959 in New Jersey, an appellate court denied Elizabeth Hanson custody after her husband claimed that she "associated with female homosexuals and refused to change her ways."[79] As proof, Elizabeth's husband submitted thirty-nine letters she had written to another woman discussing their love for each other. Even lesbian mothers who initially won custody could lose their children if their husbands secured proof of their homosexuality. In a 1959 case in California, *Immerman v. Immerman*, a divorced lesbian mother lost child custody after her ex-husband walked into her home to discover her making love with another woman.[80]

Divorced lesbians who attempted to raise their children outside of marriage during this period thus often lived in fear of losing their child custody rights. In some cases, this fear was enough to push divorced lesbians back into marriage. In 1963, for example, Vera Martin, an African American mother living in Los Angeles, learned that her ex-husband was beginning to suspect her homosexuality. Unwilling to risk losing custody of their youngest child, Vera married a gay male friend and resumed an outwardly straight life.[81]

At the same time, however, a variety of factors could work to lesbian mothers' advantage in child custody battles at midcentury. To begin with, in the early twentieth century, a strong legal preference for placing young children with their mothers replaced an earlier legal understanding of children as their fathers' property. As one authoritative family-law treatise of the 1920s put it, "Where the children are of tender years, other things being equal, the mother is preferred as their custodian."[82] Perhaps in part because of this "tender years" doctrine, coupled with their own ignorance about lesbian sexuality, some judges refused to believe that married women could desire other women. Del Martin, for example, one of the founders of the DOB, divorced in the late 1940s after her husband discovered love letters between her and a female neighbor. Though her husband sought to deprive Del of child custody on the basis of her lesbianism, the judge refused to take the letters into consideration, believing that they provided evidence only of a close friendship.[83]

In other cases, lawyers operating with a sense of sexual discretion made sure that such allegations never made it into the courtroom in the first place. Shirley Maser separated from her husband, Fred, in Oregon in the late 1940s, when her daughter was only a few months old. When Fred served her with divorce papers, he requested custody of their daughter on the basis of Shirley's lesbianism. But Shirley was not intimidated. She went to her husband's lawyer and admitted that she was gay, but insisted that she would not give up custody without a fight. "I'm not going to just sit there and sign her over," Shirley told him. If he wanted to take her to court and air the details of her lesbianism publicly, she would oblige. The lawyer went on to ask her a series of invasive questions about whether she and her daughter had separate bedrooms, and even whether or not she used "tools" for sex. Satisfied with her answers and wanting to avoid a sordid scene in court, he talked Fred into giving Shirley joint custody: "Which I thought was pretty nice," Shirley noted, "Seeing it was his lawyer."[84]

Most mothers, though, were unwilling to take such a chance. Fearful of losing her children and unable to support herself, Lilly choose a different path when her husband confronted her about her lesbian affair in the late 1950s. The child of upper-middle-class Jewish parents, Lilly married David, an aspiring lawyer, around 1951 in Cleveland, Ohio. Unfortunately, David was unable to make a living as a lawyer or to remain sexually faithful. Still, by her daughter's later account, Lilly remained deeply in love with him. The couple had two children and David earned extra money by helping out at his parents' restaurant. Then, in the late 1950s, Lilly somehow managed to meet Jo, a white, outspoken butch who managed a lesbian bar in the city. Years later, Jo recalled how smitten she was with Lilly and how what may have begun as a friendship soon became a sexual affair. Jo regularly visited Lilly in the family's apartment when David was out. Lilly would signal to her lover, waiting outside, when it was safe to come up by raising or lowering the window shades, thus turning to her own ends one of the household goods that have become a symbol of white, middle-class housewives' lives in the 1950s. Lilly also became acquainted with Jo's group of lesbian friends, either by attending house parties or by visiting the bar where Jo worked. Whether this continued for months or even a year is unclear, but eventually David learned of the relationship. Despite his own infidelities, he threatened to divorce Lilly and take custody of their children if she did not end her affair.

Lilly, like all the wives described here, was able to control much of what occurred inside her home, but she could do little about the forces beyond it. If her husband had produced evidence of her homosexuality in court as threatened, she could have lost custody of her children and her only source of income as well. Lilly was a housewife with little employment experience and a limited education, leaving her ill-prepared to find a well-paying job. Faced with an unhappy marriage on the one hand and an uncertain future without her children on the other, Lilly responded to her husband's ultimatum by attempting to kill herself. Giving even darker meaning to the concept of women's "domestic containment" at midcentury, she shut herself inside their apartment and turned on the gas.[85] Thankfully, Lilly's suicide attempt was not successful; her sister discovered her and took her to the hospital before it was too late. Whatever Lilly's initial feelings upon coming to—shock, anger, sadness—she gathered herself together, ended her affair with Jo, and made a renewed effort to save her marriage. Shortly after her suicide attempt, Lilly and her husband moved out of the city and bought a house in the suburbs, far away from the lesbian community Lilly had briefly encountered. The couple's marriage did not improve, and decades later she and David divorced. Lilly never identified as a lesbian, and there is no evidence that she ever had another homosexual relationship. Yet despite the trauma Lilly and Jo's sexual affair caused, the women's friendship persisted and they remained in touch through letters for the rest of Lilly's life.[86]

Husbands, as well as other family members, compelled wives to end their affairs and recommit themselves to marriage. In the late 1940s Irene Weiss, a young Jewish nurse in Pittsburgh, fell in love with one of her married patients, Phyllis. "I actually seduced her, I guess," Irene recalled decades later.[87] The women were able to continue their relationship for some months after Phyllis was released from the hospital, but eventually— out of guilt or because she wanted to begin a new life with Irene—Phyllis told her husband about their relationship. He responded by kicking her out of the house in her nightgown at two o'clock in the morning. Irene then sneaked Phyllis into her room in the nurses' residence where she was living. Phyllis did not return to her husband the following day to beg his forgiveness, and her husband did not come to Irene's residence to demand his wife's return. Instead, Phyllis stayed with Irene for several weeks until her father called and asked to meet with her. When Phyllis went to speak with her father outside the nurses' residence, Irene watched helplessly as "he grabbed her and like kidnapped her."[88]

Perhaps suspecting that physical force alone was not enough to keep the women apart, Phyllis's father then called the director of nurses at the hospital where Irene worked and threatened to publicly reveal her affair with his daughter unless she discharged Irene immediately. This was not an empty threat, as Phyllis's father owned a small local newspaper and could surely have crafted a salacious story about an aggressive lesbian nurse taking advantage of her innocent, married patient. Unsurprisingly, Irene lost her job and left Pittsburgh for New York City shortly thereafter. We cannot know for certain what Phyllis's father's motives were in terminating Irene's employment and forcing Phyllis to return to her old life. He may have believed he was protecting his daughter's reputation and future happiness, or he may have been concerned about the way her divorce and consensual lesbian relationship would reflect on him. In either case, he showed little interest in hearing what Phyllis wanted. When Phyllis and her husband gave no sign of reconciling on their own, he took it upon himself to force them back together.[89]

It would be inaccurate, though, to suggest that wives ended their same-sex relationships only when others compelled them to do so. When wives' priorities shifted or children were born or lovers changed or threatened to leave, combining marriage and lesbian affairs could become more difficult and less desirable. After more than a decade together, Muriel ended her affair with Mary Crawford when she decided to become a mother. Throughout their relationship in the 1940s and 1950s, Mary had repeatedly asked Muriel to leave her husband. At one point, in part to make Muriel jealous, Mary even threatened to find a husband herself. Yet despite these pressures, it seems that Muriel was content to balance her marriage and her relationship with Mary until she decided to start a family. After nearly fifteen years together, Muriel began to put space between Mary and herself. She took a full-time job that left her little free time, and she stopped returning Mary's calls. Mary did not know for sure that their relationship was over, however, until the women met and Muriel informed her that she was going to have a baby. Mary understood the pregnancy as a sign that Muriel was planning to begin a more conventional married life without her. Just as Mary suspected, after their meeting Muriel ceased contact entirely.[90]

❧ ❧

Lesbian history has tended to highlight the radical implications of love and sex between women, but married women's same-sex affairs cannot be understood wholly as a type of protest against the institutions of marriage and heterosexuality.[91] For the most part, the wives described here had no intention of challenging 1950s marital norms. By secretly but persistently acting on their same-sex desires, they were struggling to meet their needs for emotional intimacy and sexual pleasure, as well as their responsibilities as wives and mothers. Their actions grew out of both their pervasive discontentment and their commitment to conventional ideas about women's roles within marriage. Indeed, from the harshest perspective, we might even see such wives' same-sex affairs counterintuitively as tactics that they employed in their attempts to fulfill the nuclear-family ideal and make their marriages work. There is evidence that some wives who engaged in heterosexual extramarital relationships also understood their actions as reinforcing, rather than undermining, their marriages.[92] Yet wives who engaged in extramarital relationships with women had even more reason to see their actions as compatible with, if not beneficial to, their marriages. Their relationships with women were of an entirely different nature from those they had with their husbands—born, more often than not, out of friendship—and the possibility of divorcing one's husband for a female lover, as opposed to a male one, was even more remote. Tellingly, most wives did not use terms like "infidelity" or "cheating" in describing their relationships with women, suggesting that they did not see these relationships in the same way they might have understood a heterosexual romance.

Although many wives still experienced guilt about acting on their same-sex desires and worried about the effects their actions could have on their families, the women described in this chapter were not ruled by such negative emotions. Venturing into a lesbian bar or party, confessing one's passionate feelings to a close friend: these are optimistic acts. Through such acts, women resisted feelings of depression, despair, helplessness, and isolation. They forced themselves to look beyond the present moment and into the future—to the next chance they would have to get to that bar, or the next quiet moment with the mother of three down the block. With such acts, women sought human connection and understanding, emotional sustenance, and physical pleasure. Whether or not they found what they were looking for, taking those steps was an act of faith. In order to kiss a friend or speak the words "I love you," these women had to believe that the connection they were looking for *might* exist. One wife and mother who was searching for a female lover in Iowa in the mid-1960s used a favorite saying that captured her situation and that of many others: "There's no solution; seek it lovingly."[93] In seeking the solution—to their continuing lesbian desires and their continuing commitment to their families—these wives elicited within themselves the hope they needed to carry on with their daily lives and persevere in marriages that "worked" but fell far short of their dreams. In the process, they challenged, if only privately, the intense stigmatization of their feelings for other women.

Of course, viewing the actions of the wives in this chapter through a black and white lens, understanding them *either* as a form of protest or conformity, reduces the complexity of such wives' desires and experiences. In acting on their desires for women, the wives described here incited changes that they could neither foresee nor control, making these changes difficult to categorize as either simply resistance or accommodation. Some husbands who initially found their wives' lesbian affairs unthreatening eventually realized their relationships were far more serious than they thought and demanded that their wives make a choice. Women who never had any intention of divorce found they could not bear living apart from their lovers. Many others gradually began to envision a time, after their children were grown, when they would divorce and live the lives they truly wanted. Marriages that had once seemed permanent now appeared temporary; sexual relationships and identities that had once seemed sick or immoral were now appealing and affirming. In some cases, even wives who had never attributed political meaning to their intimate, sexual lives, nor understood themselves as part of a minority group, found themselves reaching out to and becoming part of a national gay and lesbian community and an emerging homophile movement.

I do not mean to suggest, however, that those women who eventually sought a connection with the gay and lesbian community were the only "really" radical ones. The case of Marie Pierce, a divorced, white nurse who fell in love with a married woman in the late 1950s in Baytown, Texas, suggests the ways in which wives could dramatically redefine the meaning of family. Marie's lover, C. Willa Brown, was a school bus driver, fourteen years her senior. Well-known for her quick wit and good humor, C. had an unusual relationship with her husband, Norman. Years before Marie and C. met, Norman had offered C. a divorce after he returned home from the military and discovered he was impotent, a common symptom of post-traumatic stress disorder.[94] C. refused to divorce and tried to find medical help for Norman, but he would not talk to anyone about his condition and was untroubled by their lack of sex life. By the time that Marie and C. became involved, Norman seemed thankful that Marie was able to provide his wife with a level of companionship he could not provide. Norman was never jealous, Marie insisted, and by her account the two bonded rather than competed over their shared love for C. "He always told me, if anythin' ever happened to him, be sure [C.] went to the beauty shop every week because she looked so pretty," Marie later recalled.[95]

Marie, C., and Norman succeeded in establishing a different kind of family unit. Norman was unfailingly kind to Marie and became, she would later explain, like a brother to her. Early in Marie's relationship with C., Norman suggested that they get a trailer home for Marie to set up on their acre of property near Galveston Bay, so that she could live with Norman and C. while having her own space. At some point later, Marie moved into the main house, but Norman never had a problem with the situation. As

Marie remembered, "We had our bedroom and he had his."[96] For about twenty years, the three lived peaceably together, until Norman's death from bone cancer in 1979. Near the end of his life, when Norman was very sick and in terrible pain, Marie and C. cared for him at home so that he could die in comfort. The women brought in two hospital beds—one for them, and one for Norman—so that they could sleep next to him and wake up at night if he needed help. When the end finally came, Marie was touched that her employer, Gulf Coast Hospital, did not hesitate to acknowledge Norman as her kin. "They gave people three days' pay for family," Marie later recalled. "They gave me three days' pay."[97] Long after Norman passed away, Marie cared for C. as she had promised she would. And when C. died at the age of eighty-eight in 2002, the women had been together for forty-four years.

If Marie's and C.'s likely exceptional experiences tell us anything, it is perhaps how thoroughly inadequate and constraining our sexual vocabulary and our definitions of love, romance, and family remain. In refusing to choose between either their lovers or their husbands, some wives who desired women rejected conventional understandings of romantic love as possible between only two people at a time, of sexuality as either heterosexual or homosexual, and of marriage as narrow and inflexible. Remaining married was not necessarily the same as remaining "closeted" or in hiding. Indeed, for some, combining marriage and lesbian relationships may have begun as a compromise, but it became an ideal, an alternative way of organizing family life and affective ties that was more fulfilling than either a strictly lesbian or heterosexual life would have been.

CHAPTER 3

The Lesbian Wife Problem

ESMÉ LANGLEY WAS FRUSTRATED. For once, the ever-capable Langley, veteran of World War II, fearless single mother, advocate for the homeless, and leader of the British lesbian rights organization the Minorities Research Group (MRG), did not know what to do.[1] In the fall of 1964, she penned a letter to fellow lesbian activist Barbara Gittings, founder of the DOB's New York chapter, asking for help. "The enormous no. of unhappy married women who want to join MRG and *relax* from the strains of a miserable 'home' life," she explained, was causing MRG a "major headache." Such women, Langley feared, put the organization at risk of becoming involved in "enticement" or "alienation of affection" lawsuits or divorce cases, and threatened its members with being publicly branded as "wife-stealers," "home-breakers," or "corrupters of the innocent."[2] Most MRG members who had been married were divorced, separated, or widowed, Langley pointed out, but in an attempt to avoid getting caught up in any legal trouble, the MRG's membership application demanded that married women's husbands sign the form. What, Langley wanted to know, did the DOB do about this group of women? Gittings replied that married women were not a problem for her organization at all. "Uninitiated married lesbians don't flock to the DOB," she claimed, continuing, "Anyway, as far as I know we've had few married members who have conflicts with their husbands, and no trouble incidents for us so far."[3]

While there is to my knowledge no evidence that the DOB was ever caught up in the type of lawsuit Langley feared, Gittings was somewhat disingenuous in insisting that married women did not pose a "problem" for her group. Soon after the DOB's founding in 1955, wives who desired women sought help and advice from the organization, subscribed to the group's monthly magazine *The Ladder*, attended DOB events, and became members of the organization. Years later, long-time leaders of the DOB, Del Martin and Phyllis Lyon, noted that whenever the organization attracted media attention the biggest response came from married women.[4] If Chapter 2 presented wives who desired women as existing largely in isolation in the 1950s and 1960s, this chapter demonstrates that some married women were able to connect with a broader lesbian community by reaching out to the DOB and other homophile groups, which, in turn, welcomed their participation. Though lesbian activists and wives who desired women were often separated by a wide cultural and geographic gulf, a few married women were able to contribute to the DOB's mission and become activists themselves.

Wives' involvement in the DOB raised serious questions for the organization's leaders and members. Whether such women were victims of circumstance or hedonists enjoying the best of both worlds; whether they should leave their marriages or seek divorce; whether they were partners in the struggle for lesbian rights or obstacles to it: these were matters of heated and enduring debate among DOB members. Due, in part, to married women's significant participation in the organization, the "lesbian wife" became a recurring and controversial figure in *The Ladder*, particularly in the late 1950s and early 1960s. The community of women who participated in the DOB did not reach a consensus during these years on any one of the myriad questions that lesbian wives engendered. Yet married women's participation in the DOB and the attendant debate within the organization about this population shed light on lesbians' understandings of the complex relationships between marriage, heterosexuality, and homosexuality. Most DOB leaders, members, and wives themselves conceived of marriage as neither a solid barrier to participation in lesbian life, nor a clear indicator of a woman's sexual desires. For them, hetero- and homosexual worlds and identities were permeable; they may have existed in tension with one another but they were not mutually exclusive.[5] The DOB's leaders understood that for many women marriage was a social and economic necessity; women's sexual desires were another matter altogether.

Forging Connections

The DOB was part of a broader postwar effort to organize on behalf of homosexual rights, which began with the creation of the Mattachine Society in Los Angeles in 1951. The Mattachine Society's founders, most notably Harry Hay, had been involved in the Communist Party, an experience that shaped their political tactics. They focused on raising homosexuals' consciousness of themselves as a minority group, developed a social analysis of homosexual oppression, and established a hierarchical and secretive organizational structure. This small organization grew substantially in 1952, when it gained nonprofit status. Another major step came that same year when a few Mattachine Society members branched off to begin an independent organization, ONE, Inc., which published the homosexual magazine, *ONE*. By the spring of 1953, the Mattachine had spawned a network of nearly one hundred groups with more than two thousand members.[6] At the same time, tensions within the group erupted over its founders' Communist Party connections, and a new, more moderate set of leaders took over. Over the next year and a half, as the Mattachine shifted its priorities—at least publicly—from mobilizing a grassroots movement to supporting the work of researchers studying homosexuality, its membership levels dropped.[7]

The Mattachine Society and ONE, Inc., had a profound influence on the DOB. In October 1955, a group of eight women in San Francisco created the DOB to serve as a secret, social alternative to gay bars. They selected the DOB's obscure name—Daughters of Bilitis, which referred to a fictional lover of the Greek poet Sappho—precisely because few people would understand its meaning. Only a few months after its founding, however, Del Martin and Phyllis Lyon—lovers, as well as the DOB's president and secretary, respectively—were reconsidering the organization's primarily social purpose. After meeting with activists involved with the Mattachine and ONE, Inc., Martin and Lyon were impressed by their cautious approach to challenging the stigmatization of homosexuals. By the summer of 1956, the DOB had a new goal and a new group of members who were, like Martin and Lyon, committed to changing social attitudes toward homosexuality. As its new statement of purpose explained, the DOB was now dedicated to "promoting the integration of the homosexual into society." Its tactics were multiple: education of the homosexual "to enable her to understand herself and make her adjustment to society," education of the public "leading to an eventual breakdown of erroneous taboos and prejudices," participation in research about homosexuality, and investigation and transformation of laws affecting homosexuals.[8] Throughout the 1950s and 1960s, though membership levels remained low, women created DOB chapters—some longer lasting than others—in cities including New

York, Los Angeles, Boston, Chicago, Cleveland, Philadelphia, and Dallas.[9] Despite these changes, the DOB's leaders remained deeply committed to helping individual women. The DOB was, as one handout for new members put it, "a home for the Lesbian. She can come here to find help, friendship, acceptance and support."[10]

In 1956 the DOB's leaders also began publishing their monthly newsletter, *The Ladder*, which they initially publicized through the Mattachine's newsletter and *ONE* magazine. Lyon served as *The Ladder*'s first editor until 1960, when Martin took over, followed by Barbara Gittings in December 1962. *The Ladder* was in many respects the most successful of the DOB's endeavors, and its reputation soon superseded that of the DOB itself.[11] While the DOB distributed the first copy of its magazine to only two hundred people, by 1964 circulation neared one thousand copies per issue between subscriptions, newsstand sales, and bookstore sales; by the time it was last issued in 1972, *The Ladder*'s mailing list reached nearly four thousand, including women across the nation and even outside of it.[12] Featuring short stories and poems, reports on academic studies of homosexuality, reviews of lesbian-themed books, updates about the activities of the DOB and other early gay rights groups, and selected letters from the magazine's readers, *The Ladder* enabled the DOB to connect and inform lesbians across the country, and to present positive depictions of female homosexuality to undermine those in the mainstream media. The magazine's illustrations, cartoons, and cover art often depicted young attractive women but always did so prudently (Figure 5), in contrast to the salacious covers of cheap lesbian-themed paperback novels, which provided the most readily available depictions of lesbians at midcentury.[13] Though women of color were not entirely absent from *The Ladder*, the magazine focused on the experiences of white, middle-class lesbians, who made up the majority of the DOB's members, and demonstrated a pointed distaste for working-class butch/femme bar culture.[14]

From the beginning, married women participated in the DOB, often by writing letters to the organization or subscribing to *The Ladder*. Wives' correspondence demonstrates that they found the DOB to be a vital means of connecting to other women like them. Indeed, the organization's existence helped many women to name their same-sex desires, and to imagine themselves as part of a larger homosexual community, as historian Martin Meeker has argued.[15] The letter of one married woman in Dubois, Wyoming, dramatically conveyed how desperately she needed the DOB in 1963: "Don't let *The*

Figure 5. The Ladder's editors were careful to present respectful, humanizing images of lesbians that would counter those in the mainstream media. Cover of *The Ladder*, October 1957. From the Phyllis Lyon and Del Martin Papers, courtesy of the Gay, Lesbian, Bisexual, Transgender Historical Society.

Ladder publication stop! It is the *best friend* we isolated folks in remote parts of the country have. Life would be unthinkable *without* it! In fact, it would be unbearable!"[16] Readers who did not know where or how to meet other lesbian-identified women clearly depended on the DOB to fill this need.

Even this limited type of outreach took great courage, as married women risked having their families discover their correspondence or magazines; but whatever the risks, married women persisted in reaching out to the DOB. One wife and mother of three from Jacksonville, Florida, was so afraid that her children would find her copies of *The Ladder* that she burned the magazine every month. Still, this woman had no intention of ending her subscription. Instead, "being thrifty as well as faint-hearted," she wrote to *The Ladder*'s editor in 1963 asking if she could return her copies of the magazine after reading them, both to avoid her "monthly conflagration" and to get a reduced subscription rate.[17] Though this woman described herself as "faint-hearted," she let neither fear of her children finding her *Ladder* copies, nor concern about the DOB leaders' disapproval—of her marriage or her stinginess—stop her.

Married women often requested that their names not be used in the DOB's materials, and that the DOB send correspondence to them on unmarked stationary. Yet to see such women as immobilized by fear would be a mistake. One wife who made a literary submission to *The Ladder* implored then editor Gittings, "Please—on pain of losing me one husband, one career and one very happy existence—I beg you not to let anyone know that I am the author of the enclosed." At the same time, within her letter she referenced an earlier phone conversation with Gittings, and she signed her note, "See you Saturday night."[18] Whether Gittings and this letter writer had plans to meet at a DOB gathering or at some other type of event is unclear, but in either case, their relationship was not limited to correspondence alone. Despite this wife's concerns about her husband's discovering her association with the organization, she contributed writing to *The Ladder*, and also spent at least one Saturday night in Gittings's company.

Wives' fear of being connected to the DOB continued into the late 1960s as the homophile movement was becoming more visible and more radical. As late as 1968, a young wife and doctoral candidate at the University of Chicago was so afraid of being connected to the DOB that she had her unknowing sister write her a membership check. "Is everyone as cowardly as I am?" she asked her readers at the DOB.[19] While concerned that her homosexuality, if discovered, could hurt her young son or endanger her burgeoning academic career, it was her husband's wrath this letter writer dreaded the most. "If [my husband] ever discovered any of this," she wrote, "he would either draw and quarter me or perhaps be less sadistic and just shoot me."[20] This statement should not be dismissed as mere hyperbole. The fear of physical punishment it dramatically conveys may have been, for this woman, quite real. Nonetheless, desperate for contact with other gay people, this wife still took the risk of reaching out to the DOB and even asked what she could do "to be useful" to their cause.[21]

The male-dominated Mattachine Society and ONE, Inc., received far fewer letters from married women during these decades, but wives' correspondence with these groups similarly demonstrates their determination to make contact with a larger gay world.[22] One wife from New Jersey wrote to ONE, Inc., in the early 1960s requesting to be put into contact with other gays or lesbians in their organization, but she was doubtful they would fulfill her request. Apparently, having already made similar requests to other homophile groups, she understood that ONE, Inc., might have a "no contacts arranged" rule, but she stressed that this was her only way of participating in the organization and that she could be trusted. "Now if you apply your rule, I suppose you won't answer me," she wrote. "But at least I tried—and, damnit, I'm going to keep on trying. Somewhere, maybe I'll persuade someone to believe me! I'll go nuts if I don't."[23] A similarly determined, though less desperate Canadian wife wrote to Irma Wolf, *ONE*'s editor in 1956, after reading a copy of the magazine at a female friend's home. "I am 29 now and have been a lesbian for many years having had my first experience in a Nudist Camp while in Europe with my husband back in 1947," she informed the editor. "We still live together and he does not mind a bit my way of thinking about my love for lovely feminine friends, on the contrary." Because of the strict laws governing homosexuality and divorce in Quebec at the time, this woman explained that it was "very difficult [for homosexuals] to get together and live together," and she worried that it would be hard for her to receive copies of *ONE*. She was, nonetheless, undaunted. She suggested that Wolf send the magazine through first-class mail so it would reach her town, and even requested that Wolf put her in contact with an American lesbian of her age.[24]

Surprisingly, some married women were involved in multiple homophile organizations. In 1956, one such woman, Esther, from Providence, Rhode Island, wrote to Del Martin to find out more about the organization.[25] Esther had heard of the DOB first through *ONE*, and then through the Mattachine Society's New York City chapter, which had recently sponsored an event she attended. Esther had met many other gay people there, though disappointingly far more men than women. Esther applauded the brave and courageous work the DOB was doing, and in response to Martin's request that she serve as a "correspondent" for her area by gathering contacts for their mailing list, she promised to send the names of other lesbians who might be interested in the organization when she could.[26] "Until a few months ago I had not known any other girls here in Providence, but have become acquainted with several since then," Esther explained. "There are a large number of homosexuals in Providence as throughout the country."[27] Eventually, Esther did forward to Martin the names of three other local women—two of whom were married—who wanted to receive the DOB's magazine.[28] Esther was neither self-hating nor isolated, neither trapped nor helpless. She may or may not have had an affair with one of the other gay "girls" she knew in Providence, or left her marriage, or publicly identified as homosexual. But she was clearly embedded in a local queer network in Providence, and she had a consciousness of herself as part of a larger, nationwide group of gays and lesbians. Indeed, it was out of a belief in the value of the DOB's work and a desire to support the organization that Esther showed the organization's publication to her friends and encouraged other women to become subscribers. Despite the risk that her husband might discover her correspondence with the DOB or her copies of *The Ladder*, she remained a member of the group and received the magazine for at least two years.

In the late 1950s, another exceptional wife from San Jose attended Mattachine, ONE, Inc., and DOB events, and had her writing published in the *Mattachine Review* and *The Ladder* under the pseudonym Jo Allyn. In a letter to Hal Call, the Mattachine Society's president, Jo described the factors—most importantly a disabled son who required her sustained care and attention—that made it difficult for her to leave her marriage. "It seems to me that if I could only adjust my home life to my gay life, the situation would be perfect," she wrote. "But I doubt very much that I can ever accomplish this." Despite her troubles, she evinced no shame or guilt about her sexual orientation and had no desire to overcome it. She even facetiously apologized to Call for being too affectionate with him at ONE, Inc.'s recent convention banquet: "Perish the thought that anyone should think we were converted."[29] Jo was not the only married woman to become involved with multiple homophile groups during this period, but she was among few.[30]

Yet another married woman was improbably able to connect with an international homophile community. Sally, a working-class housewife and mother from Pittsburgh, corresponded with Barbara Gittings in the mid-1960s. Oddly, Sally did not contact Gittings directly but first reached out to Esmé Langley, the British homophile activist mentioned earlier, who put the two Americans in touch. It is unclear how Sally found out about Langley, but it is possible that she came across a copy of *Arena Three*, the MRG's magazine, which Langley authored and which was publicized in the United States through *The Ladder*. Though in the midst of a difficult breakup with another wife and mother, Sally was developing a small circle of lesbian friends closer to home. Her correspondence to Gittings was peppered with references to lesbian "girls" and gay bars. "Our clubs in Pgh [Pittsburgh] are being raided constantly," she complained in one letter, and favorably compared the women she had recently met at a gay bar in Ohio to those in Pittsburgh.[31] In fact, Sally was making plans to open up her own lesbian bar—"a club for girls," as she put it—with her husband's help. "All the legal technicalities are being worked out and my husband is definitely for it," she informed Gittings.[32] Whether or not Sally's husband knew that her plans for a lesbian club were motivated by personal as well as financial interests remains unclear.

While most wives contacted homophile organizations to find friends and a sense of community, at least one married woman treated the DOB as a type of matchmaking service. In 1958 Pat, a married, self-identified butch living in Portland, Oregon, asked Del Martin for help in finding a lover of her own class status, or as she put it, "any femme who is in my own strata and unattached."[33] The gay bars in Portland "hold no inducements," she explained, either referring to the quality of the bars themselves or the types of women she had met within them.[34] While slight (only five feet two inches and 117 pounds), Pat, who was in her early forties, stressed that she had broad shoulders, some college education, her own Cadillac car, and a taste for the finer things in life.[35] She conceded she was married—to a man she derogatorily referred to as a "norm"—but she insisted this would not prevent her from carrying on a relationship with another woman. Although Pat was new to the gay world, she was surprisingly particular in describing the femme she was looking for: "musically inclined" and "with a fair education." This ideal femme "would not necessarily have to be financially secure," she added. "In fact I would prefer not, but from a nice background."[36]

Considering the isolation we might assume such women experienced, Pat's confidence and sense of entitlement here are significant. She had only recently "found [her]self" with the help of a "very dear girl in San Francisco," but she emphasized that she was learning about gay life quickly and that she experienced no embarrassment about her homosexuality.[37] "I realize now that it is as normal for me to be a lesbian as it would be if I were an out and out 'norm,'" Pat wrote, pointedly questioning the term "norm" by placing it in quotation marks.[38] Though married and resistant to visiting gay bars she perhaps perceived as beneath her, Pat clearly believed she could afford to be picky in selecting her future lover. Her offhand comment that she would prefer her femme to be financially *in*secure is notable as well. As she made such a point of noting her own wealth and social status, it is possible that she was looking for a woman whom she could use her wealth to court, or one who would need her financial support and might thus be compelled to remain with her. Though new to the lesbian world and still married to a man, Pat clearly envisioned a future lesbian relationship for herself in which she had the upper hand.

Not all married women who contacted the DOB were so self-assured. In the early 1960s, Bea, who lived in Cincinnati, Ohio, with her husband and two children, expressed uncertainty about her sexual identity, and also about the way she fit into the butch/femme system. Bea had married at age nineteen, despite her feelings for other women, and she had two children. Although she loved her family, her feelings for women returned after a few years of marriage. "Am I a Lesbian?" she asked the DOB in 1963 after describing her entire sexual history, from her earliest crushes on girls to her current infatuation with a female coworker. "Is it possible to be an emotional but not physical homosexual? Can I have a 'butch' appearance, but a 'fem' personality? I am so confused!"[39] Bea's confusion about her sexual identity was exacerbated by the fact that she had not yet had sex with a woman, but she was coming to the conclusion that she had a right to act on the same-sex desires that had been troubling her for decades. At thirty-one, she felt that she could no longer ignore her feelings for other women. Bea's butch coworker had made some passes at her, and Bea asked the DOB leaders how she should proceed with the relationship. "I love my family dearly and wouldn't do a thing to harm them, but what about my loyalty to 'know thyself'?"[40] While it is unclear what Bea ultimately decided to do, in her letter she stressed that she was barely able to contain her attraction to her colleague. Indeed, it seems Bea was not so much asking for the DOB leaders' advice about how to proceed with her coworker, as she was seeking their support in carrying out a course of action on which she had already settled.

Other married women reached out to the DOB after having already begun new lesbian lives. In 1965, Doreen, a twenty-five-year-old mother in Los Angeles, wrote to the DOB after separating from her husband. Again, as if contacting a matchmaking service, Doreen provided a "personal data sheet" along with her letter to DOB. The data sheet included her age, marital status (separated), height, weight, measurements, race, and complexion ("Negro-Medium light brown"), as well as her education, health, interests, and hobbies. She was currently working at the Los Angeles County Board of Education, but her ambition was "to become a Professional Legal Secretary and to find happiness and acceptance in Society being what I am."[41] Though Doreen's goals may sound modest in retrospect, her insistence that she could find "happiness and acceptance" as an unmarried, black, lesbian mother is particularly striking, considering that 1965 was the same year that Assistant Secretary of Labor Daniel Patrick Moynihan released his policy report titled *The Negro Family*, which notoriously blamed the persistence of black poverty on the weakness of black marriages and the prevalence of female-headed households.[42] Doreen may not have encountered the Moynihan report firsthand, but she could not have escaped the prejudice against unmarried black mothers that it fostered. Perhaps her unusually formal and professional letter to the DOB took the form it did precisely because she was aware of the social stigma that she faced. In any case, it was in the face of overwhelming discrimination that Doreen optimistically set out on her new life.

Lesbian Wives in *The Ladder*

As married women asserted a presence within the DOB and the broader lesbian world, they both inspired and contributed to a debate about lesbian wives in *The Ladder*. Short stories featured wives pining for lost lesbian lovers, while opinion pieces examined the problems such women faced and provided advice about the path they should take. Unmarried women weighed in on the ethical and political issues raised by married lesbians, and married women themselves contributed writings about their predicaments, sharing information about their lives and asking for more stories and articles on the experiences of others like them. Wives who desired women inspired greater representation and discussion in *The Ladder* in some years than others, and the debate became particularly heated in 1957, 1960, and 1964, in particular. In 1957 this debate appears to have unfolded organically, with one story or letter about lesbian wives inspiring another. In 1960 and 1964, however, *The Ladder*'s editors made concerted efforts to solicit material and spark a conversation about wives who desired women. By the late 1960s, as the DOB separated from male-dominated homophile groups and became more closely allied with the emerging women's liberation movement, married women and the problems they faced no longer generated the same interest on the part of *The Ladder*'s readers and editors. This may also have been due to a shifting demographic within the organization itself. By the late 1960s, the original San Francisco chapter of the DOB was focusing more on younger women who were just beginning to identify as lesbians than on married women, and middle-aged women in the Bay Area were forming their own social groups.[43] The discussion of lesbian wives in *The Ladder* that follows focuses on the three years in which the figure of the lesbian wife generated the most attention.

Most of the early nonfiction articles about lesbian wives argued that such women should and could build successful heterosexual marriages. While this may have been a response to the difficulties of securing a fault-based divorce, or the possibility that a proven lesbian mother would lose custody of her children, most contributors portrayed remaining married as a moral, rather than a practical decision.[44] In 1957, for example, contributor Nancy Osbourne insisted that women who came to a "complete understanding" of themselves after marrying and becoming mothers had little choice but to remain married for their children's sake.[45] Osbourne then attempted to explain how such wives could build healthy relationships with their husbands, and she enumerated some of the many activities that a married couple could find pleasure in together other than sex: interior decorating, gardening, even the raising of show animals. Osbourne believed that it was deceitful for a woman to hide her homosexual desires from her husband, so she encouraged such wives to share their feelings. "An accepting attitude and a willingness to be enlightened on the part of her husband is her only way to find complete peace of mind," Osbourne wrote, but she acknowledged that not all husbands were so tolerant, and that most wives found it easiest to keep their feelings to themselves.[46]

Several readers agreed with Osbourne that homosexuals who had married should fulfill their obligation to their families. Luther Allen of Baltimore, a frequent contributor to the *Mattachine Review*, sympathized with the plight of the lesbian who realized her attraction to other women only after marrying, but he compared married homosexuals who acted on their same-sex desires to self-indulgent gluttons who could not control their appetites. Using a phrase that would appear again in *The Ladder*'s discussion of lesbian wives, Allen claimed that some married homosexuals simply wanted "to have their cake and eat it too."[47] Instead, Allen argued that after having entered into marriage, homosexual men and women had a responsibility to stick with it and remain sexually faithful: "When one individual breaks his/her freely given pledge to another individual who loves and trusts him/her a genuine and serious sin has been committed," he wrote.[48] While Osbourne encouraged wives who desired women to reveal their homosexuality to their husbands, Allen felt this was asking too much of spouses who would feel betrayed and deeply hurt by such a confession. For Allen, then, cheating on a spouse or dissolving a marriage were greater moral offenses than choosing to hide one's same-sex desires.

Novelist Marion Zimmer Bradley also believed that lesbians could have successful heterosexual marriages, though she resented Osbourne's implication that such women were being untrue to themselves. In her 1957 *Ladder* article "Some Remarks on Marriage," Bradley argued that wives could recognize their desires for other women but choose not to act on them. "The married Lesbian who can say to herself, and if necessary to her husband, 'I find other women interesting; that does not in any way affect our relationship,' is making a mature attempt to accept the nature of the world she has chosen to live in," she wrote.[49] Bradley conceded that if a married lesbian could not make such a statement truthfully, she should get divorced, and she unequivocally condemned wives who engaged in same-sex affairs; but if a woman could find a way to "adjust" to her desires, Bradley concluded, "there is no reason why a woman who is, or suspects herself to be, inherently Lesbian cannot make a happy marriage."[50] Bradley herself had married at age nineteen, in part to escape an alcoholic and abusive father. She was aware of her same-sex desires when she married, and before doing so had a relationship with another woman, who told Bradley that her homosexuality was a phase. The fact that Bradley's father suspected her homosexuality and attempted to have her arrested on account of it could only have convinced her further that lesbian relationships were not a viable alternative to married life. But Bradley's attraction to women did not end after marriage and the birth of her son as she had expected. After she wrote several lesbian-themed pulp novels, her editor recognized her interest in the issue, informed her about the existence of the homophile movement, and shared with her his copies of *The Ladder*. Bradley's argument, then, that women like herself could acknowledge their homosexuality without acting on it, and without threatening their marriages, was likely one of necessity. She was not only attempting to convince her readers that lesbians could have successful marriages, she was perhaps also trying to convince herself. [51]

In the issue of *The Ladder* following the publication of Bradley's article, Lorraine Hansberry, the civil rights activist and author of the later prize-winning play *A Raisin in the Sun* (1959), argued that Bradley was denying the seriousness of lesbian desire by describing it as something that women could easily overcome. Like Bradley, and Allen for that matter, Hansberry agreed that lesbian wives who engaged in extramarital affairs deserved only contempt, but she maintained that it was "pat and even unfair" to tell such women to simply get over their troubles and make a happy marriage. "I am afraid that homosexuality, whatever its origins, is far more real than that, far more profound in the demands it makes," she wrote.[52] Ultimately, Hansberry believed that the search for an answer to lesbian wives' problems was futile and distracted from the more important task of analyzing the cultural and economic forces that compelled women with same-sex desires to marry in the first place: their financial dependence on men, and their belief that marriage and motherhood represented women's destiny. A male-dominated culture had produced the ethical quandary in which married lesbians found themselves, Hansberry boldly argued, and it was thus the entire moral system premised on women's subordination that needed to be called into question. Formulating lesbian feminist arguments that would not emerge fully for more than a decade, Hansberry suggested "that homosexual persecution and condemnation has at its roots not only social ignorance, but a philosophically active anti-feminist dogma."[53] Unfortunately, Hansberry, who died of cancer in 1965, would not take up this idea in *The Ladder* again.

Hansberry's analysis, like Bradley's, was grounded in personal experience, but her perspective on the issue differed from Bradley's. At the time Hansberry's letter was published in *The Ladder*, her marriage was falling apart. She had married white composer Robert Nemiroff in 1953, but problems in their relationship emerged quickly. In a letter to her husband the following year, she wrote vaguely, "There *are* things that do trouble me in our marriage—most of the serious ones have to do with me."[54] By the time she began writing to *The Ladder*, she and her husband were separating, but they did not divorce until a year before her death. Ending their marriage was emotionally difficult for her. "I am sorry about the holes this marriage turned out to have in it," she told Nemiroff privately in 1958, "because it was so nice in the solid places. So very nice."[55] Indeed, long after their marriage was effectively over, Hansberry and Nemiroff remained close friends and artistic collaborators.

Yet it was, most likely, more than her continuing love and affection for Nemiroff that made it so hard for her to end their marriage. After *A Raisin in the Sun* premiered on Broadway in 1959 to widespread acclaim, Hansberry became an important figure in the civil rights movement, and she may have feared that if her homosexuality were revealed publicly, it would undermine the struggle for African Americans' rights, or her role within it. Even after she and Nemiroff legally divorced, they kept their separation quiet, and it was only after her death that Nemiroff publicly revealed they were no longer married. Years later, Martin and Lyon wrote that "many black women who had been involved in the homophile movement found themselves forced to make a choice between the two 'Causes' that touched their lives so intimately." Without referring to Hansberry by name, they noted: "One of them wrote a play that was a hit on Broadway."[56]

If Hansberry worried that her sexuality could be used to undermine the civil rights movement, her fears had good cause. Gay civil rights leader Bayard Rustin's sexuality both alienated him from other black leaders and provided fodder for opponents of the civil rights movement. Most notably, in advance of the 1963 March on Washington, which Rustin organized, Senator Strom Thurmond attempted to undermine Rustin's character by reading before Congress the record of his 1953 arrest for engaging in homosexual sex.[57] As a woman, Hansberry also had to contend with enduring and virulent stereotypes about black women's sexuality that had long excused their sexual abuse and exploitation. Faced with these stereotypes, civil rights leaders of the 1950s and early 1960s consciously selected as figureheads black women whose sexual behavior and gender presentation accorded with middle-class norms and values.[58] In light of these pressures, we might understand Hansberry's commitment to maintaining her public persona as a heterosexual wife as evidence of what scholar Darlene Clark Hine has termed a "culture of dissemblance" among black women in history. In the face of pervasive and dehumanizing sexual stereotypes, black women learned how to maintain an appearance of openness while keeping their inner lives hidden and secretly nurturing an alternative sense of themselves.[59] Indeed, Hansberry's letter to *The Ladder* provides evidence that beneath her outward presentation as a heterosexual wife, she was developing both a positive understanding of her own sexuality and a radical feminist and anti-racist critique of homosexual oppression more broadly.[60]

Much the way Hansberry struggled to maintain a respectable public persona as a married woman while privately affirming her same-sex desires, *The Ladder*'s editors struggled to balance competing political demands in choosing how to portray wives who desired women. On the one hand, the DOB intended *The Ladder* to provide positive portraits of lesbians that would counteract the negative depictions of them in the mainstream media. It was most likely for this reason that the DOB refrained from publishing articles and short stories urging married lesbians to leave their husbands, which might have exacerbated stereotypes about lesbians' selfishness and their threat to marriage. On the other hand, when the DOB published stories and articles about lesbians who remained married despite enduring lesbian desires, they failed readers who wanted more hopeful depictions of lesbian relationships. Moreover, while we know married women, including Bradley and Hansberry, appreciated *The Ladder*'s depictions of women like them, other women had little patience for those hiding their homosexuality beneath the veneer of conventional married lives. One such unmarried lesbian wrote to *The Ladder* to critique the editors' use of the euphemistic term "homophile" as opposed to "homosexual," a tactical choice that she argued betrayed some gays' and lesbians' "neurotic attempt to conform and integrate into heterosexuality." This reader particularly detested the way that "men and women who have three children and a home in the suburbs" used the label to describe themselves.[61] Clearly, not all *Ladder* readers shared an interest in or sympathy for married lesbians.

Perhaps in response to such readers' frustration, the DOB published a short story in *The Ladder* in 1958, titled "Chanson du Konallis," that portrayed lesbian wives in a harsher light than before. Written by Hansberry, under the name Emily Jones, the story is a modern retelling of Richard Aldington's 1926 cycle of poems *The Love of Myrrhine and Konallis*, which depicts a relationship between Konallis, a goat-girl, and Myrrhine, a courtesan.[62] In the retelling, Konallis is a wealthy white wife, and Myrrhine a beautiful black singer. The women, both American, lock eyes at a glamorous club in Paris, prompting Konallis's memories of a former female lover. The women meet briefly after the performance is over, and clearly share an attraction, but the singer breaks off their conversation after recognizing that the other woman has chosen a more conventional life path. The fact of Konallis's marriage and her capitulation to social expectations thus prevents the women from replicating the love affair their counterparts share in the earlier cycle of poems. It is only the married woman who suffers, though. After the singer departs, Konallis drowns her sorrows in drink, and that night lies awake in bed beside her husband, cursing her life.[63]

The debate about lesbian wives in *The Ladder* heated up again in the spring and summer of 1960, when Lyon and Martin made a conscious effort to incite a discussion on the topic. As Lyon explained in the June issue by way of her introduction to an article on married lesbians, her concern with the issue of lesbian wives was motivated both by the large number of such women and by "the general climate of intolerance existing among Lesbians toward women who are married yet admit their Lesbian tendencies."[64] Similarly, soon after Martin took over as editor in July, she issued a call for more contributions on the subject of married lesbians. In a note to readers in the magazine, she wrote, "There is all too little understanding of the 'married' lesbian, and it is apparent the subject needs some airing."[65] Martin and Lyon were not interested in merely "airing" the subject, though. The pieces they selected for publication on the subject were calculated to inspire unmarried lesbians' sympathy for their married counterparts. They did not provide instruction to married lesbians but elicited compassion and understanding for them. Such writings presented wives in as positive a light as possible, emphasizing their commitment to their families despite their personal suffering, as well as the ways in which married lesbians were not solely responsible for the situation in which they found themselves. Shifting the blame onto society more broadly, these stories, letters, and articles drew attention to the ways in which misinformation about homosexuality, the stigmatization of gays and lesbians, and the social and familial pressures on women to marry all helped to create a population of wives who desired women.

The first of these more sympathetic and dramatic publications was Bradley's short story "The House on the Borderland," which she published using the pseudonym Miriam Gardner. Judging by this short story, Bradley's opinions had drastically changed since she wrote on the subject of married lesbians in 1957. No longer did Bradley argue that lesbians could build happy heterosexual marriages. Instead, her fable depicted such wives as miserably torn between their responsibilities to their husbands and children and their unremitting desires for other women. "I live in a strange house. I call it the house on the borderland," the married protagonist says, describing how she is figuratively caught between two existences.[66] Alienated from both straight and lesbian worlds, the protagonist becomes a prisoner in her home, "tied by invisible bonds, allowed to venture only a few steps either way."[67] Though the story is told in the first person, the archetypal narrator repeatedly rejects the idea that she is alone in her borderland house: "Many cluster there, drawn irresistibly to the dark moonlight, hearing the beseeching voices from the sunlit world."[68]

In the same issue of *The Ladder*, Lyon published a letter from J. E. of Illinois, which—much like Bradley's story—portrayed wives who desired women as relatively powerless. In her letter, J. E. explained that she wanted to cancel her subscription to *The Ladder* because she had recently married and did not want to risk her husband's coming across the magazine. Perhaps fearing that *The Ladder*'s staff would fault her for her choice, J. E. explained that after seven tumultuous years in the "gay life," she had decided that the "security" of marriage was more important to her than relationships with women. Though J. E. gushed, "I can't tell you how thrilling it is to be accepted by my family and by his family at face value. I've almost forgotten to be afraid of what people are saying or possibly thinking of me," she conceded, "I'm not terribly strong in my convictions yet."[69] J. E. knew it would not be easy to leave her old life behind, and she even suspected that she would eventually regret her decision. "I was fascinated with every issue of *The Ladder* and it will be hard, believe me, to replace it with 'Better Homes & Gardens,'" she conceded. "I'll probably wish I could have really been one of you. I just wasn't strong enough to face it all."[70]

What Martin and Lyon chose *not* to include about married women in *The Ladder* is just as revealing as what they did. Lucy, the New Orleans wife and mother of two whose story began Chapter 2 of this book, was responding to Bradley's fable, "The House on the Borderland," when she wrote her letter to the DOB in 1960 arguing that married women could balance marriage and affairs as long as they did so with "caution and discretion."[71] Lucy addressed her response specifically to Bradley, requesting that the DOB forward it to her, and encouraged Bradley to see her borderland house as a gateway rather than a prison. Lucy also asked that her letter be printed in

The Ladder so that it could benefit other married subscribers. Lucy's conviction, however, that wives could "without guilt, shame or conscience" accept their "homosexual leanings" as just one part of themselves, and secretly act on their homosexual desires without harm to their marriages, was not in keeping with the desperate, selfless portrait of married lesbians Martin and Lyon were attempting to paint. In contrast to the stories and articles they printed, which emphasized married lesbians' hopelessness, Lucy insisted that wives who desired women could have a "bright emotional future," by integrating their "homosexual tendencies" into their married lives.[72] The DOB may well have forwarded Lucy's letter to Bradley as she requested, but—perhaps fearing that Lucy's letter would inspire unmarried lesbians' resentment rather than their sympathy—they did not publish it.

Instead, Martin and Lyon published letters from married women that supported *The Ladder*'s sympathetic and dramatic depictions of their lives.[73] Notable among these is an open letter from Jody Shotwell, a Philadelphia wife and mother of three, addressed to her disapproving friend "Meredith." Jody served as secretary of the DOB's New York chapter when it was founded in 1958, and she participated in the Mattachine Society's chapter in Philadelphia as well. In the late 1950s and early 1960s, she also contributed poems and short stories—often featuring wives who desired women—to *The Ladder*, *ONE*, and the *Janus Society Newsletter*, a publication of the Philadelphia-based homophile organization. Apparently, Jody had an "understanding" with her husband that allowed her to engage in sexual relationships with both women and men.[74] In her letter to Meredith, she wrote that a recent piece in *The Ladder* had caused a disagreement between them on the issue of bisexuality, and the case of "the heterosexually married lesbian" in particular. "You insist upon the reaching of a decision, of a choice, irrevocable, between homosexuality and heterosexuality," Jody wrote, but then countered, "It is not that simple. Nothing involving our basic nature is that simple."[75] She believed that women who were attracted to both sexes could never wholly renounce one aspect of their sexuality, and she did not see an easy resolution for them. Instead, she concluded with a plea for friendship and understanding.

Jody's simultaneous use of the terms "bisexual" and "lesbian" in describing wives who desired women was not unique; other women who contributed to *The Ladder* during this period also muddied the line between lesbianism and bisexuality.[76] In an autobiographical article published a few months after "The House on the Borderland," Bradley referred to herself as both "a Lesbian" and "bisexual." Like Jody Shotwell, Bradley portrayed bisexuality as a burden. "I didn't ask to be bisexual," she wrote. "I would much prefer, if the truth were told, to be one thing or the other; and at my present stage of the game I wouldn't much care which it was."[77] Though Bradley believed that she was drawn to women at her "truest emotional level," she stated that she did enjoy heterosexual sex, and—if she were able to divorce and marry a man who was a better match—might be able to put her homosexual desire behind her.[78] Similarly, an anonymous, formerly married woman explained in a personal testimony titled "Why Am I a Lesbian?" that she identified as lesbian but was capable of responding sexually to either men or women. For her, being a lesbian entailed far more than sex. "It is a way of life," she wrote, "the emotional, physical and spiritual expression of the love of one woman for another."[79] Presaging the arguments of later lesbian feminists, this author portrayed lesbianism as a choice rather than an inborn characteristic.

Whereas these authors defined their sexual identities in different and sometimes multiple ways, some *Ladder* contributors attempted to draw a starker division between bisexual women and lesbians. Incensed by the formerly married anonymous letter writer's statement described above, two lesbians calling themselves "Y & A" argued that the author was truly bisexual and, therefore, "no more a spokesman for Lesbianism than many other forms of aberration."[80] Citing the Austrian psychoanalyst Wilhelm Stekel, the writers argued that bisexual women were masochists seeking punishment from both heterosexuals and homosexuals. Such women, they asserted, lacked the emotional depth required for lesbian relationships and only harmed lesbians' political cause. Clearly upset by this letter, Martin responded to it in print. She defended the formerly married author's claim to the identity "lesbian" but did not directly challenge Y & A's disparaging portrait of bisexual women.[81] Bradley, for one, personally recognized the homophile movement's failure to deal with bisexuality. In 1965 she complained to Barbara Gittings that "the very people who beg for tolerance of homosexuals lift their skirts (and eyebrows) in holy horror to avoid thinking about the problems of the genuine bisexual." She even suggested that a "new counterpart of ONE or Mattachine or the DOB" was needed to address the issue.[82]

Despite some homophile activists' hostility to bisexuals, it seems most DOB members conceived of themselves as somewhere in the middle of a continuum between hetero- and homosexuality. In 1959 the DOB published the results of a survey of *The Ladder*'s subscribers in which respondents were asked to categorize their sexual orientation based on Alfred Kinsey's six-point scale. According to the results, 91 percent of the 157 women who participated considered themselves more homosexual than heterosexual, but this percentage included those who were either "incidentally" or "more than incidentally" heterosexual. In addition, the survey found that of the one hundred respondents who described themselves as "exclusively" homosexual, the vast majority—ninety-eight people—reported having had some heterosexual relationships.[83] Florence Jaffy, the DOB's research director and the author of an article about the study, explained that the high incidence of heterosexual experience among *The Ladder*'s subscribers was a result of women's "heterosexual-homosexual balance" changing over time. Whatever the reason, though, the survey showed that married or formerly married women were not vastly different from most other *Ladder* subscribers who also felt a degree of attraction to men and had some sexual experience with them.[84]

Bisexual, lesbian, or both: how best to categorize wives who desired women remained an open and controversial question in *The Ladder* during the 1950s and 1960s, but it was not a pressing one. The fact that contributors to *The Ladder* referred to these women far more often as "married lesbians" rather than "bisexuals" suggests that there was room for married women within the category "lesbian" during this period, and that the label "bisexual" was not needed to distinguish them. Whether or not they agreed with married lesbians' choices, viewed them with sympathy or distrust, believed they should divorce or remain married, *The Ladder*'s contributors understood well that many women who experienced lesbian desires would find themselves married to men at some point. In addition, the recurrence of the terms "married lesbian" and "lesbian wife" in *The Ladder* suggests that most contributors did not see marriage as a clear indicator of a woman's most powerful erotic and romantic attachments. While Shotwell and Bradley stated explicitly that they were attracted to men as well as women, most wives who wrote to the DOB or contributed to *The Ladder* did not express being physically attracted to their husbands. In a letter, one married woman quite typically wrote of her husband, "I love him, yes—but I feel towards him the way I feel towards my children."[85] For wives like this one who engaged in sex with their husbands out of duty rather than desire, "bisexual" may have seemed an inappropriate if not inaccurate identity label.

In any case, the married lesbian, as she was most often called, continued to figure in *The Ladder* in the mid-1960s after Barbara Gittings took over as editor of the magazine. In contrast to Lyon and Martin, Gittings was more closely allied with radical homophile activists on the East Coast, including Franklin Kameny, founder of the Mattachine Society's Washington, DC, chapter. Gittings participated in some of the earliest public protests of homosexual oppression and was influenced by militant gay activists' refusal of psychiatric definitions of homosexuality and their demands for legislative change. Under her editorial guidance, *The Ladder* began to espouse more radical views and to challenge, head-on, understandings of homosexuality as sickness or sin. The word "lesbian" was printed on *The Ladder's* cover for the first time; a new column titled "Living Propaganda" called on readers to publicly identify themselves as lesbians; photographs rather than line drawings of lesbians began to appear in the magazine, as did updates about the East Coast Homophile Organization. Though readers applauded *The Ladder's* political transformation in Gittings's hands, not all of the DOB's leaders supported her choices, and the DOB's board removed Gittings as editor in 1966.[86]

During Gittings's years as editor *The Ladder's* depictions of married lesbians grew less forgiving. After Gittings announced that *The Ladder* would "soon begin a discussion on 'The Married Lesbian'" in September 1964, stories and letters written from the perspective of wives' unmarried female lovers began to appear with greater frequency, and they took an angrier, more critical tone than in years past.[87] Increasingly, the lesbian wife appeared cowardly, conformist, and greedy rather than tortured and self-sacrificing. In "Letter to an Old Friend," for example, Elizabeth Tudor wrote to Liza, a married former lover who had recently reached out to her. In the letter, Elizabeth explains that she wants no part of Liza's hypocritical life and rejects her invitation to rekindle their relationship. She accuses Liza of toying with her out of boredom, and of sacrificing her individuality for the roles of wife and mother. "You are no longer a whole being, only a part of the machine, Family," Elizabeth wrote acidly.[88] Similarly, in a short play titled "A Christmas Dialogue," an unmarried woman, Beatrice, rebuffs her former married lover who is eager to begin their affair again. "How much does it take to assure one woman of her existence?" Beatrice asks. "A husband, children, a house filled with furniture and appliances . . . and now you want me for a sister, too!"[89]

Yet while writing about married lesbians grew more severe in the mid-1960s, *The Ladder's* contributors still refrained from arguing explicitly that wives who desired women should divorce. A few authors argued that married lesbians who passed as straight were doing an injustice to other lesbians and were standing in the way of the homophile movement, but they stopped short of instructing them to leave their husbands. In "Plea to the Silent Ones," for example, a wife and mother called on others like her to admit their homosexuality to at least one other person, but not necessarily to divorce.[90] Similarly, in an article castigating "passing" women as "cruel" and "useless," Marilyn Barrow criticized married lesbians but assumed that divorce remained out of the question for such women, who often had children.[91] "By the time she discovers that the girl next door means more to her than her husband," Barrow wrote, "it's usually too late to change her situation."[92] Although *The Ladder* was beginning to demonstrate a more radical gay politics and take a more uncompromising perspective on married lesbians, demanding that these women divorce remained difficult when there were children to consider. Even as late as 1969, *The Ladder* refrained from dictating a clear course for married women with children.[93]

A few writers, however, did provide an example for others to follow by describing how they or their female lovers had left unhappy marriages and begun new lesbian lives. In 1958, for example, Barbara Grier, using the name Gene Damon, argued that lesbians who loved one another and were committed to each other could build a life together even in the face of significant obstacles. Barbara's partner had been married when the two met. Nonetheless, her partner divorced, an act made easier by her childlessness, and the two had been together for years by the time Barbara told their story.[94] Similarly, in 1964 the DOB published a letter from a woman in Indonesia, Ger van Braam, explaining how she had left her marriage after only three months. Ironically, she noted, it was her husband who "enlightened" her about herself by sharing with her several lesbian novels, including *The Well of Loneliness* and *The Price of Salt*. Even though her family disowned her, Ger insisted she had no choice but to end her marriage.[95] Such stories were rare, but the survey of DOB members conducted in 1959 found that of those lesbians who had married heterosexually, less than a quarter of them remained so.[96] Thus, beneath *The Ladder*'s repeated insistence that the situation of lesbian wives was hopeless, that they could not divorce or raise their children outside of a "normal" family, another, more optimistic message was discernable.[97]

The DOB and the Courses of Wives' Lives

While most of the letters, articles, and stories in *The Ladder* during the 1950s and 1960s stressed the hopelessness of the situation faced by lesbian wives, privately the DOB leaders—Martin, Lyon, and Gittings—did all they could to support wives who desired women and to put them in contact with a larger lesbian world. Martin, Lyon, and Gittings actively encouraged married women to participate in the DOB. They invited married women to become members, attend DOB conferences and events, subscribe to *The Ladder*, and contribute their writings to it. They did not demand that married women choose between lesbianism and marriage, nor did they suggest that such a choice was necessary. In fact, when married women expressed a desire to meet other lesbians, DOB leaders did their best to oblige without judgement. Even more important than the connections Martin, Lyon, and Gittings facilitated between married women and other lesbians, though, were the connections they made with married women themselves. Married women wrote to the DOB because they believed they had found women who cared about them and understood their situation. The DOB leaders did not intend to chastise married women for their choices or push them in one direction or the other, but rather to "give some of them confidence in themselves and the rightness of their deep feelings," as Gittings put it in a letter to one wife and mother.[98] Through letters, over the phone, or in person, Martin, Lyon, and Gittings listened to and empathized with married women's problems; they validated married women's same-sex desires and welcomed them into the DOB's community as well as, in some cases, their own circle of friends.

It is difficult to determine what impact participating in the DOB had on married women's lives, but in at least a few cases it eventually led to divorce. Nora, a working-class housewife and mother of four in Portland, Oregon, was conscious of her lesbian desires when she married, having carried on a passionate same-sex affair in her teens. Nora had an amicable relationship with her husband, who was aware of her attraction to women, and for fifteen years she was able to survive in her marriage, longing for the woman she had fallen in love with long ago. When Nora wrote to the DOB in January 1963, she expressed gratitude to the organization for helping her continue on her present path. "If I am able to see my responsibilities carried through to a successful finish, I will owe a great deal to the inspiration and companionship I have received through your publication," she wrote.[99] By November, however, Nora was asking Gittings and Gittings's lover, Kay Lahusen, how she could "drop this mask"—that is, be open publicly about her sexuality.[100] By October the following year, she had separated from her husband, and by January 1965 she had divorced, won custody of her children, and established a household with her formerly married lover.

Nora was inspired to participate in the homophile movement after reading Reverend Robert Wood's book *Christ and the Homosexual* (1960).[101] A minister in New York City, Wood argued that gays should be included in the church, permitted to marry, and allowed to take hold orders. He also criticized discrimination against homosexuals in the military and the workplace. Wood's book helped Nora, the daughter of a Nazarene preacher, to accept her lesbianism. It restored her faith in God and encouraged her to consider what higher purpose her life could serve. Nora began to feel that by "hiding" in marriage she was failing younger or troubled lesbians who needed the guidance and advice of women like herself.[102] "No one could help the wrecked, alcoholic, suicide bent Lesbians like another Lesbian," she stated in a letter to the organization. "Do we have among our group, women who would be w[i]lling to take an open stand and show the public, but more importantly, our own kind, that it is possible to find peace of mind, purpose in life, and happiness?"[103] Nora decided to be this type of woman. In 1963, although she had already been a *Ladder* subscriber for at least a year, Nora began working actively to support the organization. She started writing material for the magazine.[104] She educated women in Portland's bars about the DOB and sold copies of *The Ladder*. She sent dozens of letters about the DOB to psychiatry centers, clinics, colleges, Portland's mayor, the Oregon Council of Churches, and any other individuals or institutions she believed were in a position to help homosexuals.

Nineteen sixty-three was a turning point in Nora's life for yet another reason: it was the year she met Helen, another Portland wife and mother of four children (the exact same ages of Nora's kids) who would become her lover. Helen was also a *Ladder* subscriber, and she happened to read an article, "Plea to the Silent Ones," that Nora had published, as "Rose Marie of Portland," calling on "hidden" lesbians like herself to admit their homosexuality to at least one other person.[105] Helen felt the piece surpassed anything the magazine had published before, and she wrote a letter to "Rose Marie" asking *The Ladder*'s editor to forward it to the author.[106] Gittings did forward Helen's letter to Nora, and the women met in December. They immediately began visiting lesbian bars together and drumming up support for a local DOB chapter. "I've met [Helen] and she's fine," Nora told Gittings and Lahusen. "She is just the partner I need."[107] By January, the two were not only coorganizers for the DOB, but lovers as well.

Nora's acceptance of her homosexuality and her newfound mission to serve others like her inevitably affected her marriage. Her husband, Jim, had long been aware of her homosexuality, read her copies of *The Ladder*, and approved of the article she had written. When Nora began spending more time with Helen, however, and actively trying to start a DOB chapter, he became enraged. Jim's mental state, it seems, was shaky. He was having trouble at work, and his employer at a meat factory threatened to fire him. Neighbors accused him of being a Peeping Tom and of sexually propositioning women when they were alone late at night. Nora and Jim had sought help from marital counselors earlier in their marriage, and now they turned to psychiatrists at the University of Oregon Medical School for help. Shockingly, Nora admitted to them that she was having an affair, visiting lesbian bars, and working in Portland for lesbian rights. She refused to take any blame for her husband's current mental condition and radically insisted that she could be both a lesbian and a good mother. "My children may well have it thrown in their faces . . . that their Mother is a 'Queer,' but they will remember me as a devoted, loving and sacrificing Mother. If they remember me also as one lesbian with courage enough to try to do something, regardless how small, for my minority group, then it will not injure them."[108] Nora's psychiatrist agreed that she had "adjusted" to her homosexuality well enough to make a "perhaps most successful" attempt at life with Helen, but he urged her to remain married for her husband's sake.[109]

Initially, it seemed that Nora would balance marriage and her newfound lesbian relationship. In 1964, she told Gittings and Lahusen how greatly things had improved in her life. Tensions had lessened with her husband—even though the two had not been intimate—and her children were happier; she and Helen had even taken a recent "lesbian honeymoon" to California to visit Helen's sister.[110] "I know now beyond all doubt that one can lead a happy, fulfilled lesbian life and keep a necessary marriage going along reasonably well," she wrote.[111] (Incidentally, Gittings later highlighted this section of Nora's letter in pencil and noted in bold script in the margin "The Married Lesbian," as if with that very sentence Nora had crystallized into an archetype.)

In her next letter, however, which she sent less than three months later, Nora announced that she had filed for divorce and was moving into a new home.[112] It is unclear what exactly precipitated this decision. Nora's husband may have experienced another mental breakdown that disturbed the delicate equilibrium in their home. Or he may have improved to the point that Nora did not feel she needed to remain married in order to care for him. It is also possible that Nora made the decision to divorce apart from her husband's needs or behavior. As her relationship with Helen developed, the two may simply have decided that they were ready to establish their own household together, husbands be damned. In any case, the following year Nora published another article in *The Ladder*, explaining how she had divorced and secured child custody, despite admitting her homosexuality to the judge. Since her husband's lawyers were unable to find any evidence undermining her character, and no one could deny that she had been a good mother and a good housekeeper, she won custody of her four children and subsequently established a household with her lover.[113]

❧ ❧

While *The Ladder* portrayed wives who desired women in the 1950s and 1960s as either isolated and helpless or conformist and self-hating, married women's letters to the DOB during these years defy such easy categorizations. Wives who connected with the DOB were certainly constrained by their marriages and their children, but they also possessed significant resources and personal strength. As this chapter has shown, married women who wrote to the DOB were strikingly intent on connecting with others like them, even as they risked having their husbands, children, or neighbors discover their letters or copies of *The Ladder*. Some were surprisingly well ensconced in local gay communities and even involved in the broader homophile movement. Others freely admitted to engaging in sexual and romantic relationships with women, sometimes forcefully insisting on their right or need to do so. Significantly, most wives who contacted the DOB were not entirely cut off from other gays and lesbians but had participated to some degree in urban gay bar cultures, suggesting how these women might have heard about the DOB in the first place. The letter writers described here, then, may have been somewhat exceptional among the broader population of wives who desired women; they were likely better connected to "out" lesbian communities and more willing to take actions that could endanger their marriages. To return to the exchange between Barbara Gittings and Esmé Langley that began this chapter, perhaps Gittings stated accurately that few socially "uninitiated" married lesbians joined the DOB.

The path that wives who desired women should take and the place they should have within the lesbian community were matters of debate within the pages of *The Ladder*, but this discussion did little to push married women in one direction or the other. The letters, stories, and articles about lesbian wives that circulated within *The Ladder* are best understood as evidence in the DOB's broader argument that a social transformation in sexual norms and values was necessary. This argument became more uncompromising over the course of the 1960s and more hostile to married women who did not admit their homosexual desires openly. By fostering married women's connections with the lesbian world, on the other hand, the DOB's leaders helped wives find lesbian friends and lovers, and inspired at least a few to leave their marriages. But most wives who participated in the DOB during these years probably did not divorce, and the DOB's help and support was not contingent upon their so doing. During the many years that she participated in the DOB, for example, Marion Zimmer Bradley left one marriage only to begin another.[114] Instead, then, by attempting to connect married women with, and incorporate them into, a larger lesbian world, we might see the DOB's leaders as acknowledging and facilitating such women's ability to transform, or at least adjust their marriages. To be sure, Martin, Lyon, and Gittings would never have described their actions this way. They were fundamentally concerned with building a national lesbian community and with providing "isolated" lesbians emotional support, practical advice, and social resources. For Martin, Lyon, and Gittings, whether such women existed within or outside the institution of marriage was, in the end, beside the point.

CHAPTER 4

Scandal in Suburbia

WHETHER LOOKING FOR CHEAP entertainment or desperately seeking information about homosexuality, anyone who picked *An Authentic Report on Lesbianism* off a drugstore rack in 1966 would have encountered the lesbian wife. "It's happening in your neighborhood and mine," the pseudo-scientific paperback began. "Outwardly she appears to be a loving wife and mother. . . . Her two children are attractive and well-behaved. . . . Nevertheless, she inhabits another world . . . that dark, little understood, only whispered about domain of the female homosexual."[1] While *An Authentic Report on Lesbianism* purported to reveal the lesbian wife to an audience unaware of her existence, psychoanalysts, journalists, novelists, and filmmakers had been consistently unveiling this figure to the American public for more than a decade by the time this book was published. Indeed, in the 1950s and early 1960s the lesbian wife became an object of widespread fear and fascination within popular culture, often, but not exclusively through what are now called "lesbian pulps," cheap and sensational mass-marketed paperback novels and so-called "nonfiction" studies of lesbian life.

As we have seen, this concern was not entirely without basis. Married women did engage in lesbian sex at midcentury, but their likely limited numbers hardly justified the cultural attention they attracted. In *Sexual Behavior in the Human Female*, for example, Alfred Kinsey found that among women who had engaged in homosexual sex in their youth, "the chief effect of marriage had been to stop the homosexual activities."[2] In total, only around 1 percent of married women in each age group in Kinsey's study had actively engaged in homosexual activities to the point of orgasm.[3] Though these wives were a negligible cohort in Kinsey's broad sample, among the smaller population of self-identified lesbians, married women comprised a more noteworthy percentage. According to the DOB's 1959 study, 27 percent of the lesbians surveyed had been married at one time.[4] Still, the cultural interest in lesbian wives seems vastly out of proportion, given their numbers in society.

The depictions of menacing lesbian wives captured within this chapter thus reveal much more about cultural producers' anxieties than they do about actual wives who desired women. While wives of different races and classes found ways to act on their same-sex desires at midcentury, within popular culture the lesbian wife was almost exclusively white and middle class. Several scholars have argued that the working-class butch was the most socially threatening lesbian at midcentury, but the white lesbian wife was surely a contender for the position, linking fears about homosexual subversion and white American womanhood gone awry.[5] Often suburban and conventionally feminine in appearance, the imagined lesbian wife suggested that although a household might appear "normal" on the outside, it could shelter perversions imperceptible even to those within it. The "aggressive dyke" could, at worst, seduce or do violence to individual women, but the lesbian wife imperiled her children's welfare, her marriage's future, and the household's sanctity: the building blocks of the nation's postwar political and economic systems.[6] Like her close relative in popular culture, the overbearing white "mom," the lesbian wife suggested that beneath the surface, white middle-class wives and mothers were not all that different from the emasculating black "matriarchs" whom Daniel Patrick Moynihan, then assistant secretary of labor, accused of perpetuating black poverty in his 1965 policy report.[7] After World War II, as politicians expanded and institutionalized New Deal social welfare policies that privileged a male-breadwinner family model, both white and black women's failure to accept their subordination portended disaster.[8]

Yet even as the cultural discourse around the menacing lesbian wife portrayed married women's homosexual inclinations as dangerous and destructive, it also conveyed that women could defeat them. For every menacing lesbian wife who destroyed her husband's manhood and tore her family apart, there was another who ultimately reformed, returned to marriage, and overcame her sexual misbehavior by sleeping with her newly virile husband, escaping the influence of a predatory female lover, seeking psychiatric treatment, or simply finding a different focus for all her extra time and energy—a new baby, perhaps, or more volunteer work. In this way, popular culture's messages largely aligned with postwar policies that pushed women with same-sex desires into seemingly heterosexual marriages and kept them there. As we will see, most psychoanalytic books, novels, and films suggested that wives who desired women had two options: they could work to conquer their feelings for other women, or they could leave their marriages and die, either literally or metaphorically. Faced with these messages, it is little wonder that so many husbands saw their wives' feelings for other women as temporary, and that so many wives felt they had no choice but to remain married and fight to overcome their same-sex desires, or at least keep them quiet.

Attending to the popular discourse around the lesbian wife makes homosexuality more critical to histories of women's domestic "containment" within marriage and the household, while also making women more central to histories of homophobia in the Cold War era. Examining depictions of the lesbian wife reveals that the imagined homosexual threat at midcentury was highly gendered: if gay men endangered the nation the most within the public sphere, lesbians did so in private. By focusing on the policing of homosexuals within the government and in public cruising spots, most scholarship has implied that men were the primary victims of attacks on homosexuals during this period. According to historian David K. Johnson, only two of the first ninety-one homosexuals fired from the State Department in 1950 were women.[9] Likewise, arrests and convictions of gay men dwarfed those of lesbians during these years.[10] Though there were significant exceptions, even so, understanding why lesbians were not typically the focus of such assaults requires a new, more private starting place: the home.[11]

Demonizing the Lesbian Wife

Since the creation of the concept of homosexuality in the late nineteenth and early twentieth centuries, sexologists had acknowledged that some married women experienced lesbian desires and relationships, but they were not particularly concerned about them.[12] Indeed, both sexologists and mainstream critics alike in the interwar years interpreted married women's lesbian inclinations as evidence not of their own deviance or inadequacy, but of their husbands' failures as financial providers and sexual partners.[13] By the 1920s and 1930s, there were some hints of the menacing lesbian wife to come in scientific and pseudoscientific texts, but it was not until after World War II that researchers truly seized on this figure.[14]

In the wake of Kinsey's studies of human sexuality, accredited psychoanalysts and pseudoscientific charlatans alike were eager to capitalize on Americans' newfound interest in reading about sexuality, and few figures could inspire readers' fantasies and nightmares as effectively as the lesbian wife. Psychoanalytic psychiatrists Edmund Bergler and Frank Caprio were the first respected sex experts to warn Americans about the lesbian wife, in their popularly marketed books in the 1950s. Bergler, who came to the United States after leading the Psychoanalytic Institute in Vienna, was a prolific writer who published more than twenty books during his lifetime with leading medical publishers.[15] While some of Bergler's peers considered him to be "a publicity-seeking hack," his arguments against homosexuality had a powerful influence on the general public, and members of Congress even cited his work in hearings about homosexual government employees during the 1950s.[16] Caprio's professional reputation was more tenuous than Bergler's—psychoanalytic reviewers of his work were often critical—but he was no less popular among lay readers.[17] In the 1950s and 1960s, Caprio was a regular writer for *Sexology: The Illustrated Magazine of Sex Science*, a mass-marketed pseudoscientific magazine, and he wrote several books on sexuality with mainstream publishers, some printed in multiple editions.[18]

In their writings on female homosexuality, Bergler and Caprio insisted that married lesbians comprised a considerable, hidden, and highly dangerous population. Although other psychoanalysts suspected that latent homosexuality was common among married women, they did not believe that a large number of wives were actually engaging in lesbian sex. When homosexually active wives did appear in psychoanalytic case studies in the 1950s, most authors were not alarmed by them, in part, because they seemed so unusual.[19] Psychoanalyst Helene Deutsch, for example, even considered one married woman's happy lesbian affair to be a successful outcome of her therapy![20] But Bergler's and Caprio's arguments about the lesbian wife were not based on rigorous research. They made no attempt to provide data demonstrating that lesbian wives constituted a significant population and instead used a handful of case studies to make broad generalizations. While Bergler discussed cases drawn, it seems, from his private practice, Caprio pulled anecdotes from newspapers, books, and even confessional romance magazines. Bergler and, to a lesser extent, Caprio took the small numbers of lesbian wives they identified as proof that such women were eminently successful at hiding and lay the burden of disproving their arguments on their readers.

Bergler contended that, much like communists who supposedly passed as regular, patriotic Americans, lesbians who disguised themselves as ordinary wives greatly outnumbered those "openly admitted or recognizable ones."[21] Bergler was incensed by the emergent homosexual rights movement and by Kinsey's efforts to destigmatize homosexuality. By attacking Kinsey's research, Bergler sought to undermine any change in mainstream attitudes toward homosexuality.[22] Among Bergler's many critiques of Kinsey was his charge that the scientist had underestimated the population of lesbians in *Sexual Behavior in the Human Female* because he had failed to recognize the great numbers of lesbians hidden in marriage. Again using terms that called to mind the war against communism, Bergler argued that these "camouflaged" lesbians not only endangered their own households, but also threatened to corrupt the entire population of American women.[23] Married lesbians were so dangerous, he insisted, because their friends and family never doubted their heterosexuality, giving them free rein to sexually convert others. Indeed, Bergler cast lesbian wives as double agents in a veritable war between hetero- and homosexuality when he wrote, "It is the reservoir of married women which contributes most of the recruits to the great army of lesbians."[24]

Caprio also stressed the ease with which lesbians could penetrate and destroy the nuclear family, but he maintained that married women were more often the seduced, rather than the seducer, in lesbian affairs. "Lesbians often become intimate with wives living with their husbands," he wrote in one *Sexology* article.[25] While lesbian wives were typically the objects of homosexual seduction in Caprio's writing, they were far from innocent. They deceived their husbands, tore apart their families, and subverted the social order by establishing pseudo-marriages with "girl husband[s]."[26] Caprio even suggested that married lesbians had established communist-like networks among themselves, hidden in plain sight, and he quoted at length one husband who had lost his wife to a mysterious "woman's club" that served as a front for her homosexual affairs: "From the date of my wife's membership to this club she no longer cared for any more children. . . . [S]he finally confessed that the private club to which she belonged was nothing more than a secret Lesbian Club made up of six women (three of them married) living in the suburban section of the city. At the meetings which were held twice a month, these women paired off and indulged in lesbian practices."[27] Even though this husband succeeded in extricating his wife from this nefarious sexual network, the damage to their marriage was irreparable and they divorced. Still, for Caprio divorce was not the worst fate that could befall a lesbian's husband. Citing one extreme case of "antimale [*sic*] rebellion" in which a lesbian wife seduced dozens of schoolgirls before beating her husband to death, Caprio suggested that men who waited too long to address their wives' lesbian activity risked losing not only their marriages, but also their lives.[28]

Bergler and Caprio portrayed married women's lesbianism and related sexual frigidity as stemming from a secret revolt against their roles as wives and mothers. In this respect, Bergler and Caprio built on the work of journalist Ferdinand Lundberg and psychiatrist Marynia Farnham, who argued in their bestselling book, *Modern Woman: The Lost Sex* (1947), that married women's growing autonomy—their career aspirations, disregard for their husband's authority, and disenchantment with motherhood—was producing a dramatic increase in cases of sexual frigidity. Though Lundberg and Farnham did not explicitly allege that such women were really lesbians or were secretly engaging in sexual relationships with other women, they did claim that women who rejected their "most fundamental instinctual strivings" were becoming dangerously masculinized, a trait they associated with homosexuality.[29] Bergler and Caprio made Lundberg and Farnham's barely subtextual association between lesbian and frigid wives explicit. In his book *Counterfeit-Sex*, Bergler even listed lesbianism as a subcategory of frigidity; in other words, while not all frigid women were lesbians, all lesbians were sexually frigid. This assumption was critical to Bergler's larger argument that more lesbians than gay men married: "Since it is easier to disguise frigidity than impotence in heterosexual marriage it is easy to understand why there are so many lesbians living in 'alibi marriages,' and so few homosexuals who simulate sexual normality."[30] Bergler contended that the modern American woman's "masculine strivings" for a career instead of motherhood had disturbed her natural sexual responses, and he advised medical practitioners diagnosing frigidity to ask themselves, "To what extent does this woman accept herself as a woman?"[31]

Caprio argued similarly that many wives suffered from frigidity because of their latent homosexuality, and he categorized frigid, unconsciously homosexual women as the "masculine protest type." While such women might marry, and on the surface appear to be good wives and mothers, their inability to "accept their own femininity" emerged in their failure to enjoy sex with their husbands. As evidence, Caprio cited a "Dr. Niederland," who described the case of one likely "latent lesbian" who married at age twenty-six but could not reconcile herself to her new role as a subordinated wife. "She was angry at her husband's desire for marital relations, found no pleasure in them, and resented him for relegating her to an inferior position as his woman slave," Niederland explained.[32] Whereas Bergler believed that frigid/lesbian wives wanted to remain married in order to maintain their social and economic privilege and disguise their pathology, Caprio feared that such women would seek divorce rather than assume the responsibilities of marriage and motherhood. The real danger of lesbianism, Caprio argued, was not homosexual sex itself, but these "homosexual attitudes toward life."[33]

The majority of psychoanalysts would never exhibit Bergler's and Caprio's heightened fears about the lesbian wife, but by the early 1960s their arguments had gained some followers. A panel on overt female homosexuality at the American Psychoanalytic Association's fall meeting in 1961 demonstrated the reach of Bergler's and Caprio's ideas. At the event, the psychoanalyst Terry Rodgers insisted that it was "not uncommon for overt female homosexuality to be acted out behind the veneer of an apparently successful heterosexual life."[34] Much like Bergler and Caprio, Rodgers had little evidence. The sole source of his information was one married patient who, he claimed, seduced married men as a way of instigating homosexual relationships with their wives. Another psychoanalyst then delivered a paper on the "orgy à trois," involving a married man, his wife, and another woman, also based on just one of his clients. In a subsequent discussion of the issue, Charles Socarides—who would later become a leading opponent of homosexuality's demedicalization—agreed that the women in question were homosexuals who included husbands in their activities only to "allay their superego guilt."[35] This one panel aside, however, it would be other popular "experts" on lesbianism, rather than Bergler's and Caprio's psychoanalytic peers, who promulgated anxiety about "overt" lesbians in heterosexual marriages.

Jess Stearn, a former associate editor of *Newsweek*, took up Bergler's and Caprio's arguments about lesbian wives in his book *The Grapevine* (1964), a journalistic study of what he portrayed as a hidden lesbian world. Stearn first ventured into the public discussion about homosexuality with his bestselling book about gay men, *The Sixth Man* (1961), and with *The Grapevine* he was surely aiming for the same level of success.[36] *The Grapevine* was first published in hardcover by a mainstream press, Doubleday, and it was widely reviewed in the news media.[37] Stearn traveled across the country appearing on numerous radio talk shows publicizing *The Grapevine*, and subsequent studies of lesbianism frequently cited his book. Although Stearn had relatively little new to add to Bergler's and Caprio's portraits of the lesbian wife, he was well positioned to alert an even greater number of people to her existence.

Stearn was not as vehemently anti-homosexual as many other popular "experts" on homosexuality. In the introduction to *The Grapevine*, he portrayed himself as providing a service for lesbians who wanted to see realistic portraits of their lives. Indeed, he convinced Del Martin and Phyllis Lyon, longtime leaders of the DOB, to help him with his project and grant him personal interviews and access to their group's meetings in San Francisco. After the book was published, Martin and Lyon were happy with the publication and thanked Stearn profusely for his work, but other DOB members were less pleased with Stearn's depiction of them. One contributor to *The Ladder*, after hearing Stearn promote his book on the radio, angrily reported that he was only helping "to cement the opinion that lesbians are dangerous women, a threat to the home, to the family, to the traditional American way of life." Far from seeing Stearn as doing lesbians like her a favor, this woman considered him an opportunist, out "to tap the purses" of readers fascinated with homosexuality.[38]

Like Bergler and Caprio, Stearn maintained that lesbians were better able to hide their deviance than homosexual men and that the vast majority of them were hidden from view. Most lesbians were feminine-looking, he argued, and could express physical affection in public without drawing attention. Reflecting the inflammatory anti-communist language of the period, Stearn argued that only a "small proportion of the lesbian underground" identified themselves openly.[39] The married lesbian bore out Stearn's argument about the invisibility of lesbian women better than any other figure. For example, Stearn pointed to one "middle-aged, staid-looking" woman named Belle who had been married for years, raised a child, and passed unsuspected within straight society before one day abandoning it all for her lover Mildred.[40] Another woman, Sidney, who identified as bisexual but whom Stearn suggested was truly lesbian, informed the author that she had been married three times and that no man had ever known about her homosexual inclinations unless she wanted him to. "How could they?" she asked.[41] For Stearn, men were the ultimate victims of these uncaring wives. "Many unhappy husbands unwittingly married to lesbians," he maintained, "never suspected why their marriages didn't work."[42]

Ultimately, Stearn wanted to uphold both the institution of marriage and the conventional gender roles within it. Like those psychoanalytic experts before him, Stearn concluded that married women who turned to lesbianism were cravenly turning away from their jobs as wives and mothers. In *The Grapevine*'s final chapter, he argued that lesbianism was a side effect of other social changes: women's desire to be treated as men's equals, their insistence on having careers, their declining focus on marriage, their deteriorating femininity, and even their "widespread use of slacks."[43] Stearn even quoted Del Martin as stating that the reason her marriage had failed was not because of sexual incompatibility, but because she disliked housework and the other "female responsibilities" that came with marriage.[44] Although Stearn admitted that some exceptional, caring lesbian mothers did exist, he insisted that most were incapable of being good parents because they were fundamentally selfish and immature. As children were little more than possessions to their lesbian moms, accoutrements of a socially acceptable life, Stearn reasoned, "If the lesbian was careful about her furniture, she usually took good care of the children."[45]

Yet the menacing lesbian wife turned up within explicitly fictional stories more often than she did in journalistic books, which were constrained, if only slightly, by their authors' claims to objectivity. One of the earliest of these fictional works was Philip Wylie's sardonic novel *Opus 21* (1949), which castigated American sexual hypocrisy in what he called the "Lower Kinsey Epoch of the Atomic Age."[46] As mentioned in Chapter 1, in his bestselling book *Generation of Vipers* (1942), Wylie argued that overbearing mothers were undermining their husbands' and sons' masculinity, thereby contributing to the nation's deterioration.[47] Though Wylie did not see lesbian wives as posing quite the same threat to American masculinity as overbearing moms did, he saw both figures as emblematic of all that was wrong with American women, their families, and the nation. In *Opus 21*, Wylie reserved his greatest disdain for Yvonne Prentiss, a wealthy young blonde who has recently left her husband after discovering his affair with another man. Despite Yvonne's pretense of disgust with her husband's homosexuality and her refusal to accept his apology, she secretly harbors lesbian desires herself. By the novel's end, Yvonne has slept with a redheaded prostitute and returned to her repentant husband with plans of secretly continuing her own homosexual adventures in the future. The lesbian wife, like the overbearing mother, engendered Wylie's disgust and ridicule as well as his anxiety. His novel suggested that her posture of moral superiority disguised an inner ethical bankruptcy which would result in a perversion of the American family if left unchecked.

Hollywood took hostile depictions of lesbian wives such as those found in *Opus 21* even further. While the Motion Picture Production Code prevented Hollywood filmmakers from portraying homosexuality straightforwardly from the 1930s until the early 1960s, the menacing lesbian wife made an early, somewhat veiled appearance on-screen in the film *Young Man with a Horn* (1950). Much like other classic Cold War films such, as *Invasion of the Body Snatchers* (1956), *Young Man with a Horn* functioned as a cautionary tale, revealing the inner corruption that could lurk beneath the exterior of a seemingly normal, even beautiful individual. In the movie, Lauren Bacall plays Amy North, a wealthy, aspiring psychiatrist capable of analyzing everyone but herself. Amy possesses many of the characteristics that would define the lesbian wife for the next decade and a half. She is attractive but sexually cold—hence the name North—and uninterested in having children or taking care of a household. Nonetheless, she attracts the interest of Rick Martin (Kirk Douglas), a jazz trumpeter. Despite the fact that Amy rebuffs Rick's kisses, warns him not to fall in love with her, and implies she's not "terribly normal" like his other love interest, Jo Jordan (a squeaky-clean Doris Day), Rick is smitten, and they elope. The marriage is happy for a while, but Amy grows increasingly distant, and one night she does not come home. When Amy finally returns, she informs Rick she has a new "friend." "I met a girl the other day," she says, "an artist, maybe we'll go to Paris together."[48]

Young Man with a Horn dramatically demonstrated the damage that wives like Amy could wreak on their marriages and their husband's masculinity. Soon after Amy informs Rick about her painter friend, he sees the two women speaking intimately together at a party and becomes enraged. Rick calls Amy "confused," but she has made up her mind: "I'm sick of you trying to touch me!" she yells. Rick responds by telling Amy she is a "sick girl" and needs to see a doctor. "You're like those carnival joints I used to work in," he informs Amy. "Big flash on the outside, but on the inside nothing but filth." Rick then announces that he is leaving Amy. Save for one last shot of her alone and defeated, Amy disappears from the narrative, but their failed marriage propels Rick on an alcohol-fueled path of self-destruction. In one scene, he even smashes his horn, a symbol of his sexual virility; he has lost his ability to "perform," both as a musician and a man. At the film's end, Rick is homeless and sick with pneumonia, fighting to stay alive.

While operating within the constraints of the Motion Picture Production Code, *Young Man with a Horn*'s creators made a concerted effort to make Amy North legible as a lesbian. They based the film on Dorothy Baker's 1938 novel of the same name.[49] Baker, as previously discussed, carried on an affair with another woman for decades with her husband's knowledge and explicit permission, and homosexuality was a major theme in her writing. Baker later admitted that "homosexuality is [Amy's] trouble" in *Young Man with a Horn*, but the clues the novel provides about Amy's sexuality are so subtle as to be practically illegible.[50] In fact, after Warner Brothers purchased the rights to *Young Man with a Horn*, several screenwriters struggled to make sense of Amy's character. It required an in-person meeting with Baker herself to clear up Amy's motivations, and only then did the heightened allusions to Amy's homosexuality appear in the script: the painter friend, the discussion of moving to Paris (a longtime haven for expatriate American lesbian artists), the suggestion that Amy needs a doctor.[51]

Years later, Baker remained impressed with how the filmmakers had depicted Amy's homosexuality. "Warner Brothers played it up very high and very subtly, with Lauren Bacall and some other girl tearing off to Europe—it was quite overt, for the time. I was probably about the only one who got it, but that was actually what they meant," she explained.[52]

Baker was most likely not the sole audience member to recognize Amy as a lesbian. Though the censors, who were concerned only with the film's suggestions of extramarital heterosexual sex, remained oblivious to Amy's homosexuality, the critics were more savvy.[53] One review's title, "Trumpeter Story Lacks in Climax," used double entendre to suggest the film's thwarted heterosexual love, stating forcefully, "Ms. Bacall's assignment is in a rather repellent domain."[54] Another reviewer described Amy's character as "a confused, mentally sick wife."[55] While some filmgoers were surely blind to Amy's coded lesbianism, such critics' vehement condemnation seems unnecessary, unless they understood the character as gay.

The lesbian wife appeared on the big screen again in *Walk on the Wild Side* (1962), and this time there was even less ambiguity about both her sexuality and her threat to society.[56] Whereas *Young Man with a Horn* and its reviewers gestured to Amy North's sexual "sickness," *Walk on the Wild Side* was recognized by critics as one of a spate of new films that, thanks to a 1961 revision to the Motion Picture Production Code, depicted homosexuality more openly.[57] That very same year, however, the production code's administrators refused to grant approval to *Victim* (1961), a highly acclaimed British-made film, in part because of its "overtly-expressed plea for social acceptance of the homosexual."[58] Although the revised code allowed for more explicit representations of homosexuality, it still compelled filmmakers to portray homosexuality as either a tragedy or a threat.

Walk on the Wild Side does the latter. In the film, Jo Courtney (Barbara Stanwyck), a married brothel owner in 1930s New Orleans, is sexually infatuated with one of the girls in her employ, Hallie Gerard (Capucine). Jo's marriage is not critical to the film's plot, but near the end of *Walk on the Wild Side*, a legless man who maneuvers himself around on a rolling cart and has seemed to be nothing more than Jo's assistant is revealed to be her husband. In this scene, he encourages Jo to let Hallie begin a new life so that they can have a normal marriage again. He affirms his continuing love for Jo and attempts to touch her, but she is repulsed. "Love! Can any man really love a woman for herself without wanting her body for his own pleasure?" she responds. In *Young Man with a Horn*, the lesbian wife's destructive potential was metaphorical, but here it is inescapable. Jo, uniformly clad in a tailored suit, has assumed the masculine role in her marriage: she runs the business, pays off the police, and orders around the prostitutes in her house. Her husband, who barely grazes her waist, is literally half a man. At one point, Jo even likens him to her "retriever dog." Not only does Jo wreck her own marriage, she ruins Hallie's chance at having a "normal" family as well, when one of her thugs kills Hallie by mistake. But Jo does not escape this crime unscathed. Much like those unreformed lesbian wives in paperbacks whose lives usually end in death or alcoholism, Jo is ultimately imprisoned.

The Dangers of Postwar Affluence

Like novelists, journalists, and filmmakers, paperback writers were quick to take up psychoanalytic warnings about the lesbian wife. Pocket Books introduced the mass-market paperback in the United States in 1939. Sold for only twenty-five cents in the early years, paperbacks were available at drugstores, supermarkets, bus and train stations, and the like. Some paperbacks were reprints of literary classics and first-edition "quality" works, but many others were mysteries, thrillers, and Westerns, which by the 1950s were attracting readers with increasingly sensational covers. Lesbian-themed paperbacks, or "lesbian pulps" as they have come to be known, were particularly popular at midcentury. In fact, publishers first identified the market for lesbian pulps when Tereska Torres's memoir *Women's Barracks* sold over one million copies in 1950. Lesbian-pulp publishers most likely intended their books for heterosexual male readers, but many others, including lesbians desperately seeking representation, consumed them avidly. In fact, by putting the term "lesbian" into wider public circulation than ever before, lesbian pulps were critical to the formation of lesbian identity at midcentury, helping women far removed from urban gay and lesbian communities to conceive of a broader lesbian world and to consider themselves as potential members of it.[59] Most lesbian pulps were novels, but the genre included reprints of supposedly nonfiction studies of lesbian life, previously released in hardback, and original pseudoscientific studies as well.[60]

Paperback authors regurgitated the arguments of psychiatrists, such as Bergler and Caprio, but they often tied the lesbian wife's existence more directly to postwar affluence and suburbanization. Significantly, they emphasized the idea that boredom could engender homosexuality among privileged married women. One pseudoscientific paperback, *The Lesbian* (1963), featured among its case studies a chapter about Moira, a wealthy urban wife—dubbed the "bored matron"—in the midst of a lesbian affair.[61] In the chapter on Moira, *The Lesbian*'s author, Benjamin Morse, suggested that some lesbian wives might not be revolting from their female role but simply trying to occupy spare time. Despite Moira's insistence that she enjoys lesbian sex, the author-analyst Morse insists that she is merely frustrated with her life. Moira "had let herself grow lazy over the years," Morse writes. "She took things easy, let her mind and body soften to the point where she was 'accomplishing nothing.'"[62] Morse went on to explain that once Moira understood that she was not, in fact, attracted to women, that her lesbian affair was merely a symptom of her ennui, she began filling her time instead with unthreatening volunteer work at local hospitals and churches. Reassuringly, as Moira's life became more satisfying, her lesbian affair became unnecessary.

In *The Lesbian in Our Society* (1962), W. D. Sprague, associate director of the imaginary Psychoanalytic Assistance Foundation, struck a more panicked tone. He argued that lesbianism was on the rise—among suburban housewives, in particular—and that boredom was the cause. Emulating actual scientific texts, but with little concern for the truth, Sprague cited an apocryphal study claiming that "ONE in FOUR [wives] had experimented with homosexuality since moving to the suburbs."[63] Providing fodder for readers' erotic fantasies and sneaking suspicions, Sprague depicted the suburbs as a veritable lesbian playground with most affairs taking place within women's homes while their husbands were at work. In fact, he claimed lesbian sex sometimes occurred automatically when women met in the absence of men. As one housewife recounted, "I'll be alone with one of the other girls in our circle of friends either in my house or at hers, and before we know it, we'll get a sudden urge to have relations with each other."[64] Such statements may seem outrageous, and surely many readers recognized their absurdity, but beneath them lay real and pervasive fears about the negative effects of suburban living and the impact of housewives' discontent on their marriages.

Pseudoscientific authors' concerns about exploitative wives taking advantage of hardworking husbands were similar to those found in *Playboy* magazine at this same time. *Playboy*'s founder, Hugh Hefner, was an outspoken critic of marriage at midcentury. As the sociologist Barbara Ehrenreich has argued, his magazine, first published in 1953, celebrated the man who resisted suburban conformity and familial responsibility, and—with its bunnies and centerfolds—defended him against charges of homosexuality.[65] On the other hand, in its early years *Playboy* regularly portrayed husbands as dupes, slaving tirelessly to earn "bread, bacon, clothes, furniture, cars, appliances, entertainment, vacations and country-club memberships" for lazy, gold-digging housewives.[66]

While *Playboy* typically took such wives' heterosexuality for granted, one 1963 cartoon in the magazine implied that some married women were engaging in lesbian affairs. The cartoon, a simple line drawing, depicts three figures. In the background, a woman, clad in a long slip, covers her face with her hands in shame. In the foreground, the woman's husband—just home from work, with his hat still on and briefcase in hand—opens the closet door to find his wife's female lover, also wearing a slip, staring out at him blankly. The joke, of course, is that this wife is cheating, not with a man, as her husband might expect, but with a woman. In retrospect, it may be surprising that *Playboy* addressed the issue of homosexuality at all. In the 1950s, *Playboy* echoed widespread homophobic attitudes, but by the early 1960s the magazine—and Hefner himself—criticized the stigmatization of homosexuality and printed letters from gay men who turned to the Advisor and Forum columns for help and advice.[67] Lesbians, it seems, were among the magazine's readers as well. Although the cartoon described here was probably intended for *Playboy*'s predominantly heterosexual male readership, one DOB member, whose lover had recently left her husband, enjoyed the cartoon so much that she mailed a copy to Jaye Bell, then president of the DOB, to share with the group's members.[68]

While the lesbian wife's humorous appearance in *Playboy* was unusual, by the early 1960s she had become a stock character in lesbian paperback originals, which usually portrayed pampered lesbian wives as fleeing from adult responsibilities while emasculating their husbands. Take, for example, Allan Seager's *Death of Anger* (1960), in which protagonist Hugh Canning battles his beautiful blonde lesbian wife, Hedwig, for control in their marriage.[69] Before Hedwig reveals her sexual orientation to Hugh, her refusal to sleep with him, her disinterest in children, and her extreme indolence—effectively conveyed by the novel's cover art, which portrays Hedwig lying in bed and reaching languorously for her pretty nurse—betray her hidden "perversion" (Figure 6). *Death of Anger* casts Hedwig's laziness as a symptom of her lesbianism. Hedwig is so lazy, in fact, that she remains in bed for twelve years after Hugh rapes her. As an act of disobedience against him, Hedwig's self-imposed bed rest serves as a symbol of her failure as a woman. She grows fat eating bonbons in bed and humiliates her husband, not only by making him take on a subservient role, but also by criticizing his appearance, playing tricks on him, and even threatening to physically abuse him. Although Hedwig is a particularly vicious lesbian wife, her sexual frigidity, reluctance to have children, disinterest in household labor, and dominance over her husband are true of many such characters.

Depictions of lazy lesbian wives like Hedwig resonated with pervasive fears that Americans' affluence was contributing to their moral deterioration. Indeed, it is because of Hugh's wealth that Hedwig tricks him into marrying her in the first place. While a consumption-based economy dramatically raised Americans' standard of living after the war, President Dwight Eisenhower warned in his 1960 State of the Union address that this wealth could have undesirable effects. "A rich nation can, for a time, without noticeable damage to itself, pursue a course of self-indulgence, making

Figure 6. The cover of *Death of Anger* (Avon Books, 1960) by Allan
Seager. Hedwig, pictured here lying on the bed, is the quintessential
indolent lesbian wife. Reprinted by permission of HarperCollins
Publishers.

its single goal the material ease and comfort of its citizens," he argued, but that path would eventually lead to "internal moral and physical softness."[70] Such messages were typically directed at men and boys, but the discourse around the lesbian wife reflects a similar concern that life was becoming a bit too easy for wives and mothers as well. If a weak or sick body, lack of courage, and general effeminacy signaled a man's decline, a sloppy appearance (including but not limited to obesity) and a messy house made manifest a woman's lack of discipline and moral compass. Such female "softness" was often imagined as having a detrimental effect on husbands and marriage: marital counselors blamed messy housewives for precipitating their husbands' infidelity, and judges accused "sloppy and dirty" women of making their husbands divorce them.[71] Examining this widespread criticism of housework-averse wives at midcentury, the historian Rebecca Davis has described the domestic sphere as a veritable "battlefield," within which a simple task such as preparing breakfast could take on epic meaning about increases in women's employment and fathers' growing responsibilities at home.[72] Not only resistant to household labor, but possibly violent, and clearly "perverted," the lesbian housewife added yet another frightening layer to this broader anxiety.

Like the pseudoscientists, many pulp novelists implied that homosexuality was particularly rampant among those women who benefitted the most from postwar affluence: suburban housewives. The promotional text on the cover of George Simon's *The Third Lust* (1963), for instance, hinted at the all-too-common storyline within: "The well cared-for women in their well-tended homes had time on their hands—time to pursue the new community pastime . . . lesbianism!"[73] Another of Simon's novels, *Girls Without Men* (1964), tells of a married dance instructor who seduces no fewer than five housewives in one suburban neighborhood.[74] The titles of other lesbian pulps, such as *Scandal in Suburbia* (1960) and *Love in the Suburbs* (1963), linked suburban life and sexual depravity from the outset.[75] These novels were part of a broader trend within sexploitation film and fiction which helped to eroticize the geography of ordinary middle-class life, thus fostering the idea that an illicit sexual subculture lay within every man's reach.[76] More respectable novels, including the National Book Award finalist *Revolutionary Road* (1961), also suggested that loveless marriages and rampant infidelity lay beneath the veneer of cheery suburban conformity.[77] Lesbian pulp novelists, however, went one step further. While in popular memory the postwar suburbs were a bastion of heterosexual normalcy, pulp novels brought to the fore the queer potentiality of the female-dominated world that emerged in suburban enclaves on any given weekday. In the suburbs, such novels warned, sexual deviants could easily disguise themselves by taking advantage of the single-family homes intended to provide married, heterosexual couples with privacy and freedom.[78] Here, the lesbian wife's color is critical, for—as discriminatory housing policies, lending practices, and grassroots homeowners' associations attempted to maintain the suburbs' racial homogeneity—it was white women, for the most part, who inhabited this space.

The race and class specificity of this discourse becomes even clearer when we notice that there was a slightly different discourse around African American lesbian wives. Though lesbian wives of color appeared as supporting characters in a few paperback novels, the most significant discussion of them appeared in the pioneering, African American–owned Johnson Publishing Company's magazines.[79] Yet even here the black lesbian wife did not generate the same anxiety that the white lesbian wife did. Perhaps motivated by a desire to combat pervasive, ugly stereotypes of black women's hypersexuality and the weakness of the black family, the authors writing for African American magazines stressed that most wives who dabbled in lesbianism did not pose a serious threat to marriage. For example, "Strange Love," a short story in *Tan Confessions*, a romance magazine, tells of a married woman, Yvonne, who sleeps with her lesbian friend only once before swiftly returning to her husband with an even greater appreciation for him.[80] Similarly, an article in the pocket weekly *Jet* titled "Why Lesbians Marry Men" reassured readers that even black women with more significant lesbian experience could become "good wives," because they understood the advantages of marriage and often sought psychiatric help.[81] The article closed by emphasizing the benefits of marriage for lesbians: "Even though their adjustment to marriage may never be complete, it is an anchor and a bulwark, an institution which has its rewards for those masculine women who can assume its responsibilities."[82] Rather than condemning black lesbians who married, the author applauded their fortitude.

Countering the Menacing Lesbian Wife

African American journalists and writers were not the only ones to push back against widespread cultural depictions of menacing lesbian wives. In the pages of the DOB's magazine, *The Ladder*, many readers expressed frustration with depictions of menacing lesbian wives in paperback books like those discussed in this chapter. In a 1964 article in *The Ladder* titled "Lesbian Stereotypes in the Commercial Novel," Marion Zimmer Bradley—who, as noted in Chapter 3, was herself a married woman—bemoaned the representation of lesbians in paperback novels. A key lesbian stereotype, Bradley argued, was the predator who seduces other women. The predator "may be a married woman whose husband never satisfies her," she noted, "so she spends her days enticing other housewives into bed."[83] Attempting to correct this misconception, Bradley explained defensively, "As for married lesbians, they are often desperately secretive about their desires, and if they *do* find a sympathetic friend, they are not apt to be casual about a love affair."[84] Barbara Grier, who reviewed lesbian novels for *The Ladder* in her regular Lesbiana column, frequently criticized those lesbian wife characters she considered unbelievable or unbecoming to lesbians as a group. Grier castigated one of these as "the wolf type, interested in conquest rather than stability," but she also praised those novels in which lesbian wives were more realistic or appealing.[85] The conniving and oversexed lesbian wife was certainly a literary device whose entertaining sexual misbehavior necessitated her husband's demonstration of sexual prowess, and pulp publishers hoping to evade obscenity charges often required that lesbian characters turn straight or face dire punishment at novel's end. But the fictional lesbian wife's utility does not negate her significance. As many lesbian readers and writers recognized, this figure conveyed unmistakable messages about female homosexuality and women's roles within marriage.

Some female writers countered pulp depictions of the menacing lesbian wife with books of their own. While most lesbian pulps were written by or attributed to male authors who heeded publishers' requirements to present lesbian life as miserable and degrading, between 1950 and 1965 a group of around fifteen women writers attempted to portray lesbian life more sympathetically.[86] The lesbian author Marijane Meaker, who used the pen name Ann Aldrich, was among these writers. In her series of journalistic, mass-market paperback books—*We Walk Alone* (1955), *We, Too, Must Love* (1958), *Carol, in a Thousand Cities* (1960), and *We Two Won't Last* (1963)—Meaker described the lesbian landscape from a privileged, insider view.[87] Meaker's series differed from other sympathetic lesbian pulps in that she began her first book by identifying herself as a homosexual. As several scholars have noted, Meaker's work is marked by sometimes conflicting and contradictory ideas about homosexuality.[88] Although she cited psycho-analysts such as Bergler and Caprio in her books, she firmly contested discrimination against lesbians. Indeed, she explained that she intended her work to "bring more compassionate understanding on the part of mothers and fathers, sisters and brothers, friends, teachers, employers and strangers," and she attempted to garner tolerance for homosexual women by presenting a balanced rather than wholly positive view of them.[89]

In the same way that Meaker depicted both the good and the bad of the lesbian world, she portrayed some lesbian wives with compassion and others with disgust. Meaker was sympathetic to lesbian women who felt compelled by familial and social pressures to enter into "front marriages" with gay men, and to lesbian wives who discovered their same-sex desires only after marrying. Several of Meaker's anecdotes about such lesbian wives suggest that if their husbands had been kinder and more attentive, they would not have turned to women in the first place. Ginny serves as one example of this type. Not only did Ginny's family emotionally neglect her when she was growing up, but her husband, an alcoholic businessman who traveled constantly, was indifferent to her. Throughout her marriage, Ginny rode horses at a nearby stable, and eventually she fell in love and ran off with the female owner of the riding academy. Meaker postulated that Ginny may have found in her lover a replacement mother figure, but she also suggested that "when [Ginny] found another human being whose love was companionate as well as passionate she surrendered everything she had to it."[90] If Ginny's husband had provided that "companionate" and "passionate" love, it follows that she would not have looked outside of her marriage to find it.

Despite her compassion for wives like Ginny, Meaker's descriptions of women who knowingly entered into heterosexual marriages to secure a sexual "cover" seethe with sarcasm. Though Meaker acknowledged that some married women were truly bisexual, she claimed that these women were outnumbered by lesbians who married to "mask their abnormality" or "for economic gains."[91] She quoted one such woman as saying heartlessly, "I'd just like to get married so I could have a Mrs. before my name. . . . That would solve everything for me."[92] Meaker reserved her greatest disdain, though, for lesbian wives who pushed their husbands into cheating on them and then sued them for alimony, such as Carol in We, Too, Must Love. Despite her husband's suspicions about her sexuality and his attempts to discuss the issue openly, Carol refuses to address it. When her husband gives up on their relationship and has an affair with another woman, Carol secures a divorce and a cushy financial settlement, which she celebrates with her female lover. "Of course, I don't really believe in alimony, but Dan *was* unfaithful. . . . [H]e did take up some of my best years," Meaker quoted her as saying disingenuously.[93]

Meaker clearly felt antipathy for such wives, but as an unmarried lesbian struggling to make a living as a writer in New York City, this sentiment grew from her disapproval of women who enjoyed lesbian relationships while benefiting from marriage, rather than from a fear that they were victimizing men and destroying the American family. In fact, Meaker had firsthand knowledge of such enterprising wives. Around 1950, at only twenty-three years of age, Meaker had an affair with a much older married woman who was on her third husband at the time, a wealthy man involved with politics. Whereas Meaker lived in Greenwich Village, her lover lived uptown, and the two traveled in separate social circles. So that they would have an excuse to see each other, the wife set Meaker up with one of her single male friends, a stockbroker. Meaker and the stockbroker got along well, but to her lover's disappointment, Meaker was unwilling to marry him. Sounding much like the opportunistic wife Carol in *We, Too, Must Love*, Meaker's lover used to say to her, "Just marry him, just stick in it for two years and you'll be a millionaire."[94] Before long, Meaker's lover took her own advice; she divorced, secured alimony (even though her husband was aware of her infidelity), and eventually married for a fourth time.

As we have seen, Meaker was hardly the only lesbian to criticize wives who engaged in lesbian affairs. While some lesbian contributors to *The Ladder* attempted to defend wives who felt torn between their desires for other women and their responsibilities to their families, *The Ladder* was also filled with letters and stories, increasingly in the 1960s, by unmarried lesbians criticizing their wifely counterparts. Yet whereas critical stories and comments about lesbian wives in *The Ladder* were broadcast to a small number of lesbians and those sympathetic to them, Meaker addressed a much larger and more varied audience. *The Ladder*'s distribution did not near a thousand until 1964, but Meaker, by comparison, recalled that each of the books in her nonfiction series was reprinted three or four times at approximately four hundred thousand copies per printing.[95] Meaker undoubtedly reached individuals who understood the reasons behind her critique of married lesbians, but she mostly likely had other, less sympathetic readers who were blind to the sources of her resentment. Readers who wanted to find evidence in Meaker's books that lesbian wives were not malevolent could have done so, but those anecdotes were outweighed by stories that presented such women as scheming and dishonest.

In *The Price of Salt* (1952), the suspense novelist Patricia Highsmith, using the pseudonym Claire Morgan, defended the lesbian wife more forcefully. Though originally published in hardcover, *The Price of Salt* did not truly achieve success—Highsmith estimated it sold nearly one million copies—until it was issued in paperback in 1953, in recognizable lesbian pulp format, with the requisite suggestive cover art.[96] The novel tells the story of an affair between a wealthy wife, Carol, and a much younger shop-girl, Therese. Initially, it is unclear whether Carol is only toying with the smitten Therese; but Therese is no victim, and it is Carol who ultimately pays the price for their love. Carol is in the midst of a difficult divorce when *The Price of Salt* begins, and her husband uses evidence of her affair with Therese to blackmail Carol into giving up primary custody of their daughter. Rather than give in to her husband's demand that she renounce her homosexuality, Carol eventually admits her lesbianism to the court. In contrast to those who would call homosexuals "degenerate," Carol boldly argues, "To live against one's grain, that is degeneration by definition," and she begins a life together with Therese at the novel's end.[97]

Highsmith's depiction of the lesbian wife was clearly informed by her own experiences. According to her biographer Joan Schenkar, Highsmith drew details of Carol's life from that of a divorced female lover who had lost custody of her child. In addition, shortly before writing *The Price of Salt*, Highsmith was engaged to be married and, in an attempt to overcome her homosexuality, saw a Freudian psychoanalyst who suggested she participate in group therapy with latent lesbian wives. Highsmith, however, soon became disenchanted with psychoanalysis. When writing in her diary about the wives in her therapy group, she joked "better latent than never," and noted irreverently, "Perhaps I shall amuse myself by seducing a couple of them."[98] Shortly thereafter, she terminated her therapy as well as her engagement and began an affair with her publisher's wife.

Similarly, radical depictions of lesbian wives also appeared in the paperback novels of Ann Bannon and Valerie Taylor. Bannon and Taylor did not always present lesbian wives sympathetically, but their respective novels, *Journey to a Woman* (1960) and *Return to Lesbos* (1963), almost heroically depict suburban housewives and mothers who leave their husbands for new lesbian lives.[99] The protagonists in these novels, Beth Cullison in Bannon's and Frances Ollenfield in Taylor's, are "ambivalent heroines," as one literary scholar categorized them.[100] They experience shame about their homosexuality and engage in self-destructive behaviors. Nonetheless, in contrast to contributors to *The Ladder*, who tended to agree that wives and mothers should fulfill their obligations to their families despite their feelings for other women, both Beth and Frances, in distinctly "protofeminist" fashion, assert that their responsibility to themselves is greater than their responsibility to their families.[101] What is more, in choosing to leave their marriages, these characters do not give up their chance at happiness, as Bergler, Caprio, and Stearn would have had Americans believe. Both novels, in fact, conclude with their protagonists beginning new lives with their lesbian lovers.

Significantly, both Bannon and Taylor resembled the wives they wrote about. At the time she wrote *Journey to a Woman*, Bannon was a young housewife living with her husband and children in Philadelphia, periodically traveling to Manhattan and visiting Greenwich Village's lesbian bars to gather fodder for her novels. There, she could witness the lesbian scene without truly having the life she wanted. She later explained that on her trips to New York City she was like "the kid standing on the outside of the pet shop, wishing [she] could go in and get the puppy in the window."[102] Taylor was also a wife and mother (of three), and she engaged in at least one affair with a woman before divorcing her husband and winning custody of her children in 1953. Though Bannon later explained that she did not write her lesbian novels with a political purpose in mind, Taylor, a gay rights activist, saw her novels as an agent of social change. At a meeting of the Chicago Area Council of the Mattachine Society in 1960, Taylor argued that while direct political action might be more effective in challenging homosexual oppression, "Some of us happen to be writers, and we must use the tools at hand."[103] It was, then, perhaps with some sense of responsibility to real-life wives who desired women that Bannon and Taylor tried to counteract the widespread cultural fearmongering and condemnation of lesbian wives in their writing, while suggesting to their unhappily married readers, secretly lusting after female friends, that a different life was possible.

The lesbian author Jane Rule's novel *The Desert of the Heart* (1964) echoed these more sympathetic portraits of the lesbian wife. Cleveland's World Publishing Company released the book (originally published in Canada in 1964) in the United States in hardback in 1965, and the come-hither eyes of the dark-haired woman on the novel's original cover signaled its strikingly unrepentant tone.[104] At the beginning of Rule's novel, the protagonist Evelyn Hall's marriage has already ended and she has traveled to Reno, Nevada, to secure a divorce. Evelyn's relationship with her soon-to-be-ex-husband George appears in the novel only through flashbacks that make clear that her lesbianism was at least partly responsible for their failed union. By her own account, Evelyn is to some extent the emasculating witch that postwar psychoanalysts and journalists imagined her to be. She subverted the gender order in her marriage by taking on the breadwinner role, denied her husband a sexual relationship, and—with her continued disapproval and thinly veiled contempt—helped to drive him to a nervous breakdown. "George was the real victim of their marriage," Evelyn thinks at one point, "so much the victim that he hadn't the courage left to want a divorce."[105] Shockingly, though, Rule insists that Evelyn deserves romance, happiness, and a new life nonetheless. She falls in love with a much younger woman who works as a change maid at a local casino and ultimately decides to remain in Reno with her.

◆ ◆

The lesbian wife's widespread representation in popular psychoanalytic and pseudoscientific books, journalistic reports, novels, and films demonstrates that she reflects a broad cultural fascination, not merely a trope of psychoanalytic writing or a convention of lesbian pulp fiction. If we were to sketch a rough chronology of the lesbian wife at midcentury, we would start with her portrayal in such works as Wylie's *Opus 21*, the film *Young Man with a Horn*, Highsmith's *The Price of Salt*, and Bergler's and Caprio's writings in the late 1940s and early 1950s, move through the plethora of scandalous pseudoscientific, journalistic, and fictional pulps in the late 1950s and early 1960s, and conclude with her unmistakable presence in *Walk on the Wild Side* and Stearn's solidly mainstream *The Grapevine* and beyond. Despite some researchers' and novelists' efforts to undermine or complicate the threatening lesbian wife, this figure persisted within popular culture for at least a decade, with one story about her emasculated husband and neglected children, her indolent and even violent tendencies, inspiring another.

By the late 1960s, though, representations of lesbian wives were beginning to change. *The Killing of Sister George* (1968), a film based on Frank Marcus's London-set play, demonstrates the ways in which the public discourse around the lesbian wife was shifting.[106] As the feminist movement, the countercultural revolution, and the increasingly militant struggle for gay rights began to pose far more pressing and open threats to the male-headed nuclear-family household, *The Killing of Sister George* did not reflect nearly the same degree of anxiety about lesbian wives that earlier films such as *Walk on the Wild Side* or *Young Man with a Horn* had. The lesbian wife in *The Killing of Sister George*—British Broadcasting Corporation executive Mercy Croft (played by Coral Browne)—remains a villain. However, her victim is not her husband—for he has already passed away—but an aging, alcoholic, butch soap-opera actress named June Buckridge (Beryl Reid), who fails to mask her sexual "deviance" as deftly. Over the course of the film, Mercy informs June that she is losing her job, insultingly arranges for her to play a cow on a children's TV show, and steals her much younger lover, Childie (Susannah York). Mercy is despicable, then, not because she undermines her husband's masculinity or threatens her children's welfare, but because she lacks the courage to come out openly and engineers the downfall of another lesbian who—at the cost of her career and her relationship—refuses to deny her homosexuality or apologize for it.

The Killing of Sister George did not cast its protagonists in a flattering light, but the frankness with which it addressed homosexuality was unprecedented among mainstream movies. The film adaptation heightened the play's lesbian themes and introduced a strange and exceptionally unsexy seduction scene between Mercy and Childie, which earned the film an X rating under the new Motion Picture Association of America ratings system.[107] *The Killing of Sister George* also memorably included a scene at a long-lived lesbian bar in London's Chelsea neighborhood, the Gateways Club, for which eighty of the Gateways' regulars volunteered to serve as extras, despite the risk of being recognized by employers and family members.[108] The scene at the Gateways is the only one to provide any relief from *The Killing of Sister George*'s overwhelmingly dark tone, and the lesbian world it depicts is a vibrant one. The club is packed, and an appealing all-girl band decked out in matching blue dresses plays in the corner. Lesbians fill the dance floor, and close-ups of women dancing, smiling, laughing, and touching humanize the bar's patrons. The scene at the Gateways thus suggests that not all lesbians are as miserable as Mercy, Childie, or June.

In fact, the playwright Frank Marcus privately expressed concern that the depiction of lesbian life at the Gateways was entirely *too* positive.[109] In several ways, then, *The Killing of Sister George* marked the end of one era and the beginning of another in terms of popular representations of wives who desire women.

Before this shift began, however, the discourse around the menacing lesbian wife worked to police all married women's behavior. Much like the overbearing white "mom" and the black "matriarch," the figure of the menacing lesbian wife delimited the boundaries of acceptable behavior for women and fortified male dominance within marriage. The lesson implicit in stories about the lesbian wife was that nearly any deviation from her ascribed social role could signal a woman's sexual "perversity." If she failed to derive the appropriate pleasure from marital sex or household labor, if she was a reluctant or inattentive mother, and if she in anyway undermined her husband's authority, Americans were encouraged by the works described here to ask, "Could she be a lesbian?" Spinsters, career women, prostitutes, and working-class butches were thus not the only women vulnerable to charges of homosexuality at midcentury. Even white middle-class wives and mothers faced pressure to continually affirm their heterosexuality through more marital sex, greater devotion to their children and households, and further subordination to their husbands.

But wives who *did* secretly desire women or engage in lesbian affairs most likely felt the impact of this discourse most intensely. Joyce Pierson, then living near Lake Tahoe in California, with her husband and three children, had long tried to bury her feelings for other women. When she visited a psychoanalyst in the early 1960s to deal with her depression, she was shocked when he told her that she was "having a struggle with [her] sexual identity." Joyce later reflected that "it wasn't that far in psychoanalytic thinking that women who rejected and had difficulty with being a mother and taking care of children, they were the queer women. But I had no idea of that."[110] Though her psychoanalyst's suspicions were, in fact, true, Joyce would remain married for another decade in an effort to prove him wrong. Similarly, after falling in love with a female neighbor in the 1960s, one wife went to see a therapist who shared Bergler's and Caprio's beliefs. "[The therapist] told me that I was really sick, and that my husband had every right to divorce me and take my children and never let me see them again," she later recounted.[111] Faced with the prospect of losing her children, this woman recommitted herself to marriage and resigned herself to never having another relationship with a woman again. Even as late as the 1970s, the letter of one wife and mother in a Chicago suburb reflected the opinions of the midcentury "experts" described in this chapter: "I'm that part of society that is sneered [sic] at and joked about. A 38 year old mother of 4 children—suspect—perverted—sick—not to be trusted."[112] As this woman's letter illustrates, some wives continued to wrestle with an understanding of themselves as "sick" and as posing a danger to their families far into the future.

At the same time, however, the seemingly endless cultural repetition that the threatening lesbian wife inspired may have alerted wives to previously unforeseen sexual possibilities. Tales about the lesbian wife conveyed that marriage need not be a barrier to homosexuality; that the lesbian world stretched beyond urban bars into suburban neighborhoods and single-family homes; that lesbians sometimes had children and looked like other "normal" women.[113] The most sympathetic among these popular representations provided wives who desired women with much needed hope and affirmation. One divorced lesbian, in fact, wrote to Valerie Taylor decades later thanking her for her novels, which had helped to sustain her during a ten-year marriage in the 1960s.[114] But even less sympathetic writers, such as Edmund Bergler and Jess Stearn, who attempted to warn Americans about the legions of lesbians passing as ordinary housewives and endangering marriage, also, if inadvertently, notified a generation of wives and mothers who desired women—many of whom would leave their marriages in unprecedented numbers in the 1970s—that they were not alone.

PART II

Sexual Borders and Legible Threats,
1970–1989

CHAPTER 5

A World of Their Own

THERE WERE, AS ONE historian has written, likely "more lesbians in America during the 1970s than any other time in history."[1] The emergence of lesbian feminism as a political ideology and a distinct social movement was the most important factor behind this phenomenon. Beginning in the late 1960s, lesbians involved with the women's and gay liberation movements began to draw a connection between the oppression of women and homosexuals. They combined a liberationist gay politics with feminist analyses, merging ideas about the centrality of heterosexuality to women's oppression with beliefs about women's distinctive, shared behavioral traits and values.[2] Lesbian feminists framed lesbianism as an accomplishment rather than a flaw, and a political choice rather than an unchanging, inborn attribute. Being politically committed to other women was more important in defining lesbian identity, they believed, than either sexual attraction or experience. For lesbian feminists, choosing to become a lesbian, to build one's life around other women, and to surrender the privileges that came with heterosexuality represented the fullest manifestation of a feminist politics. Furthermore, because many white lesbian feminists identified male supremacy as the most fundamental form of social oppression, some believed that separating from men would bring an end to not only sexism and homophobia but classism and racism as well.

Lesbian feminists created a broader and more visible lesbian community than ever before. They published literature, made music, planned festivals, founded archives, and even claimed rural lands specifically for women like themselves. Lesbian "separatists" who sought to withdraw personally and politically from male-dominated, heterosexual society formed collectives across the country, including the Furies in Washington, DC, the Gutter Dykes in Berkeley, California, and the Gorgons in Seattle, Washington.[3] By the mid-1970s, lesbians had succeeded in creating a veritable world of their own. A group calling themselves "Ambitious Amazons" in East Lansing, Michigan, conveyed this idea in explaining the purpose of their newsletter, *Lesbian Connection*. "We want to provide the means for lesbians organizing a conference, publishing a book, or starting a bookstore to let the whole world, or better yet, the whole *lesbian* world know about it," they wrote.[4] That month's cover of the *Lesbian Connection* depicted an outline of the mainland United States dotted with interlocking female symbols. The message was clear: lesbians were everywhere. Less than a year after its debut in 1974, *Lesbian Connection* had reached a circulation of twenty-five hundred, including subscribers in every state.[5] It would go on to become likely the largest lesbian publication in the nation at the time, with a circulation of more than seven thousand.[6]

Once-married women were a vital part of this world. Writing in the late 1970s, the lesbian activist Jeanne Córdova claimed that thousands of "formerly heterosexual" women had joined the lesbian movement over the course of the decade. Indeed, "some of the most ardent anti-straight women," she claimed ecstatically, had been "1971's HOUSEWIVES!"[7] By leading workshops and support groups on lesbianism, publishing personal essays and position papers on the necessity of separating from men, and founding events and spaces for lesbians only, lesbian feminists empowered and encouraged married women to leave their marriages and publicly claim a lesbian identity.

At the same time, though, wives who combined marriage with same-sex relationships encountered brutal criticism within lesbian communities. In the early 1970s, unmarried lesbians' anger and hostility began to outweigh the sympathy and understanding that had once existed for wives who were reluctant to divorce despite their lesbian affairs or desires. Well-known wives who identified as lesbian were the targets of verbal, public attacks. To be sure, there were voices of disagreement: some lesbians supported a capacious understanding of lesbian "sisterhood" according to which a woman's marital status was relatively insignificant. Some argued that women should be able to combine marriage and lesbian affairs if they chose. But the overriding expectation remained that being a lesbian was incompatible with marriage. As we have seen, during the 1950s and early

1960s lesbian activists expected that most wives who came to recognize their same-sex desires would remain committed to their husbands and their families, at least until their children were grown. By the 1980s, however, lesbian feminists had made divorce politically imperative, a change that simultaneously facilitated the development of lesbian communities and left some wives who desired women feeling even more alone.

The Emergence of Lesbian Feminism and the Divorce Imperative

Even as many women were coming to recognize their sexual attraction to women through their participation in the feminist movement in the late 1960s, heterosexual leaders refused to recognize homosexuality as a feminist issue. Some straight feminists did so because they believed that butch/femme relationships recreated the oppressive power dynamics of heterosexuality. Susan Brownmiller, for example, a leading member of the New York Radical Feminists, reportedly refused to speak to the New York DOB chapter because she thought lesbians were mannish and overly sexual.[8] Other feminists feared that lesbians endangered the women's movement by validating opponents' claims that feminists were "dykes" or "man haters," and by distracting feminist activists from more pressing political goals. Ruled by such fears, leaders of the National Organization for Women (NOW) denied lesbians' presence within their organization and among their supporters. In late 1969, New York NOW omitted the DOB's name from the list of sponsors of the First Congress to Unite Women, a city-wide feminist conference NOW had planned. New York NOW leaders also attempted to silence Rita Mae Brown, a young lesbian activist and administrator at the organization who had repeatedly attempted to draw attention to lesbianism as a feminist issue. In January 1970, Brown and two other lesbian workers responded by resigning from their positions at NOW and publishing a statement in NOW's newsletter about the discrimination they had experienced.[9]

Disenchanted with mainstream feminists, Brown turned to others in New York City's Gay Liberation Front (GLF), in hopes of creating consciousness-raising groups specifically for lesbians. A group of young activists had founded GLF in the wake of the Stonewall riots in June 1969, when LGBT bar-goers violently protested a police raid of the Stonewall Inn in

Greenwich Village. Taking their name from the National Liberation Fronts of Vietnam and Algeria, the GLF's members were college-age radicals, many of whom had gained political experience in the New Left, the anti-war movement, and the black freedom struggle.[10] Unlike their predecessors in the homophile movement, gay liberationists saw themselves as part of a larger battle to overturn capitalism, imperialism, and white supremacy. Though many liberationists shared feminists' critique of the nuclear family and normative gender roles, men still dominated the movement and they often overlooked the particular issues lesbians faced. By early 1970 many lesbians involved in the gay movement were excited about the possibility of building their own political groups. In response to Brown's call, lesbian activists, including Martha Shelley and Karla Jay, who had played leading roles in the GLF, formed two consciousness-raising groups.[11]

The lesbian consciousness-raising groups had been meeting only a short time when an article appeared in the *New York Times Magazine* that spurred them to public action. In it, Susan Brownmiller quoted NOW cofounder Betty Friedan as calling lesbians within the feminist movement a "lavender menace." Brownmiller responded that lesbians were "a lavender *herring*, perhaps, but surely no clear and present danger."[12] Brownmiller later explained that she intended her remark to distinguish herself from Friedan in a humorous way, but lesbians considered her comment belittling. In response, they began planning an action to take place at the Second Congress to Unite Women in May. Once again, lesbian leaders and issues were absent from the meeting's agenda, but this time lesbians would force straight feminists to confront them. A group of women, including Brown and Jay, crafted a position paper to distribute at the event, which set out the political relationship between lesbianism and feminism. On the opening night of the conference, roughly forty lesbians, including the manifesto's authors, disrupted the scheduled proceedings. Wearing purple T-shirts stenciled with the words "Lavender Menace," they stormed the stage, passed out copies of their paper, "The Woman-Identified Woman," and held the microphone for more than two hours. Though the activists, who would eventually call themselves the Radicalesbians, anticipated a hostile response, the audience greeted their action with applause and support. By the end of the conference, several hundred attendees had voted to support the Radicalesbians' four resolutions, the first of which—like a slap in the face to the likes of Brownmiller and Friedan—stated, "Women's Liberation is a lesbian plot."[13]

"The Woman-Identified Woman" portrayed lesbianism as essential to the feminist movement. Though not the first document to do so, it was widely disseminated following the conference, and it became the most canonical text of the lesbian feminist movement.[14] "The Woman-Identified Woman" argued that women who remained committed to men in their private lives could never devote themselves fully to the women's movement. "As long as women's liberation tries to free women without facing the basic heterosexual structure that binds us in a one-to-one relationship with our oppressors," the paper stated, the feminist movement could not succeed.[15] Rather than a distraction from more important feminist issues, lesbianism was thus essential to overturning patriarchy; lesbians were not enemies of the feminist movement, but feminists par excellence. "The Woman-Identified Woman" argued that claiming a feminist politics and separating from men were more central to lesbian identity than engaging in sex with women.[16] In making sex secondary to lesbianism, the Radicalesbians sought to challenge mainstream understandings of homosexual relationships as solely sexual. They also sought to present lesbian identification as a political option for any woman willing to give up the privileges of heterosexuality and build her life around women.

While the Radicalesbians argued broadly that women needed to extricate themselves from "the basic heterosexual structure" that bound them to men, what this meant for married women became clearer in the publications of the lesbian separatist collective the Furies.[17] A group of twelve activists from Washington, DC, and New York City formed the Furies in DC in the spring of 1971. The Furies saw themselves as the radical vanguard of the feminist movement, and they were uncompromising in the connection they drew between the personal and the political. As historian Anne Valk explains, the Furies "conceived of their collective as a means to domesticate political life and politicize domestic life."[18] The twelve members shared clothing, pooled wages, and slept on mattresses on the floor. Privacy was rare. The members also engaged in painful "criticism-self-criticism" sessions in which they attacked each other's lingering racist, sexist, classist and homophobic attitudes. The Furies were an exceptionally militant group of lesbian separatists, but they were also particularly influential. Hoping that their collective would serve as a model for other lesbian separatist groups across the country, the Furies organized public discussions, held poetry readings and film screenings, and led a lesbian theory workshop. They edited a special lesbian feminist issue of *Motive*, the magazine of the

Methodist Student Movement, and in 1972 they began publishing a newspaper, also titled *The Furies*, which they sent to three thousand women across the country. *The Furies* served as a powerful venue for disseminating lesbian separatist ideas, and it even outlasted the collective itself.[19]

In their writing, the Furies portrayed married women as suffering from a false consciousness that they could overturn only through becoming lesbians. Several Furies members had been married to men, and in publicly discussing their decisions to leave their marriages they set a powerful precedent for other women. In the first edition of *The Furies*, for example, Sharon Deevey portrayed her journey from marriage to lesbianism as unfolding in tandem with her growing consciousness of female and homosexual oppression. In her essay "Such a Nice Girl," she described how she had fallen in love with Joan, a woman in her women's liberation study group. At first, Sharon had tried to balance the affair with marriage, which her straight feminist friends could accept, but when she left her husband, her friends began to fear she had been "stolen" by a "'man-hating' lesbian."[20] This experience demonstrated to Sharon that bisexuality was less radical than lesbianism. After leaving her marriage, she argued, she was finally able to understand how heterosexuality upheld male supremacy. She could afford to recognize the ways that all men benefitted from women's subordination, and she could see that truly consensual heterosexual relationships were not possible in a society that oppressed women. As she put it, "*Every* fuck is a rape even if it feels nice."[21]

Within the Furies' public political accounts of leaving their marriages, there was little room for ambivalence. Committed to a political vision of the world in which men figured solely as oppressors, the Furies described the end of a marriage only as a liberation marking the dividing line between oppressed heterosexuality and empowered lesbian feminism. Yet privately, Furies members did experience more complicated emotions than they let on. Charlotte Bunch, veteran activist of the civil rights and anti-war movements, left her husband shortly after becoming romantically involved with another woman and joining the Furies. Decades afterward, Bunch admitted how hard ending her marriage was. "I had to come to terms with the fact that I had to leave somebody that I did love and care about if I was gonna pursue this new life," she recalled in a documentary about her life. "I'm sure he was in pain. . . . I had to detach myself some from that pain."[22] Despite the sadness she felt about ending her marriage and hurting her husband, Bunch did not publicly admit or explore such potentially disruptive feelings at the time.

Village Voice columnist Jill Johnston's book *Lesbian Nation: The Feminist Solution* (1973) was even more influential than the Furies' writing in broadcasting the tenets of lesbian separatism and the political necessity of divorce. While the Furies' work circulated primarily among women who were already involved in the feminist movement, *Lesbian Nation* reached a much broader audience. Numerous reviews appeared in the mainstream press, including the *New York Review of Books*, and Johnston's portrait appeared on the cover of the *Library Journal*. [23] In *Lesbian Nation*, Johnston argued that lesbianism and a "withdrawal at every level from the man" was essential to overturning male supremacy.[24] Like the Furies members, she used her own life story to demonstrate the ways that heterosexuality oppressed women. Before marrying, Johnston had three lesbian affairs "plagued by guilt and secrecy."[25] In an attempt to sexually conform, she began sleeping with men, became pregnant twice, and had two abortions, one of which almost ended her life. Unsure of how to proceed, fighting her desire for women, and lonely in New York City, Johnston saw marriage as the inevitable answer to her problems. She "picked the first handsome intelligent sounding male that came along" and had two children with him in a period of four years.[26] But their marriage was an abject failure, "an exercise in violence interrupted by short periods of violence," as Johnston wryly put it.[27] After leaving her husband, giving up custody of her children, and engaging in affairs with women again, Johnston became involved with the GLF in New York City and came to believe that her troubles were not unique, but endemic to a sexist society.

Lesbian separatists reached married women through their public speaking as well as their writing. According to Nancy Breeze, a white mother of three then in her early forties, women decided to leave their marriages and claim a lesbian identity en masse while attending Sagaris, a feminist summer institute in Vermont in 1975. Sagaris's faculty included leading lesbian separatist thinkers such as Rita Mae Brown, Charlotte Bunch, and Ti-Grace Atkinson; by one account, it attracted two hundred faculty and students. While the institute is more often remembered for the bitter feminist infighting it provoked, Nancy recalled Sagaris fondly as a type of lesbian summer camp.[28] By the end of the event, Nancy, who was recently divorced, recalled that "all of us had come out," including many married women, among them a minister's wife.[29] This mass coming out continued even after the event had ended. One of Nancy's good friends, Marilyn Murphy, thought the institute "was all a bit much" at the time, but after flying home to her husband in Los Angeles, she felt the difference between being in a woman-centered environment and one that was not.[30] "That was the end of heterosexuality for her," Nancy explained.[31] Eventually, Marilyn ended her marriage, became involved with another woman, and began writing for the *Lesbian News*.[32]

Lesbian separatist leaders were not the only ones who argued that married women could and should leave their marriages in order to become lesbians. In *The Lesbian Tide*, for example, a lesbian newspaper first published by the DOB's Los Angeles chapter, member Sharon Zecha linked her personal transition from wife to lesbian to her political awakening in much the same way leading lesbian separatists had. "Until two years ago," she wrote in 1972, "I was a model of middle-class heterosexuality—college educated, wife and mother, politically inert, mistrustful of other women. . . . Somewhere along the way my attitudes towards women changed, and that has changed my entire life."[33] Indeed, as more women began to leave their marriages for new lesbian lives, similar essays appeared in many other lesbian and feminist periodicals in the 1970s and early 1980s, and in edited collections such as Susan Wolfe and Julia Penelope Stanley's *The Coming Out Stories* (1980).[34] So widespread were such accounts that it became possible to invoke the journey from wife to out lesbian with a kind of shorthand. "My life changed dramatically in a relatively short time from Mrs. Straight White Suburbia to Ms. Alternative Lifestyle," one woman wrote in her essay, "Diary of a Queer Housewife."[35] Yet another divorced lesbian put it even more succinctly: "My past is heterosexual."[36]

Many lesbian feminist leaders of color forcefully rejected lesbian separatism, but they too portrayed leaving a marriage as integral to becoming a lesbian and to achieving a feminist consciousness. Lesbians of color recognized the need for political alliances with men of color and felt frustrated with white lesbian separatists' failure to address racism. "We feel solidarity with progressive Black men and do not advocate the fractionalization that white women who are separatists demand," black lesbians and feminists wrote in the Combahee River Collective's widely reprinted "A Black Feminist Statement" (1977).[37] Several pieces in the groundbreaking collection titled *This Bridge Called My Back: Writings by Radical Women of Color* (1981) echoed the Combahee River Collective's stance and expanded their critique. "The lesbian separatist utopia? No thank you, sisters," wrote Chicana lesbian feminist Cherríe Moraga in the book's preface, arguing that lesbian separatist politics made sense only for white women who did not have to struggle against racial oppression in their daily lives, and who failed to appreciate the ways that racism impacted both men and women regardless of gender.[38] In a transcribed conversation that also appeared in the volume, twin black lesbian feminists and cofounders of the Combahee River Collective, Beverly and Barbara Smith, went even further than Moraga. They argued that lesbian separatism was inherently racist as white lesbian separatists who claimed that all forms of inequality would disappear in men's absence ignored their own complicity in racial oppression.[39]

While recognizing the need for political alliances with men, black lesbian feminists also celebrated their escape from marriage and condemned the institution. Pat Parker, for example, portrayed her evolution from wife and mother to woman-loving woman in her collection of poetry *Child of Myself* (1972). The poems in *Child of Myself* move clearly from topics of marriage, household labor, and disappointment in men, to describe Parker's spiritual rebirth and awakening love for women. Midway through the collection, in "Exodus (To my husbands, lovers)," Parker announces that her relationships with men are over: "i will serve you no more / in the name of wifely love / i'll not masturbate your pride / in the name of wifely loyalty / Trust me no more / Our bed is unsafe."[40] Similarly, in the special "Black Women's Issue" of *Conditions: a feminist magazine of writing by women with a particular emphasis on writing by lesbians*, published in 1979, Beverly Smith published several journal entries she wrote in the midst of her transition from wife to lesbian. Like Parker's poems, Smith's journal entries portray marriage as a tool of women's oppression and an obstacle to love between women. Smith wrote the entries while attending the wedding of a close female friend, J., whom Smith felt as though she were losing. Having recently left her own marriage, Smith saw her friend J.'s wedding with different eyes. "Celebrating a marriage is like celebrating being sold into slavery," Smith wrote. "He will try to make her into his slave, his child, in short, his wife."[41] Observing J.'s marriage beginning, only confirmed Smith's decision to end her own.

Beginning in the mid-1970s, as women of color began to create their own lesbian organizations and to challenge their invisibility in the white-dominated feminist press, accounts of lesbians of color who had left their marriages increased. Essays and poems about formerly married black and Latina lesbians appeared frequently in the late 1970s and 1980s in *Azalea: A Magazine by Third World Lesbians* and the *Salsa Soul Gayzette*, both published by the Salsa Soul Sisters, an organization for lesbians of color in New

York City. In one particularly moving essay, Rosita Angulo Miret Libre de Marulanda, a Columbian immigrant and mother of three, described choosing a new name for herself after divorcing her husband. Had she been widowed, according to Columbian custom she would have become Rosita Miret Vuido de (widow of) Marulanda. Having divorced instead, she decided to substitute "Libre" for "Vuido," thus embedding in her name a celebration of her newfound freedom. With this new name, Rosita wrote: "anuncio al mundo mi libertad / y en regocijo canto mi encuentro / con otras lesbianas en Nueva York" (I announce my freedom to the world / and in joy I sing my fellowship / with other lesbians in New York).[42] Whatever their particular angle, these writings conveyed that lesbian feminism was not solely the purview of white women, and that the decision to divorce was a difficult, but brave, and ultimately necessary choice for women who wanted to become lesbians.

Whether penned by white lesbian separatists or anti-separatist lesbians of color, recognized lesbian feminist leaders or lesser-known activists speaking out for the first time, these ubiquitous wife-to-lesbian narratives served purposes both personal and political. In writing and sharing their coming out stories, once-married women made sense of their life histories and sexual experiences; they justified their claims to lesbian identity and their inclusion in lesbian community. Such writing thus functioned as a type of lesbian "identity work," through which many formerly married women sought to redefine their identities both internally and externally.[43] In creating new lesbian selves, these women helped to construct and convey to others what it meant to be a "lesbian" at this particular moment in time, and their stories bore out the tenets of lesbian feminist ideology.[44] They demonstrated that lesbian identity could be willfully chosen, that it was a political as well as a sexual choice, and that it required renouncing heterosexuality and the institution of marriage entirely. In telling their stories publicly, these activists surely gave confidence and support to other unhappily married women who longed to join the lesbian community. Yet, at the same time they contributed to an understanding that wives who chose differently, who sought some way of combining marriage and lesbian relationships, were not really lesbians at all.

"Will the Real Lesbian Please Stand Up?"

Within this political context, lesbian feminists became more hostile toward wives who engaged in sex with women but were unwilling to leave their marriages. In their essential lesbian feminist text *Sappho Was a Right-On Woman: A Liberated View of Lesbianism* (1972), authors and Radicalesbians members Sidney Abbott and Barbara Love devoted significant attention to married women whom they accused of burying their lesbian desires beneath a heterosexual façade. "Many women who fear lesbianism in themselves plunge into marriage or try to drown their guilt in numerous relationships with men," they stated. "Others build super-respectable lives, conservative in all aspects, including the political, and contain their Lesbianism in a small, dark closet. Through tactics like these, Lesbians try to anesthetize guilt."[45] For Abbott and Love, "guilt" was a type of "parent within" preventing women from achieving true happiness as liberated lesbians.[46] Women who sought to escape guilt by fulfilling the roles of wife and mother could never truly be happy, Abbott and Love argued, because the knowledge of their own sexual "deviance" would plague them forever. Such women were a subset of a group Abbott and Love termed "debt-paying" lesbians, women who tried to make up for their homosexuality by working exceptionally hard to conform. Only by rejecting convention, refusing gay guilt, and wholeheartedly claiming a lesbian identity, could married or other "debt-paying" lesbians hope to find fulfillment.

Abbott and Love's criticism of married women echoed the arguments of gay liberationists who criticized men and women who did not come out publicly. Whereas many homophile activists had gone to great lengths to ensure the anonymity and privacy of their members, gay liberationists made coming out imperative to gay politics. The title of the GLF's journal, *Come Out!*, made this abundantly clear. Reflecting this political shift, divorced gay activist Carl Wittman vociferously attacked married men in his widely reprinted political statement *Refugees from Amerika: A Gay Manifesto* (1970) and demanded unequivocally that they stop hiding: "Closet queenery must end. Come out."[47] Like Abbott and Love, who called closeted lesbians "the good niggers of the homosexual world," Wittman used racialized language to denigrate men who engaged in gay sex while married. Comparing "the married guy who makes it on the side" to an "Uncle Tom," Wittman argued that "pretending" to be straight was "the most harmful behavior in the [gay] ghetto."[48] With such invidious racial analogies, white activists clearly sought to compare the gay and lesbian movement to the black freedom struggle. In doing so, however, they perpetuated racist stereotypes and betrayed their own understanding of the gay and lesbian community as implicitly white.

Just as many white gay and lesbian activists failed to acknowledge the intersectionality of racial and homosexual oppression, so too did they fail to acknowledge the complex feelings and desires of married men and women they deemed simply "closeted." Activists like Wittman, Abbott, and Love put their jobs, their relationships, and even their safety at risk by openly declaring themselves to be gay and standing on the front lines of the gay liberation and lesbian feminist movements. They were, understandably, growing more frustrated and impatient with those who did not. Yet these activists mistakenly assumed that fear and self-hatred were the only important factors tying men and women who experienced same-sex desires to marriage. In an effort to mobilize people to action and foment social change, liberationists' rhetoric reduced the world to black and white. Struggling in a very real sense for their survival, their right to live as they wanted, gay and lesbian activists saw only two options. Married men and women who experienced same-sex desires could come out publicly as gay and leave their marriages, or they could stay married and remain complicit in homosexual oppression.

Lesbian feminists criticized wives who engaged in lesbian relationships not only because such women could "pass" as straight and enjoy the privileges of heterosexuality, but also because they were participating in the nuclear-family structure that lesbian feminists understood as a central mechanism of women's oppression. Such ideas were clear in DOB leaders Del Martin and Phyllis Lyon's book *Lesbian/Woman* (1972). While Martin and Lyon discussed at length the challenges that once-married lesbians faced in beginning new lives, they also unabashedly disparaged those who refused to divorce. In a tirade against wives who engaged in lesbian affairs— atypical in its tone and style from the rest of the book—Martin and Lyon argued that wives and mothers who remained married despite their same-sex desires were little more than the dupes of a patriarchal society:

> Such mothers have swallowed, hook, line and sinker, society's male-imposed dictum that the role of woman is to serve man as his wife and mother of his children. They have been brainwashed into believing heterosexuality is the only viable way of life, have never accepted themselves, live in constant threat of exposure, and carefully steer their children into stereotyped sex roles. Obviously heterosexuality was not "easier" for them. Have they, as Lesbians, been happy in their self imposed traditional roles? With all their lies, with

all the pretense and deceit, with all their fears and the guilt they heaped upon themselves, did they really lead constructive, fulfilling and satisfying lives? Or did they, in eagerness to conform, end up full of bitterness self pity and martyrdom?[49]

In concluding this attack, Martin and Lyon presented themselves as having evolved beyond such wives into their more liberated selves. "We cry for these women who pay homage to the great god They. We pity them for their slavery to the Jones family. We have shared their agonies, their anguish and their despair. We *have been there* too."[50] In Martin and Lyon's account, wives who remained married despite their lesbian desires thus appeared as vestiges of the past, holdovers from the 1950s, out of place in the more politically evolved present.

In an effort to encourage women to come out as lesbians, Martin and Lyon painted a brutally reductive picture of wives who desired women and their marriages. As we have seen, not all wives lived in fear of exposure or passively accepted conventional definitions of marriage. What is more, remaining married did not necessarily reflect a wife's beliefs about gender roles. Many such wives struggled to build egalitarian marriages, to raise daughters and sons unhindered by conventional gender expectations, to combat homophobia in their families and their communities. While Martin and Lyon portrayed wives who remained married as fools, ignorant of entrenched gender and sexual inequalities, in fact, wives who had doubts about leaving their husbands were grappling with complex moral and ethical questions for which there are no clear answers: Do I risk my children's well-being because I am not sexually or romantically satisfied? Should I break the vows I made to my husband even though I knew about my desires for women when we married? For Martin and Lyon, women who answered "no" to these questions were not adults capable of making their own decisions, but victims, unwilling or unable to protest their own oppression.

Martin and Lyon were well aware of the sticky, gray area such women inhabited, having read and responded to countless letters from married women. The few remaining drafts of letters Martin and Lyon wrote to wives weighing precisely these questions reflect a far more nuanced understanding of the pain and complexity involved in leaving a marriage and breaking up a family. In a draft of one such letter, written in 1973 to a woman having doubts about leaving her husband for her female lover, Martin and Lyon scribbled a few sayings, gently encouraging the woman to leave her husband: "You can't have it both ways." "Can't live a façade." "Don't feel guilty."[51] But they also warned this woman that her husband could contest her divorce and fight for custody of their children. In another draft of a response to a different married woman that same year, Martin and Lyon jotted down, "Know women who have denied L[esbian] feelings because of children, and have felt, in actuality, this is harmful because not being true to selves or children."[52] Though their belief that wives who desired women should leave their husbands and identify publicly as lesbian was apparent in notes like these, Martin and Lyon never, in any of the writings I have come across, told married women exactly what to do. Perhaps Martin and Lyon refrained from doing so out of a desire to protect themselves, legally and emotionally, from responsibility if a woman did lose child custody, suffer financially, or even commit suicide. But *Lesbian/Woman* was a political manifesto not a therapeutic missive; in it, Martin and Lyon could lay bare their political perspective unencumbered by the specificity of individual wives' personal situations.

Lesbian feminists' animosity for wives who engaged in lesbian relationships was connected to the anger and distrust they held for all bisexual women, whether married or not. Lesbian feminists typically argued that bisexual women enjoyed the benefits of lesbian relationships without sacrificing their heterosexual privilege or making a full political commitment to other women. "They stick to men and don't lose security and acceptance in the male world but still groove on their sisters—avoiding the political issue of choosing the oppressed over the oppressor," as the Furies put it.[53] Lesbian feminists argued that bisexuals threatened to undermine lesbian feminist politics and could not be trusted. The Berkeley-based lesbian separatist Gutter Dyke Collective even stated that bisexual women who simultaneously engaged in lesbian and heterosexual relationships posed a danger to their lesbian lovers by indirectly involving them in a relationship with a man.[54]

Unsurprisingly, lesbian feminists often explicitly excluded bisexual women from lesbian culture, conferences, and community centers branded "for lesbians only." Indeed, lesbian feminist artists of all kinds, including musicians, writers, and jewelry makers, sought to create a separate lesbian culture and economy in the 1970s.[55] In 1977, for example, *Tribad: A Lesbian Separatist Newsjournal*, which was published in New York City, boldly declared on its front cover, "TO BE SOLD TO AND SHARED BY LESBIANS ONLY."[56] Lesbian feminist spaces could become particularly heated battlegrounds. In the mid-1970s in Chicago, for example, bisexual women found themselves excluded from the Women's Center after its leaders redefined it more narrowly as a Lesbian Feminist Center.[57] Such policies would seem to run counter to lesbian feminists' aim of broadening the lesbian community, but women who disregarded these restrictions suffered nonetheless. Around the same time, a conflict arose at the Lesbian Center in East Lansing, Michigan, when two bisexual women ventured into the center's opening dance. Because only lesbians were welcome at the event, two lesbians in attendance asked the bisexual women asked to leave. Soon afterwards, the center's members clarified their policies. They affirmed that a sign stating "This place is for lesbians only" would remain on the center's door, but created particular times for women in the process of coming out to visit.[58] As one Midwestern feminist later recalled of the 1970s, it was "a bad time to be bisexual."[59]

Not all lesbians saw bisexual women as enemies. Like many gay liberationists, some lesbian feminists argued that all people were inherently bisexual and that once the stigma of homosexuality had been overturned, it would be possible for all men and women to fully realize their bisexual potential. Martha Shelley, for instance, wrote in the first issue of *Come Out!*, "Maybe after the revolution, people will be able to love each other regardless of skin color, ethnic origin, occupation or type of genitals."[60] As the queer theorist Steven Angelides has argued, such utopic conceptions of bisexuality conveniently worked to exclude bisexuality from the "present tense," thus allowing more seemingly pressing issues of gay and lesbian liberation to take political precedence.[61] Yet a few lesbians did allow bisexuality some political space in the "here and now," by recognizing the particular discrimination that bisexual women faced and by claiming them as allies in a struggle against male domination.[62] A woman who learned of bisexual women's exclusion from the Lesbian Center in East Lansing, for example, protested their treatment in a letter to *Lesbian Connection*: "Will sisters ever be able to stop hurting each other and put the energy toward the real oppressor?" she wrote.[63] Abbott and Love also briefly noted in *Sappho Was a Right-On Woman* that bisexual women had important contributions to make to feminist discussions about sexuality (albeit after they prefaced that some women claimed a bisexual identity as a "cop-out").[64] Still, even as bisexual women began to speak out on their own behalf to discuss the discrimination they encountered among gay and lesbian activists, lesbian feminist expressions of sympathy for or solidarity with bisexual women remained rare.[65]

Several scholars have argued that lesbian feminists' antipathy to bisexual women was due to the ways in which bisexuality brought to the fore contradictions and inconsistencies inherent to lesbian feminist ideology and the definition of lesbian identity itself. By criticizing and excluding bisexuals, lesbians validated and shored up the boundaries of their own identity, making lesbianism seem a more stable identity category than it actually is. [66] This is in some ways an inevitable part of claiming *any* sexual identity.[67] But while lesbian feminists often derided bisexuality as an "inauthentic" form of lesbianism, a political cop-out, an intermediary or even an illusory identity, through their continual refusal and denigration of bisexual women, they ironically helped to define female bisexuality more clearly.[68] Indeed, the many testimonies of bisexual women who came out in and through the lesbian community, in the face of significant discrimination, suggest this transformation.[69] Bisexuality, as an identity category, was so indistinct in the postwar period, in part, because lesbian identity was so flexible. Terms like "lesbian inclinations" and "lesbian tendencies," which showed up in scientific and pseudoscientific books as well as in wives' letters to the DOB, made it difficult to conceptualize bisexuality as a distinct identity category. In the 1970s, however, as lesbian feminists sharpened the boundaries around lesbian identity and the lesbian community, the once amorphous "ghost" of female bisexuality solidified.[70]

Wives who desired women figured centrally in this shift. Lesbian feminists often imagined wives who engaged in same-sex relationships to be the archetypal bisexual traitors. As DOB president Ruth Simpson declared at a 1971 meeting in New York City, "In my experience . . . if someone says they're bisexual, they're hanging onto their insurance policy of a husband or something."[71] Likewise, in an article in the underground feminist newspaper *Rat*, one young lesbian mother claimed to know many wives who were sexually involved with women. "They say that their sexual life with their husbands [is] so bad, and they enjoy sex with a woman more," she wrote.[72] Rather than seeing such women as allies, the author considered them adversaries. By entering into a relationship with another woman for "purely sexual reasons," wives who engaged in relationships with women perverted what it meant to be a lesbian, sexually exploited their lovers, and used them as sexual objects.[73] By this woman's account, wives who engaged in lesbian relationships were no less oppressive than heterosexual men.

Faced with such damning portraits, wives who wanted to express the feelings of love and commitment that tied them to marriage struggled to make their voices heard within lesbian and feminist publications. In 1972, *Sisters*, a publication of the DOB's San Francisco chapter, ran an unusual letter from two married women—"O and S"—describing how they had become friends and lovers after one woman moved in with her family next door to the other. "We have considered leaving our husbands and making a life of our own, but we seem trapped by the security our husbands represent and unable to face the social and familial pressures that would result from our divorces. So we have decided to remain friends and lovers and enjoy the situation as it is now."[74] To lesbian activists, such public expressions of helplessness and isolation may have appeared not merely politically "useless" but potentially destructive, in so far as they undermined lesbian feminist demands to divorce and sapped women's political motivation.[75] Sure enough, in the following month's issue a married woman in the process of leaving her husband chastised O and S for resigning themselves to marriage. Reiterating arguments like those found in Abbott and Love's book, she wrote they were choosing to burden themselves with feelings of guilt that would only get worse over time. "You say your husband doesn't know; but YOU know and you will suffer," she concluded almost menacingly.[76]

Lesbian feminists criticized married women who attempted to participate in lesbian communities in person as well as in print. In 1970, feminist activist Kate Millett was speaking on a panel at Columbia University about her recently published book, *Sexual Politics*. The event came on the heels of series of articles in the mainstream news media that documented Millett's marriage to Japanese sculptor Fumio Yoshimura while downplaying her involvement in lesbian feminism. *Life*'s September 4 piece, in fact, included a large photograph of Millett kissing her husband and quoted her—incorrectly she later claimed—as saying of lesbianism, "I'm not into that."[77] New York lesbian feminists who knew Millett through her participation in the New York City DOB chapter and Radicalesbians were not pleased. At the Columbia panel, in front of an audience of hundreds, they confronted her about her desire for women. As Millett later remembered it, a woman took the microphone and shouted, "Say it! Say you are a Lesbian." Knowing that lesbian feminists would see the identity "bisexual" as a cop-out, Millett conceded and said, "Yes." But the unavoidable fact of her marriage complicated her assertion of lesbian identity in any narrow sense.[78]

A mere two days after the event at Columbia, *Time* magazine attempted to use Millett's sexual confession to undermine her theories and the feminist movement as a whole. Although *Time* had featured Millett on its cover and lauded *Sexual Politics* only a few months earlier, it now castigated her work, quoting one noted literary critic who called her book "crude simplification," and who insisted that he had long suspected Millett's "sexual ambiguity." The article contended that Millett's sexuality was "bound to discredit her as a spokeswoman for her cause, cast further doubt on her theories, and reinforce the views of those skeptics who routinely dismiss all liberationists as lesbians."[79] Rather than caving in to *Time*'s lavender-baiting by distancing themselves from Millett, a number of feminist activists and collectives issued statements of support for her and claimed the fight for lesbian rights as a critical issue of women's liberation. In response to the attack on Millett, feminist leaders including Susan Brownmiller, Gloria Steinem, and Florynce Kennedy, as well as Abbott and Love, held a press conference at the Washington Square Methodist Church and argued that women's liberation and gay liberation shared a common goal of creating a society in which people would be categorized by neither their gender nor sexual preference.[80]

Yet not all lesbian feminists agreed with this argument. Ti-Grace Atkinson, former president of New York NOW and a DOB member, attended the press conference to defend Millett but, in an op-ed later printed in her own collection of writings, she asserted that the statement presented there had contained "evasions" and had not adequately captured the "unique political and tactical significance of lesbianism to feminism." Atkinson recognized Millett as bisexual but excluded her from the category "lesbian," which she defined as a "commitment, by choice, full-time, of one woman to others of her class." Women like Millett who were active in the feminist movement and had sexual relationships with women while remaining married were "not lesbians in the political sense," Atkinson argued; "they are collaborators."[81] The response to Millett's outing is typically remembered as the moment when straight feminists publicly claimed homosexual oppression as a feminist issue. But Millett's place among *lesbian* feminists was less secure. Even as straight women rallied behind her, as Atkinson's statement suggests, some lesbians remained wary of Millett because of her ongoing marriage.

Millett was not the only married woman to encounter such hostility. Even as lesbian feminists urged married women to come out, in some cases they made wives who were in the process of doing so feel unwanted in lesbian spaces. Karen, a white wife and mother of two living on a farm in Charlotte, North Carolina, discovered as much after becoming acquainted with a group of lesbians in the nearby city of High Point through her participation in the feminist movement in the early 1970s. One Valentine's Day, the High Point women planned a conference on lesbianism which Karen attended. At the time, Karen was sexually involved and "madly in love" with another neighborhood wife, and she was unsure how to make sense of her sexuality.[82] At first Karen thought of herself as bisexual, but after the Valentine's Day conference, Karen became convinced that she was a lesbian and that she belonged with the women in High Point. The following weekend she packed up her two sons and drove to visit the High Point group only to discover that she was not as welcome there as she had anticipated. Karen was, as she put it, "a straight woman to them," and their treatment briefly convinced her that she was not a lesbian after all.[83]

The fact that Karen brought her two sons along may have been another part of the reason the High Point lesbians were reluctant to accept her; many mothers felt alienated from lesbian feminist spaces in this period because they had male children. A divorced mother of two from the Bay Area, for example, complained that the lesbian community there was "too filled with both anti-children and anti-male vibes."[84] Invitations for "women only" events often excluded children or failed to take into consideration the need to provide childcare, and lesbians who were not mothers often became frustrated with children's behavior. Eventually this woman came to find friends and a community of support among older lesbians in particular. "I found I had a lot in common not just with women who were lesbians, but women who were lesbians and who had lived in this world something like as long as I had," she later explained.[85] Such women were more likely to have been involved with men at some point in their lives, to have male children, and to be less "dogmatic" regarding the issue of connection with men.[86] Race as well as age shaped lesbians' attitudes toward lesbians with sons. One biracial lesbian in New York found that because lesbians of color were committed to working with men in the fight against racism, they tended to be more accepting of formerly married mothers of male children like herself.[87]

Wives who balanced marriage and lesbian relationships were not alone in attracting lesbian feminists' ire during the 1970s and early 1980s, and many scholars have discussed the intense political battles that erupted in this period.[88] Rules, often unspoken, governed everything from dress to sexual practice in lesbian feminist communities. Blue jeans, flannel shirts, and thrift store finds were the norm, and clothing that looked too expensive, too masculine, or too feminine tended to attract negative attention.

"You wouldn't dare wear nail polish. You really wouldn't," recalled one woman.[89] Some accused butch lesbians of seeking male privilege and aping heterosexual relationships with their femme lovers. Others criticized those who sought leadership roles, or whom the media anointed as movement leaders. Lesbian mothers with male children and transgender women were subject to particularly vicious "trashings," but as sociologist Arlene Stein put it, anyone who "dared step out of line—however the 'line' was configured at any particular place and time" was in danger of being attacked.[90] In seeking to create a unified lesbian world, in some ways lesbian feminists produced a brittle notion of lesbian identity that could not easily accommodate, much less celebrate, the differences among them.

Dissenting Voices

Many women did contest what they understood to be the rigidity of lesbian feminist identity, and some leaders challenged the notion that lesbians had no choice but to divorce. In 1973 the longtime feminist leader Robin Morgan delivered the keynote address at the first West Coast Lesbian Conference, a meeting of over twelve hundred lesbians in Los Angeles (Figure 7). Despite being married to a man who identified as a "faggot effeminist," Morgan identified as a lesbian and she defended her right to speak at the event.[91] Morgan portrayed lesbian feminists' concern with sexual identity labels, and with distinguishing between lesbians and straight women, as politically misguided and a waste of energy. She claimed that members of the Radicalesbians had attacked her at some moments for identifying as a lesbian and at other moments for failing to do so. "Don't you dare call yourself a lesbian—you live with a man and you have a child," Morgan remembered being told at one point. Though she did not agree with this demand, as "statistically most Lesbians are married to men and have children," Morgan conceded to it. Six months later, a different group of Radicalesbians attacked her yet again. "'We notice that you stopped calling yourself a Lesbian,' they said, 'what's the matter—you gone back in the closet? You afraid?"[92] For Morgan, these conflicting attitudes reflected the futility of placing women in narrow sexual identity categories.

Morgan sought to ameliorate the friction between lesbian and heterosexual women by broadening the category of "lesbian" to include "any woman who had ever loved a woman," as she wrote in 1972. But even

Figure 7. Special issue on the West Coast Lesbian Conference at which activist Robin Morgan, who was then married to a man, gave the controversial keynote speech. *The Lesbian Tide*, May/June 1973. From the Jeanne Córdova Papers, courtesy of ONE Archives at the USC Libraries. Reprinted by permission of Jeanne Córdova's estate.

Morgan's vision of female unity had its limits. Rather than a "gay-straight split," what the feminist movement needed, Morgan argued, was a "feminist-collaborator" split between those women who were truly committed to the feminist movement and those who had "adopt[ed] the patriarch's style."[93] According to Morgan, such collaborators included women who listened to the Rolling Stones, objectified other women, criticized lesbian monogamy, and allied with transgender people.[94] Thus even as Morgan argued for her right to participate in a lesbian conference despite her marriage, she actively attacked and excluded others, including transgender singer Beth Elliott, who had performed just the night before. Elliott had, in fact, helped to organize the conference and most attendees welcomed her attendance, but Morgan argued that "if even *one* woman" objected to Elliott's presence, she should have left.[95] Ironically, by this same logic, Morgan would have been forced to leave as well.

As demonstrated by the issue of *The Lesbian Tide* devoted entirely to the conference, the response to Morgan's speech was mixed. While some lesbian feminist writers supported Morgan's calls to get beyond the gay-straight divide and accepted her decision to identify as a lesbian despite being married, others did not. In an article titled "The Living Contradiction," Pat Buchanan viciously attacked Morgan as a "wolf in sheep's clothing." Why "does she need the identification with the *real* Lesbians?" Buchanan asked.[96] Buchanan went on to accuse Morgan of undeservingly claiming the label lesbian because she was in danger of losing her position as a leader of the feminist movement. According to Buchanan, Morgan's claim to lesbianism was based on neither sexuality nor politics. It was rather a last, desperate bid for power as her leadership within the feminist movement was becoming obsolete. Another woman, writing in the feminist journal *off our backs*, similarly rejected Morgan as a lesbian and complained that she had delivered the keynote address: "How come we didn't have a *lesbian* speaker, like Del Martin or one of us?"[97] While this author failed to define precisely who "us" was, it seems married women were not included.

Like Morgan, Kate Millett refuted the idea that her ongoing marriage was a sign of false consciousness or political failure in her memoir *Flying* (1974). The book focuses on the year of Millett's life after she was public outed at Columbia University in 1970. *Flying* details Millett's relationship with her husband, as well as her affairs with women and the difficulties involved in balancing them all. Yet Millett denied that she had to choose between her marriage and her lesbian life. Instead, she presented the complexity of her romantic and erotic relationships in *Flying* as part of an attempt to build a new way of being in the world, unconstrained by convention or social institutions, gender or sexual binaries: a way of living based entirely on love. "What I want is outrageous," she states at one point, "all the possible pleasures of freedom."[98] At different moments in the book, Millett refers to herself as gay, lesbian, *and* bisexual, but clearly none of these labels were adequate, and this precisely was the point. *Flying* concludes as Millett and a female lover travel together to Provincetown, Massachusetts. Lest this seem some clear statement about her sexual identity or life plans, however, Millett eventually invites her husband to join them. Rather than "coming out" in a narrow sense as a lesbian, Millett's goal with *Flying* was to "come out as myself," as she put it, to counter the "Kate Millett" figure created by the news media with a messy and painfully honest self-portrait. In doing so, she sought to expose not only the constructedness of her own social and political persona, but the inevitable partiality of any identity label. [99]

In doing so, Millett opened herself up to even more criticism than she had encountered before. *Flying* was tremendously successful. Within the first ten days of its release, the paperback edition sold more than a hundred thousand copies.[100] But reviewers were brutal. Mainstream critics disapproved of her unconventional, stream-of-consciousness style, the detail with which she described her love affairs, and her seeming self-absorption.[101] Feminist reviewers were not uniformly kinder.[102] While one lesbian separatist called *Flying* "one of the artistic achievements of the twentieth century," others were more critical of her "failure to fault the grossly piggish behavior of most males she describes, and . . . perennial attachment to Fumio."[103] Even in light of such disapproval, though, Millett refused to apologize for her ongoing commitment to a man. In an interview several years after *Flying* was released, a journalist asked Millett whether or not her marriage had created a fundamental power imbalance between her and her lesbian lovers. "I don't know," Millett responded, "I suppose it did have its effect, but I couldn't stop loving Fumio—I'd lived with him ten years and he'll go on being the closest person to me all my life."[104] Though Millett remained unrepentant, the response *Flying* generated demonstrates the criticism women risked when they spoke openly about combining marriage and lesbian relationships.

Morgan and Millett were not entirely alone, however, in arguing that wives could also be lesbians. In her essay "With All Due Respect: In Defense of All Lesbian Lifestyles," which appeared in the 1975 collection *After You're Out*, the novelist Jane Rule shared a story of organizing a women's studies seminar through the University of British Columbia titled "Lesbian Lifestyles," which attracted a large and diverse group of women. "There were monogamous couples, married women living with their husbands and female lovers, single parents who hid their lovers or explained their lovers to their children, women who had never dared approach the women they loved for fear of rejection." Rather than celebrating their differences, however, the women attacked one another: "Every woman who was willing to speak was disqualified by others in the room as inauthentic, not a 'real' lesbian."[105] The difficulty, as Rule saw it, was that although all of the women in the room shared a desire to reverse and reject the stigmatization of homosexuality, they had fundamentally different values, and one woman's choices all too easily offended another. Such conflicts, Rule pointed out, were not only taking place in private contexts but in more public ones as well, and she summarized some of the well-known battles that had erupted among lesbian feminists, particularly around women who were or had been married. Rule's response to this hyperpolicing of lesbian identity was to insist that authentic lesbians were everywhere, even "asleep in their husbands' arms."[106]

Poet and activist Adrienne Rich, like Rule, resisted the inclination to institute ever-narrower definitions of who "counted" as lesbian. Rather, she argued that it was possible to see lesbian relationships in varying degrees among all nurturing and supportive female relationships, whether sexual or not. Rich introduced this concept of the "lesbian continuum" in her tremendously influential and widely reprinted 1980 *Signs* article "Compulsory Heterosexuality and Lesbian Existence." Rich wrote the essay in response to a series of important feminist academic studies that ignored the possibility of lesbianism and failed to consider the central role of heterosexuality in securing male dominance. Rich intended the idea of the "lesbian continuum" to counteract these erasures and bring together disparate historical examples of women's resistance to heterosexuality. Explicitly building on the Radicalesbians' reconceptualization of lesbianism, Rich defined the term "lesbian continuum" as referring to "a range—throughout each woman's life and throughout history—of woman-identified experience; not simply the fact that a woman has had or consciously desired genital sexual experience with another woman."[107]

Rich pointedly included married women within the category "lesbian." She noted that "there is no statistical documentation of the numbers of lesbians who have remained in heterosexual marriages for most of their lives," and she even cited Lorraine Hansberry's earlier letter to *The Ladder* about the forces that compelled women who experienced lesbian desires and relationships to marry.[108] Within Rich's article, then, lesbian wives appear primarily as victims, trapped within marriage by social and economic forces beyond their control. Rich did not address the question of whether or not such women might have *wanted* to combine marriage and lesbian relationships, because she was most concerned with drawing attention to the compulsory nature of heterosexuality for women. "The absence of choice remains the great unacknowledged reality," she wrote, "and in the absence of choice, women . . . will have no collective power to determine the meaning and place of sexuality in their lives."[109] For Rich, whether "good" marriages were possible was a distraction from the more fundamental issue: women's enduring lack of sexual autonomy.

In an interview published a few years later, the black feminist theorist Audre Lorde addressed some of the questions Rich chose to avoid and suggested—based on her own experiences—that lesbianism and marriage might be made compatible. Lorde married in the 1960s, after having several lesbian relationships. Yet she explained in a 1983 interview with the black lesbian activist Anita Cornwell that she did not see her marriage as symbolizing a rejection of her lesbian life or even as marking an end to it. "I had never really made the kind of distinction between *heterosexual* and *homosexual* that so many people make. I really felt that was another kind of smoke screen that people erect to hide behind," she stated.[110] Yet, while Lorde told Cornwell that she was not invested in the hetero-homosexual binary, she did not use the word "bisexual" to describe herself either.

In the late 1960s, Lorde engaged in an affair with Frances Clayton, a professor she met during her time as a writer-in-residence at Tougaloo College. Initially, she planned to remain married. Lorde's husband, Edwin Rollins, had long known about her love for women and was under no misconception that her feelings for Frances were a phase. Lorde did eventually decide to leave the marriage and divorced in 1970, but she insisted that her affair was not the reason for her divorce. Rather, she and her husband had grown apart in ways that her husband's response to her relationship with Frances made clear. Lorde did not portray Edwin as an oppressive patriarch, nor did she cast her marriage as an utter failure. In fact, she told

Cornwell that her relationship with her husband was no different from any of her other romantic relationships. "I don't go into relationships where I can't dig the person completely," she explained, thus resisting the lesbian feminist idea that her love affair with Frances was inherently more politically evolved than her relationship with Edwin had been.[111]

Lorde's suggestion that marriage and lesbianism might be combined and her refusal to denigrate her relationship with her husband were in keeping with her broader political vision. She repeatedly challenged the homogenizing tendencies of various political movements, particularly the tendencies of white middle-class feminists to ignore differences of race and class. "As a black lesbian feminist comfortable with the many different ingredients of my identity, and a woman committed to racial and sexual freedom from oppression, I find I am constantly being encouraged to pluck out some one aspect of myself and present this as the meaningful whole, eclipsing or denying the other parts of myself," she wrote in 1980.[112] As this statement suggests, Lorde advocated an intersectional politics that could embrace multiple identities and address multiple forms of oppression at once, "without the restrictions of externally imposed definition."[113] Even though Lorde did identify as a lesbian feminist, in her interview with Cornwell she was unwilling to reject the heterosexual parts of her life in a way that might have made her sexuality easier for others to understand. Still, she did not often speak publicly about her marriage. Only after her death did her biographer describe in detail how she and Edwin had consciously sought to create a new kind of marriage together, one in which they both had the freedom and opportunity to engage in homosexual relationships and communities, while maintaining a stable and politically radical domestic life for their children.[114]

◆ ◆

The discussions that circulated around married women in the 1970s highlight a central tension within lesbian feminists' definition of lesbianism. On the one hand, lesbian feminists argued that lesbians were everywhere. They believed that any woman could and indeed *should* choose to be a lesbian; that love, affection, and political commitment rather than sexual desire defined lesbian identity the most. "Every woman can be a l-e-s-bian," folk singer Alix Dobkin famously crooned in the 1970s, and many unhappily married women heard her call. On the other hand, many lesbian feminists maintained that in order to be "truly" lesbian in a political sense, women needed to renounce their heterosexual privilege and separate from men. In this sense, a "real" lesbian simply could not be married. Lesbian feminists who sought to restrict lesbian identity and community to only those women who were willing to leave their marriages, seem to have been engaging in a tactic of "strategic essentialism."[115] That is, they were making a conscious effort to ignore the differences within their community and the instability of the category "lesbian" itself in an effort to overturn the stigma of homosexuality, to protest male dominance, to resist the compulsory nature of marriage and heterosexuality, and to create a way for women to lead lives in which their sexual and emotional relationships with other women were central.

This political tactic did undoubtedly help many wives who desired women leave unhappy marriages and embark on new lesbian lives; it fostered their sense of community and their political consciousness. But it also stigmatized women whose sexual desires, romantic relationships, and family ties included men as well as women at one time or another. And it fed tensions that persisted long after the peak of the movement had passed, both between lesbians and bisexual women, and among lesbians themselves. Indeed, some lesbians continued to fear long after divorce that they were not lesbian *enough*. As the feminist science-fiction writer and once-married lesbian Joanna Russ wrote in a personal essay, the question "Am I a 'real' Lesbian?" plagued her for years after coming out and getting divorced. The idea that she could not be a lesbian because she had experienced attraction to men was precisely what Russ had heard for years in psychoanalytic treatment during her marriage: "You aren't a Lesbian. You can't be a Lesbian. There aren't any Lesbians. Real Lesbians have horns." By policing the boundaries of lesbian identity, Russ argued, lesbian feminists were "simply doing the culture's dirty work for it," chipping away at the category "lesbian" until there was nothing and no one left.[116]

In some cases, the idea that lesbians could not be married made it even harder for wives to publicly express their same-sex desires. In the late 1970s, about a year into her marriage, J. Lapis Springtree, a white woman living in suburban Pennsylvania, slept with her close female friend. The experience was not a happy one, but it did confirm J.'s sense of being attracted to women. Soon after, she became involved in the Women's Resource

Center of Delaware County in hopes of connecting with women like her. When the center conducted a survey asking members what topics they would like to see covered at events in the future, J. seized the opportunity and wrote "lesbians." Before long, the center's codirector called J. into her office. "I understand you're married with a small child," the codirector began, "so I don't understand why you wrote this." J. explained that she was interested in the issue and believed that other members were too, but the center's codirector was unmoved. She informed J. that lesbians did not "mingle" with wives and mothers like herself. Their lives were very different from hers, and they had a "whole world" of their own. "Basically she called me a wannabe," J. recalled, and she left the meeting feeling so ashamed and embarrassed that she did not act on her same-sex desires again for years after attempting suicide no fewer than six times.[117]

Certainly, the views of the center's codirector were extreme and her lack of sympathy striking, but her response to J.'s interest in lesbianism is nonetheless revealing of the extent to which the lesbian feminist movement had transformed understandings of lesbian identity. By the early 1980s, for better and for worse, marriage and lesbian identity seemed far less compatible than they had in the postwar period. The discursive separation between marriage and lesbianism that lesbian feminists instated, however, never produced an absolute boundary at the ground level. In the 1970s and 1980s, wives continued to find ways of engaging in sexual and romantic relationships with other women. How ordinary wives navigated their relationships with their husbands and their desires for other women differently in this era is the subject of the next chapter.

CHAPTER 6

Opened Marriage

IN 1972, LIN, a Chinese American woman from Fresno, California, wrote to Del Martin and Phyllis Lyon because she wanted to "quit living this lie of nineteen years of marriage." She had recently read Martin and Lyon's book *Lesbian/Woman* (1972), which helped her realize she was "not some kind of freak, or the 'one' and only."[1] Over the course of a year, Lin came out to her three children and her husband, who "accepted the idea" of her homosexuality but did not want to divorce.[2] Lin and her husband remained legally married, but within a few months she had moved into her own apartment and connected with a broader gay and lesbian community in Fresno. Before long, Martin and Lyon were asking Lin for advice about where to direct another Fresno woman in the process of coming out. Her chatty response reveals just how rich and widespread the contours of her lesbian world had become: "I could refer her to our Tuesday night gay rap group (not a part of NOW) or she could go to the Underground Railroad Coffeehouse (gay guys and gals) at nighttime—there is a Thursday night rap meeting (7:30 pm) sponsored by the MCC [Metropolitan Community Church] at the coffee house also for guys & gals—then there is always the bar at Pine Lake Lodge, old highway 99—good for meeting women on Friday & Saturday nights. Then there's the Fresno Rockets women's softball team. If they're playing in town—practically the whole lesbian community is sitting in the stands cheering for our team."[3]

Lin's letter demonstrates the multiple ways in which marriage *opened* for wives who desired women in the 1970s and 1980s. As they had in the past, married women continued to develop sexual relationships with women they met in the course of their daily lives, but these relationships now connected wives to a lesbian world that was more vibrant and more visible than they had imagined possible. Marriage and the household, in other words, now opened out into a broad lesbian geography. These lesbian and/or feminist spaces were not without their problems, and not all married women experienced them as welcoming or affirming. But the sense of community that wives—particularly white, middle-class ones—found in gay and lesbian bars and rap groups, women's centers and bookstores, and lesbian feminist dances and conferences helped convince them that it was possible to build a rich and fulfilling lesbian life.[4]

Marriage *opened* for wives who desired women in this period with regard to communication as well as geography. In a striking change from the previous era, by the 1970s wives who desired women often communicated with their husbands about their sexual desires and identities plainly and unambiguously, just as Lin did. For some women, this communication took the form of a conventional "coming out" as lesbian. But for others, the move to a lesbian identity took place slowly over time. Rather than moving through this process alone, wives increasingly chose to include their husbands as they tried to make sense of their desires and negotiate their sexual identities. Furthermore, despite the significant stigmatization bisexual women faced within the lesbian community, the media's sudden interest in bisexuality in the 1970s helped to make this identity category more available to wives who desired women, and they increasingly used it to describe themselves.

Finally, marriage *opened* in a sexual sense. As marital advice books—including Nena and George O'Neill's best-selling *Open Marriage: A New Life Style for Couples* (1972)—seemed to endorse sexual nonmonogamy, some of the women in this study were able to balance marriage and same-sex relationships far more transparently than they had before, with their husbands' explicit rather than implicit permission and support. Lin and her husband may not have been familiar with *Open Marriage*, but they could have found inspiration and encouragement for their unconventional marital arrangement in the growing number of advice and self-help books on open marriage, group marriage, and bisexual marriage, among other marital "experiments."

While in Lin's case the historical record is unclear, nearly all of the women described in this chapter did ultimately leave their marriages, despite the multiple ways in which marriage and the household opened. This chapter thus reveals the somewhat contradictory forces that reshaped the lives of wives who desired women in the 1970s and 1980s. For just as it became possible for wives who desired women to connect with lesbian-identified women, to share their feelings with other people—including their husbands—and to remake their marriages to accommodate their lovers more publicly and openly, the women in this chapter overwhelmingly came to see marriage and lesbian identity as incompatible. This transformation was due to not only lesbian feminists' insistence that wives who desired women leave their marriages, but also broader changes in the meaning of marriage itself. By the 1980s, psychologists and marital advisors no longer considered remaining married for marriage's sake to be an unequivocal good, and they encouraged married couples to expect far more emotional intimacy from each other than they once had. Whereas in the postwar period wives who combined marriage and same-sex relationships typically remained married, in the 1970s and 1980s, this arrangement was more often a prelude to divorce.

The New Geography of Wives' Lesbian Worlds

Wives who engaged in sexual relationships with women they met in the context of their daily lives found it much easier in the 1970s and 1980s to connect with a broader lesbian community by participating in lesbian and feminist groups.[5] In doing so, many found both affirmation of their lesbian desires and confirmation that there were others like them. Marty Elkin, for example, a white, middle-aged wife and mother, fell in love with another mom in Springfield, Illinois, in the early 1980s. She later recalled how greatly attending a lesbian feminist group for women over forty at the Sangamon State University Women's Center helped her in the process of coming out. "Everyone had a voice," Marty explained. "And everyone was respected equally. And everyone was encouraged to be honest about who they were and where they were in their process."[6] As we have seen, some married women experienced significant hostility in lesbian feminist spaces, but for Marty, who recalled her coming out group in almost idyllic terms, this was clearly not the case.

Feminist groups proved vital for younger women too. In the early 1970s, Sharon, a twenty-something wife and mother of a young son, fell in love with a woman who was rooming with her and her family at their home in San Diego. Yet, in contrast with wives who desired women in the past,

Sharon never felt alone. "I'd been involved in the women's movement and felt supported by that—I didn't feel like I was weird or anything," she later explained.[7] Specifically, Sharon found support by attending feminist meetings at the San Diego YMCA, as well as a retreat in the San Francisco Bay Area. Of the retreat, in particular, Sharon recalled, "There were a lot of lesbians and women around, and I just felt great—there was this whole community of women up here who were political, and that really felt good about themselves as being gay, and mothers, too."[8] The support and sense of community Sharon found among these women helped convince her that it would be possible to divorce her husband and begin a lesbian life, which she eventually did.

Unlike Marty and Sharon, who became involved in the feminist movement after beginning lesbian relationships, many wives came to recognize, verbalize, and act on their lesbian desires entirely within the context of feminist spaces. Feminist consciousness-raising groups were particularly important spaces for married women in this respect.[9] In consciousness-raising groups, small numbers of women met periodically to examine the ways that gender and sexual politics shaped their personal lives. Though young, radical feminists were the first to form these groups in the late 1960s, such groups soon spread to include women well beyond this particular demographic group. By 1970, consciousness-raising groups were present in every major American city, and in 1973 alone, more than one hundred thousand people nationwide claimed membership in a consciousness-raising group.[10] Still, those who participated in these groups were overwhelmingly white, middle-class, college-educated women who had the time and inclination to attend them. This route to lesbian identity and community was, therefore, not equally accessible to wives of all races and income levels.

Because consciousness-raising groups encouraged women to explore their dreams and desires, to reconsider their relationships with both men and women, and to voice feelings they might have never before put into words, many wives felt safe expressing secret lesbian desires within them. Others found that the intimacy and openness inspired by such groups sparked unanticipated sexual feelings between members.[11] A policy of confidentiality further enabled wives to examine their lesbian desires without fear of being judged or "outed" publicly. Bea Howard, a Jewish housewife and mother of two in her early forties, joined a consciousness-raising group in the early 1970s in New York City. Bea had long been aware of her attraction to women and internally identified as a lesbian, but she had never discussed her feelings with anyone else. After several months, she found the courage to come out to her group, which inspired other members to do so as well.[12] Another married woman, also in her forties, later explained how participating in a consciousness-raising group with other lesbians in small-town Malone, New York, in the mid-1970s helped her to "come out" to herself and to realize that it was possible to live a different kind of life. "It was very, very helpful to talk to other lesbians," she later recalled, "to find that they were living on farms and creating a life together. . . . I found out there is a viable lifestyle here, that you can actually *be* this thing."[13]

Feminist courses taught at colleges, universities, and other venues were also important spaces in which married women came to recognize lesbian desires and begin lesbian relationships. For these women in particular, claiming a lesbian identity was often based on both their sexual attraction to women and their political beliefs about the inherent inequality of hetero-sexual relationships. Aleah, a young mother of Egyptian and Iraqi descent, met her first female lover when she took a women's studies course at San Francisco State University. Women's studies was just emerging as a field in the 1970s. Cornell University offered the first for-credit women's studies course in 1969, but by 1973 more than five hundred colleges and universi-ties were doing the same.[14] Aleah, a psychology student, later claimed that she "accidentally" wandered into an early women's studies course on women and madness and soon discovered that "90 percent of the women in there were dykes." She had never before been consciously attracted to women, but upon entering the classroom, she remembered being instantly "turned on."[15] The course also provided Aleah's first exposure to feminist thought, and she welcomed the idea that her life did not need to center around men. Before the semester was over, she had become sexually involved with another woman in her class.

Older women, too, found lovers in feminist courses. Around the same time that Aleah enrolled at San Francisco State, Deedy Breed, a white housewife and mother of three who had been married for nearly twenty years, began meeting "all these wonderful Yale lesbians" after taking courses at the New Haven Women's Liberation Center. Deedy first took a six-week course called Growing Up Female, which served as her introduction to the feminist movement. "My eyes were opened," as she later put it. "I could not get enough."[16] So Deedy enrolled in another feminist course at the local community college, and another, and she soon became involved in a range of feminist causes at the Women's Liberation Center as well. As discussed in Chapter 1, Deedy had once engaged in a lesbian affair before getting married in the 1950s, but she rejected those feelings for decades until she became involved in the feminist movement. At some point during her feminist education, she promised herself that she would act on her attraction to women again before turning fifty. Sure enough, just a few days before her fiftieth birthday, Deedy slept with one of her teachers.[17]

Although NOW leaders' initial resistance to the issue of lesbianism convinced many women of the need for a separate lesbian feminist movement, by the late 1970s and early 1980s NOW chapters across the country provided older married women in particular with a vital conduit to a lesbian community and identity. Some women joined NOW with the intention of connecting with lesbians, but others discovered, through NOW, the possibility of living a life they had never imagined before. Henrietta Bensussen, a white mother of two then in her late forties, was already considering leaving her marriage of nearly thirty years when she became involved with NOW in San Francisco in the early 1980s. Before long, many of the married women in Henrietta's meetings began coming out as lesbians. One day, an older woman who usually wore dark, somber clothes and who looked to Henrietta like a nun, suddenly arrived at their meeting wearing jean pants and a new top. "I finally left that horrible Ralph after thirty some years of marriage. I'm a lesbian!" she announced.[18] If this woman could leave her marriage and begin a new life as a lesbian, Henrietta thought, surely she could too.

Henrietta soon began taking steps toward a new life. At a NOW conference, she danced with a woman for the first time, and afterward she ventured to a lesbian nightclub in Santa Clara—Club Savoy. Henrietta was nervous heading to the club for the first time. She had only ever been to a few bars with her husband, and she had never entered one alone. But she discovered that she enjoyed meeting women, talking, dancing, and drinking at Club Savoy, and she soon became a regular there, giving her husband the excuse that she had a meeting to attend. In her journal, Henrietta described feeling quite at home at the Savoy as a middle-class, middle-aged wife. "I go to this bar, each time meeting and talking with women who seem very much like me," she wrote. "Some are married, some divorced, some have children, some are young and running away from a bad experience, others looking for a new woman. Some married mothers have found neighborhood lovers, but are restless with their secrets and ponder the pros and cons of a split from suburbia. We all seek connection and adventure within the world of women."[19] That Henrietta was able to find so many women like her at Club Savoy is striking, but not as surprising as it may at first seem.

Henrietta's story and her description of the clientele at Club Savoy reflects the fact that middle-class married women of multiple generations were becoming more willing to visit gay bars in the 1970s and 1980s. This was likely a result of gay and lesbian activists' success in challenging the police harassment of gay bars, the expansion of lesbian bars in particular, and the fact that it had become more acceptable for women to visit bars in general.[20] In fact, several white, middle-class, married women later described visiting a gay bar for the first time in this period as a critical moment in the development of their lesbian or bisexual identity. "It was like, Wow, this is going on? I mean it's a whole new world, opening up for me," recalled one woman of her first experience stepping into a gay bar in Madison, Wisconsin, during this period.[21] Another housewife, living in the Bay Area, described visiting a gay bar in nearly identical terms: "The first time I walked into a gay bar it was just like, Wow! This is where I belong. This is the place that I should be."[22] As these women's very similar statements suggest, by the 1970s gays and lesbians increasingly understood going to a gay or lesbian bar for the first time as an expected step in the process of coming out. This had, of course, long been the case for working-class lesbians, but it marked a significant change for white, middle-class, middle-aged wives like those just quoted.

Some married women of color described bars as integral to their coming out as well, despite the fact that many owners of gay and lesbian bars continued to practice racial discrimination in the 1970s and 1980s.[23] One married black actress and mother, then in her twenties, later described how she became deeply attracted to another woman for the first time while visiting a gay bar in Los Angeles with some lesbian friends in the early 1970s. It was, as she later explained, "my first crush on a woman, that I was really, totally acknowledging the full potential of it."[24] While it was not necessarily the case nationwide, white flight from Detroit to the suburbs following World War II had the effect of opening up many formerly white, urban, gay bars to lesbians of color by the 1970s.[25] This transition in the racial composition of Detroit's gay bars came at just the right time for Anita, a Mexican American nurse who married at the age of sixteen in the late 1960s. Anita had long felt that something was "wrong" with her sexually, and after visiting several doctors about her problem, she confided in a neighbor with whom she was also friendly. "I don't think you're frigid," the friend replied. "I think you need to come with me and go somewhere with me."[26] The friend, who identified as bisexual, brought her to the Casbah, a lesbian bar less than a mile away from where the women lived. The Casbah was located in a neighborhood that was transitioning from white to black in the early 1970s, and the many different types of people Anita met at the Casbah, from "different walks of life, different backgrounds," made her feel at home.[27] She ended up meeting her first female lover there and eventually divorced her husband.

Yet not all wives of color felt comfortable in gay and lesbian bars or clubs, even when they did cater to people of color. In the 1980s, Mistinguette Smith, an African American wife in her twenties, often felt uncomfortable at the black lesbian parties or clubs in her home city of Cleveland, Ohio, such as the Eight Ball Club. Although the people, music, and food in these specifically black, lesbian spaces felt familiar to Mistinguette, there were other aspects of this world she did not share or welcome. For example, she did not drink, and she did not fit easily into the butch/femme culture that predominated in these spaces. As she later explained, "My demeanor and my dress tend to be really feminine, but I've always worn trousers, and I remember being at these sets and having people walk up and say, 'What are you?'" Mistinguette was a feminist activist. She worked at a reproductive health clinic and at a domestic violence shelter, and she helped organize public protests of violence against women in Cleveland. But she did not feel at home within these almost exclusively white, feminist spaces either, where she was "suspect, not welcome, racially isolated, and culturally always having to lean in and understand somebody else." Feeling alienated within both white feminist groups and black lesbian clubs, it was not until Mistinguette discovered the writings of the once-married lesbian feminists Pat Parker and Audre Lorde in the 1980s that she truly came to believe she could be both "black and lesbian at the same time."[28]

Organizations for politically active lesbians of color like Mistinguette may not have existed in Cleveland in the 1970s and 1980s, but they were taking shape in other cities. In 1974, a group of black and Latina women involved with the Black Lesbian Caucus of New York City's Gay Activists' Alliance founded Salsa Soul Sisters with the intention of bringing lesbians of color together. Several of the organization's founders, including Achebe Betty Powell and Reverend Dolores Jackson had been married, as had other members of the group.[29] Following the National Lesbian

Feminist Organization conference in Santa Monica in 1978, a group of women founded a similar organization, Lesbians of Color, in Los Angeles. The next year, Annette "Chi" Hughes, who had been involved in the Lambda Student Alliance at Howard University, helped create Sapphire Sapphos in Washington, DC, to provide lesbians of a color with an alternative to the bars as well as the male-dominated National Coalition of Black Gays, later renamed the National Coalition of Black Lesbians and Gays. Significantly, Sapphire Sapphos made a point of welcoming children at dances and support groups, which would have made it particularly appealing for women who were or had been married.[30] In the late 1970s in San Francisco, Zee Wong and Lisa Chun formed a small group for Asian American lesbians called the Asian Women's Group, and beginning in 1984 Lesbianas Unidas, a task force of Gay and Lesbian Latinos Unidos, sought to empower Latina lesbians in particular.[31]

These organizations provided married women of color who were struggling to make sense of their sexuality with a sense of community, support, and understanding they could not find in white-dominated lesbian groups. In the late 1970s, Alberta Ashley, a black mother of two in her fifties, then separated from her husband, described the importance that Salsa Soul Sisters had in her life. "I'm very concerned with what I like to identify as the triple wammy [sic], being Black, woman, and Lesbian," she explained in an interview for the organization's *Gayzette*. "Here at Salsa, I've found women coming from the same place." In fact, Alberta portrayed her first Salsa Soul Sisters meeting as nothing less than a dream come true: "I had at last found women who think and have attitudes the same as my own."[32] Saundra Tignor, a formerly married woman from Los Angeles, described first finding a social group for black lesbians in the late 1970s in similar terms. "Thought I'd died and gone to heaven," she later told an interviewer, adding that lesbians of color like herself were "just hungry" for such spaces at the time.[33]

Despite the many tensions and problems inherent in lesbian and feminist spaces, by the 1970s the lesbian feminist and gay liberation movements had reshaped the places in which wives who desired women expressed their sexuality, as well as the possibilities such women saw for themselves in the future. Joan Biren, a lesbian feminist activist and cofounder of the Furies collective in Washington, DC, later explained that their organization had sought "to make space in the world to live as lesbians."[34] As Biren and countless other activists did so, the household became less central to married women's lesbian lives. Gay and lesbian support groups; feminist consciousness-raising groups, courses, and retreats; gay and lesbian bars and dances—in these venues and many others, wives who had long been aware of their attraction to women were able to voice their feelings for the first time, while others suddenly became conscious of desires they had not recognized before. For both groups of women, lesbianism began to appear as a real and viable alternative to married life.

No More Secrets, No More Lies

In the 1950s and 1960s, the women in this study tended to think of their same-sex desires as merely a part of themselves, one that should be subordinated to their more central identities as wives and mothers and remain unspoken. In the 1970s and 1980s, however, wives began to experience their feelings for other women as revealing an authentic inner self that could not and should not be denied. This change reflected a growing political emphasis on personal transparency which could be found in the grassroots feminist movement's demands to make the personal political, as well as in politicians' increasing openness with the media about their intimate, private lives.[35] In keeping with this broad social shift, the women in this study increasingly felt that they owed it to themselves and their husbands to convey the truths of their newfound identities. Married women thus began moving away from an earlier strategy of sexual discretion to a policy of openness with their husbands, much as gay and lesbian children did with their parents during this same period.[36]

This transformation in communication was due in large part to the importance gay and lesbian activists placed on coming out, but it was also due to a new explicitness around homosexuality within mainstream culture. The 1967 United States Supreme Court ruling in *Redrup v. New York* narrowed the definition of obscenity and made possible more explicit depictions of sex in American fiction. In the late 1960s, homosexuality also moved to the forefront of the news. On October 31, 1969, *Time* magazine featured a series of articles on the topic of, as the issue's cover stated, "The Homosexual in America," and in December 1971, *Life* published an eleven-page spread titled "Homosexuals in Revolt," which depicted the gay liberation movement as one of the most significant happenings of the year.[37] By the 1970s, the Motion Picture Association of America had replaced the Motion Picture Production Code with the modern film rating system, enabling more straightforward, if still stereotypical, portraits of homosexuality in Hollywood films. Among these films was the pioneering *The Boys in the Band* (1970), which focused on a group of gay male friends. Within two years of its release, more than a dozen films dealing with homosexuality made their way into theaters. Such films included both major studio pictures and small-budget, independent films. Television reflected this new frankness about homosexuality as well, and many married women who corresponded with Martin and Lyon in the 1970s explained they had learned of the couple's existence through their 1972 appearance on the *Phil Donahue Show*—a daytime talk show dealing with controversial issues and aimed at housewives.

Wives' new openness with their husbands also reflected the emergence and sweeping cultural influence of humanistic psychology. Beginning in the 1950s and 1960s, psychologists Abraham Maslow and Carl Rogers placed a new emphasis on personal growth and self-realization. In contrast with psychoanalytic and behavioral psychologists who took a rigid, hierarchical approach to counseling and aimed to help patients fulfill their social roles, these humanistic psychologists urged therapists not to judge their patients, interpret their feelings for them, or tell them what to do. They defined psychological health not by people's "adjustment" to social norms, but by their "self-actualization,"—that is, their ability to fulfill their own unique potential, to free themselves from anxiety and guilt, and to develop their own ethical standards independent of society. This approach transformed American psychology and social work and influenced leading countercultural thinkers, including the psychologist and LSD advocate Timothy Leary and the Youth International Party leader Abbie Hoffman. Humanistic psychology was also closely linked with what became known as the human potential movement, which aimed to help people achieve their full potential—emotionally, intellectually, and spiritually—through a range of treatments: encounter groups, Gestalt therapy, yoga, meditation, and psychedelic drug use.[38]

Humanistic psychology had a major impact on marital counseling as well. Rather than seeing marriage as inherently positive, humanistic psychologists warned that marriage and family ties could get in the way of personal autonomy and independence. In *Pairing* (1970), for example, which sold more than seven hundred thousand copies in the 1970s, clinical psychologist George Bach and writer Ronald Deutsch denounced the cultural emphasis on marriage, which, they argued, prevented most people from ever achieving truly intimate romantic relationships.[39] Valuing marriage above all else compelled men and women to disguise their "authentic" selves in an attempt to satisfy their romantic partners and to hide their true feelings in order to avoid conflict. Such patterns of behavior produced marriages that were for the most part, "confining, unfulfilling associations with good potential for divorce should serious crises emerge."[40] Only by reinventing the norms that shaped romantic couples' interactions, they argued, could couples achieve lasting, loving relationships. In their book, as in Bach's therapeutic practice at the Institute of Group Psychotherapy in Beverly Hills, California, the authors advised couples against suppressing their feelings in an attempt to avoid conflict. Instead, they recommended that couples recognize their feelings and share them with each other, whatever the repercussions.[41]

Humanistic marital advisors did not simply urge couples to talk more; rather, they emphasized the importance of communication around precisely those issues that were hardest to put into words and most tempting to leave unsaid. The unapologetically confrontational psychologist Will Schutz, for instance, advised married couples in his therapeutic encounter groups at the Esalen Institute—a mecca of the human potential movement in Big Sur, California—to tell each other three secrets that could possibly end their relationship.[42] The authors of more accessible marital-advice or self-help books did not go to quite this extreme, but neither were they very far behind. One humanistic author, for example, stated that the most important and most terrifying statements to say to one's spouse included "I'm having an affair," "I'm sexually attracted to your best friend," and "You don't always sexually satisfy me."[43] As this list suggests, humanistic authors considered matters of sexuality to be particularly revealing of one's inner self and especially important to convey to one's spouse. They advised couples to share sexual fantasies and past sexual experiences as a means of learning about one another and making marital sex more pleasurable. According to the authors of *Pairing*, while couples might manage to keep up the pretense of happiness in other realms of marriage, "in sex the truth tends to emerge in a merciless manner."[44] Humanistic relationship experts thus framed holding back when it came to matters of sexuality as misguided and ultimately detrimental to one's self and one's marriage.

As Americans came to understand honesty and openness—especially with regard to sex—as integral to marriage, some wives confided in their husbands almost immediately after initiating lesbian relationships. Rachel, an Italian Jewish nurse and mother of three in Berkeley, California, became infatuated with a female coworker in the early 1970s. She looked for opportunities to be with her crush at work, and she even invited her coworker to dinner at home with her family. Eventually Rachel told her coworker how she felt. In response, her coworker asked her if she had ever acted on her attraction to women before. "I said no, and so she said she felt that I had a right to find out," Rachel later recalled.[45] Their conversation convinced Rachel that she was in love, and when her husband came home that evening she told him "right away" what had happened. "I guess I thought that would be the end of my problems," Rachel later conceded. "I was very naïve."[46] Likewise, artist Rainbow Williams, then living in Deland, Florida, came out to her husband, Chas, the very next day after sleeping with her best friend, Sue. Chas had been traveling, and when Rainbow went to pick him at the airport she immediately told him what had transpired. Initially, he responded with humor: "I always wanted to do that," he said, referring to his own desire to sleep with Sue. But Rainbow made clear to him that her sexual experience was no joke; it had reshaped her sense of self and she now identified as a lesbian. Soon after, Rainbow and her husband began the process of splitting up.[47]

Other women moved from a strategy of discretion to openness with their husbands more slowly, over a matter of months or years. Rosa, a Latina woman living in Orlando, Florida, was miserable for the first decade of her marriage, largely because of sexual incompatibility with her husband. "Ten years sex is no good. I am frustrated, with bad disposition," she explained in a letter to Lyon in the early 1970s.[48] After carrying on several unsuccessful affairs with men, Rosa began sleeping with her female next-door neighbor and finally found the sexual satisfaction she had been searching for. Both her mood and contentious relationship with her husband improved, but when her lover moved away, Rosa's marriage deteriorated again. Finally, she told her husband what had been going on. Rosa wrote, "I confess to my husband. He not condemn me. I find another and it is alright with him."[49] The marriage continued for another two years after she met her second female lover, but ultimately, the women's relationship became emotional as well as physical, and Rosa left her marriage.

Older women, who had long been conscious of their attraction to women, also began to communicate these feelings to their husbands more explicitly in the 1970s, demonstrating that this transformation cannot be understood simply as a matter of a generational difference between the baby boomers and their parents. Changes in the meaning of marriage and in gay politics facilitated older women's coming out to their husbands much as they did for younger women. But older women's particular life stage also made it easier for them to communicate more openly with their husbands about their sexuality. At a practical level, as their children neared adulthood, middle-aged wives no longer had to worry about financially supporting them or fighting for child custody if they divorced.[50] In addition, as their kids grew up and demanded less attention, wives had greater opportunities to take time for themselves and reevaluate their life choices. Betsy McConnell, a white middle-class housewife and mother of three living in Rochester, New York, came to recognize her attraction to women in the early 1980s after two decades of marriage. By then, her oldest child was in college and her youngest in high school, and Betsy had the emotional space to think about her own needs and desires. As she later recalled, "I suppose I was beginning to really look at myself, and feeling, looking at women and saying, 'Those two women—that's really where I want to be. I don't—I can't do this anymore.'"[51] Despite her unhappiness in their marriage, Betsy still considered her husband to be her best friend. Aside from her therapist, he was the first person she told about her attraction to women. Soon after coming out to him, when he suggested to her that they get divorced, she was initially shocked and sad.

Some men, including Betsy's husband, responded to their wives' sexual confessions with kindness and support. Pat Gandy's husband was particularly wonderful. Pat, mentioned in Chapter 1, had identified internally as a lesbian nearly her entire life, but she buried her feelings for decades during the course of two marriages. Not until the 1980s, when she was in her fifties and her adult daughter was living on her own, did she tell her husband, Rivers, that she was attracted to women. For Pat, admitting her homosexuality was synonymous with getting divorced, and she was reluctant to do so because Rivers had always been so good to her. "It's easy to get up and leave a sob," she later explained.[52] For a time, Pat dealt with her unhappiness by drinking, but once she gave up alcohol she felt she had to tell her husband the truth about her sexuality. So she wrote him a letter, which he read over the breakfast table one morning. In response he stood up, turned to Pat, gave her a hug, and asked, "What can I do to help you?"[53] This was no empty offer. Pat and Rivers lived outside of Houston with Pat's elderly mother, and Pat told her husband that she planned to take her mom and move into an apartment in the city. Concerned that a move would be too disruptive for Pat's mother, Rivers generously suggested that her mother continue living with him, which she did.

Wives were not the only ones to initiate these difficult conversations about their sexuality. Sensing that their spouses were experiencing emotional challenges, some husbands forced their wives to communicate. Husbands' increasing willingness to begin such conversations demonstrates how gender roles within marriage were changing and how communication was becoming more widely understood as the key to marital success. For most of the twentieth century, wives had typically undergone marital counseling by themselves, reflecting the idea that it was women's responsibility to save an unhappy marriage from divorce.[54] As feminists critiqued the pressure women faced to make their marriages work, however, counselors increasingly urged husbands to accompany their wives to "conjoint marital therapy" sessions and take on greater responsibility for their relationships. Meanwhile marital experts and couples themselves increasingly cited "communication" as a—if not *the*—central problem of unhappy marriages.[55] The word "communication," of course, may simply have been a new way of referring to the same problems couples had faced before, but this language at least suggested that fixing marital problems now required both spouses' active involvement.[56]

It was perhaps because of these new ideas about marital communication that Beverly Todd's husband finally confronted her about her unhappiness in the mid-1980s, after they had been married for more than three decades. Beverly, a white woman, married in the 1950s after a traumatic military investigation convinced her to renounce her homosexuality. For thirty-two years, Beverly denied her same-sex desires while raising her three sons and two daughters. But once her children were grown, she began to lead a more independent life. She finished her college degree and eventually began working at an independent bookstore in Colorado where she met several lesbians. Soon Beverly's feelings for women returned, and she began to see that a different life for herself was possible. Still, she was emotionally distraught about ending her marriage and did not know how to proceed. It was only after her husband sat her down and asked her what was going on that she told him the truth. As Beverly later explained, "He knew me when the Air Force was pressing charges against me. And I said, 'Well, you know, I tried really hard but I never really changed.' "[57] The couple separated, and Beverly's children were uniformly supportive of her, but her husband remained upset. Eventually, in an attempt to hurt her, Beverly's husband outed her to her very conservative brother without her knowledge or consent.

Despite marital experts' sometimes cavalier faith in honesty and openness, confession carried risks, and some men, like Beverly's husband, responded to news of their wives' lesbian relationships or desires with anger and even violence. In the early 1970s, when one woman's husband found out that she had been involved a lesbian relationship before marrying, he called her "a queer," pushed her down a flight of stairs, and, "in a saner moment, said, 'Sex is for procreation.' "[58] Around the same time, Martha, a twenty-something woman living in upstate New York, told her husband that she did not enjoy having sex with him because she was still attracted to women, despite her attempt to renounce these feelings. Even though Martha had not engaged in an extramarital affair and "didn't want to be a Lesbian," in response to her confession, her husband attempted to rape her. When he passed out in a drunken stupor, she escaped to her parents' home in a different state.[59] Communicating with their husbands openly about their attraction to women came as a relief for many wives who had once felt it necessary to hide this part of themselves. But in some cases, doing so antagonized controlling and abusive husbands who might have been better left in the dark.

The Marriage Experiments

Although violent reprisal was always a possibility, more husbands became willing to explicitly accept and consciously create space for their wives' lesbian desires in this period. Demonstrating this shift, wives who wrote to lesbian organizations and leaders in hopes of finding other women for potential relationships or sexual encounters now often insisted that their husbands knew and approved of their activities. Framing her letter to Cambridge's Lesbian Liberation group as a type of personal ad, one married, lesbian-identified woman from Massachusetts asked the group's members for help locating other lesbians and included a detailed description of her physical appearance: her height, weight, measurements, and hair color. While wives in the past had once stressed the need for secrecy in such letters to lesbian organizations, this woman claimed that her husband knew of her feelings for women but "d[id]n't mind," and she gave the Lesbian Liberationists her home phone number along with instructions to call in the evening when she was available, and her husband was likely home as well.[60]

As in the past, some men may have been willing to condone their wives' same-sex relationships because they did not take them very seriously, but others were genuinely accepting.[61] Take the case of Rebecca, a fifty-something mother of six from Arizona. When Rebecca contacted Martin and Lyon in 1974, her lover Joanne was in the process of leaving her husband and moving in with Rebecca's family. Rebecca and Joanne had fallen in love five years earlier at a church where Joanne's husband was the minister and Rebecca was the church organist. When the women eventually told their spouses about their relationship, Joanne's husband was hostile, but Rebecca's husband agreed to financially support Joanne and let her live in their home if only Rebecca would "stay close" for four more years until their two youngest children were finished with high school.[62] Rebecca informed her husband that once their children were grown, she and Joanne would move into their own home, "though not exclude him entirely, unless or until he finds another close relationship, which we hope he'll do."[63] Rebecca's husband was so understanding and supportive of the women's relationship, in fact, that she told Martin and Lyon he was going to read their book *Lesbian/Woman* next.

In publicly redefining their marriages, couples like Rebecca and her husband heeded the advice of marital advisors who argued that the institution of marriage needed to transform in order to survive. As rates of divorce and extramarital cohabitation rose dramatically in the 1970s, some marital experts applauded husbands and wives who gave each other the freedom to engage in sexual relationships with other people. Historians have argued that efforts to redefine marriage in the 1970s were never very widespread, but wives who desired women were particularly amenable to these ideas.[64] Humanistic psychologist Carl Rogers was one of the earliest marital experts to endorse nonmonogamous marriage with his book *Becoming Partners: Marriage and Its Alternatives* (1972). Rogers envisioned *Becoming Partners* as a guide to help young people in the process of creating "new kinds" of marriages or other romantic relationships.[65] How couples might balance their commitment to each other with their sexual interest in other people was a central theme of the book, and Rogers interviewed several couples in a range of unconventional and nonmonogamous relationships. In Rogers's mind, these men and women were pioneers for a new age. "Just as the frontiersman kept pushing on, endeavoring to open up unknown territory, so these two are exploring the terra incognita which lies ahead in a modern marriage," he wrote of one such couple.[66] Other relationship experts endorsed nonmonogamy for more practical reasons. In *How to Live with Another Person* (1974), David Viscott—who would become one of the first psychiatrists to dispense advice to callers over the radio a few years later—argued that demanding sexual fidelity of one's partner was not only an ill-advised attempt to control and take ownership of another person, it was also profoundly ineffective in preventing extramarital sex.[67]

By far the most influential book on marital nonmonogamy during this period, as mentioned earlier, belonged to the anthropologists Nena and George O'Neill. The O'Neills' *Open Marriage* spent more than forty weeks on the *New York Times* best-seller list and sold nearly two million copies in the United States by 1980.[68] With *Open Marriage*, the O'Neills aimed to help couples make their marriages more egalitarian and more responsive to their emotional needs. The O'Neills defined an "open" marriage as one in which both spouses were open to rewarding relationships with other people and to changes within themselves and each other. Clearly influenced by humanistic psychology, the authors emphasized catch phrases such as "personal growth," "individual freedom," "flexible roles," and "mutual trust."[69] Their book provided mostly uncontroversial marital advice about the importance of self-disclosure and the value of fighting, for example; but one brief chapter explored marriages that were "open" in a sexual sense. The O'Neills refrained from taking a moral position on sexual infidelity, but at the same time they suggested that combining marriage with potentially sexual outside relationships could make "marriage a still deeper, richer, more vital experience."[70] In a later interview, Nena O'Neill insisted that she and her husband had never seen sexually open marriage as "a concept for the majority," and in a second book of her own she defended sexual fidelity as an ideal.[71] Nevertheless, many of *Open Marriage*'s readers believed the authors were endorsing nonmonogamy, and it was, unsurprisingly, the sexual meaning of "open" marriage that had the most lasting impact.

The possibility of wives' sexual contact with other women did sometimes come up within advice literature on marital nonmonogamy, but it typically did not appear as a threat to marriage, as most authors took for granted that wives' homosexual activity would include their husbands in some way. In *Becoming Partners*, for example, Carl Rogers described one wife, Lois, who developed a sexual relationship with another woman living in her communal household. While Lois's husband was somewhat threatened by the emotional intimacy between the women, he was also "turned on" by their sexual activity, she said, and often participated in it. "It's sort of like . . . a masturbatory fantasy thing with him," Lois explained.[72] In their advice book, *Making Love Work: New Techniques in the Art of Staying Together* (1979), Zev Wanderer and Erika Fabian similarly argued that marriage could refer to an array of more than a dozen sexual and/or domestic arrangements, and they claimed to know of cases in which "two homosexuals chose to have a third person of the opposite sex live with them."[73] In one example they described, including a husband, his wife, and her female lover, Wanderer and Fabian took for granted that the husband would enjoy watching the women have sex, and might even "be allowed to join."[74] In the parallel example they sketched, however, involving a wife, her husband, and his male lover, the authors assumed that the men would engage in sex privately. These casual anecdotes convey the broader logic that structured most experts' understandings of wives' versus husbands' homosexual encounters—that is, that sex between women would remain open and available to men's gaze and participation, while sex between men was entirely their own.

Nevertheless, engaging in group sex with other women and their husbands did help some wives to recognize their attraction to women.[75] Even some wives who participated in sex with other women in swinging groups, in which their activities were highly circumscribed by men's gaze, came to identify as lesbian or align themselves with lesbian politics as a result of their experiences. One waitress and mother from Southern California later explained how sexual experiences she had with female swingers during the course of two marriages allowed her to consider the possibility of having a full-fledged romantic relationship with another woman. As her second marriage was ending, this possibility became more real, and she joked to her estranged husband that rather than finding another man, she might "just fall in love with women."[76] Soon after, she began attending coming out groups, as well as a lesbian Alcoholics Anonymous group in San Francisco. In the process, she became involved with another woman and came to identify as lesbian. Another married woman from Milwaukee, Wisconsin, wrote to Martin and Lyon in the early 1970s explaining how she had become sexually involved with other women after joining a swingers group with her husband. "Surprising although the husbands are not bi they seem to approve if not encourage it," she noted. Though this woman identified as bisexual, she wrote to express support for Martin's and Lyon's work and to thank them for their courage.[77] It is important to note, though, that stories like these are uncommon. Wives' sexual experiences with other women were generally condoned within the context of the swinging world only so long as they disavowed any affiliation with lesbian community or politics, and at least appeared to be primarily attracted to men.[78] But even so, the women's stories described here do seem to support historian David Allyn's claim that "the swinging world expanded the boundaries of the 'normal'" in ways that benefited wives who desired women.[79]

Other wives came to recognize their same-sex desires through experiments with group marriage or open marriage. Suzanne, a mother of two from the Bay Area, had an unhappy sex life with her husband for much of their marriage. In an attempt to revive their sexual intimacy, she and her husband embarked on what they called "The Great Sexual Experiment" in the mid-1970s.[80] As Suzanne explained, "The book *Open Marriage* came out, and all these things were just in the air. There were groups, or books, and encounters, and therapies, and all this stuff that was available and we began to explore some of it."[81] Initially Suzanne's marriage was "open" only in a heterosexual sense, but soon Suzanne's husband became involved with men, and Suzanne developed a relationship with a younger woman who worked for her. While Suzanne's earlier heterosexual affairs never posed "a threat to the basic structure of the marriage," once she became involved with another woman things changed, and Suzanne "began to see some other possibilities in [her] life."[82] Suzanne and her lover went to women's dances and bars for the first time, and Suzanne eventually began attending bisexual groups at the Pacific Center, a gay and lesbian community center in Berkeley. All the while, Suzanne and her husband remained completely frank about their sexual lives and entirely supportive of one another's relationships.

Yet even for Suzanne, balancing marriage with lesbian relationships proved more difficult than she had expected. Within a few years, Suzanne and her husband were living apart. In explaining the reasons for their separation, Suzanne later pointed to "a certain feeling of pressure from the lesbian community" and stated that many lesbians she knew were "very suspicious" about her continuing to live with her husband.[83] Although her husband was willing to accept her lesbian relationships and did not expect their own sex life to continue, Suzanne's prospective female lovers could not countenance her sharing a home with her husband and feared she would ultimately return to him. Faced with these pressures, Suzanne moved out of her family home, but she had no plans to divorce and secretly hoped that she, her husband, and her lover would be able to establish a home together one day. "I have my little fantasies," she conceded in an interview, "that somehow we would find a duplex or a very big house. Something [that] would allow the kids to be with us both and allow us not to be with each other."[84] While it is unclear whether or not Suzanne was able to make this dream into a reality, her story illustrates some married women's continued desires to combine marriage and lesbian relationships as well as the challenges involved in doing so.

The Bisexual Possibility

The "discovery" of bisexuality in the mainstream media in the 1970s, discussed in greater detail in Chapter 8, provided wives like Suzanne, who wanted to have relationships with women while remaining married, with an alternative to divorce and lesbian identity. In 1974, the *New York Times*, *Newsweek*, and *Time* all published articles on bisexuality, which generally presented bisexuality's increasing visibility as a type of fad—a side effect of feminism, gay liberation, the counterculture, and even the rise of gender-neutral clothing.[85] But more nuanced popular depictions of bisexuality could be found. In 1975, for example, Barbara Walters devoted an entire week to the issue of bisexuality on her TV show *Not for Women Only*, which featured a diverse group of bisexual men and women.[86] At least one book, *Barry and Alice: Portrait of a Bisexual Marriage* (1980), combined this new attitude toward bisexuality with the ethos of *Open Marriage*. In this combination memoir and marital advice book, Barry Kohn and Alice Matusow, a lawyer and social worker, respectively, from Philadelphia, argued that while many couples of their generation were getting divorced, they had avoided this fate by moving beyond conventional ideas of marital monogamy and heterosexuality and making space for their bisexual identities and sexual relationships with other people. Although it was Barry's desire for other men that spurred a change in their marriage, his newfound bisexuality coupled with Alice's participation in the feminist movement encouraged her to recognize the erotic potential in her relationships with women as well.[87]

In response to these changes, wives who desired women began to use the term "bisexual" with greater frequency in their correspondence with lesbian organizations and leaders. For some women, bisexuality provided a new way of making sense of sexual desires and emotional attachments that did not fit neatly into either straight or lesbian categories. In a letter to Cambridge's Lesbian Liberation group, an Iowa mother in the midst of a divorce and a same-sex relationship wrote, "I'm not sure that I would classify myself as a Lesbian or a homosexual or as Straight, probably the closest thing or word or classification I could be labeled (augh!) is Bisexual." With her exasperated "augh!" this woman seemed to suggest her reluctance to claim any sexual label. For her, "bisexual" may not have been an entirely satisfying identity category, but it was better than any of the other options.[88] Writing to this same group, another woman, from Lincoln, Nebraska, who had been in a lesbian relationship before marrying similarly struggled to define herself. "I could be a latent homosexual or even bi-sexual," she suggested. Although this woman explained that she was not "unhappy" with her husband and had no plans to divorce, she fantasized about women while having sex and wanted to be put in touch with a woman who could understand her feelings.[89]

Other wives defined themselves as bisexual with more confidence and certainty. One bisexual woman from Springfield, Ohio, whose husband also identified as bisexual, expressed her frustration with the absence of a bisexual subculture in a letter she wrote to Lesbian Liberation in 1970. While she and her husband were happy together, they experienced painful judgment and rejection from straight as well as gay people. "Gay women are hesitant to really become close to me because of my husband," she wrote, noting that a similar barrier had emerged between her husband and his gay friends. Sensing "a certain hostility" in gay bars but recognizing that they could not be open about their sexuality within straight bars either, she and her husband struggled to find friends.[90] Suspecting that the Lesbian Liberationists might also disapprove of her bisexual marriage, this wife entreated her readers, "Please do not call us 'closet cases.' We are what we are." But the problem of where and how to meet people who would understand their sexuality and unconventional marriage remained: "So where do we go from here, any suggestions?" she asked.[91] While the Lesbian Liberationists' response to this letter does not remain, it was a question with no easy answer.

Social and political groups explicitly for bisexuals were just beginning to emerge in the 1970s.[92] In 1972, Stephen Donaldson, a Buddhist Quaker, started a bisexual group at that year's Friends General Conference in Ithaca, New York. The group adopted the "Ithaca Statement on Bisexuality," one of the earliest public declarations of the bisexual movement, which later appeared in the *Advocate*.[93] That same year, New York City psychotherapist Don Fass started a National Bisexual Liberation group, which only three years later had expanded to include ten chapters and more than five thousand five hundred members nationally.[94] In 1975, the psychiatrist and sex researcher Fritz Klein, together with activist Chuck Mishaan, founded the Bisexual Forum in New York City, which had more than two hundred active members at its peak in 1980. Klein claimed that the men and women who attended the Bisexual Forum felt keenly the lack of a bisexual subculture, but they often had difficulty putting that feeling into words or even envisioning what more institutionalized bisexual community spaces would look like. He recalled one bisexual man asking, "What do you mean by 'subculture' . . . You mean like a bar or something?"[95] In the late 1970s, not long after the Bisexual Forum began, bisexual activists began to form smaller groups across the nation such as Chicago's Bi-Ways and San Francisco's Bisexual Center, the longest lasting of these early bisexual groups.[96]

Following these foundational, male-dominated bisexual organizations, a new generation of feminist bisexual groups took shape. The largest of these groups included the Boston Bisexual Women's Network, Chicago's Action Bi-Women (ABW), and San Francisco's BiPol, but by 1984 bisexual women's support groups existed in New York City, Portland, Oregon, and Hartford, Connecticut, as well.[97] These female-led bisexual organizations worked hard to build alliances with feminists and gays and lesbians, and they offered much-needed support for married bisexual women. In 1984, ABW organized potlucks and coffee hours, as well as meetings and panels on reproductive rights, coming out, and the challenges of building a women's community. ABW typically held events in feminist and gay community spaces, including the local women's bookstore, women's coffee shop, women's center, and gay community center, thus geographically marking the group's connection to feminist and gay and lesbian communities. ABW leaders also planned events to facilitate connections between bisexual and gay and lesbian people in Chicago, including a community dance celebrating "gay/lesbian/bisexual" pride and a workshop about building bridges among lesbian, bisexual, and heterosexual women. They offered a support group for married bisexual women and a discussion group titled "Marriage: Past, Present, Future or Never?" In addition, their newsletter, *Bi-Lines*, examined the ethical issues married bisexual women faced in balancing marriage and relationships with other women.[98]

The divorced, bisexual activist Lani Ka'ahumanu was among those at the forefront of this wave of bisexual activism, and her experiences demonstrate the particular challenges involved in coming out as bisexual in this period. A Catholic woman of Japanese, Hawaiian, Irish, and Polish descent, Lani married her high school sweetheart at age nineteen in 1962. By the time she was twenty-three, she was a full-time housewife with two children and a caring husband. Although her life appeared perfect, Lani was desperately unhappy. In 1974, after eleven years of marriage, she divorced, moved to San Francisco, and became involved in the feminist movement. Lani had been aware of her attraction to women since adolescence, and she soon came out as a lesbian. "I didn't think there was such a thing as bisexuality. You either were this or that," she later recalled.[99] Lani's sense of herself as a lesbian was disrupted in the late 1970s, however, when she fell in love with a man. In coming out as a lesbian, she had felt supported, but coming out as bisexual was an entirely different experience. "When I said I was bisexual it was not empowering; it didn't feel good. And of course when you said you were bisexual after having identified as a lesbian, you weren't coming out into a community. You were losing a community."[100] Lani's experiences of discrimination and stigmatization as a bisexual radicalized her and she became a major figure in the bisexual movement. A cofounder of BiPol, she helped organize the San Francisco Bay Area Bisexual Network in 1987, and she was one of the planners of the first National Bisexual Conference, held in San Francisco in 1990.[101]

Lani Ka'ahumanu and bisexual activists like her forced gays and lesbians to confront their own biphobia and to broaden the parameters of the gay movement, but their actions came somewhat late for the women in this study, who tended to conceive of their bisexuality as a phase en route to lesbianism rather than a permanent identity. Rachel, a nurse who, as mentioned earlier, fell in love with her female coworker, explained that after reading an article about bisexuality in the newspaper she initially thought, "This is me."[102] Eventually, though, she began to identify as lesbian, and to see her brief identification as bisexual as a psychological step she needed to go through on the way to homosexuality. She later likened this process to a type of "ladder." "It's very hard to jump from being straight to being gay, and so many people go through this transition of thinking, yes, they're bisexual. That explains everything. And then that maybe gives you the courage to have that first encounter, and then you find out that maybe you're really not, maybe you're just gay."[103] For

Rachel, in other words, bisexuality was a less evolved and less stable form of sexuality than lesbianism.

Such understandings of bisexuality clearly reflected the views of the lesbian community Rachel came to join. One early sociological study of female bisexuality published in 1974 reported that lesbians typically understood bisexuality as a failure to accept one's "true" homosexuality, a belief that compelled women who were attracted to both women and men to either conceal their bisexuality or deny it by committing themselves to a lesbian life.[104] The decisions of the majority of the women in this study to divorce and identify as lesbian rather than bisexual reflect the historical sources I have depended on, which privilege the stories of women who eventually identified as lesbian. But these women's choices and their understandings of their sexuality also reflect the sexual possibilities that were available to most wives at this moment—that is, the pressure they faced from the gay and lesbian community to choose between heterosexuality or homosexuality, marriage or divorce.

Even married women who did claim a bisexual identity could not avoid this pressure. Gretchen Courage, a white middle-class woman, who married at age twenty in the late 1960s, had several relationships with women during the course of her more than forty-year marriage. But participating in the lesbian world while remaining married and identifying as bisexual was not always easy. At a women's music festival in Asheville, North Carolina, Gretchen remembered someone saying to her much younger girlfriend, who identified as lesbian, "Why'd you bring her here?" The feeling that she did not belong in lesbian spaces because of her marriage and bisexual identity weighed heavily on Gretchen. "There was definitely this feeling of being in two worlds," she recalled, "which is eventually what got, really got me out of my marriage."[105] Gretchen was hardly unique. Even Barry Kohn and Alice Matusow, coauthors of *Barry and Alice: Portrait of a Bisexual Marriage*, divorced just a few years after their book came out.[106] And in the early 1980s, sex researcher Eli Coleman struggled simply to find still-married bisexual women for an interview study. In the end, almost all of the forty-five women who appeared in his 1985 article "Bisexual Women in Marriages" were divorced and "relating almost exclusively to other women" by the time he spoke with them.[107]

❧ ❧

Just as bisexuality came to seem like an impermanent identity to most of the women in this study, a stopgap between a straight life and a lesbian one, so too did open marriage. For wives who temporarily balanced marriage and lesbian relationships, the decision to divorce and to identify as lesbian was often based on their feminist politics and their frustration with the inequality in their marriages. Mare Chapman, for example, a white therapist in Madison, Wisconsin, decided to divorce after briefly trying to maintain an open relationship, in part because of the inequality in her marriage and her husband's unwillingness to change. Mare tried to make their relationship more egalitarian, and her husband seemed amenable, but when it actually came to making changes "there was no follow through," as Mare later explained. Mare's husband would agree to take on a fair share of the household chores but would then practice what she later called "creative incompetence." He would, for example, deliberately do a bad job of cleaning the floor or doing the dishes so that Mare would have to do the chore anyway in the end. Despite her more genuine desire to change, Mare too felt trapped by her marital role. "I realized that I was so caught in these habituated patterns, these habits of conditioning, that I couldn't get totally free of them either," she recalled.[108] In contrast, she believed a relationship with a woman would be inherently egalitarian and "mutually empowering."[109]

Yet the decision to end a marriage, of course, was not solely in wives' hands. In some cases, husbands who initially sought to create space for their wives' lovers within their families and households simply changed their minds. In the late 1970s, Carol Hoke, a thirty-something housewife and mother of three in Indiana, fell in love with her children's horseback-riding teacher, Susan. Over more than a year, Susan became a close friend of the family, and Carol, who had never before had a lesbian relationship, began to realize she was attracted to her. One night, they kissed, and Carol told her husband, Howard, what had happened. To her surprise, Howard was unconcerned, and he even invited Susan—who had recently lost her apartment—to move into their home. The arrangement worked for a time, but when it became clear to Howard that the women's relationship was more significant than he had thought, he asked Carol to choose between him and Susan. She chose Susan.[110]

For multiple reasons, then, open marriage was more often a stepping-stone on the path to divorce than a permanent solution for the wives described here. It is quite possible that more women than are reflected here were able to balance marriage and lesbian relationships for extended periods of time in some way. Such women were perhaps more likely to identify as bisexual and less connected to lesbian and feminist communities than those represented within archival and oral history collections geared toward recovering the lives of gays and lesbians. Still, despite these limitations, the experiences of the women in this chapter likely reflected the temporariness of "open marriage" itself in this period. In *The Marriage Premise* (1977), Nena O'Neill's single-authored follow-up to *Open Marriage*, O'Neill wrote that she and her husband had found "very few" couples in their research for whom sexual nonmonogamy was a "long-term viable life-style."[111] In fact, she once confided to a friend that of the one hundred or so couples she and her husband interviewed for *Open Marriage*, the longest a husband and wife stayed together in an open relationship was two years.[112]

At a more fundamental level, though, the short life span of the open marriages described here was due to a transformation in the laws and attitudes governing divorce, one that lessened the pressures that might have held such relationships together. If the idea that couples could openly and explicitly redefine their marriages in new ways in the 1970s brought the contractual aspect of the institution to the fore, so too did the broad social and legal changes that together became known as the "divorce revolution."[113] Marriage *opened*, then, in yet one more sense for wives who desired women: that is, it became far easier to leave.

CHAPTER 7

The Price They Paid

CAMILLE AND DOYLE MITCHELL married in 1955 and had three children together. Outwardly, they had a conventional middle-class marriage. Doyle worked as an instrumentation technician, while Camille stayed home and took care of their children. Together they owned a house in San Jose, a station wagon, a motorcycle, and an extensive record collection.[1] Still, their marriage was not without its problems, and by the late 1960s Camille was having an affair with her married next-door neighbor, Darlene Reynolds. Although Camille did not speak openly with Doyle about her relationship, he "strongly" suspected it.[2] To some extent, Doyle even seemed to enjoy the women's intimacy. In court, Doyle admitted to taking pictures of the women sunbathing nude together in the backyard and to kissing Darlene's breasts on that occasion.[3] In 1970—the very same year that California's new "no-fault" divorce legislation went into effect—Camille and Darlene made plans to leave their husbands and begin a new life together. Doyle may have been willing to turn a not-so-blind eye to his wife's relationship with their pretty brunette neighbor during their marriage, but when Camille announced that she wanted a divorce, he did not hesitate to use her sexuality against her. He immediately told her that he possessed letters providing evidence of her lesbianism, which he would use to take the children away from her. "I would rather give the children to the grandfather," he said publicly at one point, "than have them be raised with a bunch of queers."[4]

Camille was one of the "lucky" ones. Untold numbers of lesbian mothers in the 1970s and 1980s lost custody of their children, but against all odds, Camille succeeded in winning custody of her three children in 1972.[5]

While the national gay news media celebrated Camille's win, proclaiming her to be the first "acknowledged lesbian to win custody" in the country, her victory was only partial.[6] Wanting to prove that he was not "soft on homosexuality," Judge Gerald Chargin, who presided over the case, awarded Camille, then unemployed, punishingly low child custody and alimony payments, totaling less than a quarter of her husband's monthly income.[7] Furthermore, Chargin prevented Camille and Darlene from living together and even from spending time together when the children were present. Only by sneaking around, much as they had before their divorces, were the two women able to see each other at all.[8]

Camille's story suggests the paradoxical situation that wives who desired women faced in the 1970s. As divorce became more common and less stigmatizing, and as the gay liberation and lesbian feminist movements challenged discrimination against gays and lesbians, many of the forces that had worked to keep these women within marriage abated. Yet, while legal reform made getting divorced significantly easier, it also exacerbated gender inequality between divorcing couples when it came to child custody and financial matters. In the late 1960s and early 1970s, divorce reformers began to replace the earlier alimony system, which had often required husbands to support their ex-wives long after divorce, with a gender-neutral rhetoric of equality and mutual self-sufficiency. As legal scholars Deborah Rhode and Martha Minow have written, these reforms "secured equality in form, but not equality in fact."[9] The new ideology of economic equality negatively affected divorced women in terms of alimony, as well as the division of assets and child support payments.[10]

In addition, beginning in the late 1960s, the judicial preference for placing minor children with their mothers declined, leaving *all* divorcing mothers at increased risk of losing primary custody of their children. Mothers who openly identified as lesbians were particularly vulnerable. But depriving lesbian mothers of custody was merely one of the ways that the courts punished and policed such women's sexuality. In child custody cases of the 1970s, the courts began to intervene in lesbian mothers' lives more intimately than they had before. Lesbian mothers had certainly lost custody of their children in the 1950s and 1960s, and a great many others chose to hide their homosexuality and their relationships with other women for fear that the courts would take their children away from them. But it was not until the 1970s, *after* it became possible for wives who desired women to lead openly lesbian lives outside of marriage, that the state, through child custody rulings, began regularly preventing lesbian mothers from living with their lovers, seeing their lovers while in their children's presence, or participating in gay and lesbian activism and communities. Such rulings were part of a broader legal and political attack on "homosexual house-holds" in the 1970s, but they also represented a specifically anti-feminist means of punishing women who dared to build homes and families without men.[11] It was in leaving their marriages, in other words, that the women in this study encountered the full force of the state's power to control their lives and punish their sexual behavior.

The Divorce Revolution

Beginning in 1963, the divorce rate, which had remained stable since the mid-1950s, began to rise again until it peaked in 1979. In 1958, when the divorce rate reached a postwar low, there were 368,000 total divorces. By 1970, that number had climbed to 708,000; in 1981, it reached a new high of 1,036,000.[12] Both the baby boomers and their parents contributed to this tremendous increase in divorce. Though the generation that married between 1945 and the late 1950s slowed the long-term twentieth-century trend of rising divorce rates, these couples were still more likely to divorce than their predecessors.[13] And while we might imagine that it was only younger married couples who chose to divorce in the 1970s, middle-aged Americans who had married in the postwar years contributed to the divorce revolution as well. Once their children were grown and out of the house, some parents of the baby-boom generation no longer felt the need to remain in unhappy relationships. For wives, in particular, divorce became more economically feasible when they no longer had to worry about finan-cially supporting their children.[14]

There were many reasons behind the divorce rate's climb in the 1960s and 1970s. To begin with, marriages forged in the wake of World War II tended to last much longer than they had in the past, as Americans' life expectancy increased. One historian has even suggested that Americans turned to divorce in growing numbers because early death ended marriages less often.[15] A 1973 *Readers Digest* article interpreted this correlation some-what differently: "Living longer, [couples] have more time to be disap-pointed."[16] Ending a marriage informally, or rather, extralegally, also became more difficult after the war than it had been beforehand. The necessity of

drivers' licenses, Social Security numbers, and health insurance plans compelled couples to appear in court instead of simply parting ways.[17] The growing numbers of married women who worked outside the home after the war
also contributed to the long-term increase in divorce, by reducing women's
economic dependence on their husbands.[18]

Yet the rising divorce rate reflected more than just Americans' rising
life expectancy, the growth of state and federal bureaucracy, and married
women's growing participation in the workforce. Even more importantly,
Americans began to reject the idea that remaining married at all costs was
a personal responsibility and a social good. Feminists, of course, played an
important role in this shift. The most radical contingent of the feminist
movement, including many lesbian feminists, compared marriage to legal-
ized prostitution and slavery. "Here come the slaves / off to their graves,"
members of the Women's International Terrorist Conspiracy from Hell
(WITCH) famously chanted at a 1969 bridal fair at Madison Square Garden
in New York City.[19] Other feminists believed that marriage could be
reformed, and they called on husbands to take responsibility for their fair
share of childcare and housework.[20] Whether they believed that marriage
could be reformed or not, though, feminists on all sides of the issue challenged the idea that marriage and motherhood represented women's natural destiny, ultimate achievement, and most important means of personal
fulfillment. This intervention in and of itself enabled many wives to imagine
a life for themselves outside of marriage.

Feminist activists also shattered the silence surrounding domestic violence and argued that that violence and abuse were not acceptable parts of
married life. Before the 1970s, marital counselors were reticent about violence between married couples and even lacked the phrase "spousal
abuse."[21] Counselors and social workers were not entirely ignorant of
domestic violence, however. Descriptions of domestic violence had long
appeared in case records and complaints in women's divorce petitions, but
marital advisors either willfully ignored the problem or encouraged women
to find ways of dealing with the abuse.[22] In sharp contrast, feminist activists
argued that the silence around domestic violence derived from understandings of wives and children as men's property. They informed victims of
domestic abuse that the violence they suffered was not their fault. They
provided legal aid to women seeking divorces from or orders of protection
against violent spouses, and they founded domestic violence shelters to help
women escape. In 1973, the first domestic violence shelter in the United

States opened in Phoenix, Arizona. Only five years later there were more than three hundred such shelters across the country.[23]

As feminists challenged the teachings of postwar marital experts, even wives who had been married for decades began to realize that they no longer had to "adjust" themselves to their husbands' violent tempers and verbal abuse. For some wives who desired women, like Doreen Brand and Edith Daly, an increasing awareness of their attraction to women accompanied this realization. Doreen and Edith worked together for years in Yorktown Heights, New York, before falling in love in the mid-1970s. Doreen was a grade school teacher, and Edith was a teacher's aide who often helped out in Doreen's class. Both women were white and in their forties with children of approximately the same ages. Both had also endured years of domestic abuse.[24] For decades, Edith and Doreen discounted the possibility of divorce and believed they had no choice but to make their marriages work. But their attitudes began to change in the 1970s as domestic violence became less acceptable, divorce became more common, and their children reached their teens. Edith's and Doreen's attitudes also changed as they confided in each other about their marriages and their hopes for the future. Eventually Edith and Doreen were making gifts for one another, sharing special breakfasts before work, and playing footsie at dinner parties. In 1974, they expressed their love for one another. Their marriages ended soon after—Edith's husband left, and Doreen's husband passed away suddenly— and the women embarked on a new life together (Figure 8).

While feminists drew attention to the role marriage played in women's oppression and the danger they suffered within it, humanistic psychologists critiqued the institution as a barrier to individual development and fulfillment. From their perspective, helping individuals to achieve happiness and reach their fullest potential was more important than simply holding a marriage together. A 1972 *New York Times* article about a "new breed" of marriage counselors suggested the reach of such ideas. These counselors considered themselves to be in the business of "saving" spouses rather than marriages. For them, a client's decision to remain in an unhappy and unfulfilling relationship was a far greater "failure" than his or her divorce. As one emblematic psychology professor and marital counselor explained, "Our job is to help people understand how they are interreacting in a relationship. What they choose to do with that understanding is *their* business. . . . We are certainly not in the business of gluing them together."[25] Such attitudes marked a dramatic shift in marital

Figure 8. Doreen Brand (*left*) and Edith Daly at the wedding of Doreen's foster son, 1978. From the Old Lesbian Oral Herstory Project Records, Sophia Smith Collection, Smith College. Printed by permission of Edith Daly.

counseling, which, for most of the twentieth century, had focused on keeping couples together at all costs.

Humanistic psychology and the human potential movement idealized masculine behavioral traits and ignored gender inequality, but in some ways its critiques of marriage aligned with feminist ones, and many women—including those struggling with same-sex desires—found the ideology appealing.[26] By the mid-1970s, in fact, the idea that it was more important for women to achieve personal happiness than to avoid divorce had reached the pages of some of the most popular women's magazines— the very same magazines that had previously instructed wives to swallow their feelings and do whatever necessary to make their marriages last.[27] Although women's magazines never entirely rejected this earlier ideology, there were major signs of change. In an anonymous personal essay in *Good Housekeeping* in 1974, for example, a middle-aged bank executive explained why she had decided to divorce her husband after twenty-five years together. The problems that had plagued their marriage, including her husband's drinking and infidelity, were those that most wives would have tolerated in the decades beforehand. In fact, the author admitted her marriage was probably better than those of many others. But for her, and perhaps for *Good Housekeeping*'s readers as well, this was no longer enough.[28]

As marital experts and ordinary married couples came to believe that remaining in an unhappy marriage was detrimental, wives who desired women, in their letters to lesbian groups and leaders, began to reason that doing so was "unfair" not only to themselves, but also to their husbands.[29] On the surface, this argument was a complete reversal of wives' earlier ideas about the necessity of remaining married for their husbands' sakes, a line of reasoning which never entirely disappeared from their writing. Yet with both arguments, wives who desired women struggled to make their choices—whether to stay married or to get divorced—compatible with normative understandings of "good" women's sensitivity, compassion, and selflessness. Arguing that they should divorce for their husbands' benefit, rather than, or in addition to, their own, may have helped wives feel that their decision was not a selfish one. They sought to convince themselves that, despite the pain and disruption they were causing, their husbands would be better off for it in the end.

Telling themselves that their children would be better off after divorce was somewhat more difficult for wives who desired women. Notwithstanding custody issues, mothers worried about the negative impact that leading an openly lesbian or bisexual life might have on their children. In the early 1970s, one middle-aged mother from outside of Dayton, Ohio, feared that her seventeen-year-old son, who was studying to become a minister, "would be totally destroyed with the truth" about her.[30] Although this woman had been in a same-sex relationship for years and desperately wanted to leave her marriage, she could not justify hurting her son by doing so. Other mothers worried about harming their children's relationships with their fathers. In one typical letter to Phyllis Lyon, for example, an officer's wife in Fort Dix, New Jersey, explained that she was planning to leave her husband and begin a new life with her children and her lover. She still had doubts about this decision, though, as her husband had threatened that he would have nothing more to do with their children if she left. "My only question to myself is who am I to take the boys' father from them?" she wrote. "I have already lost them their only grandmother."[31]

Yet even with regard to divorce's impact on children, such mothers could find reassuring messages within popular culture. As early as the late

1950s some researchers began to argue that divorce was less traumatic for children than unhappy, stressful marriages.[32] In the late 1970s, pioneering longitudinal studies of divorced children and their parents showed that while divorce was traumatic for children, two years after the fact, most had adjusted and restabilized.[33] Among the most optimistic commentators on divorce's impact on children were Susan Gettleman and Janet Markowitz, social workers and authors of the book *The Courage to Divorce* (1974). In a chapter titled "Divorce Can Liberate Children," Gettleman and Markowitz rejected the ideas that parents should stay together for their children's sake and that divorce negatively impacted children's relationships with their parents. In contrast, they argued that divorce could free children from oppressive nuclear-family relationships and even "enrich children's lives" by forcing them to become less dependent on their parents.[34]

As feminist activists and women's magazine writers, psychologists and relationship experts alike advised women against reconciling themselves to unhappy unions—even for their children's sake—the legal process of divorce became significantly easier. Lawyers began calling for legal reform of the adversarial, fault-based divorce process in the early twentieth century as Americans increasingly understood marriage as an egalitarian relationship, ideally based on mutual love and concern. In 1927, for example, noted marriage reformer Judge Ben B. Lindsey of Denver, Colorado, suggested that the law should allow couples to enter into trial marriages, which they could decide to end at will.[35] Such legal critiques increased in the 1940s, when the divorce rate spiked following the war. Reformers argued that by requiring one spouse to be found "at fault," divorce law unfairly punished couples whose relationships simply did not work.[36] Legal reformers also pointed out that the adversarial divorce process encouraged men and women to commit perjury in order to successfully secure a divorce.[37] Faced with such criticism, many states chose to make fault-finding less important to the divorce process in the 1960s by permitting couples to divorce without citing wrongdoing, after living separately for a certain period of time. By the mid-1960s, eighteen states and the District of Columbia allowed couples to use the fact that they lived apart as grounds for divorce.[38]

Within this shifting legal context, California became the first state to permit "no-fault" divorce. In 1969, California's legislature approved the Family Law Act, which replaced the state's previous seven grounds for divorce with two no-fault options: marital breakdown or incurable insanity. The law completely removed fault as a basis for divorce and as a factor judges could consider in awarding alimony or dividing marital assets. Instead, judges were supposed to divide property equally, taking into consideration one spouse's financial need and the other's ability to pay. The innovation of no-fault divorce had national effects. In 1970, the Commissioners on Uniform State Laws created the Uniform Marriage and Divorce Act (UMDA) as a model for state divorce law. California's legislation significantly influenced the UMDA, which similarly replaced the search for blame in divorce with an attempt to uncover "whether the marriage has ended in fact."[39] Three years later the American Bar Association finally ratified a version of the UMDA. This model divorce legislation differed from California's "pure" no-fault divorce law by allowing judges to take fault into consideration when dividing marital property. By the end of the 1970s, thirty-seven states provided some way for couples to end their marriages without finding fault. By 1991, this was true of every state.[40]

These legal changes allowed some wives who desired women to leave their marriages with relative ease. As no-fault divorces did not regularly require witnesses, private detectives, or drawn-out trials, the cost of divorce dropped. The 1977 US Supreme Court ruling in *Bates v. State Bar of Arizona* reduced the cost of divorce even further, by upholding the right of lawyers to advertise their services. Though lawyers advertised divorces for as little as $29 in Georgia, the national median for a simple, uncontested divorce was $150 nationally in the late 1970s. The minimum cost of more complicated contested divorces, or those involving children or property, ranged from $300 to $400 nationally.[41] Ann Marevis was among those wives who secured a no-fault divorce after recognizing her attraction to women. Ann left her husband in 1987. Although she considered suing him for "mental cruelty," she sought a no-fault divorce because it was faster and cost less. Ann had to live apart from her husband for eighteen months, but after that her lawyer went ahead with the paperwork, and her husband did not resist it. "It was a done deal," as Ann put it. By 1989 their divorce was final.[42]

In light of these changes, the idea that divorced men and women were destined for unhappiness and social exclusion began to crumble. In his book *The World of the Formerly Married* (1966), author Morton M. Hunt rejected the notion that divorced people were failures and encouraged Americans to see divorce as "painful but necessary," and even as an "act of courage," suggesting one's faith in the possibility of a finding a more fulfilling relationship.[43] That same year, a *Newsweek* cover story titled "The Broken Family: Divorce U.S. Style" portrayed divorce as difficult and undesirable, but hardly disastrous. One divorced father of three interviewed for the article stated that divorce had improved both his and his ex-wife's lives: "She's developing her independence and I've got the joys of having my family. We're both happier now. We've both gained fuller lives."[44] Indeed, during the 1970s and 1980s a range of divorce self-help books argued that those who divorced could not merely survive, but thrive. In one of the earliest of these books, *Creative Divorce: A New Opportunity for Personal Growth* (1973), divorce therapist Mel Krantzler acknowledged the feelings of loss and guilt that often followed divorce, but he argued that men and women who divorced could, after mourning their relationships, begin a process of rebirth and rebuilding.[45] As his book's title made clear, Krantzler presented divorce as an opportunity rather than a disaster, and a beginning rather than an end.

Some of this divorce literature was specifically for women and decidedly feminist in tone. In 1972, for example, the Philadelphia Women's Center published the *Women's Survival Manual: A Feminist Handbook on Separation and Divorce.* The book was a national version of the guidebook that the center's staff had developed for African American, Puerto Rican, and low-income women who were in the process of separating from their spouses or partners.[46] Jane Wilkie's *The Divorced Woman's Handbook* (1980) provided advice targeted at newly divorced women. It included instructions on everything from fixing a broken toilet to dining out alone and becoming sexually active again (don't sleep with your ex-husband, Wilkie warned).[47] In 1986, even *New Woman* magazine published an article titled "The Complete Guide to Divorce—American Style," which provided practical advice as well as uplifting emotional reassurance. "Will you will win?" the article asked, before concluding firmly, "You've already won. You've gotten out of a marriage that wasn't working, and you've got your health, your career, your self-esteem, and the love of your family and friends to get you through this trauma."[48] Such optimistic advice was a far cry from the demonizing and pathologizing messages that unhappily married women had encountered in the pages of similar magazines just a few decades beforehand.

While most of these authors took divorcing wives' heterosexuality for granted, they likely provided much needed encouragement for some of the women in this study, particularly those who were more isolated from lesbian and feminist communities. Janet Lathrop, who came out as a lesbian in the late 1980s in Munising, Michigan, was among these more isolated women. Subscribing to older ideas about divorce as a type of social death, Janet was initially quite nervous about divorcing her husband, and she believed that in leaving her marriage she would be entering a type of "wasteland." "I don't know anybody, I'm going to be completely alone and it's going to be really, really, drab, gray, frightening, lonely," she feared at the time.[49] A therapist's help proved vital in getting Janet through her divorce. And her life improved dramatically after she entered graduate school at the University of Wisconsin and discovered the lesbian feminist community in Madison. Soon Janet was attending lesbian picnics, barbeques, and concerts every night. She easily met a lesbian lover, became involved in the university's women's studies program, "fell in love" with Alix Dobkin's music, and attended the Michigan Women's Music Festival. In fact, Janet's post-divorce life was better than she had ever imagined possible. It was, she later explained, as if she had been "reborn."[50]

Other wives needed little reassurance in getting divorced, knowing full well that a better life awaited them. Barbara Kalish fell within this group. As mentioned in Chapter 2, Barbara and her lover, Pearl, carried on a relationship for more than a decade in the suburbs of Los Angeles, beginning in the late 1950s. The women had agreed to leave their marriages once their children were grown, and around 1970, at forty years old, Barbara decided she was ready. Pearl chose not to leave her husband. She was ill at the time and worried about losing health insurance if she divorced, but Barbara was done. "I went to Chuck Kalish and said, 'I'm going.' And I went," she recalled.[51] By this time, Barbara had discovered the Star Room, a lesbian bar on the outskirts of the city at the corner of Main and El Segundo. In fact, Barbara invested some of her own money in the bar, making her a part owner; and when she left her marriage, she moved into a "cute little house" directly behind the bar, where she was particularly well situated to begin a new lesbian life. She swiftly embarked on a series of lesbian relationships with women half her age, and she eventually began selling dildos, which she made out of mattress stuffing and electrical tape, at the bar. As Barbara later recalled of this time, "I was in hog heaven."[52]

"The Full Weight of the Power That He Had"

Despite the elation many women experienced upon leaving their marriages, it was in the process of divorce that the inequality between wives who desired women and their husbands became most pronounced. In some ways, the women described here were like many others, for no-fault divorce put women at a distinct financial disadvantage, regardless of their sexual orientation. In her landmark 1985 book, *The Divorce Revolution: The Unexpected Social and Economic Consequences for Women and Children in America*, sociologist Lenore J. Weitzman argued that no-fault divorce laws failed to take into consideration the fact that most husbands earned far more than their wives, and that wives who took care of their children and households full-time typically earned little money, if any. Adversarial divorce provided some financial protection for women whose husbands were found "at fault," as husbands were typically "punished" through lifetime alimony payments to their ex-wives. But under the no-fault paradigm, alimony payments became less common and short-term, based on the assumption that a woman would swiftly become financially independent. Assuming that husbands and wives would share the financial costs for their children equally, judges also began requiring husbands to pay only half of what was needed to support their children. According to a 1975 federal government poll, only 14 percent of divorced women received alimony, and only 44 percent received child support. Among both groups of women, less than half received the full amount of either alimony or child support on a regular basis.[53] The result, according to Weitzman, was that most wives who divorced were worse off economically, while their husbands' income increased.[54]

Because they felt guilty about breaking up their marriages or simply wanted to divorce as quickly as possible, some wives who desired women contributed to the resulting economic inequality between themselves and their ex-husbands by choosing not to fight over financial assets. Harriet Marks-Nelson, a Jewish woman from Brooklyn, New York, left her physically abusive marriage in 1978. Harriet and her husband owned a hardware store together that had originally belonged to her parents. When Harriet divorced, she wanted no part of the business, but she did want to leave it intact for her son. So, rather than selling her share of the business to someone else, she allowed her husband to buy her out slowly over the course of several years at what was a significant financial loss. "You could be a very rich woman today," Harriet remembered her friends telling her, but Harriet did not care.[55] Despite her personal financial loss she was happy because she had helped to ensure her a financial future for her adult son and his family. Henrietta Bensussen, mentioned in Chapter 6, similarly deprioritized her own economic needs when she and her husband divorced in the mid-1980s. Henrietta was in her late forties at the time, and she had stayed home taking care of two children for most of her married life. At the time she divorced, though, she had a job at Stanford University Press, a steady paycheck, and her own bank account, credit card, and car. "I had a budget. I could manage," she recalled thinking, so she decided not to push for alimony, and she willingly gave up the house she and her husband had shared.[56]

Of course, even those women who were more willing to fight still suffered financially. In the late 1970s, after nearly three decades of marriage, Avis Parke's husband, a Unitarian minister, announced that he wanted a divorce so that he could marry his much younger lover. Avis, meanwhile, had fallen in love with a woman her husband had hired to help her around the house. Avis's Massachusetts divorce was technically no-fault, and Avis's husband had been unfaithful to her throughout their marriage. Even so, he still brought up her lesbian affair in their divorce proceedings. Avis thus had to fight "tooth and nail" to retain a home on Cape Cod that she and her husband technically owned together, but which she had inherited from her parents.[57] Avis succeeded in gaining her husband's share of the home and some child support, but with no marketable job skills and three of her six children still at home, she applied for public assistance. Eventually, she became a spokesperson for the displaced homemakers' movement, which fought for greater recognition of women's household labor and drew attention to the economic challenges faced by primarily white, middle-aged, middle-class housewives after divorce.[58] Avis's lesbianism rarely came up in public coverage of her story, however, which portrayed her as a "representative" displaced homemaker, a "deserving" member of the "nouveau poor."[59]

As Avis's story suggests, the transformation in divorce law made the legal process of divorce easier, but it did not completely remove fault-finding from the process. While fifteen states made "marital breakdown" or incompatibility the only ground for divorce, sixteen others—Alabama, Alaska, Connecticut, Georgia, Hawaii, Idaho, Indiana, Maine, Massachusetts, Mississippi, New Hampshire, North Dakota, Ohio, Rhode Island, Texas, and Tennessee—more conservatively added the no-fault standard to their existing list of grounds. In these states, one spouse could bring up the other spouse's misbehavior and threaten to initiate a fault-based divorce, in order to pressure the "misbehaving" spouse into giving up child custody, alimony, or assets during negotiations. Many of the no-fault divorces in these states, therefore, could and did involve behind-the-scenes allegations of misconduct. Furthermore, most states continued to allow judges to consider either spouse's fault or merits in awarding property. A wife whose husband proved that she had been unfaithful could thus still lose receiving alimony or suffer in the awarding of marital assets in most states.[60]

Significantly, child custody was the one sphere in all states in which fault continued to matter. In states that took fault into consideration in awarding alimony and dividing marital assets, custody was one more realm in which fault came into play. But in states like California, where couples could not raise fault in other aspects of a divorce, lawyers often encouraged husbands to fight for child custody even if they did not want it, in order to get their wives to make other, typically financial, concessions. In effect, then, the no-fault divorce revolution made child custody a *more* important tool for vengeful spouses whom divorce reform had left with fewer means of making their ex suffer, financially or emotionally.

Child custody also became a more important battleground between divorcing husbands and wives in this period as courts began to replace the maternal preference, or "tender years," principle that had prevailed for most of the twentieth century with a more gender-neutral concern for the "best interests of the child."[61] In the late 1960s, as divorce rates increased, fathers' rights groups began to protest the courts' preference for granting child custody and child support payments to mothers. By the late 1970s, studies found that when fathers in Minneapolis, New York, and North Carolina demanded custody, they were nearly or equally as successful as mothers.[62] By 1981, thirty-seven states had rejected the tender years doctrine, either by statute or court decision.[63]

On the surface, this transformation in family law appeared to be more egalitarian and less sexist than the earlier maternal preference, but several feminist researchers have shown that it often resulted in mothers being unjustly deprived of their parental rights. For example, judges in contested custody cases tended to place children with the higher-earning parent, thus penalizing mothers who had given up careers in order to serve as their children's primary caretaker. At the same time, family court judges often assumed that mothers with full-time jobs had prioritized their careers over their parental responsibilities and would be unable to care for their children. Needless to say, judges typically did not hold fathers' full-time jobs against them in this way.[64] After interviewing sixty mothers who fought for child custody in the United States and Canada in the 1960s and 1970s, the feminist psychologist Phyllis Chesler concluded that women tended to lose custody when their husbands challenged them because of the impossible cultural standards to which all mothers are held. "An ideal father is expected to legally acknowledge and economically support his children," she wrote. "Fathers who do *anything* (more) for their children are often seen as 'better' than mothers—who are, after all, supposed to do every-thing."[65]

Mothers who had engaged in lesbian relationships or identified openly as lesbian were particularly vulnerable to custody challenges from ex-husbands. The "best interests of the child" doctrine thus conveniently served as a "smoke screen" for legal bias against both gay and lesbian par-ents in this period.[66] A 1967 case involving Ellen Nadler of California set the precedent for rulings in lesbian mothers' custody cases during the 1970s and early 1980s and demonstrates how judges used a concern for children's welfare to justify discrimination. In the case, Judge Joseph Babich of Sacra-mento County initially granted custody of Ellen's five-year-old daughter to her ex-husband purely on the basis of her lesbianism, without hearing any additional evidence. Ellen challenged the decision, and a California court of appeals overturned the ruling, not because of its outcome, but because of Babich's decision not to hear all the evidence in deciding where "the best interests of the child" lay. The appeals court thus forced Babich to hear the case again, and again he awarded child custody to Ellen's husband. Rather than stating that her lesbianism *itself* made her unfit, however, this time he determined that there was a potential link or "nexus" between Ellen's homosexuality and harm to her daughter, which made placing her in a heterosexual household preferable.[67]

While many husbands in this study had tolerated or even enabled their wives' lesbian relationships during their marriages, they often became more hostile once divorce was immanent or their ex-wives began leading openly lesbian lives. Many used the legal bias against lesbian mothers to their advan-tage. In the midst of a custody battle in the early 1980s, one woman from DeKalb, Illinois, told Martin and Lyon how her estranged husband had earlier helped her to recognize her lesbianism. "Once upon a time, my husband bought me a copy of your book *Lesbian/Woman*. Until that time, I did not have a name for how I felt about this coworker, or that friend," she recalled.[68] This woman and her husband divorced for reasons unconnected to her sexu-ality, but once she began openly living as a lesbian several years later, her husband became hostile and revisited their custody agreement. "Why or how

[his] attitude changed I don't know," she explained.[69] Another woman, from California, later recalled how her husband had quietly encouraged her lesbian affair, believing that she would remain in the marriage if she could have a "little dalliance on the side."[70] Once she decided to end the marriage, he sued for child custody on the basis of her homosexuality.

There were likely many reasons behind such men's change in attitude. When formerly married women began to put their relationships with women ahead of those with their husbands, when they began to identify as lesbian openly and raise their children in unconventional female-headed households, their homosexuality likely became more real to their husbands, more threatening, and perhaps publicly embarrassing. In some cases, grandparents and other extended family members pressured husbands to fight for child custody when they learned of a mother's homosexuality. In 1974, one Iowa mother, whose husband knew of her homosexuality when they married, sued for custody of their two children, in part because of her own father's influence. "My father has pledged $20,000 to my husband's side in what he rationalizes as his duty to save his innocent grandchildren from their perverted mother," she wrote in a letter to Del Martin.[71] A husband's increasing religiosity could also prompt him to challenge child custody. In the early 1970s, for example, a married couple in South Dakota became sexually involved with another woman. As the relationship between the two women intensified, the husband left. The couple eventually divorced, and the mother was granted child custody in 1975, but when the father became a Jehovah's Witness, he began to see his ex-wife's relationship as "evil" and filed a petition seeking custody.[72]

More often, though, once-understanding husbands were motivated by purely financial concerns. In the late 1960s, Margaret, a California mother, and her husband embarked on a group marriage with another couple. Eventually, Margaret and the other wife in their group marriage became sexually involved and fell in love. Although Margaret's husband had been willing to have a sexually open marriage, after Margaret initiated a divorce he attempted to use her lesbian relationship against her to secure a more favorable financial settlement. "The trade-off became, that if I wanted his daughter, I couldn't have his money too," she recalled. Ultimately, Margaret received $125 a month in child support for her daughter, and $150 a month in alimony for just two years.[73] Another woman, who had married an openly gay man in the late 1960s, had a similar experience. After her divorce was final, in the midst of a fight about child support, this woman threatened to take her ex-husband to court to make him pay. "If you do that, I'm a queer and you're a lesbian and I'll scream it all over the place," he retorted.[74] Had he done so, both parents could have lost custody of their infant daughter. Unwilling to take this risk, and recognizing that her ex-husband was financially unstable anyhow, this woman decided to drop her demands for financial support entirely.

Fathers were not the only ones who could contest lesbian mothers' custody. Though such cases were less common, some lesbian mothers faced custody challenges from their own parents. After her divorce in the 1960s, Lynda Chaffin had secured custody of her two daughters. In 1968, Lynda left her daughters, then six and eight years old, in her parents' care in Washington State while she regained her health and her economic stability in Los Angeles. A few years later, after Lynda moved her children to California to be with her, her parents sued for custody. In 1973, a trial court judge granted custody of Lynda's daughters to her parents, largely because of her homosexuality. In response, Lynda and her two daughters went underground. A year later, when Lynda turned herself in and appealed the custody order, the appellate court again denied Lynda custody of her children.[75] Aware of cases like Lynda's, another lesbian mother in California so feared that her parents might attempt to have her declared unfit that she had made up her mind to go to great extremes to protect her custody rights. "I could, and am quite capable of going underground with eight hours' notice," she told an interviewer in the late 1970s. "I'd do that before I lost custody."[76]

In the 1970s and 1980s, family court judges across the country ruled against lesbian mothers based on claims that their homosexuality could cause harm to their children in some way. Typically, judges expressed concern that placing children with lesbian mothers would expose them to ridicule and social isolation or thwart their normative gender and sexual development. All of these issues came into play in the case of a Dallas mother named Mary Jo Risher, who famously lost custody of her nine-year-old son, Richard, after a jury trial in 1975. The testimony of a court-appointed psychologist, Robert Gordon, weighed powerfully against Mary Jo. Gordon claimed Mary Jo's older teenaged son, Jimmy, had been in a "homosexual panic" when they met because his mother occasionally dressed in masculine attire and supposedly once took him to a gay bar.[77] In addition, Gordon expressed concern that Richard had attended a meeting with him wearing a YWCA T-shirt and a pair of jeans belonging to the daughter of Mary Jo's lesbian partner. By allowing Richard to wear this clothing, Gordon argued that Mary Jo showed poor parental judgment and was not doing a sufficient job of "encourag[ing] . . . masculine identifications" in her son.[78] It did not help matters when seventeen-year-old Jimmy took the stand and claimed that he had chosen to live with his father because his mother's homosexuality was a source of shame and embarrassment.

Stereotypes about homosexuals as child abusers also had an impact on lesbian mothers' custody rights. Lawyers often insinuated that lesbian mothers might sexually molest their children by asking these mothers whether they had engaged in sexual activity in front of their children.[79] In at least one instance, widely described as a "witch hunt" in the feminist press, a social worker falsely accused Cynthia Forcier, a lesbian mother of two, of sexually abusing her daughter. In the mid-1970s, Cynthia placed her five-year-old daughter, Kristi, with foster parents in Orange County, California, while she struggled to get her life together. After Kristi spent Christmas with her mother, her foster parents took her to a doctor, who noticed bruising around her pelvic area. Kristi explained that a little boy had kicked her, but the doctor disregarded her explanation and assumed that her mother had sexually abused her. The doctor notified Kristi's social worker, who sent a letter about the "violence of [Cynthia's] lifestyle" to Orange County authorities who, in turn, pressed charges against her.[80] Orange County authorities offered to drop the charges if Cynthia relinquished parental rights to both her children, but Cynthia refused. Only after a superior court judge ruled that Cynthia's lesbianism could not be used against her did Orange County authorities drop the charges against her for lack of evidence.

As these examples suggest, any sense of propriety or discretion that affected how judges and lawyers dealt with wives' lesbianism in the 1950s and 1960s had disappeared by the 1970s. Taking its place in the courtroom was a new obsession with such women's sexual behavior. While Ellen Nadler, mentioned earlier, was on the stand, the opposing lawyer asked her how frequently she engaged in sex and if she had ever had sex while her children were present. He demanded that she give the names and addresses of her previous female sexual partners and he inquired if she had ever worked as a prostitute. If this was not enough, Judge Babich demanded to know precisely what Ellen did in bed. Even after Ellen's lawyer responded that answering such questions could expose her to criminal prosecution, as sodomy remained a crime in California at the time, Babich persisted with mock ignorance, "I would like to know what she does with other women that constitutes the act. Maybe she just shakes hands with them."[81] Though Babich claimed to be uninterested in whether or not Ellen's sexual activities constituted sodomy, in many other cases lawyers and judges invoked sodomy laws to argue that lesbian mothers were in effect criminals and therefore unfit. Women were rarely convicted of sodomy laws, and, beginning with Illinois in 1961, states were slowly repealing these laws across the country. Nevertheless, judges and lawyers continued to reference sodomy laws to threaten and intimidate lesbian mothers.[82]

In general, judges and lawyers focused in far greater detail on lesbian mothers' sex lives than gay fathers' sex lives in custody cases.[83] This discrepancy may be due in part to the greater attention judges and lawyers paid to all mothers' sexual behavior in child custody battles, regardless of their sexual orientation.[84] But judges' and lawyers' detailed scrutiny of lesbian mothers' sexual experiences and activity also, undeniably, reflected their own fascination with lesbian sex. In a 1976 case in Washtenaw County, Michigan, for instance, a lawyer advised one lesbian mother's lover to restrict her presence in court in order to prevent sexual fantasies on the judge's part.[85] Other lesbian mothers encountered this objectifying behavior on the part of their own lawyers. Upon seeking advice from a legal aid service in California, one lesbian mother found that her male lawyer was more interested in learning about the details of her sex life than in protecting her parental rights. "He really got off on that, and started asking me all these questions, about did I lust after women, and all that crap, it was really awful," she recalled.[86] Despite his offensive behavior, because her financial resources were so limited, this woman felt she had no choice but to use this lawyer to represent her in her divorce.

Ironically, judges and lawyers tended to portray lesbian mothers as the ones who were sex-obsessed. In explaining his decision to deny lesbian mother Larraine Townend custody of her three children, Judge Albert Caris of Ohio argued that it was not Larraine's lesbianism, per se, that made her an unfit mother, but her decision to raise her children in a lesbian household. Caris believed that Larraine should have given up her lesbian relationship in order to maintain custody, and damningly declared of all lesbians, "Orgasm matters more to them than children or anything else."[87] Judges also asked lesbian mothers more often than gay fathers to choose between their children and their lovers. For example, in *Jacobson v. Jacobson* in 1981, the North Dakota Supreme Court reversed a district court ruling that had granted Sandra Jacobson custody of her two children, not because she was a lesbian, which the judges conceded might well be "beyond her control," but because she had chosen *to act* on her lesbianism by living with her lover. "We need no legal citation to note that concerned parents in many, many instances have made sacrifices of varying degrees for their children," they concluded.[88] The subtext of such a statement seemed to be that "good" mothers should be willing to surrender their sexual and romantic lives for their children.

Anticipating legal discrimination in court, lawyers working on behalf of lesbian mothers often advised women to hide or deny their lesbianism in court if they could. In 1972, one mother in the midst of a custody battle over her six-year-old son in Connecticut decided to take this path after her lawyer informed her that her husband did not have sufficient evidence to prove her homosexuality. "I grappled for a long time about whether to make this a political issue," she explained in a letter to Del Martin, "but finally I decided for the sake of my child, who needs me, I would not prejudice the case against me by making any unnecessary confessions. If my own welfare were the only issue, I would have made a stand for justice." Doing so, however, meant that she would no longer be able to participate in lesbian life and would have to "resume the façade indefinitely," as she put it. Even attending a lesbian workshop, her lawyer warned, could endanger her case, and communicating with Martin was itself a risk.[89] Likewise, another lesbian mother, from Berkeley, lied on the stand and said that her homosexuality was a passing phase in order to win custody of her children. Because she did not want to risk losing her kids, for years afterward this mother hid her relationships with women while publicly performing the role of a "flaming heterosexual." "That's what I had to do, 'cause I wanted my kids. . . . So I just paid that price, and got what support I needed from women, covertly," she explained.[90] Such women found that in leaving marriage, they had effectively traded one form of confinement for another.

Because courts could reassess child custody decisions even after an initial determination, lesbian mothers remained legally vulnerable so long as their children were minors. Though most states required proof of a "material change in circumstances" to revisit a custody ruling, a husband could meet this standard simply by claiming to have discovered his ex-wife's homosexuality. A husband could also argue after remarrying that he and his new wife could provide a more "stable" heterosexual family life for his kids.[91] This legal vulnerability pushed some lesbian mothers into isolation for years. One Bay Area mother of two, Beth, succeeded in winning full custody of her children because her ex-husband assumed her lesbianism was temporary. Sometime after the divorce, a lesbian friend and her son moved in with Beth and her children. At that point, Beth's ex-husband suddenly began "to question the moral atmosphere" she was providing their children. "I remember it was quite late at night when he phoned me, and I was alone," Beth recalled. "I felt the full weight of the power that he had. Before that time, I was kind of trusting along, and suddenly I realized—just being a lawyer, being who he was, being a man, being a white man—having everything on his side. There was like a moment of panic."[92] This experience convinced Beth that the possibility of living with a female lover was out of the question.

Surprisingly, even mothers who *lost* primary custody could find their lives legally constrained. In a 1976 case, *In re Jane B.*, a New York trial court judge denied a lesbian mother child custody because she lived with her lover, and imposed major restrictions on her visitation rights as well. The judge ruled that her child could not stay overnight with her, visit her when other gay people were present, or accompany her to places where gay people were even likely to be present. In addition, the court ordered that this mother could not involve her child in gay rights activism, or what it termed "homosexual activities or publicity."[93] Writer, activist, and Chilean immigrant Mariana Romo-Carmona faced similar constraints after losing custody of her two-year-old son, Cristian, in Connecticut in 1976. In fact, her legal battle and the government's intrusion into her life continued for years as the courts restricted her visitation rights further and further. "Every time I move, I am forced to give an account of my living situation," she wrote in 1982. "Being a visiting lesbian mother, everything I do is subject to scrutiny, my faults are magnified as under a microscope, and accordingly, my anxiety rises with each incident in which my privacy is violated."[94] Painfully, Mariana found that just as the courts denied her parental rights, her ex-husband denied her very identity as a mother, leading Cristian to believe that Mariana was "just a friend."[95] Only when her son was four years old, after Mariana made a formal request through her lawyer, did Cristian's father tell him the truth. Even so, Mariana ultimately lost the right to have Cristian visit her on the weekends when she moved to New York City in 1985.

While most media coverage of lesbian mothers' custody cases focused on white, middle-class women, mothers like Mariana found that racism and economic marginalization only increased their legal vulnerability.[96] In fact, after Mariana briefly received public aid following her divorce, a family court judge restricted her visitation rights on the grounds that she was providing her son with "inadequate meals."[97] As the editors of *Azalea*, a magazine for lesbians of color, explained in a special issue on lesbian mothers in 1980, the discrimination they experienced because of their lesbianism was part of a much larger social system that regularly denied women of color the right to bear and raise children either directly, through forced sterilization, or indirectly, through employment discrimination and a lack of basic social support. "All too often we have neither the funds to decide to have a child since we are most often employed in the lowest paying jobs or not employed at all and present day necessities such as day care and proper health care is generally unavailable to us," the editors wrote.[98] Furthermore, as the editors noted, the stigmatization of lesbian mothers of color was inextricable from the hostility that *all* mothers of color encountered when raising their children in families without men for whatever reason. As one black mother who battled her ex-husband for child custody in Philadelphia in 1978 put it, "You're aware of the odds against you. You're aware that the deck is stacked." Although this woman luckily succeeded in winning primary custody of her daughter, a year after her custody battle, she could name only one other black lesbian mother in the nation who had done so.[99]

It is important to acknowledge here that not all fathers were antagonistic and homophobic. Rachel, mentioned in the previous chapter, divorced in the 1970s in California and found the process nearly painless. Rachel and her husband had a joint custody agreement, and they divided their property equally. "He was very chivalrous about the whole thing," Rachel recalled, and neither one of them revealed her lesbianism to the court.[100] When her ex-husband's parents found out about her homosexuality, they wanted to have Rachel declared an unfit mother, but her ex refused. Because the stories of lesbian mothers who were forced to fight for child custody have attracted attention from scholars and the media, there were likely far more men like Rachel's husband than we know. Lesbian mothers who won primary custody or agreed to joint custody with their ex-husbands tended not to discuss their divorces in great detail in oral history interviews. Furthermore, *contested* custody battles are the ones that have made it into the historical record through court cases or letters that women wrote to lesbian mothers' advocacy groups. The existence of men like Rachel's husband, however, does not diminish the overriding systems of inequality that structured lesbian and bisexual mothers' experience of divorce. Rachel's husband was clearly kind, respectful, and egalitarian in ending their marriage. As her comment about his "chivalry" suggests, though, the choice about how their divorce would play out remained his to make.

Even the experiences of women who chose *not* to fight for custody of their children suggest the oppression that lesbian and bisexual mothers faced. Women who chose to give up custody of their children often doubted their own ability to be good parents. Some women's reasoning was purely economic; they believed that their children would be better off with their husbands because they earned more money. But the idea that gays and lesbians could not be good parents, or rather that they could not be *as good* as heterosexual parents, may also have shaped these women's sense of themselves as mothers. In the early 1980s, for example, a divorced bisexual woman from Cleveland, Ohio, whose ex-husband was openly gay, was considering marrying again for her daughter's sake, despite the fact that she preferred relationships with women. "I've been told by other people, that because my X husband [*sic*] is gay, that at least one of us should be straight to give her a healthy outlook on life," she wrote.[101] Similarly, another lesbian mother who had recently separated from her husband told an interviewer in the late 1970s how difficult it had been for her to overcome the idea that heterosexual families were best for children. Although this woman had come a long way in her thinking about lesbian parenting, she recalled that for many years, on hearing about lesbian mothers' custody cases in the news, she would side with straight fathers and the state. "You can't expect society to really just sit back and allow her to do her mothering and leave her alone when there is a nice heterosexual alternative," she recalled thinking. That wives who desired women could themselves remain convinced of the superiority of straight families suggests just how insidiousness such beliefs were.[102]

Legal Change and the Lesbian Mothers' Rights Movement

It was precisely these types of ingrained attitudes that lesbian mothers' rights activists sought to change. Beginning in the early 1970s, a range of lesbian mother activist groups took shape across the country. The first of these groups was the Lesbian Mothers Union (LMU). A group of women founded the LMU in 1971 following a panel for lesbian mothers at the Gay Women's West Coast Conference. In talking to each other, the dozens of women at the workshop began to realize the many issues they had in common, including their sense of marginalization within the lesbian community. "We realized that we never talked about our problems before because of the fear—fear that is still very real: fear that the courts will take our children away, fear that our children will suffer from the cruelties of straight world oppression . . . fear and paranoia that all those who know us as lesbians will use our motherhood against us," one article about the organization's founding explained.[103] By the conference's end, thirty women had signed up to participate in what became the LMU. While the LMU did not focus solely on lesbian mothers' custody battles, these cases were a priority from the beginning. With an initial donation from Del Martin and Phyllis Lyon, the LMU started a legal defense fund to help lesbian mothers and held auctions and benefits to raise money for it. Martin, an LMU cofounder and grandmother, unsurprisingly became one of its most outspoken members. During the 1970s, she delivered public lectures, published articles in the gay and feminist press, and spoke to the mainstream media about the challenges, legal and otherwise, that lesbian mothers faced.

Other lesbian mothers' groups soon followed. In 1974, Geraldine Cole and Lois Thetford helped to found the Lesbian Mothers' National Defense Fund (LMNDF) in Seattle, Washington. The LMNDF, like the LMU, raised money to support lesbian mothers' legal battles: "A Dollar a Day Keeps the Husbands Away," one call for donations wryly promised.[104] LMNDF members also organized auctions, dances, concerts, and performances with the help of well-known lesbian artists and musicians such as Pat Parker, Meg Christian, and Holly Near. The group's bimonthly newsletter, *Mom's Apple Pie*, served as an important venue for spreading the word about lesbian mothers' custody issues in Seattle and beyond. The same year that the LMNDF began, Rosalie Davies founded Custody Action for Lesbian Mothers (CALM) in Philadelphia. After losing custody of her children to her ex-husband because of her homosexuality, Rosalie, who compared her custody case to "an ancient witchcraft trial," returned to law school in order to defend women like her.[105] With the help of a private endowment and the pro bono services of its legal staff, CALM was able to offer mothers in Pennsylvania free legal counseling and representation. In 1976, Dykes and Tykes of New York City joined the movement. Dykes and Tykes created a lesbian mothers' defense fund of its own, and also ran a hotline which received twenty-five to thirty-five calls a week from mothers seeking legal advice.[106]

Complementing the efforts of these organizations, activists formed smaller, short-lived groups to support individual lesbian mothers' cases across the country. Such case-specific support groups emerged in cities such as Ann Arbor, Austin, and Denver, to name a few.[107] After Mary Jo Risher famously lost custody of her son Richard after a jury trial in Dallas in 1975 (see earlier discussion in this chapter), an activist group known as Friends of Mary Jo Risher came together to help raise money for her legal appeals. They planned fund-raisers, published articles, and secured opportunities for Mary Jo to speak on television and radio. Although she never secured custody of her son, she did regain the right to see him every other weekend.[108] Furthermore, the national media attention these activists— including Mary Jo herself—brought to the case helped to elicit sympathy for lesbian mothers and shift public attitudes toward them.

Lesbian mother activists insisted that the discrimination and oppression lesbian mothers faced in court was not an isolated issue. "Lesbian custody concerns all of us," one LMNDF fund-raising letter argued. "If we ignore the lesbian mother we are helping the homophobics [sic] to maim and rape our hearts and our humanity."[109] Lesbian activists thus framed lesbian mothers' custody issues as part of a much broader attack on gay and lesbian rights, but they connected their struggles to other battles for social justice too. One issue of *Mom's Apple Pie*, for example, compared the struggles lesbian mothers faced to those that formerly incarcerated women experienced, and noted that the LMNDF had begun working together with the Women Out Now Prison Project in Seattle.[110] In 1977, the defense committee for Jeanne Jullion, a lesbian mother in San Francisco, joined together with the Black Panthers, as well as activists protesting police violence and working for women's wage equality, in planning a July 4 "March and Rally for Jobs and Justice."[111] While this broad political coalition seems somewhat atypical, many lesbian mother activists linked the fight for child custody to a range of other reproductive justice issues. As historian Daniel Rivers has argued, such activists' efforts should be understood as part of the broader struggle for reproductive freedom in the 1970s.[112]

The advocacy and support that the lesbian mothers' movement provided was critical, and by the late 1970s lesbian mothers were making some progress in the courts.[113] In 1978, the Washington State Supreme Court ruling in the case of Sandy Schuster and Madeleine Isaacson represented a major victory. Initially, in 1974, Judge James Noe of Seattle had awarded each of the women primary custody of their children—Sandy had two children, and Madeleine four—on the condition that they cease living together in the home they had shared for the past two years. Sandy and Madeleine came up with a creative solution to this legal requirement and rented adjoining units in an apartment building. But when the women's ex-husbands learned of their new living arrangement, they petitioned for a custody modification. They also alleged that the women had violated the court's order by living together and harmed their children by speaking out about their relationship publicly.[114] Following a custody modification trial in September 1974, Superior Court Judge Norman Ackley ruled in the mothers' favor and lifted the requirement that they live apart, finding no evidence that the women's relationship had harmed the children whom he described as "healthy, happy, normal, and loving."[115] In 1978, though narrowly, the Washington State Supreme Court affirmed Ackley's decision not to grant custody to the fathers, and, by default, allowed Sandy and Madeleine to continue living together.[116]

In 1979, lesbian mothers in New Jersey and Michigan won two more significant cases in the higher courts. That year a New Jersey Superior Court judge awarded Rosemary Dempsey unconditional custody of her two children in the first-ever ruling in the state in favor of a lesbian mother who lived with her partner. In his decision, Judge William J. D'Annunzio wrote that Rosemary was "not to be denied continued custody of the children merely because of her sexual orientation." He also stated forcefully of the children, "There is no evidence of any social, emotional or psychosexual damage as a result of their mother's sexual orientation."[117] Likewise, after a two-and-a-half-year battle, the Michigan State Supreme Court granted Ann Arbor mother Margareth Miller custody of her adopted twelve-year-old daughter, Jillian. This decision overturned four earlier court rulings that had awarded custody of Jillian to Margareth's ex-husband, despite Jillian's stated desire to remain with her mother. By arguing that a parent's sexual status alone was not sufficient to deny him or her child custody without evidence of "proven detrimental effect," the ruling set an important national precedent.[118]

Despite lesbian mothers' increasing success in custody cases in the late 1970s and early 1980s, their right to be both lesbians and mothers was by no means guaranteed. And judges remained most likely to grant custody to mothers who did not have romantic or sexual partners and were not politically active.[119] One recent study of lesbian mothers' custody cases between 1973 and 1998 has demonstrated that there was no "steady progression" for formerly married lesbian mothers in court. Such women's chances improved in the late 1970s after a series of research studies showed that the children of lesbian mothers were no more likely to be gay or gender nonconforming than others. Yet these gains were primarily limited to lesbian mothers on the East and West Coasts, and lesbian mothers' likelihood of winning child custody never reached much beyond 50 percent. What is more, this legal progress proved short-lived. In the mid- to late 1980s and early 1990s, formerly married lesbian mothers' chances of winning child custody decreased nationally.[120]

◆ ◆

As the economic, legal, and cultural forces keeping wives who desired women within marriage waned in the 1970s, another architecture of repression emerged to take their place and to restrain the public growth of the lesbian community. This system of repression built on long-lived discrimination in the courts against lesbian mothers, but it went beyond this as well, by preventing women from building households with their lovers, from seeing their children in their lovers' presence, and from participating openly in gay and lesbian communities. The increased economic vulnerability that most women faced upon divorcing in the 1970s was a part of this system. Fear of angering ex-husbands and losing meager child support payments helped to keep divorced mothers in hiding, separated from their female lovers and the broader lesbian community. Being unable to afford experienced, sympathetic lawyers and expert witnesses hamstrung many mothers in contested custody cases as well.

Because so many lesbian mothers' cases have not been made public, we have no real way of knowing the numbers of women who lost child custody or visitation rights in court.[121] Those lesbian mothers whose ex-husbands compelled them to give up child custody outside of court are even harder to trace. The emotional and material impact of the discrimination that lesbian mothers and their partners experienced in court is also impossible to measure. One lesbian mother from Mississippi, writing to thank women across the country for their support during her continuing custody battle in 1979, explained that due to the stress of the case her partner had experienced "a complete nervous breakdown" and had been in and out of the hospital for months.[122] Though Carol Whitehead won custody of her daughter in Maine in 1976, the fallout from the case persisted long afterward due to the notoriety she attracted in the local news. A year after her custody case concluded, her antiques business fell apart. She was unable to find employment, her phone was disconnected, and she was in danger of losing her farm.[123] Perhaps hardest to grasp is the trauma and confusion that such custody cases caused the children who were at once at the heart of such battles and so utterly unprepared to understand them. "If I have to live with my daddy I will cry and run back to my mom. She will cry too I think," the seven-year-old subject of one such custody case wrote.[124]

Leaving marriage exposed the women in this study to more severe state discrimination than they had experienced before, but it also made the oppression they had faced within marriage more visible. The legal, financial, and emotional punishment meted out by the state, as well as by ex-husbands and other family members, on lesbian and bisexual wives who dared to leave their marriages swiftly and painfully disabused them of the notion that they were at liberty to live as they wished. This realization inspired many to political action and analyses that might have otherwise remained out of reach. One twenty-one-year-old bisexual-identified mother in Ottumwa, Iowa, for example, married in the 1970s believing that her husband would tolerate her sexual relationships with women. At the time they married, her husband knew that she and her maid of honor were involved in an affair. After that relationship ended, and this young mother found another female lover, her husband was no longer so accepting. Still, it was only in leaving her marriage and losing custody of her son to her parents that "the whole political aspect" of her sexuality became real to her.[125] Seeking legal help from Del Martin in her continuing fight to regain custody of her son, she wrote with newfound political conviction: "I want the law to give me my right as a mother. And I want my sexual privacy protected."[126]

Your Best Fantasy
and Your Worst Nightmare

BILL AND LISA, A WHITE, working-class married couple had a satisfying sex life. Even so, Bill secretly entertained fantasies of "swinging" or swapping partners with other people. One day he purchased a copy of *Select*, a regional swinging magazine that couples used to find each other and stashed it in the trunk of his car. Before long, Lisa discovered the magazine. To Bill's surprise she was not angry, but in fact proved quite amenable to the idea. After simply talking about swinging together, Bill and Lisa found that their sex life went "from *great* to fantastic."[1]Eventually, Lisa came upon a picture of a woman in *Select* whom she found attractive and admitted to Bill that she had always been turned on by the idea of a ménage à trois. The couple, who lived in an apartment near Queens, became obsessed with the idea of engaging in a threesome. Soon they began cruising Greenwich Village looking for a woman to pick up. Their efforts to enlist a stranger in their sexual adventures came to no avail, though, so Bill and Lisa half-heartedly approached a woman much closer to home: their friend and upstairs neighbor, Rhonda, who eagerly accepted their proposal.

Bill, Lisa, and Rhonda's resulting sexual encounter is just one of the titillating stories in Julius Fast and Hal Wells's book *Bisexual Living*, published in 1975. Fast, an award-winning mystery writer and author of the best-selling nonfiction book *Body Language* (1970), claimed to have spoken with "hundreds of bisexuals across the country" in researching *Bisexual Living*, but the book betrays little evidence of such rigorous research.[2] It includes only nine narrated interviews with bisexual couples and individuals, and it is difficult to establish whether the interviews are real or fabricated by Fast. Following each interview is a short analysis penned by Wells, a clinical psychologist, and the book as a whole concludes with a question-and-answer session about bisexuality between Fast and the sexologist Wardell Pomeroy, Alfred Kinsey's collaborator. Yet despite its hardcover format, accomplished authorship, and legitimate expert ties, *Bisexual Living* provided readers with soft-core pornographic stories about its interviewees' edgy sex lives, stories that might have been all the more exciting because Fast claimed they were true.

Bisexual Living did more than simply provide readers with a thrill, thinly disguised as journalism, however. It also taught them how to discern the difference between various types of wives who desired women. Though Lisa and Rhonda are both wives and mothers who find their experience together mutually satisfying, Fast portrays Rhonda as a repressed lesbian and Lisa as a swinging bisexual. While Lisa is blonde and feminine, Rhonda is mannish. "Rhonda is the butch type, masculine and kind of threatening," Bill tells Fast after their encounter. "She didn't really turn me on."[3] Lisa, meanwhile, goes on to sleep with other women, but Fast's coauthor, Wells, affirms that Lisa is "truly" bisexual rather than lesbian. Lisa does not seek out her bisexual experiences but enters into them as a result of her husband's urging, Wells points out, and although she clearly "enjoys the lesbian part of bisexuality," her main objective continues to be her husband's happiness. "If it's good for Bill, she will continue bisexual experiences; if it's not good for him, she will stop," Wells concludes.[4]

Fast and Wells were part of a larger cultural conversation that sought to distinguish bisexual and lesbian wives in the 1970s and early 1980s. Indeed, while postwar cultural anxieties around the figure of the menacing lesbian wife had manifested as an almost compulsive need to uncover a hidden and invisible threat, in the 1970s this compulsion had been largely, if not entirely, superseded by a new need to classify and categorize a diverse population of queer wives whose social and political presence was now entirely unavoidable. As lesbian mothers' custody battles captured newspaper headlines, memoirs about open marriages made best-seller lists, and social scientific researchers celebrated swinging wives who engaged in sex with other women before their husband's very eyes, deciphering which wives were *truly* bisexual and which were *truly* lesbian, became an issue of pressing cultural concern.

In making these distinctions a range of cultural producers sought to clarify the relationship between marriage, love, and sex between women. If, at the middle of the twentieth century, psychoanalysts, novelists, and filmmakers almost uniformly understood wives who engaged in lesbian affairs as a threat to marriage and the family, how to make sense of these women in the wake of the sexual revolution was far less clear. Did swinging housewives threaten their marriages if they engaged lesbian sex to please their husbands? Was it possible to balance marriage and ongoing lesbian relationships openly and happily? And were such women lesbians or bisexuals? Of course, not all Americans were invested in the answers to these questions. In the eyes of those most hostile to the women's rights, gay liberation, and sexual freedom movements, the difference between lesbianism and bisexuality simply did not matter. But even so, a range of thinkers—from academic scholars and journalists to feminist novelists and Hollywood filmmakers—did seek to clarify these issues, and to reinstate some sense of order over what had become a muddy, gray territory.

Researchers, filmmakers, novelists and journalists concerned with categorizing wives who desired women held a variety of political perspectives. Some sought to emphasize the threat lesbian sex and desire posed to marriage and male dominance while others sought to minimize it. Some celebrated and fetishized bisexual wives while others branded them as traitors and cowards. Some idealized wives who chose to leave their marriages and claim a lesbian identity while others pitied or feared them. Whether lesbian or bisexual wives were the stuff of fantasy, nightmare, or both, depended entirely on where one stood. Yet despite their many differences of opinion, the cultural producers described here all demonstrated a mutual concern with fleshing out the differences between one particular type of wife and another, and they shared strikingly similar definitions of *who* each of these women were and *what* set them apart. Together they helped to construct the meaning of female bisexuality in "the glory years of bisexual chic."[5] They also, if inadvertently, helped to lay the groundwork for more flexible understandings of female sexuality that would emerge in the 1990s.

Real Lesbians Leave

By the 1970s, a number of articles in the mainstream news media reflected lesbian feminists' arguments that wives who discovered they were lesbians should, and ultimately would, divorce. As early as 1969, a *New York Times* article, "The Woman Homosexual: More Assertive, Less Willing to Hide," stated that lesbians were increasingly coming out of the shadows and leaving their marriages. Several of the women featured in the article had been married, including Jean and Ruth, lovers and divorced "Long Island matrons" with five children between them. Though the article quoted psychiatrist Charles Socarides who described women like Jean and Ruth as "ill," it countered Socarides's opinion by also quoting a pair of psychologists who insisted that homosexuality was not a disease but a choice. In addition, the article featured statements by lesbians themselves who denied that they were "sick" or wanted to change.[6] In 1971, divorced lesbians figured significantly in yet another *New York Times* article about lesbian feminism by Judy Klemesrud, who frequently covered the women's movement and was quite sympathetic to feminist activists.[7] Though Klemesrud suggested that lesbians were better able to "function" in heterosexual marriages than gay men, such women were of less interest to her than the numbers of those who had left marriage behind them. Klemesrud profiled several such women in her piece, including "Mrs. Betty J.," a forty-five-year-old nurse and mother from Westchester County who had never been completely happy in her marriage. "I just kept thinking of women," Betty J. explained. The same article profiled Marcia Moyano, a thirty-two-year-old college student who had recently introduced her lover to her ex-husband. "He didn't seem very surprised," Marcia noted, suggesting that her ex-husband had long ago recognized her "true" homosexuality, and, by extension, that other husbands could recognize their wives' lesbianism as well.[8]

Though such news articles were somewhat sympathetic to lesbian-identified women who left their marriages, feminist fiction of the 1970s and 1980s unequivocally celebrated these women. In Marge Piercy's *Small Changes* (1973), Alix Kates Shulman's *Burning Questions* (1978), and Carol Anne Douglas's *To the Cleveland Station* (1982), protagonists Beth Walker, Zane IndiAnna, and Brenda Anne Dougherty, respectively, begin lesbian relationships that cement their feminist politics and heighten their understanding of the patriarchy. It is, for example, only when Beth's lover, Wanda, is imprisoned and loses custody of her children, that the meaning of the word "oppression" finally becomes clear to her.[9] Similarly, when Zane and her friend and fellow activist suddenly become conscious of a mutual attraction and sleep together, all the lesbian feminist arguments Zane has read and empathized with from afar as a wife and mother of three, suddenly make sense. "It was like the difference between reading music and hearing it; reading recipes and tasting them," she reflects.[10] And at the conclusion of *To the Cleveland Station*, Brenda vows to devote her life to educating lesbians about the dangers facing them, after seeing firsthand how her former black lover was subjected to electroshock therapy and raped by a racist, homophobic psychiatrist.[11]

While most wife-to-lesbian novels of the 1970s and early 1980s featured white, middle-class characters, a few wives of color appeared in pioneering novels written by black and Latina women, including Ann Allen Shockley's *Loving Her* (1974) and Sheila Ortiz Taylor's *Faultline* (1982).[12] These novels, like those mentioned above, celebrated lesbian wives who left their marriages and condemned male dominance while also critiquing black and Chicano nationalism. In *Loving Her*, by many accounts the earliest novel to explicitly and positively depict a black lesbian character, Renay Lee leaves her abusive husband Jerome for her white lover Terry.[13] The novel addresses head on the myth of black matriarchy and undermines the idea that the key to overturning racial oppression lay in reinstating the black man to his proper place at the head of the family.[14] *Faultline* similarly challenges Chicano nationalism's idealization of the heterosexual, male-dominated family through the figure of Arden Benbow, a Chicana, Indian, and white mother of six who leaves her husband for a new lesbian life. At novel's end, Arden celebrates wining custody of her children and marries her lover, surrounded by their eccentric group of friends and family, both biological and chosen. Indeed, by placing a lesbian mother at its center, *Faultline* transforms the meaning of *la familia*, a symbol more often used to subordinate women and erase the existence of Chicano gays and lesbians.[15]

Loving Her and *Faultline* likely had limited audiences, but a similar character, Celie, made her way into the mainstream in Alice Walker's Pulitzer Prize–winning historical novel *The Color Purple* (1982).[16] Set in rural Georgia, *The Color Purple* traces Celie's life from the early 1900s to the 1940s. Abused first by a stepfather who impregnates her twice and takes away her children, and then by her husband, Albert, who beats and denigrates her, Celie is a prototypical victim of male dominance. *The Color Purple* never uses the term "lesbian," as Walker had earlier expressed her belief that the word was unsuitable for black women whose own history of "woman-bonding" had little to do with the ancient Greek poet Sappho of Lesbos. Even so, Celie travels much the same path as the characters described above.[17] That is, she evolves from a subordinated wife into a more confident and independent woman as a result of a sexual and romantic relationship with another woman, Shug Avery, Albert's longtime lover.

Although *The Color Purple* does not use the words "lesbian" or "bisexual," like many of the works discussed in this chapter, the novel seems to make precisely this distinction between Celie and Shug's sexuality. Celie never expresses any romantic or sexual interest in men, while Shug has relationships with several men throughout the course of the novel, including Albert, her husband Grady, and later a much younger lover, Germaine. "I know how you feel about men. But I don't feel that way," she tells Celie at one point. "Some mens can be a lots of fun."[18] Walker does not condemn Shug's sexuality, and she ultimately justifies the pain Shug causes Celie in temporarily leaving her for Germaine as a necessary step in her evolution and independence. But Walker does portray Shug's relationship with Germaine as a kind of personal failure and a reflection of her vanity: "I'm gitting old. I'm fat. No body think I'm good looking no more, but you. Or so I thought," Shug tells Celie in asking for permission to have one last fling with Germaine.[19] Though sex functions as a source of pleasure and power for Shug throughout the majority of the novel, her late-life affair with Germaine signals a major shift: sex, in this instance, reveals Shug's neediness and desperation.[20] While *The Color Purple*, then, does not portray Shug's attraction to both men and women as necessarily negative, it does portray her relationship with Germaine as a result of her flaws and weakness.

Several literary scholars have argued that feminist literature was integral to the growth of the feminist movement in the 1970s, reaching women who may never have participated in an organized feminist group and helping them to see their seemingly unique and personal experiences of oppression as shared and political.[21] Feminist literature also helped to express the particular messages of lesbian feminism to a broad audience, and thus to constitute the lesbian community. As scholar Bonnie Zimmerman has written of the efflorescence of lesbian novels in the 1970s and 1980s, "The purpose of this writing is to create lesbian identity and culture, to say, *this* is what it means to be a lesbian, *this* is how lesbians are, *this* is what lesbians believe."[22] The recurring character of the subordinated housewife who eventually leaves her marriage for a lesbian relationship conveyed that lesbianism could be willfully chosen, that lesbian relationships offered a more egalitarian alternative to heterosexual ones, and that separating from men would allow women to better understand gender and sexual oppression.

By the 1980s, sympathetic wives who left their marriages for new lesbian lives even appeared on screen in John Sayles's *Lianna* (1983) and in Donna Deitch's *Desert Hearts* (1985). *Lianna* tells the story of an ordinary wife and mother whose marriage dissolves after she falls in love with another woman, who, in turn, leaves her. The more hopeful *Desert Hearts*, an adaptation of Jane Rule's 1964 novel *The Desert of the Heart*, discussed in Chapter 4, focuses on a college professor who arrives in 1950s Nevada to secure a divorce and unexpectedly begins a lesbian affair. *Lianna* and *Desert Hearts* were part of a new genre of "femme films" produced in the early to mid-1980s, including *Personal Best* (1982) and the more sexually ambiguous French film *Entre Nous* (1983), which enabled multiple readings: while heterosexual viewers might watch the erotic relationships depicted voyeuristically, lesbian viewers could identify with them.[23] Film scholars have thus accused such films of depoliticizing lesbian identity, utilizing the tropes of heterosexual romance to negate lesbian difference, and perpetuating the sexual objectification of lesbians on screen.[24]

Nevertheless, most feminist and lesbian critics at the time recognized *Lianna* and *Desert Hearts*, in particular, as groundbreaking in their humanizing depictions of lesbians, and the films quickly became "classics" among lesbian viewers, who eagerly awaited their release in VHS.[25] Of the two, lesbian and feminist reviewers tended to prefer *Desert Hearts* for its more positive portrayal of lesbian life and more erotic sex scenes. One leading queer film critic writing for the *Village Voice*, for instance, compared *Desert Hearts* favorably to *Lianna*, which she described as a "punish-me morality play."[26] Another lesbian reviewer raved about *Desert Hearts*' sex scene in the feminist news journal *off our backs*, writing that it "beats out anything from *Lianna* or *Personal Best* by a mile."[27] Still, at least one married woman who, much like Lianna, came to recognize her attraction to women after returning to college and falling in love with a female professor, felt that the film quite accurately reflected her own lesbian awakening.[28] Such widely accessible depictions of wives who left their marriages and claimed a lesbian identity in the 1970s and 1980s, thus affirmed and encouraged women going through the same experiences. At the same time, they inherently differentiated such women from bisexual wives who engaged in sex with other women without feeling the need or desire to divorce.

Bisexual Swinging Wives

Just as these positive portraits of lesbians who left their marriages emerged within popular culture, hypersexualized, apolitical bisexual wives who engaged in same-sex acts within the context of swinging and group sex also grabbed the public's attention. In the late 1960s the bisexual wife had intermittently appeared in the same pseudoscientific pulps in which the menacing lesbian wife had featured so prominently. Initially, the bisexual wife did not appear to be entirely distinct from the lesbian wife, but rather a synonym for her, as the title of David Lynne's *The Bisexual Woman: A Timely Examination of Lesbians Trapped in Conventional Marriages* (1967) suggested.[29] But in other purportedly scientific paperback studies, the bisexual wife became more distinct, associated in particular with swinging culture and group sex. Emblematic here is an extended quote from a bisexual character in *The Bi-Sexual Female* (1968), by one supposed "Roger Blake, PhD": "I'm definitely *not* a Lesbian, doctor . . . but at the swinging parties my husband and I go to . . . well, I always end up being Frenched by one of the wives, and . . . I've done it myself, too. . . . I do like it, but I'm *not* a Lesbian."[30] Although Blake went on to discuss this woman among others as evidence of the muddy line between lesbianism and bisexuality in women, more reputable scholars of swinging and group sex would later affirm such swinging wives' declarations that they were not lesbians.

When and how the phenomenon of "wife-swapping" or "swinging" with other couples emerged is unclear, but by the 1970s this phenomenon had become a legitimate—though still controversial—topic of academic research as scholars began to focus on a range of alternative forms of marriage and family life.[31] Anthropologists, psychologists, and sociologists who studied swinging in the 1970s and early 1980s before this body of research on "alternative lifestyles" tapered off, often noted with surprise how common sex between women was among otherwise conventional, middle-class, white couples. While homosexual encounters between men were for the most part verboten in swinging circles, swingers often encouraged sex between women at parties and frequently sought "versatile" or "AC/DC" wives in advertisements for sex partners.[32] In one of the earliest academic articles about swinging, anthropologists and later the authors of *Open Marriage*, George and Nena O'Neill found that more than half of the women in their study of fifty married and unmarried swingers from the New York area reported engaging in same-sex sexual activity including genital contact.[33] Other researchers put the percentage of female swingers who engaged in same-sex sex near 100 percent.[34]

While earlier paperback studies of swinging presented the boundary between bisexuality and lesbianism as tenuous at best, academic researchers of the 1970s endorsed it completely and emphasized repeatedly that swinging women did not see themselves and should not be seen by others as lesbians.[35] According to James W. Ramey, founder and director of the Center for the Study of Innovative Lifestyles, women were able to engage in same-sex contacts more freely than men within swinging communities precisely because they did not have to fear that other people present would categorize them as "homosexual." According to Ramey the vast majority of female swingers did not consider themselves lesbians "by any stretch of the word."[36] Likewise, the O'Neills eschewed the word "homosexual" entirely in their research, arguing that it implied a regular if not exclusive pattern of sexual behavior quite different from that which they observed among swinging women, whose sexual encounters with other women they described instead as "bi-sexual," "ambi-sexual," or "same-sex."[37]

Researchers also distinguished swinging wives from lesbian ones by describing their sexual encounters with other women as reflecting *men's* desires rather than their own. The O'Neills, for example, wrote that the "active encouragement of the males" was the most important factor behind women's involvement in same-sex activity.[38] Ramey similarly accounted for such behavior at swinging parties by explaining that watching two women together allowed men to "re-cycle" sooner after orgasm.[39] Yet another scholar argued that swinging wives "learn[ed] to enjoy" sex with women in an effort to please their husbands and "to be sociable."[40] There was, without doubt, truth to such arguments. Some women *did* engage in bisexual group sex for their husbands' sake. And men *did* often act as spectators while their wives engaged in lesbian sex at swinging parties. But the fact that men derived pleasure from watching their wives does not mean that this was such women's only motivation.

In fact, in the two most extensive, book-length studies of swinging, wives rejected the idea that they engaged in sex with women primarily to please their husbands. In *Group Sex: A Scientist's Eyewitness Report on the American Way of Swinging* (1971), based on interviews with 280 white, middle-class, suburban swingers, the anthropologist Gilbert Bartell noted with consternation that "no matter how closely" he questioned the women about their sudden participation in homosexual sex after years of hetero-sexuality, "they came up with no reasons other than, 'I just enjoy it.' "[41] This answer was clearly insufficient for Bartell who went on to propose a series of reasons *he* believed swinging wives claimed to enjoy sex with women. He suggested that sex with women was, for swinging wives obsessed with cleanliness, appealingly less "messy" than sex with men; that it was an effect of wives' aversion to performing fellatio on strangers; and that it was a result of men's and women's inherently different capacities for orgasm, which led male swingers to circulate quickly between women at parties, leaving their female partners aroused but unsatisfied.

Yet even as Bartell questioned swinging wives' accounts of their same-sex encounters, he could not ignore their sexual pleasure, which was, as he put it, "plainly evident" at every event he and his team of researchers attended.[42] In fact, 65 percent of the women in Bartell's study admitted that they would rather "turn on" with women than with men at swinging par-ties.[43] Some of the wives Bartell studied even began to take female lovers outside of the swinging world, with and without their husbands' knowl-edge. Bartell wrote vaguely that if such wives continued to show an increas-ing interest in sex with women "some questions may become more and more pertinent," but whether swinging was in fact leading these women down a path to lesbianism was an issue he chose not to pursue.[44]

Like Bartell, social psychologist Brian G. Gilmartin found in his later study of one hundred suburban swinging couples in Southern California that wives' self-professed "enjoyment" was the chief motivating factor behind their sexual experiences with other women.[45] While most wives admitted that arousing their husbands was *a* motive, they insisted that it was a minor one. Several women even accused Gilmartin, much to his surprise, of being a "male chauvinist pig" for suggesting that they had sex with each other purely to please men.[46] Still, Gilmartin, like Bartell, again found ways to undermine the significance of sex between swinging women. He stated, for example, that the husbands of wives who enjoyed sex with women the most were inadequate lovers. And he referred to same-sex sex throughout his book as "sex *play*," while describing heterosexual sex as simply "sex."[47] Gilmartin's careful though unexplained word choice clearly conveyed his belief that sex between women was not equivalent to hetero-sexual sex. But the fact that he felt the need to trivialize lesbian sex as mere "play," suggests some concern on his part that the difference between swinging wives' lesbian and heterosexual encounters was not entirely self-evident. What is more, Gilmartin also felt the need to reassure his readers that while swinging wives frequently engaged in same-sex activities, doing so did not negatively impact their marital sex lives, nor discourage them "from wanting to continue living with their husbands and caring for their children."[48]

Academic and amateur scholars of swinging thus portrayed the bisexual wife as capable of harnessing the changes of the sexual revolution for her husband's benefit without threatening marriage or men's power within it. As she figured within these texts, the bisexual wife allowed white, middle-class husbands to engage openly and without social repercussion in sexual acts which, under the postwar moral code, would have been wholly unacceptable. Game for anything, the bisexual wife gave her spouse license to engage in extramarital sex freely, to experiment with group sex and relationships, and to derive pleasure directly or indirectly from her sexual experiences with other women. Her sexual relationships with women were unserious (that is, purely sexual), unfettered by lesbian or feminist politics, and undertaken with her husband's explicit approval, if not encouragement. Still, despite the bisexual wife's clear potential in this respect, the possibility always remained that she might come to enjoy sex with women too much, that she might cross over the boundary separating tame, sexy bisexuality from threatening and unattractive lesbianism.

Such anxieties were usually left unspoken, but they came to the fore in one interview with a married couple in the *The Groupsex Tapes* (1971), a journalistic study of swinging in California. In the interview, Mike and Karyn, a couple in their thirties who renounced swinging after a period of about six months explained that the sexual encounters they witnessed between swinging women had been a major detractor. As Mike told the authors, "I mean, seeing two women pleasuring each other, married women, was something that quite frankly shook me up. . . . Seeing a woman pleasure another woman as well as a man could or better, well for me at least, it led to a negative effect. I assumed that it's the man's role to pleasure a woman, and I was seeing those roles changing quite a bit." Karyn too disapproved of this behavior which seemed to her distinctly "unfeminine."[49] Expecting the swinging scene to provide her and other married couples with an opportunity for "normal sex," she was appalled to see wives having sex with each other. According to Karyn, women who turned to each other after their husbands were unable to continue sexually performing, should have ceased swinging when their husbands did instead of using other women "as male substitutes."[50] In other words, while academic researchers denied that swinging wives' sexual activities with each other posed any sort of social threat, Mike and Karyn understood this behavior as undermining such women's gender and sexual normality.

Despite such underlying concerns, articles in the mainstream news perpetuated the idea that sex between swinging women, both married and not, was more a product of men's desires than their own. In an early report on swinging for *Playboy* in 1969, journalist Richard Warren Lewis implied that swinging wives' same-sex contacts were merely a manifestation of their compulsive sexual exhibitionism, one of their many ploys for male attention akin to the revealing outfits or sexy costumes they donned at swinging parties.[51] Likewise, several articles on swinging in the *New York Times*, the *Los Angeles Times*, and *Newsweek* quoted anthropologist Gilbert Bartell and discussed his research, but they uniformly ignored his findings about married women's admitted enjoyment of sex with women. Instead, they emphasized the pleasure swinging women's same-sex activities provided male onlookers while allowing men to "conserve" their own sexual energy.[52] In a 1977 article for the *Village Voice*, author Michael Tolkin conceded that some swinging women found it annoying when men tried to "interfere" in their sexual relations with each other. Nonetheless, he too undermined such women's same-sex desires by insisting that swinging women gravitated to one another purely out of "boredom" when men were unable to attain an erection or bring them to orgasm.[53]

Scholarly studies and media coverage of swinging helped contribute to a broader cultural understanding of wives who dabbled in sex with women as hip, sophisticated, and sexy—so long as they retained a primary attraction to men. In her 1974 *Cosmopolitan* article "Bisexuality: The Newest Sex-Style," for example, writer Jane Margold celebrated wives who engaged in same-sex relationships as the vanguard of the sexual revolution, but the article's subheading conveyed that Margold's positive analysis was qualified: "Could *you* be ready for a lesbian encounter? Well, a surprising number of perfectly 'normal' man-loving females *are*."[54] Paula, whose husband had pressured her to engage in a threesome, was one of several bisexual wives Margold profiled in the article. Annoyed by her husband's constant pestering, Paula slept with another woman while he was out of town, and then went on to sleep with several other female friends. According to Paula while her first lesbian experience "liberated" her sexually, it was the feminist movement that taught her "bisexuality has to involve your head and your heart, not just your body."[55] In contrast with news coverage about bisexual swinging wives which described their experiences with women as purely sexual, Margold's article emphasized bisexual wives' emotional connections to other women, and focused in particular on an affair between two married women, Elena and Jill, who described their relationship in idyllic terms, as loving and passionate, but "free of competition and jealousy."[56]

Lest such wives' loving relationship trouble the line between lesbianism and bisexuality, Margold made clear that bisexual wives were easily distinguishable from lesbians who did not want to remain married and whose homosexuality was physically apparent. In the article, Margold described meeting one formerly married lesbian, Mary, who led a workshop titled "Loving Women" at a San Francisco women's conference. Margold described Mary as visibly different from the conventionally feminine bisexual women in her piece: "a husky woman with close-cropped hair and sneakered feet splayed carelessly in front of her chair; she looked so outrageously, militantly 'butch' that many of us made a determined effort not to stare."[57] While bisexual wives like Paula, Elena, and Jill were thus broadening the definition of acceptable or "normal" female sexuality, they were still distinct from divorced butches like Mary who were clearly outside the norm.

Similar representations of bisexual wives appeared in erotic novels of this era, which took pains to separate hip, sexy, bisexual wives who experimented with same-sex sex from married, closeted lesbians who became emotionally attached to other women. One such set of characters appears in Harold Robbins's raunchy novel *The Lonely Lady* (1976), which ranked number eight on the *Publishers Weekly* list of best sellers in 1976.[58] *The Lonely Lady* follows the adventures of JeriLee Randall, a white girl from small-town Long Island with an unquenchable sexual appetite and big dreams of becoming a writer. Over the course of the novel, JeriLee divorces her much older husband and has an ill-fated affair with a married African American woman, Licia Lafayette. *The Lonely Lady* explicitly distinguishes JeriLee's bisexuality from Licia's lesbianism. In one scene in particular, Licia unabashedly informs a detective looking for JeriLee, that while the women once had an affair together they are sexually different: she is a lesbian while JeriLee is bisexual. "It took me a long time to understand that her reaction to our sex was purely physical," Licia explains. "It was never like that for me at all. I really loved her."[59] For Robbins, then, as for many swinging scholars, bisexual women appeared distinct from lesbians in so far as their same-sex encounters were "purely physical" and unaccompanied by lasting romantic feelings.

Yet another erotic writer of the 1970s, Erica Jong, demonstrated the difference between bisexual and lesbian characters in *How to Save Your Own Life* (1977), the much-anticipated sequel to her infamous best seller *Fear of Flying* (1973). *How to Save Your Own Life*, which ranked among the top-ten best-selling novels of 1977, picks up on protagonist Isadora Wing's life after *Fear of Flying* ends. Still desperately unhappy in her marriage, Isadora embarks on a range of extramarital sexual relationships, including a summer affair with another married woman, Rosanna Howard.[60] Like *The Lonely Lady*, *How to Save Your Own Life* emphasizes the boundary between lesbian and bisexual women through reference to more visible and seemingly stable differences. In *The Lonely Lady* race helps to distinguish JeriLee and Licia, while in *How to Save Your Own Life*, ethnicity and religion divide Isadora and Rosanna. Isadora is a Jewish New Yorker, an accomplished author and intellectual, while Rosanna is an obscenely wealthy, Midwestern WASP with time on her hands. The two improbably cross paths when Rosanna, toying with the idea of becoming a writer, enrolls in one of Isadora's courses.

Isadora's and Rosanna's significant personal differences extend into the realm of sex and relationships. While Isadora is sexually uninhibited—"man or woman, vibrator or shower spray, I come in three minutes flat"—Rosanna is nearly inorgasmic.[61] And while Jong presents Rosanna as a repressed lesbian, she makes clear that Isadora is merely sexually curious. She sleeps with Rosanna not because she is deeply attracted or romantically attached to her, but because bisexuality happens to be *en vogue*. Perhaps the most important measure of Isadora's bisexuality, indeed of her fundamental *heterosexuality*, is how repulsive she finds Rosanna's vagina and how profoundly she dislikes performing oral sex. Rosanna, on the other hand, is "an expert cunt-eater," who also truly cares for Isadora.[62] Even in the very act of sex then, the boundary between bisexuality and lesbianism remains secure. And while Isadora finds the courage to divorce her husband and take a chance on a new, much younger man, Rosanna remains trapped in her unhappy marriage. As *How to Save Your Own Life* makes clear, Rosanna is no liberated bisexual adventurer but a closeted lesbian whose marriage is little more than a façade. "Every reluctant lesbian needs an absent husband to cover her," Isadora notes at one point. "I never heard *any*one use the phrase *my husband* as often as Rosanna."[63] By explicitly distinguishing Isadora's and Rosanna's sexuality, Jong helped her largely female readership map out the differences between bisexual and lesbian women.

That bisexual wives who slept with women were also becoming a staple of pornographic films—which began attracting larger audiences and greater critical attention in the midst of the sexual revolution—only added to their cultural cachet in the 1970s.[64] The earliest "sexploitation" or soft-core films to feature such characters, like Joe Sarno's *Sin in the Suburbs* (1964), were basically adaptations of homophobic, moralizing lesbian pulps.[65] Yet, as public attitudes toward sexuality shifted, porn films began reveling in the bi-curious wife's same-sex adventures without vilifying or punishing her. Such characters appeared in Radley Metzger's *The Lickerish Quartet* (1970) and *Score* (1972) which combined sexual storylines with art house stylistics and European backdrops.[66] Another bi-curious wife appeared in Metzger's *The Private Afternoons of Pamela Mann* (1974), which signaled the director's move into hardcore territory.[67] *The Private Afternoons of Pamela Mann*, like *The Lickerish Quartet*, *Score*, and most other porn films, concluded with the bisexual wife returning to marital heterosexuality, thus shutting down the possibility of such characters' same-sex relationships ever excluding men. But there were important exceptions within this genre. At the end of *Just the Two of Us* (1975), for instance, a film written and codirected by the feminist filmmaker Barbara Peeters, two bored and neglected California housewives who have been having an affair walk off screen together, suggesting that they will not be resuming their married lives.[68] Even in porn, then, the boundary between bisexuality and lesbianism remained somewhat unstable.

Fence-Sitters, Failed Lesbians, and Fatal Women

Bi-curious wives may have found champions among scholars of swinging, erotic fiction writers, and pornographic filmmakers, but they still had a significant number of detractors. While some journalists echoed the tolerance social scientists showed for bisexual swingers, as we have seen, other journalists found bisexual wives who engaged in sex with women outside the context of the swinging world to be far more disconcerting. One 1974 *New York Times* article, "Bisexual Life-Style Appears to Be Spreading and Not Necessarily Among 'Swingers,'" warned that while celebrities like Kate

Millett and David Bowie might declare their bisexuality openly, most bisexuals were married and "remained carefully underground," for fear that their "homosexual activities would hurt their families and possibly wreck their marriages."[69] A similar *Time* article published only a few months later also mentioned Kate Millett and her forthcoming memoir *Flying*, but quoted a range of even more hostile psychiatric experts, including psychologist John Money, who claimed that "bisexuals generally do not have the capacity to fall in love with one person." According to this article, while bisexuality happened to be hip, it was a type of psychological illness akin to, but worse than homosexuality, because it involved a distrust for both sexes. According to one Manhattan psychoanalyst bisexuals' "constant ricocheting from one sex to the other" ultimately produced unstable relationships and chaotic homes unsuitable for children who could find their sense of sexual identity disturbed.[70]

Such skepticism about the stability of bisexual identity was pervasive, and journalists often portrayed bisexual wives who engaged in ongoing lesbian relationships as untrustworthy. One 1974 Associated Press article, "Bisexuality: A Phase or an Alternative Lifestyle?," expressed a sense of unease in describing the case of a bisexual-identified, fifty-year-old suburban housewife and mother of three named Lydia. Lydia, who was in love with another woman but intended to stay married, had long known she was attracted to women but feared ruining her marriage. At her psychiatrist's suggestion, Lydia first acted on her desires for women in the context of group sex with her husband, but she had since moved on to pursue relationships with women independently of him. "My ultimate goal, is to be able to function as freely as possible with a woman, my husband, and any other man who may come on to the scene," Lydia explained. Though the author of this article did not explicitly disparage Lydia's choices, she concluded that bisexuality was typically a phase that people passed through as they tried to decipher their "real" sexual orientation.[71]

Advice columnist Ann Landers was even less evenhanded toward bisexual wives, and in letters to bisexual-identified women and their husbands she made her disapproval for such women's lifestyles clear. In 1975, for example, when the husband of a bisexual woman who had been carrying on a lesbian relationship for most of their sixteen-year marriage asked Landers if there was hope for him, she replied that any man who could stay married to a bisexual woman that long was in need of psychological help.[72] A few years later, Landers published a letter from a bisexual woman who explained that she had left her husband after he proved unwilling to accept her lesbian relationship. Now divorced, this woman was finding it hard to find a man who could tolerate her girlfriend, and she asked Landers if she ever received letters from the husbands of bisexual women. "Yes—they tell me they are divorcing them," Landers replied. "Maybe I'm square as a chair, but I think it's asking a lot of a husband (or a gentleman friend) to accept, with equanimity, the fact that his wife or sweetheart has a female lover on the side."[73]

Many feminist novelists shared this negative opinion of wives who sought to balance marriage and lesbian relationships, albeit for different reasons. In keeping with lesbian feminist ideology, these writers did not explicitly distinguish between bisexuals and "closeted" lesbian wives who refused to leave their husbands. Rather they drew a more fundamental boundary between "real" lesbians, that is, those who built lives apart from men, and those who failed to do. This distinction is apparent, for example, in Rita Mae Brown's classic lesbian novel *Rubyfruit Jungle* (1973) which sold around 70,000 copies in its first year alone.[74] During the course of her adventures in the Big Apple, Molly Bolt, *Rubyfruit Jungle*'s brazen young lesbian protagonist, develops a crush on Polina, a forty-something wife, mother, and college professor. Though Polina has an open marriage and considers herself sexually liberated, she is appalled to learn that Molly is a lesbian. Only after several meetings with her psychiatrist does Polina decide that as long as Molly has "adjusted as a mature, healthy human being" her sexuality need not ruin their relationship.[75] Eventually the women sleep together but, despite Polina's position of moral superiority, she is in fact the more sexually maladjusted of the two. For all her talk of maturity and adjustment, Polina must engage in bizarre sexual fantasies to reach orgasm, and she even expresses incestuous desires for her teenaged daughter.

In their respective novels *Final Payments* (1978) and *Some Do* (1978), authors Mary Gordon and Jane DeLynn similarly distinguished between "real" lesbians and those who engage in sex with women while remaining committed to men. Liz O'Brian of *Final Payments* is the wife of a promising young politician and the mother of two beautiful children. From the outside, their life is picture-perfect, but in actuality both Liz and her husband are engaged in extramarital relationships. Though Liz is in love with a young, unmarried lesbian-identified woman who desperately wants to begin a new life with her, Gordon portrayed Liz as too invested in the privileges her marriage brings to make a change. At the novel's end, Liz promises a friend that she will leave her husband, but her words sound hollow and Gordon provided the reader no reason to believe that she will actually do so. "Proud of her house, proud of her children, proud of her boyish body and her good manners," it seems most likely that Liz will remain precisely where she is.[76] DeLynn likewise portrayed Bettina of *Some Do* as lacking the courage and the political conviction to leave her marriage despite the intensity of her desire for women. At the beginning of the novel, set in the late-1960s, Bettina has recently escaped her stultifying life as a wife and mother in Columbus, Ohio, and moved to Berkeley in the hopes of completing her education and building a new life. After her black lesbian roommate, Maria, takes her to a gay bar, Bettina begins sleeping with other women, but she remains embarrassed about her "surely temporary" lesbianism. She denies that she is "a 'real' lesbian" like Maria and continues to identify inwardly as heterosexual.[77] Sure enough, when life in Berkeley becomes too difficult, Bettina rushes back to her husband in Columbus who writes off her lesbian experiences as "very sexy." [78]

Despite such harsh portraits of bisexual—or more accurately "failed lesbian"—wives in feminist fiction, Hollywood depictions of wives who attempted to balance marriage and same-sex relationships were even more disapproving. Indeed, in a series of moralistic films from the early 1970s swinging, bisexual wives served as a convenient symbol of the dangers of the sexual revolution.[79] In *Doctors' Wives* (1971), for example, a soapy murder mystery loosely based on Frank G. Slaughter's 1967 novel of the same name, a blonde and beautiful bisexual wife, Lorrie Dellman (Dyan Cannon), wreaks havoc on her community (Figure 9). Lorrie is the youngest, most attractive and vivacious of a group of desperately unhappy doctors' wives in some affluent, nameless suburb. When the film begins the women are engaged in a deadly boring card game at their country club. "God, I feel horny," Lorrie blurts out and asks her friends only somewhat facetiously, "Would one of you like to slip out to the parking lot for a little while?" The women are appalled at Lorrie who, in return, accuses them all of being sex-deprived and admits to having bedded half their husbands. Lorrie's sexual misbehavior is swiftly punished (her husband shoots and kills her in flagrante), but her destructive influence continues even after death.[80]

One of the women in Lorrie's circle, Della Randolph (Rachel Roberts), is particularly haunted by memories of her, and eventually Della admits to her husband that she and Lorrie once slept together. In a trope we have seen now several times before, while the film portrays Lorrie as a sex-obsessed,

Figure 9. Dyan Cannon as the seductive and dangerous bisexual wife in *Doctors' Wives* (1971). From the Core Collection, Margaret Herrick Library.

swinging bisexual Della appears as a repressed lesbian, a distinction which the women's differences in nationality and appearance help to highlight. Della is British, dowdier, and more masculine than the late Lorrie. By Della's account, Lorrie teased and cajoled her into sex without considering the experience to be particularly meaningful. As Lorrie put it, "Some people are star-struck. Some people are clothes-struck. I'm sex-struck." But Della, by contrast, was deeply affected by the encounter and tearfully admits to her psychiatrist husband that "it was wonderful." Della possesses some striking similarities with the menacing lesbian wife of postwar popular culture: she is caustic and bitter toward her husband, rebuffs his sexual advances, and refuses to have another child with him. Yet even so, the film portrays Della as more pathetic than menacing. Following her confession, Della's husband reasserts his authority by hitting her with a rolled-up newspaper like some misbehaving pet. The couple then bizarrely embraces, suggesting that their marriage is saved.[81]

The following year the crime caper *They Only Kill Their Masters* (1972) reiterated the idea that bisexual women like Lorrie were taking the ethos of sexual liberation to dangerous extremes and perhaps unleashing other wives' repressed lesbianism. In the movie a middle-aged wife much like Della becomes mentally unhinged as a result of her relationship with a younger, more sexually adventurous divorcee, Jenny Campbell. The movie begins when Jenny's dead body washes up on the shore of a sleepy California beach town. Eventually the police come to suspect—and accidentally kill—the town's middle-aged veterinarian, Dr. Watkins (Hal Holbrook), but it turns out his reclusive wife is to blame (Figure 10). At the end of the film, while standing over her husband's dead body, Mrs. Watkins (June Allyson) attempts to account for her actions. Initially she and Jenny were lovers, she explains, but their relationship was not enough for the greedy younger woman who seduced Mr. Watkins as well. While Mrs. Watkins could stand to share her lover with her husband, she reached her breaking point when Jenny became pregnant with Mr. Watkins' child. "There was nothing left of him. Nothing left of me," Mrs. Watkins utters. "I had no choice." As in *Doctors' Wives*, then, murder is the inevitable way of dealing with bisexual wives.

They Only Kill Their Masters clearly condemns the social changes wrought by the sexual revolution, which had, it suggested, made their way to small-town America with dire consequences. Throughout the film, the police chief and protagonist Abel Marsh (James Garner) comments on the sexual immorality of "city people" like Jenny, a Los Angeles transplant who took up a permanent residence in her husband's vacation home after their divorce. The film thus portrays Jenny as a conduit of moral depravity who introduced urban licentiousness to an otherwise peaceful town, none-too-subtly named Eden Landing. During her short lifetime, Jenny appears to have crossed all manner of sexual boundaries: she was divorced, bisexual, and pregnant with a married man's child. She engaged in group sex and even photographed her sexual encounters. Jenny's moral disease, then,

Figure 10. June Allyson as a murderous, repressed lesbian in *They Only Kill Their Masters* (1972). From the Museum of Modern Art Film Stills Archive.

unleashed the baser instincts of the otherwise boring Dr. and Mrs. Watkins, played by sweet-faced Hal Holbrook and classic Hollywood film star June Allyson, best known for portraying ideal wives to leading men like Jimmy Stewart in films of the 1940s and 1950s. While Mrs. Watkins moves from a lesbian relationship to murder in just a few short steps, her devoted husband resorts to arson and violence in an ill-fated attempt to protect her.[82]

It was not only cheesy crowd-pleasers like *Doctors' Wives* and *They Only Kill Their Masters* that linked bisexual wives, violence, and tragedy together. This theme also emerged in *Lenny* (1974), director Bob Fosse's arty, more serious biopic about the late countercultural comedian Lenny Bruce.[83] In the movie, Lenny (Dustin Hoffman) falls in love with and marries Hot Honey Harlow, a stripper. Lenny describes Honey (Valerie Perrine) as an idyllic combination of a kindergarten teacher and a "five-hundred-dollar-a-night hooker." Eventually, though, their love story takes a darker turn: they begin using drugs and Lenny pressures Honey to engage in a threesome with him and another woman. The film then jumps to a later fight between the two over Honey's continued infidelity with at least one other woman. Honey's behavior, it seems, has threatened to cross the line between hip bisexuality and secretive lesbianism. "It's really hard to spot dykes," Bruce informs the audience at a comedy club soon after. "You know why? Because sometimes we're married to 'em."

The issue of Honey's sexuality recedes from the storyline after the pair reconcile and have a child, but her detrimental impact on Lenny continues. Ultimately, the film portrays Honey as largely responsible for Lenny's death from a drug overdose. While *Lenny* does not directly condemn Honey's bisexuality, then, it does use her sexuality to portray her as a weak and dissolute woman who readily gives in to temptation—whether sexual or chemical—and who cannot be trusted. Honey's character is, in one critic's words, "a stripper without a heart of gold."[84] Doe-eyed and soft-voiced, Honey at first appears as harmless as her name would suggest, but her influence on Lenny is devastating. Meanwhile Honey survives their troubled life together relatively unscathed. At the conclusion of the film, she feebly sums up the tragedy of Lenny's death: "He was just so damn funny." The bisexual wife of 1970s Hollywood film was thus just as destructive as the postwar menacing lesbian wife had been.

Anxieties about the tenuous distinction between bisexual and lesbian wives play a critical role in Woody Allen's 1979 Oscar-nominated film *Manhattan* as well.[85] When the movie begins, Jill Davis (Meryl Streep) has recently divorced Isaac Davis (Allen) and is raising their son, Willy, together with her lover, Connie. Unlike *Lenny*, *They Only Kill Their Masters*, or *Doctor's Wives*, *Manhattan* mines Jill's unstable sexuality as a source of comedy. During the course of the film we learn that Jill informed Isaac about her bisexuality before they married, and that the couple once engaged in a threesome with another woman. As Isaac later explains, "[Jill] wanted to. . . . I didn't want to be a bad sport." Even Isaac's psychoanalyst warned him about becoming involved with Jill, but Isaac was set on pursuing her, believing he could "straighten her out" under the strength of his "personal vibrations." "Under your personal vibrations she went from bisexuality to homosexuality," his friend retorts. In retrospect, then, Jill's claims to bisexuality seems to have been a type of denial of her "true" lesbianism, which neither she nor Isaac wanted to admit.

Yet despite the film's humor, *Manhattan* still portrays Jill's relationship with Connie as dangerously disruptive and painfully emasculating. Jill injures Isaac, not by physically attacking or lying to him, but by publishing a humiliating, tell-all memoir in which she accuses him of being paranoid and nihilistic, and states that making love with a "more masterful female" revealed how empty her sex life with Isaac was. Adding insult to injury, Jill warns Isaac near the end of the movie that her memoir may be adapted into a film. Furthermore, Jill's sexuality threatens not only Isaac's masculinity, but also that of their young son. Throughout the film, Isaac worries about the effect that Jill's lesbianism will have on their son, and at one point, he asks Jill of Willy, "Does he play baseball? Does he wear dresses?" None of the other characters in the film share Isaac's concern, but the film suggests that Isaac's fears are justified when, in one of the final scenes, Connie mentions in passing that Willy is at ballet class.

Bisexual Activists and Allies Respond

While bisexual wives typically appeared within popular culture as either hypersexual, dangerous, or confused, a different portrait of them emerged in popular and academic publications that sought to challenge stereotypes about bisexuality. In 1975, for example, the anthropologist Margaret Mead published an article titled "Bisexuality: What's It All About?" for *Redbook* magazine, which boldly begins, "The time has come, I think, when we must recognize bisexuality as a normal form of human behavior."[86] Although Mead remained skeptical about the possibility of a distinct bisexual political movement, she celebrated the increasing cultural awareness of bisexuality. As evidence of this new cultural attitude she pointed to British author Nigel Nicolson's best-selling memoir, *Portrait of a Marriage* (1973), about his famous parents, novelist Vita Sackville-West and diplomat Harold Nicolson, who carried on same-sex relationships while remaining committed to one another for decades. *Portrait of a Marriage*, and Mead's brief summary of it, provided a powerful counterpoint to hypersexualized and demonized representations of bisexual wives. As she wrote of Sackville-West and her husband with clear admiration, "Theirs was a marriage founded on a deep, abiding trust and a community of interest symbolized by the house and great garden they created together."[87]

More sympathetic and complex portraits of bisexual wives also appeared in the mid-1970s in a series of articles by sociologists Pepper Schwartz and Philip Blumstein. Schwartz and Blumstein's findings were based on interviews they conducted with one hundred and fifty people who had sexual experiences with both men and women. Some, but not all of their interviewees identified as bisexual. Schwartz and Blumstein published their findings in academic outlets, but they also attempted to intervene in popular representations of bisexuality as a fad or a threat to the gay movement. In an article for *Ms.* magazine, "Bisexuals: Where Love Speaks Louder Than Labels," the researchers included several examples of currently or formerly married women who experienced sexual attraction to both women and men. They mentioned one woman who engaged in sex with women only while swinging with her husband, another who secretly slept with women without her husband's knowledge, and yet another who fell in love with a woman only after getting divorced and becoming a feminist. In pointing to this wide range of experiences among those they categorized as "bisexual," Schwartz and Blumstein undermined the idea that there was one type of bisexual woman or wife.[88]

In the late 1970s, a series of popularly marketed books on bisexuality, including Janet Bode's *View from Another Closet* (1976), Charlotte Wolff's *Bisexuality: A Study* (1977), and Fritz Klein's *The Bisexual Option* (1978), also complicated reductive portraits of bisexual wives while even more forcefully contesting the discrimination they encountered among gays and lesbians. In *View From Another Closet*, author Janet Bode compiled interviews with roughly a dozen bisexual women in an effort to challenge many lesbians' conceptions of them as anti-feminist and tied to heterosexuality. Though Bode did not identify as bisexual, she stated at the beginning of her book that she was a feminist, that she believed in the "validity of bisexuality as a lifestyle," and that she was concerned with bringing women together.[89] British psychotherapist and lesbian scholar Charlotte Wolff was similarly critical of gay and lesbian antipathy toward bisexuals and she argued that by failing to ally with bisexual men and women, gays and lesbians worked against their own political interests. "Only in a bisexual society can human beings get rid of the sexual compartments in which they are entrenched and understand that we are all in the same boat, only in different attire," she wrote.[90] Fritz Klein, a psychiatrist and bisexual activist, likewise drew attention to the discrimination bisexuals faced, while also arguing that bisexuals were less sexually repressed than either homosexuals or heterosexuals.[91]

Married women figured significantly in this more politically oriented literature on bisexuality. A notable proportion of the bisexual women in

Bode's study—17 percent—were married. She also estimated that more than half of the women were married at a bisexual women's rap group she attended in Berkeley, California.[92] Klein and Wolff discussed married bisexual women as well, often in comparison with married bisexual men. Klein believed that husbands rather than wives were typically more "open" to exploring their bisexuality and had more opportunities to do. Wolff, on the other hand, argued that the bisexual wives in her study were more "independent" of their spouses and less afraid of incurring social stigma. The married women in her sample also tended to be much more open with their husbands about their bisexuality than their male counterparts. Of these women, Wolff wrote, "They did not attempt to hide their love for women from husbands, who, on the whole, accepted the situation, and, in a number of cases encouraged it," sometimes inviting their wives' lovers to live with them or engage in threesomes. Yet such husbands' accepting attitudes, Wolff argued, were likely influenced by their deeply ingrained sense of superiority which led them to possess "a false sense of security" with regard to their wives' lesbian relationships. "Not many could believe that another woman could drive them out of the marriage bed, except those who actually experienced it," she noted, before going on to describe several such cases.[93]

The picture of bisexual married women that emerged in Bode's, Wolff's, and Klein's in-depth studies was thus quite different from that in academic research on swinging and group sex. Most studies of swinging and group sex sought to present married women's sexual experiences with women as entirely unthreatening to marriage. But Bode's, Wolff's, and Klein's studies betrayed no underlying investment in marriage as an institution or in bisexual wives' primary attraction to men. These scholars and activists did not attempt to undermine the seriousness of wives' desires for other women, or to portray their relationships or sexual experiences with other women as any less pleasurable or meaningful than those they had with men. And while researchers writing about bisexual wives within the context of "alternative lifestyles" typically denied such women's political affiliation with feminists and gays and lesbians, Wolff, Klein, and Bode affirmed them.

This body of literature on bisexuality was deeply connected to the emergence of the bisexual movement in the mid-1970s. As bisexual rights groups took shape across the country, formerly or currently married bisexual women increasingly began to speak out on their own behalf. In telling their stories publicly, these activists forcefully challenged stereotypes about bisexual wives as apolitical and anti-feminist. In 1978, for example, a divorced bisexual woman known as "Orlando" wrote an essay in *Ms.* magazine, about her decision to identify as bisexual after leaving her husband and falling in love with another woman. In the essay, Orlando affirmed her commitment to feminism and denied that her bisexuality was a trend. Instead she argued the label "bisexual" reflected her sexual experiences more accurately than the label "lesbian." Lesbian was, thus, for her, a more honest and truthful identity. In doing so, Orlando subtly countered representations of bisexual women as dishonest and duplicitous. Lesbian feminists typically argued that women who chose bisexuality rather than lesbianism were taking an easier path by retaining some of their heterosexual privilege. Orlando argued instead that living as a bisexual was in many ways more difficult than living as a lesbian. Despite the challenges she had encountered, however, Orlando ultimately portrayed her bisexuality in a positive light: "As a state of mind for me, bisexuality somehow *fits*. Like feminism or motherhood or work, it also happens to have been a conduit for changes I never planned on but which are now such a part of me that I can't imagine life otherwise."[94]

By the mid-1980s, bisexual women's organizations across the country were beginning to publish newsletters which provided yet another venue in which bisexual wives could represent themselves and their experiences in ways that countered hostile or hypersexualized depictions of them in popular culture. In 1984, the formerly married Elissa M. published a notable essay about her life in the newsletter of the Boston Bisexual Women's Network. In contrast with mainstream media representations of bisexual women as highly feminine and conventionally attractive, Elissa noted at the outset of her piece that, as a young woman, she eschewed miniskirts and felt most attractive when she was wearing her father's ties. In many ways, her essay reflected lesbian feminist themes and arguments by describing how she had survived significant sexual exploitation and abuse by the men in her life. Her father sexually abused her as a child, and her physically and emotionally abusive husband raped her repeatedly in an attempt to impregnate her. When she eventually came out as bisexual to her controlling husband, he found her attraction to women annoying and inconvenient. "Does that mean I have to feel jealous when you look at men as well as women?" he responded.[95] Elissa finally escaped her abusive marriage, but her essay ended on an ambivalent note. Beginning to date again after her divorce, she found that straight men tended to deny the importance of her feelings for women, while lesbians held out hope that she would one day be "fully gay."[96] Divorce, then, did not bring an end to her sexual struggles.

While Elissa remained secure in her bisexual identity, by the late 1980s, other once-married women were beginning to question the need for sexual labels all together. In 1987, formerly married Natalie Bacon wrote an essay titled "Who Am I?" about her sexual history for the newsletter of the Women's Bisexual Drop-In Rap Group at the Pacific Center in Berkeley. By closely analyzing her sexual history, Natalie, then fifty-nine years old, suggested the futility of searching for one sexual label that fit. For the first thirty-four years of her life, she had been inorgasmic and had identified as asexual, even though she had experienced sexual pleasure with her husband. "Am I a lesbian woman because I discovered how to have orgasms with a woman, gave up my husband and children for this woman and lived in a monogamous marriage with her?" she asked. "Am I heterosexual because my orgasms [were] enhanced by the clitoral caresses of my male partner and by rubbing my clitoris against his penis . . . ? Or am I bisexual because I have a history of being orgasmic with a woman and continue to enjoy being sexual with women?" Ultimately, Natalie concluded that confining herself to any one of these sexual labels was less important than accepting herself and recognizing her ability to change. "Do labels have any meaning? After due consideration, I prefer to be who I am at the moment, without fear or judgement."[97] Despite, or perhaps because of the intense cultural effort that went into policing the boundary between bisexual and lesbian wives, some women like Natalie Bacon, were beginning to reject sexual identity categories entirely.

◆ ◆

Representations of wives who desired women were integral in imagining and constructing a boundary, unstable as it was, between bisexuality and lesbianism in the 1970s and 1980s. In nonfiction studies, newspaper articles, novels, and films—from *Bisexual Lives* to *The Color Purple*, from *Group Sex* to *Doctors' Wives*—one woman's lesbianism enabled and made visible the other's bisexuality, and vice versa. In fact, many women's assertions of their own sexual identity, whether bisexual or lesbian, depended on a negation of the other. One bisexual swinging wife featured in *The Extra-marital Sex Contract*, for instance, recounted of her initial sexual experience with a woman, "The first time it happened I was absolutely shook up, I wondered if I was a Lesbian, but it was very clear to me that I'm not."[98] Conversely, the protagonist of *To the Cleveland Station* ultimately decides to leave her marriage because she wants to prove herself to be a "real" lesbian, and fears being "denounced as some kind of married bisexual dreadful."[99] The many cultural texts examined here thus support theorist Clare Hemmings's argument that "bisexuality and lesbianism are conceptualized *only* ever in relationship (though not only to one another)."[100]

As social scientific studies, newspaper articles, novels, and films worked to distinguish bisexual and lesbian wives, they helped to construct a distinct bisexual option for wives who desired women. At the same time, they also reflected, reinforced, and exacerbated political tensions and divisions between lesbian and bisexual women. Pop cultural depictions of bisexual and lesbian wives helped to produce broader social stereotypes about bisexual women as sex-crazed and apolitical, and lesbians as sexless, man-hating feminists, thus further pitting these women against one another, downplaying their shared experiences, and making it more difficult to for them join forces. As we saw in the previous chapter, whether mothers who desired women identified as lesbian or bisexual made no difference at all in terms of the legal discrimination that they encountered in family court.

The prodigious cultural effort that went into shoring up the differences between these women, however, also betrayed a sense of unease—by turns subtle and overt—that these groups were not as distinct as many people wanted to believe. The labels researchers, journalists, novelists and filmmakers ascribed to the women described here, whether fictional or real, often proved misleading. Identities and experiences failed to align and shifted over time as wives moved from one category to another and back again. Boundaries blurred, categories collided, and at some moments the purported differences between various types of wives who desired women threatened to collapse altogether. The lines between these wives, then, may have seemed so important in part because they were so tenuous. If the cultural obsession with dividing and differentiating one wife from another stemmed from a desire to impose some sense of sexual order in a moment of dramatic social transformation, to disentangle the complex relationship between marriage and lesbian desire, it was inevitably in vain. Cultural representations of wives who desired women in the 1970s and 1980s, then, and debates about which label fit them best, forecast the more fluid understandings of female sexuality that would emerge at the turn of the twenty-first century.

Epilogue

IN LATE 2016, ELIZABETH GILBERT and Glennon Doyle Melton, the authors of the best-selling, Oprah's Book Club memoirs *Eat, Pray, Love: One Woman's Search for Everything Across Italy, India and Indonesia* (2006) and *Love Warrior* (2016), respectively, revealed that they were ending their marriages.[1] A few months later, both writers announced in Facebook posts that they were in relationships with women: Gilbert with her longtime friend, the Syrian-born writer Rayya Elias, and Melton with US Women's National Soccer Team star Abby Wambach. Though Gilbert's friendship with Elias had been public knowledge for years, Melton's relationship with Wambach came as a greater surprise to the media, in part because Melton first came to the public's attention through her Christian "mommy blog," *Momastery*. In their Facebook posts, Gilbert and Melton (who are also close friends) avoided ascribing a sexual label to their identities and relationships. In fact, the words "lesbian," "gay," "bisexual," and "homosexual" are entirely absent from their posts. Both authors also explained that their newfound relationships reflected an inner truth they could not deny. "Here is the thing about truth: Once you see it, you cannot un-see it," Gilbert wrote in explaining how she realized that she was in love with Elias, who was fighting an incurable form of cancer.[2] Likewise, Melton wrote that she and her ex-husband told their children about her new relationship by saying, "In our family, we live and tell the truth about who we are no matter what, and then love each other through it."[3]

In their resistance to claiming a limiting sexual identity label, and their emphasis on living their own personal truths, Gilbert's and Melton's posts reflect the public discourse around wives who desire women at the turn of the twenty-first century; one that is grounded in therapeutic rhetoric and stresses the changeable nature of women's sexuality. For the most part, the news media, as well as Gilbert's and Melton's online readers, reacted to their announcements with support and affirmation. So, too, did other women who have begun relationships with women after years of being married to men. Andrea Hewitt, the Nashville-based creator of the blog *A Late Life Lesbian Story* and the leader of a support group for women coming out later in life, reported that the women in her group were "thrilled" with Gilbert's revelation. "Many of them have been told 'you're confused, you're having a midlife crisis', so for them this really validates their experience."[4] Another woman—a formerly married therapist and blogger in a long-term same-sex relationship—responded in particular to Gilbert's decision not to label herself as a lesbian, or to argue that she was now revealing an aspect of herself that she had previously hidden. "We aren't disregarding the relationships we previously had with our male partners, we did love them, and it was a real love for that time in our lives. It wasn't forced, or fake."[5] For this woman, Gilbert's shifting romantic attachments, like her own, were part of a broader, and never-ending personal journey of "becoming."[6]

Gilbert, Melton, and the growing list of famous women like them who have begun same-sex relationships after years of marriage or partnership with men, are emblematic of the cultural embrace of female sexual fluidity.[7] Psychology professor Lisa Diamond, in her book *Sexual Fluidity: Understanding Women's Love and Desire* (2008), was the first to introduce many people to the concept of female sexual fluidity—that is, the idea that women's sexual desires are more likely to shift over the course of their lives in ways that defy stable identity categories.[8] Citing Gilbert's and Melton's cases, a recent article in *Cosmopolitan* magazine asked, "Is Sexual Fluidity Actually on the Rise?" Rather than examining the topic as some titillating and exotic new form of sexuality, the article's author attempted to demystify the concept. She described how she had dated men exclusively before falling in love with a woman, and how neither the term "gay" nor "bisexual" really fit her experiences. "That gray area is where the concept of sexual fluidity stems from," she explained. "Attractions can swing back and forth—sometimes once or twice in a lifetime, other times more frequently." In concluding, the author applauded the extent to which the public conversation around fluidity has helped to make it more common and socially acceptable.[9] British psychotherapist Susie Orbach responded to the news of Gilbert's relationship with Elias similarly, by praising the extent to which female sexual fluidity has become more visible. According to Orbach, who is now partnered with a woman after years of living and raising two children with a man, "We are finally beginning to recognize that sexuality is neither a binary nor fixed. . . . That, as their complexity is opened up to us, the crudity of realising you were always gay or always straight is for many people a nonsense."[10] As the ongoing public conversation around female sexual fluidity suggests, today's wives who desire women do not face nearly the same pressure to choose between bisexuality and lesbianism, or even between marriage and divorce, as they once did.

This more flexible, open-ended understanding of wives' sexual identities, as well as their life choices, emerged long before Gilbert's and Melton's recent sexual revelations, in memoirs and self-help books targeting wives who desired women. Beginning in the 1990s, a group of female counselors and writers—many of whom had come to recognize their own same-sex desires while married—built a small but significant body of literature dedicated to providing emotional and psychological support for wives who desired women. Among the earliest of these authors were social worker Barbee J. Cassingham and psychologist Sally M. O'Neil. Their book, *And Then I Met This Woman: Previously Married Women's Journeys into Lesbian Relationships* (1993), includes dozens of interviews with a range of mostly white middle-class women who left their marriages in the 1970s and 1980s, and who struggled to find a place for themselves in the lesbian world.[11] Two years later, after recognizing the dearth of coming out stories like their own, two formerly married lesbian mothers, Deborah Abbott and Ellen Farmer, published *From Wedded Wife to Lesbian Life: Stories of Transformation* (1995), a collection of personal essays, poems, and interviews about a more racially, economically, and politically diverse group of women.[12] Wife and mother Carren Strock was similarly motivated to write about wives who desire women after coming out as a lesbian in 1990, after twenty-five years of marriage. Her book, *Married Women Who Love Women* (1998), a group biography and self-help guide now in its second edition, provides concrete advice for wives who desire women, interspersed with Strock's reflections about her experiences and excerpts from interviews with women like her.[13]

Perhaps the most influential of these authors is Joanne Fleisher, who appeared on the "Wives Who Confess They Are Gay" episode of *The Oprah Winfrey Show* in 2006.[14] After coming out as a lesbian and leaving her own marriage in the late 1970s, Fleisher became a clinical social worker and began treating married women attracted to other women through individual counseling sessions and wives' support groups at her private practice in Philadelphia. As her reputation grew, she began counseling women over the phone and even traveling across the country to provide weekend conferences for wives who desire women. Eventually, she created a website, Lavender Visions, where women could contact her with their questions. By the time Fleisher was invited to appear on *The Oprah Winfrey Show*, her book, *Living Two Lives: Married to a Man and in Love with a Woman* (2005), had been published by the LGBT publisher Alyson Books. Since then, Fleisher has published a second edition of her book, contributed a half dozen articles to the *Huffington Post* about the challenges faced by wives who desire women, and created an online, public message board (Ask Joanne) where wives who recognize their feelings for other women can provide support directly to one another.[15]

The women featured in these books do not all identify as lesbian. Though several of the titles mentioned include the word "lesbian," most authors are careful not to label the sexual identities of the women they discuss. Strock, for instance, refers to the women in her study as "married women who love women," or "MWLW." While some of the women in these books claim the identity "lesbian" happily and publicly, many admit to having a more ambivalent relationship with the label and with the lesbian community. Some describe themselves as lesbian while admitting to enjoying sex with men; some identify as bisexual; others continue to think of themselves as primarily heterosexual; and yet others disavow sexual identity labels altogether. "I have struggled with the term 'lesbian,'" Jan of *And Then I Met This Woman* explains. "I simply don't like having a label. I'm the same person, but I happen to love a woman."[16] Years before Diamond's *Sexual Fluidity* attracted widespread media attention, several of the books described here encouraged married women to accept the unstable and ambiguous nature of their sexuality rather than assume that their fundamental desire for women had simply been "repressed."[17]

Likewise, while the stories of wives who leave their marriages for other women certainly predominate this literature, none of the books listed here presents divorce as the single or best option. In *Living Two Lives*, for example, Fleisher directly challenges the idea that wives can choose only between remaining married or getting divorced. "In reality, women find many different solutions to their dilemma," she explains. "If you can imagine a solution, then it's a possibility."[18] Having an "in-house separation," recommitting to marriage, putting off divorce until children are grown, or having an open marriage are all options she discusses.[19] And in *Married Women Who Love Women*, Strock, who was still married and living amicably with her husband at the time she published her book, emphasized repeatedly that wives who come to recognize their attraction to women *do not* have to divorce. "I didn't believe those who told me, 'You have to leave your marriage,' " she writes. "I remembered the love and the caring we once had for each other, and I refused to throw away those things I held dear. . . . So, I set about to find another way to make my marriage work."[20] In many ways, such writers are responding to and rejecting the moral emphasis that earlier lesbian feminists placed on separating from men and getting divorced.

Drawing on a combination of popular psychology, self-help culture, and New Age spirituality, this literature almost uniformly describes wives who desire women as "traveling" on personal "paths" or "journeys" toward greater self-understanding, more honest and intimate relationships, and generally happier lives. These books also routinely stress the importance of "authenticity" or being "true" to oneself in a way that is clearly indebted to humanistic psychology and the human potential movement. "Good luck on your path. May you meet many travelers who are ready for your truth," the foreword to *Living Two Lives* concludes.[21] Carroll of *And Then I Met This Woman* explains similarly, "Part of coming out is a spiritual commitment to being one's true self. It's making a choice for authenticity and growth."[22] Likewise, Strock emphasizes the transformational nature of wives' discovery of their "true" sexuality, which she argues often brings other buried feelings to the surface, resulting in a more passionate, fully awakened existence. Some wives, she notes, have even "likened their evolution to having gained a third dimension" to their lives.[23] Reflecting the idea that they are embarking on an epic personal transformation, the women who offer anonymous support to one another on Fleisher's online message board, Ask Joanne, refer to the female crushes or lovers who prompted their reevaluation of their own sexuality as "catalysts," or "C's." Wives who have been through the experience of coming out to their husbands are "on the other side," or "OTOS."[24]

To some extent, however, the language of fluidity, freedom, truth, and authenticity that we can see in self-help literature, online support groups, and even Gilbert's and Melton's Facebook posts, can distract us from the structural challenges and gendered expectations that continue to shape the choices that wives who desire women make. This is not to say that nothing has changed. As we have seen, across the time period I have covered in this work, activists helped to change mainstream attitudes toward lesbianism and bisexuality, to shift cultural representations of wives who desired women, and to improve lesbian mothers' chances of winning child custody in court. While at the beginning of the period covered in this study, most women considered divorce unimaginable, by the 1980s it had become a real legal option, and lesbian mothers had proven that it was possible, although not easy, to raise children in alternative families. Moreover, couples who went public with open, group, or bisexual marriages transformed the meaning of married life, making it easier for wives to balance marriage and lesbian relationships more honestly and transparently. Yet scholars of women's history often focus on positive changes and transformations in the past with regard to women's rights and social movements, disguising the more depressing reality of patriarchy's relatively unblemished historical continuity.[25] For example, while mothers' participation in the labor force has increased significantly since the 1950s, women's hourly wages still lag behind those of men, and men still earn more than women in a majority of married and partnered couples.[26] This persistent economic inequality inevitably shapes the choices that wives who desire women make. Likewise, despite the gains that have been made in gay and lesbian parents' custody cases, in the absence of a rule holding that sexual orientation is not relevant to child custody cases *at all*, lesbian and bisexual mothers will remain at risk of losing their kids.[27]

Where, then, do wives who desire women ultimately stand today? On the one hand, they have at their disposal tools that were entirely unavailable to women in the past: counselors and self-help books devoted to supporting wives who desire women without dictating any one clear "right" path or identity label; online message boards that allow them to communicate with and support each other immediately and anonymously across unknown distances; and, of course, the possibility of legally marrying their female lovers and securing, without men, the social and economic benefits that marriage entails. At the same time, while the stigmatization of lesbianism as decreased and the resources available to wives who desire women have grown, many wives' economic dependence on men and legal vulnerability as mothers continues to fundamentally constrain their life options and to give their husbands the upper hand in both marriage and divorce. A 2018 article in the *New York Times*, "When Living Your Truth Can Mean Losing Your Children," about a lesbian mother in Brooklyn who had recently lost custody of her children in state supreme court aptly captures this tension between the heady language of self-help literature and the harsh realities of family law.[28]

While some women, such as Gilbert and Melton, seem to leave their marriages and begin same-sex relationships with relative ease, many wives who lack the privileges of these high-profile women struggle to live the lives they truly want. A reading of Fleisher's online forum suggests that the challenges faced by wives in the 2010s, once they have recognized their desires for other women, are quite similar to those experienced by their predecessors. To begin with, women's sense of responsibility to their children clearly continues to tether them to marriage. As one young mother explained in 2016, "I decided that the time simply isn't right for me just yet to come out. I have lots of very little children and my H [husband] and I coparent well. . . . Perhaps we can unpick this situation in a few years' time, but for now, we are making it work."[29] And, as in the past, husbands who are accepting of their wives' attraction to women during their marriage often become more combative in the process of divorce. One formerly married woman shared her experiences as a warning to a wife who was considering coming out to her verbally abusive husband: "My ex husband—who was my best friend & confidant for almost 15 years—turned on me during our divorce & claimed that I lied about my sexual ID when we were married. . . . As a bi woman who has always been OUT (especially to him), this claim was absurd. Do not underestimate the potential cruelty that your partner's attorney could unleash & do NOT provide them with ammunition to be used against you."[30]

My own conversations with women who came to recognize their same-sex desires in the 1990s and early 2000s suggest that many wives continue to navigate their marriages and their feelings for other women in very familiar ways. Some remain in unhappy marriages and quietly engage in sexual relationships with other women until their children are grown, or until they feel legally and economically prepared for divorce.[31] Others more openly negotiate space in their marriages for their same-sex desires. Some women are lucky enough to find understanding men who are willing to remake their marriages in innovative and egalitarian ways. One wife I spoke with has lived in a house next door to her husband in Michigan since the late 1990s. Both spouses have engaged in same-sex relationships, but they have remained legally married for economic and emotional reasons.[32] More often, though, husbands remain willing to tolerate their wives' relationships with other women only so long so long as those outside relationships do not get in the way of their own needs. The husband of one woman in Pennsylvania I spoke with was strikingly supportive of her feelings for women and even helped her to start a support group for wives who desired women in the early 1990s. This woman went on to have a serious relationship with another married woman, with her husband's knowledge and permission, but as soon as she refused to continue sleeping with her husband, he became less tolerant. Eventually, like so many other estranged husbands, he used evidence of her same-sex relationship in his child custody case against her.[33]

The concept of sexual fluidity and the new therapeutic emphasis on "living one's truth" are powerfully appealing and clearly resonate with many women. But they cannot help us to understand the enduring structures of oppression that continue to bind so many women to their marriages, whether redefined or not. While the blogs and books described here surely provide much needed validation, support, and inspiration to wives who desire women, they may also inadvertently imply that wives are at liberty to create their lives as they choose, unhampered by economic need, social stigmatization, or legal discrimation. This literature often suggests that with enough love, courage, and persistence, wives who desire women can remake their lives however they see fit. But doing so risks making the challenges faced by the women reading this literature appear internal rather than external—the results of their own personal failures and shortcomings rather than broader issues of social and political inequality.[34] Indeed, the specific guidance and advice that most self-help books offer is highly individualized and often banal: find a therapist or a marital counselor, keep a journal, analyze your own motivations, be honest with yourself and others, weigh your decisions carefully, don't let your fear control you. Yet legal and financial resources, in addition to courage and emotional support, are necessary to escape an unhappy or abusive marriage. And these personal coping tactics will do little to change the situation for wives who desire women as a whole.

As *Her Neighbor's Wife* has shown, wives struggling with these issues today are part of a much longer history and a much broader population than the contemporary media's focus on a handful of well-known women would make it seem. Indeed, when seen through the lives of wives who desired women, the histories of marriage and homosexuality in the second half of the twentieth century appear far less distinct than we typically imagine. The women's stories captured in this book reveal how marriage and lesbian communities have been mutually constituted and deeply intertwined. Their experiences should give us pause before assuming the straightness of any marriage between a man and a woman, particularly those that began before the emergence of the gay liberation and lesbian feminist movements. Long before the federal legalization of gay marriage was imaginable, the wives in this book found ways to act on their desires for other women. They negotiated with their spouses, through words spoken and silences sustained, an array of sexual and romantic configurations that defied expectation. Their actions tell us about the multiple meanings of marriage as well as the shifting contours of lesbian and bisexual identity. Lost in the continuing debates over gay marriage is the fact that limiting marriage to one man and one woman never truly assured the institution's heterosexuality. It never prevented husbands or wives from expressing same-sex desires, engaging in same-sex relationships, or connecting with broader queer communities. The state may legislate marriage, but the sexual desires and romantic attachments of those within it will always evade control.

BP	Dorothy and Howard Baker Papers, Stanford University Libraries, Stanford, CA
BWHBC	Boston Women's Health Book Collective, SL
DLLP	Documenting Lesbian Lives Oral History Project, SSC
DLP	Doris ("Blue") Lunden Papers, LHA
GLBTHS	GLBT Historical Society, San Francisco, CA
GLP	Barbara Gittings and Kay Lahusen Papers, NYPL
HP	Lorraine Hansberry Papers, SC
HSC	Human Sexuality Collection, Cornell University Library, Ithaca, NY
JLP	Julie Lee Papers, LHA
LHA	Lesbian Herstory Archives, Brooklyn, NY
LMP	Phyllis Lyon and Del Martin Papers, GLBTHS
LP	Ellen Lewin Papers, GLBTHS
MC	Mattachine Society Project Collection, NGLA
MP	Isabel Miller Papers, SSC
NGLA	ONE National Gay and Lesbian Archives, University of Southern California Libraries, Los Angeles, CA
NYPL	New York Public Library, New York, NY
OHC	GLBT Historical Society Oral History Collection, GLBTHS
OLP	Old Lesbian Oral Herstory Project Records, SSC
OR	ONE Inc. Records, NGLA
RP	Adrienne Rich Papers, SL
SC	Schomburg Center for Research in Black Culture, New York, NY
SL	Arthur and Elizabeth Schlesinger Library, Radcliffe Institute for Advanced Study, Harvard University, Cambridge, MA
SSC	Sophia Smith Collection, Smith College, Northampton, MA

TF   Rochella Thorpe Oral History Project Files, HSC
VFP   Voices of Feminism Oral History Project, SSC
VTP   Valerie Taylor Papers, HSC
WBP   Warner Bros. Archive of Historical Papers, University of
            California School of Cinematic Arts, Los Angeles, CA
WWP   World War II Project Papers, GLBTHS

NOTES

Introduction

1. Alma Routsong, diary entry, October 31, 1961, typed diary entries, box 13, folder 1, MP, accession no. 07S-39.

2. Elisabeth Deran, "Patience and Sarah Come to Life," appendix in *Patience and Sarah*, by Isabel Miller [Alma Routsong] (Vancouver: Arsenal Pulp Press, 2005), 207–214, at 207.

3. In her secret diary, Alma repeatedly referenced Bruce's lover, whom she hoped he would marry after they divorced. See, for example, Alma Routsong, diary entry, November 26, 1961, box 13, folder 1, MP, accession no. 07S-39.

4. Ibid.

5. Isabel Miller [Alma Routsong], "Strangers in Camelot," in *A Dooryard Full of Flowers and Other Short Pieces* (Tallahassee, FL: Naiad Press, 1993), 81–94. Deran notes that this short story was a retelling of their experiences in Washington, DC, in Deran, "Patience and Sarah Come to Life."

6. Isabel Miller, *A Place for Us* (New York: Bleeker Street Press, 1969); Isabel Miller, *Patience and Sarah* (New York: McGraw-Hill, 1972). For scholarly analyses of the book see, for example, Bonnie Zimmerman, *The Safe Sea of Women: Lesbian Fiction, 1969–1989* (Boston: Beacon Press, 1990), xii.

7. For discussions of women who left their marriages in the 1970s, see John D'Emilio and Estelle B. Freedman, *Intimate Matters: A History of Sexuality in America* (Chicago: University of Chicago Press, 1997), 316; Lillian Faderman, *Odd Girls and Twilight Lovers: A History of Lesbian Life in Twentieth-Century America* (New York: Columbia University Press, 1991), 208–209; Arlene Stein, *Sex and Sensibility: Stories of a Lesbian Generation* (Berkeley: University of California Press, 1997), 40; and Ruth Rosen, *The World Split Open: How the Modern Women's Movement Changed America* (New York: Penguin, 2000), 170–171. The following studies include discussions of married women who were able to participate in postwar lesbian communities: Elizabeth Lapovsky Kennedy and Madeline D. Davis, *Boots of Leather, Slippers of Gold: The History of a Lesbian Community* (New York: Penguin, 1994), 336–345; Esther Newton, *Cherry Grove, Fire Island: Sixty Years in America's First Gay and Lesbian Town* (Boston: Beacon Press, 1993), 38 and chap. 8. Important recent studies in which wives who desired women play a major part include: Daniel Winunwe Rivers, *Radical Relations: Lesbian Mothers, Gay Fathers, and Their Children in the United States Since World War II* (Chapel Hill: University of North Carolina Press, 2013); Alison Lefkovitz, "'The Peculiar Anomaly': Same-Sex Infidelity in Postwar Divorce Courts," *Law and History Review* 33, no. 3 (August 2015): 665–

701. For scholars who have paid much more attention to the same-sex desires and relationships of married women *before* the postwar period, see Carroll Smith-Rosenberg, "The Female World of Love and Ritual: Relations Between Women in Nineteenth-Century America," *Signs* 1, no.1 (Autumn 1975): 1–29; Lillian Faderman, *Surpassing the Love of Men: Romantic Friendship and Love Between Women from the Renaissance to the Present* (New York: William Morrow and Company, 1981); Blanche Wiesen Cook, *Eleanor Roosevelt:* vol. 2, *1933–1938* (New York: Viking, 1999); and Lisa Cohen, *All We Know: Three Lives* (New York: Farrar, Straus and Giroux, 2012). In the British context, see Martha Vicinus, *Intimate Friends: Women Who Loved Women, 1778–1928* (Chicago: University of Chicago Press, 2004); Sharon Marcus, *Between Women: Friendship, Desire, and Marriage in Victorian England* (Princeton, NJ: Princeton University Press, 2007).

8. For a further discussion of my methodology and experiences conducting these interviews, see Lauren Jae Gutterman, " 'Not My Proudest Moment': Guilt, Regret, and the Coming-Out Narrative," *Oral History Review* 46, no. 1 (Winter/Spring 2019): 48–70.

9. Specifically, I use interviews in the Ellen Lewin Papers (cited as LP), Allan Bérubé's World War II Project Papers (cited as WWP) and the GLBT Historical Society Oral History Collection (cited as OHC), all at the GLBT Historical Society (cited as GLBTHS). I also use interviews in the Voices of Feminism Oral History Project (VFP), the Documenting Lesbian Lives Oral History Project (DLLP), and Arden Eversmeyer's Old Lesbian Oral Herstory Project Records (OLP) at the Sophia Smith Collection (SSC) at Smith College. I also use interviews in the Rochella Thorpe Oral History Project Files (TF) in the Human Sexuality Collection (HSC) at Cornell University.

10. On the limitations and potential of queer oral history, see Nan Alamilla Boyd, "Who Is the Subject? Queer Theory Meets Oral History," *Journal of the History of Sexuality*, 17, no. 2 (May 2008): 177–189; Nan Alamilla Boyd and Horacio N. Roque Ramírez, *Bodies of Evidence: The Practice of Queer Oral History* (Oxford: Oxford University Press, 2012).

11. On coming out narratives, see Kenneth Plummer, *Telling Sexual Stories: Power, Change, and Social Worlds* (London: Routledge, 1995), chap. 6.

12. Biddy Martin, "Lesbian Identity and Autobiographical Difference(s)," in *Femininity Played Straight: The Significance of Being Lesbian* (New York: Routledge, 1996), 137–162.

13. Adrienne Rich, "Compulsory Heterosexuality and Lesbian Existence," *Signs* 5, no. 4 (Summer 1980): 631–660, at 654.

14. Dorothy Baker to Alma Routsong, January 13, 1964, p. 2, correspondence CD-ROM, Dorothy Baker to Miller, 1946–64, MP, accession no. 09S-46.

15. Alma Routsong, diary entry, March 9, 1991, box 1, no folder, MP, accession no. 09S-33.

16. Historical studies of urban queer communities include: Kennedy and Davis, *Boots of Leather*; George Chauncey, *Gay New York: Gender, Urban Culture, and the Making of the Gay Male World, 1890–1940* (New York: Basic Books, 1994); Marc Stein, *City of Sisterly and Brotherly Loves: Lesbian and Gay Philadelphia, 1945–1972* (Chicago: University of Chicago Press, 2000); Nan Alamilla Boyd, *Wide Open Town: A History of Queer San Francisco to 1965* (Berkeley: University of California Press, 2003); Lillian Faderman and Stuart Timmons, *Gay L.A.: A History of Sexual Outlaws, Power Politics, and Lipstick Lesbians* (New York: Basic Books, 2006); Daniel Hurewitz, *Bohemian Los Angeles and the Making of Modern Politics* (Berkeley: University of California Press, 2007); Kwame A. Holmes, "Chocolate to Rainbow City: The Dialectics

of Black and Gay Community Formation in Postwar Washington, D.C., 1946–1978" (PhD diss., University of Illinois, 2011); Genny Beemyn, *A Queer Capital: A History of Gay Life in Washington, D.C.* (New York: Routledge, 2015); Timothy Stewart-Winter, *Queer Clout: Chicago and the Rise of Gay Politics* (Philadelphia: University of Pennsylvania Press, 2016); and Julio Capó Jr., *Welcome to Fairyland: Queer Miami Before 1940* (Chapel Hill: University of North Carolina Press, 2017).

17. Other historians have attempted to broaden the geography of LGBT history beyond urban areas. On the history of queer life in the suburbs, see Tim Retzloff, "Gay Organizing in the 'Desert of Suburbia' of Metropolitan Detroit," in *Making Suburbia: New Histories of Everyday America*, ed. John Archer, Paul J. P. Sandul, and Katherine Solomonson (Minneapolis: University of Minnesota Press, 2015), 51–62. On rural queer history, see John Howard, *Men Like That: A Southern Queer History* (Chicago: University of Chicago Press, 1999); E. Patrick Johnson, *Sweet Tea: Black Gay Men of the South* (Chapel Hill: University of North Carolina Press, 2008); Brock Thompson, *The Un-Natural State: Arkansas and the Queer South* (Fayetteville: University of Arkansas Press, 2010); and Colin R. Johnson, *Just Queer Folks: Gender and Sexuality in Rural America* (Philadelphia: Temple University Press, 2013).

18. On the discrimination gays and lesbians faced after World War II, see John D'Emilio, *Sexual Politics, Sexual Communities: The Making of a Homosexual Minority in the United States, 1940–1970* (Chicago: University of Chicago Press, 1998), chap. 3; Estelle B. Freedman, "'Uncontrolled Desires': The Response to the Sexual Psychopath, 1920–1960," *Journal of American History* 74, no. 1 (June 1987): 83–106; Jennifer Terry, *An American Obsession: Science, Medicine, and Homosexuality in Modern Society* (Chicago: University of Chicago Press, 1999), chap. 11; David K. Johnson, *The Lavender Scare: The Cold War Persecution of Gays and Lesbians in the Federal Government* (Chicago: University of Chicago Press, 2004); and Margot Canaday, *The Straight State: Sexuality and Citizenship in Twentieth-Century America* (Princeton, NJ: Princeton University Press, 2009).

19. Of the thousands of gay and lesbian GIs dishonorably discharged from the army during World War II, the vast majority were men. Similarly, those fired from the State Department in its initial attack on suspected homosexual employees were almost all men, and far fewer women than men were arrested at midcentury for homosexual behavior. See Allan Bérubé, *Coming Out Under Fire: Gay Men and Women in World War Two* (New York: Free Press, 1990), 201; Johnson, *Lavender Scare*, 12; and Alfred Kinsey, Wardell B. Pomeroy, Clyde E. Martin, and Paul H. Gebhard, *Sexual Behavior in the Human Female* (Philadelphia: Saunders, 1953), 484–485.

20. Canaday, *Straight State*, 13.

21. Lefkovitz, "Peculiar Anomaly," esp. 667–669.

22. Canaday, *Straight State*, chap. 5. Valerie Traub makes a similar argument about the stigmatization of erotic relationships between women in a very different time and place; see Valerie Traub, *The Renaissance of Lesbianism in Early Modern England* (Cambridge: Cambridge University Press, 2002), 181.

23. Nan D. Hunter and Nancy D. Polikoff, "Custody Rights of Lesbian Mothers: Legal Theory and Litigation Strategy," *Buffalo Law Review* 25, no. 3 (Spring 1976): 691–734, at 692. On the policing of lesbian mothers' sexuality, see Rivers, *Radical Relations*, 229n8.

24. Terry Castle, *The Apparitional Lesbian: Female Homosexuality and Modern Culture* (New York: Columbia University Press, 1993), 2.

25. Historian and theorist David Halperin's genealogical model of how to "do" the history of homosexuality has influenced a generation of scholarship, but scholars have not heeded as closely his call to examine the history of sexuality between women separately from that between men. As Halperin wrote nearly two decades ago, "To see the historical dimensions of the social construction of same-sex relations among women, we need a new optic that will reveal specific historical variations in a phenomenon that necessarily exists in a constant and inescapable relation to the institutionalized structures of male dominance." David M. Halperin, "The First Homosexuality?," in *How to Do the History of Homosexuality* (Chicago: University of Chicago Press, 2002), 48–80, at 79.

26. Betty Deran, interview by Len Evans, May 7, 1983, p. 17, box 1, folder 21, OHC.

27. Several scholars have examined the flexibility or "play" built into marriage in the United States and Europe in earlier time periods. See, for example, Alan Bray, *The Friend* (Chicago: University of Chicago Press, 2003); Marcus, *Between Women*; Timothy Stewart-Winter and Simon Stern, "Picturing Same-Sex Marriage in the Antebellum United States: The Union of 'Two Most Excellent Men' in Longstreet's 'A Sage Conversation,'" *Journal of the History of Sexuality* 19, no. 2 (May 2010): 197–222; Rachel Hope Cleves, *Charity and Sylvia: A Same-Sex Marriage in Early America* (New York: Oxford University Press, 2014); and Rachel Hope Cleves, "'What, Another Female Husband?': The Prehistory of Same-Sex Marriage in America," *Journal of American History* 101, no. 4 (March 2015): 1055–1081.

28. On the federal government's explicit sexual categorization of men and women in the military, welfare policy, and immigration law, see Canaday, *Straight State*.

29. On the history of anti-miscegenation laws, see Peggy Pascoe, *What Comes Naturally: Miscegenation Law and the Making of Race in America* (Oxford: Oxford University Press, 2009).

30. George Chauncey makes a similar argument about the wave of antigay policing in New York City in the 1920s and 1930s. See Chauncey, *Gay New York*, 9.

31. On the spread of information about transsexuality in the postwar era, see Joanne Meyerowitz, *How Sex Changed: A History of Transsexuality in the United States* (Cambridge, MA: Harvard University Press, 2002).

32. Serena Mayeri, "Marital Supremacy and the Constitution of the Nonmarital Family," *California Law Review* 103, no. 5 (October 2015): 1277–1352.

33. Michel Foucault, *The History of Sexuality*, vol. 1, *An Introduction*, trans. Robert Hurley (New York: Random House, 1990), 69–70.

34. Howard, *Men Like That*, xvii. On the limitations of the modern hetero/homo binary, see also Regina G. Kunzel, *Criminal Intimacy: Prison and the Uneven History of Modern American Sexuality* (Chicago: University of Chicago Press, 2008); Nayan Shah, *Stranger Intimacy: Contesting Race, Sexuality and Law in the North American West* (Berkeley: University of California Press, 2011).

35. Respondent #105, interview by Terrie Lyons, p. 14, box 1, folder 105, LP; emphasis in the original.

36. Phoenix Wheeler, interview by Arden Eversmeyer, March 24, 2006, pp. 22–23, OLP.

37. Respondent #104, interview by Terrie Lyons, p. 33, box 1, folder 104, LP.

38. See David M. Halperin, "Forgetting Foucault: Acts, Identities, and the History of Sexuality," *Representations*, no. 63 (Summer 1998): 93–120, at 109.

39. Steven Angelides, *A History of Bisexuality* (Chicago: University of Chicago Press, 2001), 93–94.

40. Linda Francke, "Bisexual Chic: Anyone Goes," *Newsweek*, May 27, 1974, 90.

41. Martha Vicinus, "Lesbian History: All Theory and No Facts or All Facts and No Theory?," *Radical History Review*, no. 60 (Fall 1994): 57–75.

42. On women's domestic containment in the postwar period, see Elaine Tyler May, *Homeward Bound: The American Family in the Cold War Era* (New York: Basic Books, 2008).

43. Here I heed Susan Lanser's call to pay greater attention to the ways women have "exploited heteronormative economies" while operating within them. Susan S. Lanser, *The Sexuality of History: Modernity and the Sapphic, 1565–1830* (Chicago: University of Chicago Press, 2014), 7.

Chapter 1

1. Adrienne Rich, journal entry, January 29, 1950, carton 2, folder 40, RP. Rich's ideas here reflected the intense pressure to marry that Radcliffe women experienced at this moment; see Beth L. Bailey, *From Front Porch to Back Seat: Courtship in Twentieth-Century America* (Baltimore: Johns Hopkins University Press, 1988), 44–46.

2. Adrienne Rich, journal entry, May 8, 1952, carton 2, folder 41, RP.

3. Adrienne Rich to Helen and Arnold Rich, November 9, 1948, p. 3, carton 4, folder 91, RP.

4. Adrienne Rich to Helen and Arnold Rich, October 21, 1948, carton 4, folder 91, RP.

5. Adrienne Rich, journal entry, January 11, 1952, carton 2, folder 41, RP. See Alfred Douglas, "Two Loves," in *Penguin Book of Homosexual Verse*, ed. Stephen Coote (Harmondsworth, UK: Penguin Books, 1983), 262–264, esp. 264.

6. Steven D. McLaughlin, Barbara D. Melber, John O. G. Billy, Denise M. Zimmerle, Linda D. Winges, and Terry R. Johnson, *The Changing Lives of American Women* (Chapel Hill: University of North Carolina Press, 1988), 56.

7. William Chafe, *The American Woman: Her Changing Social, Economic and Political Roles, 1920–1970* (London: Oxford University Press, 1974), 217.

8. Lois G. Gordon and Alan Gordon, *American Chronicle: Seven Decades in American Life, 1920–1989* (New York: Crown, 1990), 399.

9. Jean Benge and Eugene Benge, *Win Your Man and Keep Him* (Chicago: Windsor Press, 1948), 24.

10. Adrienne Rich, journal entry, January 29, 1950, carton 2, folder 40, RP.

11. On *Playboy* magazine and the glamorization of the urban bachelor, see Barbara Ehrenreich, *The Hearts of Men: American Dreams and the Flight from Commitment* (New York: Anchor Press/Doubleday, 1983), chap. 4; Elizabeth Fraterrigo, *Playboy and the Making of the Good Life in Modern America* (Oxford: Oxford University Press, 2009). On the pressure to marry in this period, see May, *Homeward Bound*; Stephanie Coontz, *Marriage, a History: From Obedience to Intimacy or How Love Conquered Marriage* (New York: Viking, 2005), chap. 14; Kristin Celello, *Making Marriage Work: A History of Marriage and Divorce in the Twentieth-Century United States* (Chapel Hill: University of North Carolina Press, 2009), chap. 3; and Rebecca L. Davis, *More Perfect Unions: The American Search for Marital Bliss* (Cambridge, MA: Harvard University Press, 2010), chap. 3.

12. Julia Kirk Blackwelder, *Now Hiring: The Feminization of Work in the United States, 1900–1995* (College Station: Texas A&M University Press, 1997), 152.

13. US Department of Labor, *1975 Handbook on Women Workers*, Women's Bureau Bulletin 297 (Washington, DC: Government Printing Office, 1975), 4. For more on women's

workforce participation during and after the war, see William Chafe, *The Paradox of Change: American Women in the 20th Century* (New York: Oxford University Press, 1991); Karen Anderson, *Wartime Women: Sex Roles, Family Relations, and the Status of Women During World War II* (Westport, CT: Greenwood Press, 1981); and Alice Kessler-Harris, *Out to Work: A History of Wage-Earning Women in the United States* (New York: Oxford University Press, 1982), chaps. 10 and 11.

14. John D'Emilio, "Gay Politics and Community in San Francisco Since World War II," in *Hidden from History: Reclaiming the Gay and Lesbian Past*, ed. Martin Duberman, Martha Vicinus, and George Chauncey Jr. (New York: Penguin Group, 1990), 458.

15. On officials' willingness to overlook or reenlist homosexuals, see Bérubé, *Coming Out Under Fire*, 179–183. On "undesirable" discharges see, Bérubé, *Coming Out Under Fire*, chap. 8; Canaday, *Straight State*, chap. 4. On the number of undesirable discharges during the war, see Bérubé, *Coming Out Under Fire*, 147.

16. US Senate, 81st Cong., 2d sess., Committee on Expenditures in Executive Departments, *Employment of Homosexuals and Other Sex Perverts in Government* (Washington, DC: Government Printing Office, 1950), 4. See Johnson, *Lavender Scare*; D'Emilio, *Sexual Politics*, 40–49.

17. On the discrimination gays and lesbians faced after World War II, see D'Emilio, *Sexual Politics*, chap. 3; Freedman, "Uncontrolled Desires"; John D'Emilio, "The Homosexual Menace: The Politics of Sexuality in Cold War America," in *Passion and Power: Sexuality in History*, ed. Kathy Peiss and Christina Simmons (Philadelphia: Temple University Press, 1989), 226–240; Terry, *American Obsession*, chap. 11; and Johnson, *Lavender Scare*.

18. See Lanser, *Sexuality of History*, 17.

19. For a critique of the essentializing nature of lesbian coming out stories and autobiographical narratives, see Martin, "Lesbian Identity."

20. Linda, interview by Rochella Thorpe, August 28, 1992, p. 6, box 2, folder 2, TF.

21. Respondent #212, interview by Terrie Lyons, p. 13, box 2, folder 212, LP. All of the interviews in the Ellen Lewin Papers (LP) collection were conducted between 1977 and 1979 for a study of lesbian mothers. Exact dates are unavailable. Any names provided in the text for respondents in this study are pseudonyms of my own creation. For more about this project, see Ellen Lewin, *Lesbian Mothers: Accounts of Gender in American Culture* (Ithaca, NY: Cornell University Press, 1993).

22. Lee Rainwater, *And the Poor Get Children: Sex, Contraception, and Family Planning in the Working Class* (Chicago: Quadrangle Books, 1960), 64–65.

23. Susan K. Freeman, *Sex Goes to School: Girls and Sex Education Before the 1960s* (Urbana: University of Illinois Press, 2008), 4, 44.

24. Sandy Warshaw, interview by the author, May 10, 2010.

25. Marjory Nelson, interview by Kate Weigand, May 18–19, 2005, p. 13, VFP.

26. Philip Wylie, *Generation of Vipers* (New York: Farrar and Rinehart, 1942). See also Edward A. Strecker, *Their Mothers' Sons: The Psychiatrist Examines an American Problem* (Philadelphia: Lippincott, 1946); Ferdinand Lundberg and Marynia F. Farnham, *Modern Woman: The Lost Sex* (New York: Harper and Brothers, 1947). On masculinity and the Cold War, see Robert L. Griswold, "The 'Flabby' American, the Body and the Cold War," in *A Shared Experience: Men, Women and the History of Gender*, ed. Laura McCall and Donald Yacovone (New York: New York University Press, 1998), 323–348; Robert D. Dean, *Imperial*

Brotherhood: Gender and the Making of Cold War Foreign Policy (Amherst: University of Massachusetts Press, 2003); and K. A. Cuordileone, *Manhood and American Political Culture in the Cold War* (New York: Routledge, 2005).

27. Rebecca Jo Plant, *Mom: The Transformation of Motherhood in Modern America* (Chicago: University of Chicago, 2010).

28. Betty Friedan, *The Feminine Mystique* (New York: W. W. Norton, 1983), 276.

29. Kinsey et al., *Sexual Behavior in the Human Female*; on "homosexual play," see 113; for statistics on girls who engaged in homosexual versus heterosexual play, see table 11, figure 5, and 107; on the percentage of girls who engaged in vaginal penetration and genital exhibitions, see 114.

30. Ruth Debra, interview by Arden Eversmeyer, January 20, 2009, pp. 4–5, OLP.

31. Alta Fly, interview by Arden Eversmeyer, March 23, 2006, p. 9, OLP.

32. Jill Johnston, *Lesbian Nation: The Feminist Solution* (New York: Simon and Schuster, 1974), 59.

33. Respondent #220, interview by Terrie Lyons, p. 29, box 2, folder 220, LP. For a similar example, see Respondent #207, interview by Terrie Lyons, p. 16, box 2, folder 207, LP.

34. Kennedy and Davis, *Boots of Leather*, 336.

35. Linda, interview by Rochella Thorpe, August 28, 1992, pp. 4–5, 7, box 2, folder 2, TF.

36. For statistics on premarital sex, see Robert R. Bell, *Premarital Sex in a Changing Society* (Englewood Cliffs, NJ: Prentice Hall, 1966), 12, 57–58; D'Emilio and Freedman, *Intimate Matters*, chaps. 11 and 12. On wartime concerns about sexual promiscuity, see Allan M. Brandt, *No Magic Bullet: A Social History of Venereal Disease in the United States Since 1880* (New York: Oxford University Press, 1985), chap. 5; Marilyn E. Hegarty, *Victory Girls, Khaki-Wackies, and Patriotutes: The Regulation of Female Sexuality During World War II* (New York: New York University Press, 2008).

37. See Rickie Solinger, *Wake Up Little Susie: Single Pregnancy Before Roe v. Wade* (New York: Routledge, 2000); Regina Kunzel, *Fallen Women, Problem Girls: Unmarried Mothers and the Professionalization of Social Work, 1890–1945* (New Haven, CT: Yale University Press, 1993).

38. See Amanda H. Littauer, *Bad Girls: Young Women, Sex, and Rebellion Before the Sixties* (Chapel Hill: University of North Carolina Press, 2015), 153–154.

39. Shirley Maser, interview by Arden Eversmeyer, November 29, 2009, p. 2, OLP. See also Respondent #110, interview by Terrie Lyons, p. 13, box 1, folder 101, LP.

40. Wini Breines, *Young, White, and Miserable: Growing Up Female in the Fifties* (Chicago: University of Chicago Press, 2001), 118.

41. Nancy Sahli, "Smashing: Women's Relationships Before the Fall," *Chrysalis: A Magazine of Women's Culture*, no. 8 (Summer 1979): 17–27; Martha Vicinus, "Distance and Desire: English Boarding School Friendships, 1870–1920," in Duberman et al., *Hidden from History*, 212–229.

42. Girls who engaged in relationships with older women were particularly likely to describe these relationships in romantic terms. See, for example, Elizabeth "Betty" Shoemaker, interview by Arden Eversmeyer, January n.d., 2001, p. 15, OLP; Sally Duplaix, interview by Arden Eversmeyer, May n.d., 2001, pp. 15–16, OLP.

43. Alma Routsong, diary entry, June 13, 1942, box 9, no folder, MP, accession no. 07S-39.

44. Pat Parker, "Funny," in *Movement in Black*, expanded ed. (Ithaca, NY: Firebrand Books, 1999), 207–211, at 211.

45. For more on psychiatric understandings of homosexuality at midcentury, see Ronald Bayer, *Homosexuality and American Psychiatry: The Politics of Diagnosis* (New York: Basic Books, 1981) chaps. 1 and 2; Terry, *American Obsession*, chaps. 9 and 10.

46. Sally Duplaix, interview by Arden Eversmeyer, May n.d., 2001, p. 18, OLP.

47. Ibid., pp. 18–19.

48. Ibid., p. 19. On Sally's attempted escape, see Lillian Faderman, *The Gay Revolution: The Story of the Struggle* (New York: Simon and Schuster, 2015), 11–12.

49. Portia "P. J." Fagan, interview by Arden Eversmeyer, February 3, 2006, p. 7, OLP.

50. Ibid., p. 8.

51. Ibid.

52. For a similar story, see Muriel Crisara, interview by Rochella Thorpe, June 23, 1992, p. 48, box 2, folder 7, TF.

53. Virginia "Gini" Morton, interview by Arden Eversmeyer, April n.d., 2003, p. 7, OLP.

54. Ibid., p. 10.

55. Ibid., p. 11.

56. Elizabeth "Deedy" Breed, interview by Arden Eversmeyer, May 23, 2001, p. 10, OLP.

57. Ibid.

58. On the way happiness directs people toward normative life paths, see Sara Ahmed, *The Promise of Happiness* (Durham, NC: Duke University Press, 2010), esp. 59.

59. Coontz, *Marriage, a History*, 313. On Americans' expectations for married life in the postwar era, see also, May, *Homeward Bound*, esp. 13–18 and 31–38; and Jessica Weiss, *To Have and to Hold: Marriage, The Baby Boom, and Social Change* (Chicago: University of Chicago Press, 2000), esp. chap. 1.

60. Otis Stiese, "Live the Life of McCall's," *McCall's*, May 1954, 27.

61. Respondent #309, interview by Terrie Lyons, p. 5, box 3, folder 309, LP.

62. Respondent #112, interview by Terrie Lyons, p. 6, box 1, folder 112, LP.

63. Bea Howard, interview by Arden Eversmeyer, March n.d., 2003, 13, OLP.

64. Achebe Betty Powell, interview by Kelly Anderson, July 6 and 7, 2004, pp. 45–46, VFP. For similar stories, see Respondent #117, interview by Ellen Lewin, box 1, folder 117, LP; Letter to Phyllis Lyon and Del Martin, April 25, 1973, p. 1, box 23, folder 8, LMP.

65. Canaday, *Straight State*, 175. On the discrimination that lesbians faced during the war, see Bérubé, *Coming Out Under Fire*; Leisa D. Meyer, *Creating G.I. Jane: Sexuality and Power in the Women's Army Corps During World War II* (New York: Columbia University Press, 1996).

66. Bérubé, *Coming Out Under Fire*, 20; Canaday, *Straight State*, 197.

67. Respondent #213, interview by Terrie Lyons, p. 6, box 2, folder 213, LP.

68. Ibid. For a similar story, see Beverly Todd, interview by Arden Eversmeyer, April n.d., 2001, p. 4, OLP.

69. Ann Allen, interview by Arden Eversmeyer, March 1, 2008, p. 2, OLP.

70. Larraine Townend to Del Martin and Phyllis Lyon, January 12, 1974, box 25, folder 3, LMP. I have included Larraine Townend's full name here because her identity was revealed in a highly publicized custody battle.

71. Nicholas L. Syrett, *American Child Bride: A History of Minors and Marriage in the United States* (Chapel Hill: University of North Carolina Press, 2016); on teenage marriage rates among white and nonwhite girls at midcentury, see 247–248.

72. Virginia "Gini" Morton, interview by Arden Eversmeyer, April n.d., 2003, p. 4, OLP.

73. For a discussion of the politics of respectability among African American women, see Evelyn Brooks Higginbotham, *Righteous Discontent: The Women's Movement in the Black Baptist Church, 1880–1920* (Cambridge, MA: Harvard University Press, 1994).

74. Thaddeus Russell, "The Color of Discipline: Civil Rights and Black Sexuality," *American Quarterly* 60, no. 1 (March 2008): 101–128. On the earlier acceptance of queer sexual and gender expression in working-class black culture, see Hazel Carby, "It Just Be's Dat Way Sometime: The Sexual Politics of Women's Blues," *Radical America* 20, no. 4 (June–July 1986): 9–22; Eric Garber, "A Spectacle in Color: The Lesbian and Gay Subculture of Jazz Age Harlem," in Duberman et al., *Hidden from History*, 318–331; and Chauncey, *Gay New York*, chap. 9.

75. Gladys Bentley, "I Am a Woman Again," *Ebony*, August 1952, 92–98. See also David Serlin, *Replaceable You: Engineering the Body in Postwar America* (Chicago: University of Chicago Press, 2002), 111–157.

76. Thelma, Diane, J. P., group interview by Rochella Thorpe, n.d., 1992, tape no. tr7937a–tr7943a, TF.

77. See Premilla Nadasen, *Welfare Warriors: The Welfare Rights Movement in the United States* (New York: Routledge, 2005), 6–13.

78. Virginia "Gini" Morton, interview by Arden Eversmeyer, April n.d., 2003, p. 13, OLP.

79. Respondent #218, interview by Ellen Lewin, p. 3, box 2, folder 218, LP.

80. Ibid.

81. Pat Gandy, interview by Arden Eversmeyer, January 7, 2009, p. 9, OLP. For a similar case, see Alta Fly, interview by Arden Eversmeyer, March 23, 2006, p. 35, OLP.

82. Letter to Del Martin and Phyllis Lyon, August 14, 1973, p. 4, box 23, folder 12, LMP. The names of all letter writers from this collection are excluded here. First names provided in the text are pseudonyms of my own creation.

83. Ibid., p. 5.

84. Suzanne Reed, interview by Arden Eversmeyer, October 13, 2007, p. 7, OLP.

85. Ibid., p. 8.

86. For example, see Portia "P. J." Fagan, interview by Arden Eversmeyer, February 3, 2006, p. 11, OLP; Elizabeth "Betty" Shoemaker, interview by Arden Eversmeyer, January n.d., 2001, p. 23, OLP.

87. Respondent #214, interview by Terrie Lyons, p. 7, box 2, folder 214, LP.

88. Ibid.

89. Ernest W. Burgess and Leonard S. Cottrell Jr., *Predicting Success or Failure in Marriage* (New York: Prentice-Hall, 1939), 345–346.

90. Elizabeth "Deedy" Breed, interview by Arden Eversmeyer, May 23, 2001, p. 10, OLP.

91. Connie Kurtz, interview by Arden Eversmeyer, December 31, 2007, p. 20, OLP. On Connie Kurtz's life and activism, see also the Ruth Berman and Connie Kurtz Papers, SSC; *Ruthie and Connie: Every Room in the House*, directed by Deborah Dickson (New York: The Orchard, 2002), film.

92. Bea Howard, interview by Arden Eversmeyer, March n.d., 2003, p. 13, OLP.

93. Dorothy Hoffman, interview by Elli Gobrecht, April n.d., 2001, p. 3, OLP.

94. Ibid.

95. Sandy Warshaw, interview by the author, May 10, 2010.

96. Mirra Komarovsky, *Blue-Collar Marriage* (New York: Random House, 1964), 331.

97. Friedan, *Feminine Mystique*, 15.

98. Eva Moskowitz, " 'It's Good to Blow Your Top:' Women's Magazines and a Discourse of Discontent, 1945–1965," *Journal of Women's History* 8, no. 3 (Fall 1996): 66–98.

99. See, for example, Barbara Kennedy, interview by Arden Eversmeyer, April 4, 2008, p. 24, OLP; Marie Pierce, interview by Arden Eversmeyer, March 17, 2006, p. 8, OLP; and Edith Daly, interview by Arden Eversmeyer, January n.d., 2004, p. 11, OLP.

100. Komarovsky, *Blue-Collar Marriage*, 83.

101. Ibid., 85.

102. May, *Homeward Bound*, 126.

103. Carolyn Herbst Lewis, *Prescription for Heterosexuality: Sexual Citizenship in the Cold War Era* (Chapel Hill: University of North Carolina Press, 2010), 98; emphasis in the original.

104. Barbara Gerber, interview by Arden Eversmeyer, January 17, 2007, p. 18, OLP.

105. Letter to Phyllis Lyon, November 15, 1972, p. 3, box 24, folder 9, LMP.

106. Connie Kurtz, interview by Arden Eversmeyer, December 31, 2007, pp. 22–23, OLP.

107. Anonymous, interview by the author, December 10, 2013.

108. Ibid.

109. See, for example, Letter to Del Martin and Phyllis Lyon, August 14, 1973, p. 6, box 23, folder 12, LMP.

110. Shaba Barnes, interview by Arden Eversmeyer, January n.d., 2003, p. 15, OLP.

111. Marilyn, interview by JoAnn Castillo, October 22, 1981, p. 15, OHC.

112. Kiki Santikos, interview by Arden Eversmeyer, February 9, 2010, p. 13, OLP. On women and marital property laws in Texas, see Thomas M. Featherston Jr. and Julie A. Springer, "Marital Property Law in Texas: The Past, Present and Future," *Baylor Law Review* 39, no. 4 (Fall 1987): 861–908; Joseph W. McKnight, "Texas Community Property Law: Conservative Attitudes, Reluctant Change," *Law and Contemporary Problems* 56, no. 2 (Spring 1993): 71–98.

113. Marion Coleman, interview by Arden Eversmeyer, July 22, 2008, p. 17, OLP. For a similar story, see Respondent #214, interview by Terrie Lyons, p. 7, box 2, folder 214, LP.

114. Respondent #309, interview by Terrie Lyons, p. 9, box 3, folder, 309, LP.

115. Edith Daly, interview by Arden Eversmeyer, January n.d., 2004, p. 13, OLP.

116. Ruth Silver, interview by Arden Eversmeyer, January n.d., 2001, p. 33, OLP.

117. For a similar example, see Jo Hiner, interview by Arden Eversmeyer, April n.d., 2002, OLP. On the degree to which children took precedence over husbands' and wives' relationships with each other in the postwar period, see Weiss, *To Have and to Hold*, 124–128.

118. For a further discussion of this ideology, see May, *Homeward Bound*, chap. 6.

119. Connie Kurtz, interview by Arden Eversmeyer, December 31, 2007, p. 27, OLP.

120. On changing standards of fatherhood and gendered responsibilities for childrearing in the postwar period, see Robert L. Griswold, *Fatherhood in America: A History* (New York: Basic Books, 1993), chap. 9; Steven Mintz and Susan Kellogg, *Domestic Revolutions: A Social History of American Family Life* (New York: Free Press, 1988), chap. 9.

121. Elizabeth "Deedy" Breed, interview by Arden Eversmeyer, May 23, 2001, p. 14, OLP.

122. See Connie Kurtz, interview by Arden Eversmeyer, December 31, 2007, p. 32, OLP.

123. Phoenix Wheeler, interview by Arden Eversmeyer, March 24, 2006, p. 26, OLP.

124. Ruth Silver, paper presented at Vantage Point Panel, Passages VII Conference, Washington, DC, March 16, 1991, p. 3. The text of Silver's paper is included in Ruth Silver,

interview by Arden Eversmeyer, January n.d., 2001, OLP. "Passages" was a yearly multiracial conference on aging for lesbians first held in 1985.

125. See, for example, Edward A. Strecker and Vincent Tibbals Lathbury, *Their Mothers' Daughters* (Philadelphia: Lippincott, 1956), 71, 160.

126. Silver, paper presented at Vantage Point Panel, p. 3.

127. Alma Routsong, diary entry, November 26, 1961, box 13, folder 1, MP, accession no. 07S-39.

128. On postwar perceptions of homosexuals, predominantly male, as pedophiles and sexual predators, see Freedman, "Uncontrolled Desires"; George Chauncey, "The Postwar Sex Crime Panic," in *True Stories from the American Past*, ed. William Graebner (New York: McGraw-Hill, 1993), 160–178.

129. Alma Routsong, diary entry, November 26, 1961, box 13, folder 1, MP, accession no. 07S-39.

130. Letter to Phyllis Lyon and Del Martin, April 26, 1973, p. 2, box 23, folder 12, LMP.

131. Letter to Phyllis Lyon and Del Martin, September 14, 1972, p. 1, box 23, folder 2, LMP.

132. Bérubé, *Coming Out Under Fire*, 6.

133. On the multiple meanings of sexual normalcy at this moment, see Chauncey, "Postwar Sex Crime Panic," 167. On the postwar understanding of normalcy as a condition rather than an inborn state, see Anna G. Creadick, *Perfectly Average: The Pursuit of Normality in Postwar America* (Amherst: University of Massachusetts, 2010).

134. Julian B. Carter, *The Heart of Whiteness: Normal Sexuality and Race in America, 1880–1940* (Durham, NC: Duke University Press, 2007), esp. 153–155.

135. See, for example, May, *Homeward Bound*, chap. 8; Celello, *Making Marriage Work*, 83–84; and Davis, *More Perfect Unions*, chap. 3.

136. Adrienne Rich, "It Is the Lesbian in Us . . . ," in *On Lies, Secrets, and Silence: Selected Prose, 1966–1978* (New York: W. W. Norton, 1995), 199–202, at 199; emphasis in the original. "It Is the Lesbian in Us . . ." was first published in *Sinister Wisdom* 1, no. 3 (Spring 1977): 6–9. Rich originally presented the essay in 1976 at a Modern Language Association event.

137. Historian Colin Johnson notes similarly that "silence works as both a regulatory technique *and* a condition of possibility." Johnson, *Just Queer Folks*, 119.

Chapter 2

1. On the founding and history of the DOB, see D'Emilio, *Sexual Politics*; Martin Meeker, *Contacts Desired: Gay and Lesbian Communications and Community, 1940s–1970s* (Chicago: University of Chicago Press, 2006); and Marcia M. Gallo, *Different Daughters: A History of the Daughters of Bilitis and the Rise of the Lesbian Rights Movement* (Emeryville, CA: Seal Press, 2007).

2. Letter to Leslie Stanton, November 5, 1960, p. 2, box 11, folder 12, LMP.

3. Ibid., p. 3.

4. On women's postwar "containment" within marriage, see May, *Homeward Bound*. For limits and resistance to the domestic ideal, see Breines, *Young, White, and Miserable*; Joanne Meyerowitz, ed., *Not June Cleaver: Women and Gender in Postwar America, 1945–1960* (Philadelphia: Temple University Press, 1994).

5. Several scholars have argued that discretionary tactics were particular to middle-class lesbians, but among wives who desired women they appear more widespread. See, for example, Elizabeth Lapovsky Kennedy, " 'But We Would Never Talk About It': The Structures of

Lesbian Discretion in South Dakota, 1928–1933," in *Inventing Lesbian Cultures in America*, ed. Ellen Lewin (Boston: Beacon Press, 1996), 15–39.

6. D'Emilio, *Sexual Politics*, 98. For additional evidence of how married men participated in gay subcultures, see, for example, Nicholas L. Syrett, "A Busman's Holiday in the Not-So-Lonely Crowd: Business Culture, Epistolary Networks, and Itinerant Homosexuality in Mid-Twentieth-Century America," *Journal of the History of Sexuality* 21, no. 1 (January 2012): 121–140.

7. Heather Murray, *Not in This Family: Gays and the Meaning of Kinship in Postwar North America* (Philadelphia: University of Pennsylvania Press, 2010), chap. 1; Deborah Cohen, *Family Secrets: Shame and Privacy in Modern Britain* (Oxford: Oxford University Press, 2013), chap. 5; and Johnson, *Just Queer Folks*, chap. 4.

8. May, *Homeward Bound*, 181.

9. Case 244, E. L. Kelly, *Kelly Longitudinal Study, 1935–1955*, Henry A. Murray Research Center of Radcliffe College, quoted in May, *Homeward Bound*, 196.

10. On this therapeutic approach to marriage, see May, *Homeward Bound*, chap. 8; Coontz, *Marriage, a History*, chap. 14; Celello, *Making Marriage Work*, chap. 3; and Davis, *More Perfect Unions*, chap. 3.

11. Paul H. Landis and Helen Judy Bond, *Your Marriage and Family Living* (New York: McGraw-Hill, 1946), 162.

12. Talcott Parsons and Robert Freed Bales, *Family, Socialization, and Interaction Process* (Glencoe, IL: Free Press, 1955), 315; Talcott Parsons, "The Kinship System of the United States," in *Essays in Sociological Theory* (Glencoe, IL: Free Press, 1954), 177–196.

13. Nora Johnson, "The Captivity of Marriage," *Atlantic Monthly*, June 1961, 38–42, at 40; emphasis added.

14. For a more thorough discussion of lesbian and gay bar cultures in various cities at midcentury and even earlier, see D'Emilio, *Sexual Politics*, chap. 2; Kennedy and Davis, *Boots of Leather*; Chauncey, *Gay New York*; Marc Stein, *City of Sisterly and Brotherly Loves: Lesbian and Gay Philadelphia, 1945–1972* (Chicago: University of Chicago Press, 2000), chap. 2; and Nan Alamilla Boyd, *Wide Open Town: A History of Queer San Francisco to 1965* (Berkeley: University of California Press, 2003). On the flexibility of butch-femme culture, see Alix Genter, "Appearances Can Be Deceiving: Butch-Femme Fashion and Queer Legibility in New York City, 1945–1969," *Feminist Studies* 42, no. 3 (2016): 604–631.

15. Brandt, *No Magic Bullet*, 165–170; D'Emilio and Freedman, *Intimate Matters*, 260–261; Bérubé, *Coming Out Under Fire*, 113; and Hegarty, *Victory Girls*, 28.

16. Reba Hudson, interview by Roberta [no last name given], n.d, 1981, p. 13, OHC.

17. Marijane Meaker, introduction to *We, Too, Must Love*, by Ann Aldrich [Marijane Meaker] (New York: Feminist Press, 2006), x.

18. Kennedy and Davis, *Boots of Leather*, 332–333.

19. Audre Lorde, *Zami: A New Spelling of My Name* (Watertown, MA: Persephone Press, 1982), 220.

20. Martin Duberman, *Stonewall* (New York: Plume, 1994), 42–43.

21. Rochella Thorpe, "'A house where queers go': African-American Lesbian Nightlife in Detroit, 1940–1975," in Lewin, *Inventing Lesbian Cultures*, 40–61.

22. Ruth Ellis, interview by Rochella Thorpe, January 16, 1992, audio recording, RT. For more on Ellis's life, see *Living with Pride: Ruth Ellis @100*, directed by Yvonne Welbon, (1999; Chicago: Our Film Works, 2003), DVD.

23. Beverly Dale, interview by Rochella Thorpe, February 8, 1992, cassette tape no. tr9721a, TF.

24. Letter to Del Martin and Phyllis Lyon, October 21, 1975, p. 1, box 24, folder 9, LMP.

25. Barbara Kalish, interview by Arden Eversmeyer, January n.d., 2001, p. 10, OLP.

26. Sandy Warshaw, interview by the author, May 10, 2010.

27. Marge Frantz, interview by Kelly Anderson, November 3–5, 2005, p. 80, VFP.

28. Letter to Phyllis Lyon, November 15, 1972, p. 3, box 24, folder 9, LMP.

29. Letter to Phyllis Lyon and Del Martin, November 20, 1972, p. 1, box 23, folder 9, LMP.

30. Margaret Killough, interview by Arden Eversmeyer, April 10, 2003, p. 8, OLP.

31. Ibid.

32. Letter to Del Martin, February 4, 1973, pp. 5–6, box 25, folder 3, LMP.

33. For other examples of women meeting potential lovers at work during this period, see Letter to DOB, October 17, 1960, p. 3, box 8, folder 16, LMP; Lanice Levy, interview by Arden Eversmeyer, May n.d., 2006, p. 6, OLP.

34. Newton, *Cherry Grove, Fire Island*, 38 and chap. 8.

35. Kenneth "Ken" Sofronski, interview by the author, June 1, 2010. See also Ken Sofronski, *Old, Gay, and Fabulous: A Memoir* (self-pub., CreateSpace, 2011). In my article " 'The House on the Borderland': Lesbian Desire, Marriage and the Household, 1945–1969," *Journal of Social History* 46, no. 1 (Fall 2012): 1–22, I created pseudonyms for Della and Violet. Considering the fact that Sofronski revealed the women's names and identities in his memoir, pseudonyms are no longer necessary.

36. Beverly Dale, interview by Rochella Thorpe, February 8, 1992, cassette tape no. tr9721a, TF.

37. Kathy Martinez, interview by JoAnn Castillo, September 25, 1981, p. 14, OHC.

38. Alma Routsong, unbound typed journal entry, April 24, 1962, box 13, folder 1, MP, accession no. 07S-39.

39. For an example of the violence and police harassment that could occur even at home, see Blue Lunden, interview by Quinn [no last name given], December n.d, 1989, p. 84, box 1, folder 2, DLP.

40. Irene Weiss, interview by Arden Eversmeyer, January n.d., 2003, p. 4, OLP.

41. Geraldine "Gerry" Cooper, interview by Arden Eversmeyer, March n.d., 2006, p. 7, OLP.

42. Syrett, "A Busman's Holiday."

43. AB v. CD, 74 Pa. D. & C. 83 (1950). See also H. v. H., 59 N.J. Super. 227; 157 A.2d 721 (1959). For more on these legal cases, see Lefkovitz, "Peculiar Anomaly."

44. Letter to Julie Lee, July 22, 1971, p. 3, JLP. For a similar case, see Geraldine "Gerry" Cooper, interview by Arden Eversmeyer, March n.d., 2006, p. 10, OLP.

45. Mary Crawford, interview by Allan Bérubé, February 17, 1983, p. 62, WWP.

46. Ibid., p. 96.

47. Ibid.

48. Ibid., p. 94.

49. Carlos Ulises Decena, *Tacit Subjects: Belonging and Same-Sex Desire Among Dominican Immigrant Men* (Durham, NC: Duke University Press, 2011), 19–22.

50. Beverly Dale, interview by Rochella Thorpe, February 8, 1992, cassette tape no. tr9721a, TF.

51. Kathy Martinez, interview by JoAnn Castillo, September 25, 1981, p. 15, OHC.

52. Virginia "Gini" Morton, interview by Arden Eversmeyer, April n.d., 2003, p. 15, OLP.

53. Muriel Crisara, interview by Rochella Thorpe, June 23, 1992, p. 7, box 2, folder 7, TF.

54. Kennedy and Davis, *Boots of Leather*, 340.

55. Dorothy Baker, unbound journal entries, p. 49, box 13, folder "Baker (Dorothy) Journal," BP.

56. Ibid., p. 56.

57. On this bar raid, see Richard Clark, "City of Desire: A History of Same-Sex Desire in New Orleans, 1917–1977" (PhD diss., Tulane University, 2009), 118–119.

58. Elly Bulkin, "An Old Dyke's Tale: An Interview with Doris Lunden," *Conditions: Six* 2, no. 3 (Summer 1980): 26–44, at 29.

59. Ibid., 30.

60. Ibid.; emphasis added.

61. According to Kennedy and Davis, this was the case in Buffalo in the 1950s as well. See Kennedy and Davis, *Boots of Leather*, 96–104.

62. Blue Lunden, interview by Quinn [no last name given], December n.d., 1989, p. 70, box 1, folder 2, DLP. For more on Lunden's life and later career as an activist, see Blue Lunden, interview by Jonathan Ned Katz, January 4, 1974, Spoken Word Audio Files 844, LHA; Bulkin, "An Old Dyke's Tale"; Rivers, *Radical Relations*, 39–41, 45; and *Some Ground to Stand On: The Story of Blue Lunden*, directed by Joyce Warshow (1998; New York: Women Make Movies, 2013), DVD.

63. Blue Lunden, interview by Quinn [no last name given], December n.d., 1989, p. 90, box 1, folder 2, DLP.

64. Ibid.

65. Ibid.

66. For an example of a similar, though less exploitative marriage, see Christopher Stone, "Kids of Gays: A Lesbian's Daughter Straightens Out the Children of Homosexual Parents," *Us*, July 6, 1982, 267.

67. Muriel Crisara, interview by Rochella Thorpe, June 23, 1992, p. 2, box 2, folder 7, TF.

68. Lefkovitz, "Peculiar Anomaly." See also Rhonda R. Rivera, "Our Straight-Laced Judges: The Legal Position of Homosexual Persons in the United States," *Hastings Law Journal* 30, no. 4 (March 1979): 799–955.

69. Marvin M. Moore, "The Diverse Definitions of Criminal Adultery," *University of Kansas City Law Review* 30 (1962): 219–229. In fact, lesbian sex remains a less clear violation of the marriage contract than heterosexual infidelity, depending in part on how a given state defines the term "adultery." See Peter Nicolas, "The Lavender Letter: Applying the Law of Adultery to Same-Sex Couples and Same-Sex Conduct," *Florida Law Review* 63, no.1 (2011): 97–128, at 98.

70. See for example, Gilmore v. Gilmore, 45 Cal. 2d 142; 287 P.2d 769 at 770 (1955).

71. *AB v. CD*, 74 Pa. D. & C. at 85.

72. Ibid., 84.

73. Ibid., 85.

74. *Gilmore*, 287 P.2d at 772, 773.

75. Ibid., note 1.

76. Benkowski v. Benkowski, 203 Pa. Super. 347, 350; 201 A.2d 444 (1964).

77. Ibid., at 351.

78. Ibid.

79. Unidentified newspaper (AP) article, "New Jersey Legal Precedent: Divorce Granted—Wife Homosexual," 1959, Passing 10010 folder, Subject Files, LHA, quoted in Rivers, *Radical Relations*, 28. Rivers suspects this case was *H. v. H.*, 59 N.J. Super. 227. Alison Lefkovitz discusses this case as well in Lefkovitz, "Peculiar Anomaly," 665–701.

80. Immerman v. Immerman, 176 Cal. App.2d 122 (1959). This case is discussed in Kimberly D. Richman, *Courting Change: Queer Parents, Judges, and the Transformation of American Family Law* (New York: New York University Press, 2009), 55.

81. Vera Martin, interview by Daniel Rivers, Apache Junction, AZ, September 22, 2006, quoted in Rivers, *Radical Relations*, 27.

82. Frank H. Keezer. *A Treatise on the Law of Marriage and Divorce*, 2nd ed. (Indianapolis: Bobbs-Merrill, 1923), 408. For more on these changes, see Mary Ann Mason, *From Father's Property to Children's Rights: The History of Child Custody in the United States* (New York: Columbia University Press, 1994), 111–118.

83. On the breakup of Martin's marriage, see Gallo, *Different Daughters*, xlii; Meeker, *Contacts Desired*, 80–81.

84. Shirley Maser, interview by Arden Eversmeyer, November 29, 2009, p. 10, OLP.

85. May, *Homeward Bound*.

86. Jean [pseud.; Lilly's daughter], interview by the author, November 14, 2010.

87. Irene Weiss, interview with by Arden Eversmeyer, January n.d., 2003, p. 4, OLP.

88. Ibid.

89. Ibid.

90. Mary Crawford, interview by Allan Bérubé, February 17, 1983, WWP.

91. For examples, see Faderman, *Surpassing the Love*; Faderman, *Odd Girls*; Kennedy and Davis, *Boots of Leather*; and Vicinus, *Intimate Friends*. For a major exception, see Marcus, *Between Women*.

92. For examples, see Case 118, E. L. Kelly, *Kelly Longitudinal Study, 1935–1955*, Henry A. Murray Research Center of Radcliffe College, quoted in May, *Homeward Bound*, 189; Weiss, *To Have and To Hold*, 136.

93. Letter to Barbara Gittings, October 8, 1964, box 58, folder 1, GLP.

94. See, for example, Jana K. Tran, Gina Dunckel, and Ellen J., Teng, "Sexual Dysfunction in Veterans with Post-Traumatic Stress Disorder," *Journal of Sexual Medicine* 12, no. 4 (April 2015): 847–855.

95. Marie Pierce, interview by Arden Eversmeyer, March 17, 2006, p. 13, OLP. For a similar case, see Marge Frantz, interview by Kelly Anderson, November 3–5, 2005, VFP.

96. Marie Pierce, interview by Arden Eversmeyer, March 17, 2006, p. 12, OLP.

97. Ibid., p. 13.

Chapter 3

1. On the history of the MRG, see Jill Gardiner, *From the Closet to the Screen: Women at the Gateways Club 1945–85* (London: Pandora, 2003), 96–102, 118–123; Rebecca Jennings, *Tomboys and Bachelor Girls: A Lesbian History of Postwar Britain, 1945–1971* (Manchester, UK: Manchester University Press, 2007), 134–172. Though Langley did not identify as lesbian or bisexual, at least one woman, Diana Chapman, claimed to have been her lover; see Hall

Carpenter Archives, Lesbian Oral History Group, *Inventing Ourselves: Lesbian Life Stories* (London: Routledge, 1989), 53.

2. Esmé Langley to Barbara Gittings, November 6, 1964, pp. 1–2, box 57, folder 12, GLP.

3. Barbara Gittings to Esmé Langley, November 9, 1964, p. 2, box 57, folder 12, GLP.

4. Del Martin and Phyllis Lyon, *Lesbian/Woman* (San Francisco: Glide Publications, 1972), 123.

5. Rivers, *Radical Relations*, 12.

6. D'Emilio, *Sexual Politics*, 71.

7. On the rise of the homophile movement, see D'Emilio, *Sexual Politics*; Boyd, *Wide Open Town*, chap. 4; Meeker, *Contacts Desired*; Gallo, *Different Daughters*; Marc Stein, *Rethinking the Gay and Lesbian Movement* (New York: Routledge, 2012), chap. 2; and Stewart-Winter, *Queer Clout*, chap. 3.

8. For the DOB's statement of purpose, see *The Ladder*, October 1956, 4.

9. On the DOB's membership figures, see D'Emilio, *Sexual Politics*, 115, 173, 204; on the DOB's chapter expansion, see Gallo, *Different Daughters*, 34–35, 41–45, 71, 130, 162–163, 192–193.

10. "What Is DOB?," DOB file, LHA, quoted in D'Emilio, *Sexual Politics*, 104.

11. Marcia M. Gallo, "Celebrating the Years of *The Ladder*," *off our backs* 35, no. 5–6 (May–June 2005): 34–36, at 34.

12. Statistics from Meeker, *Contacts Desired*, 99; Kristin Gay Esterberg, "From Illness to Action: Conceptions of Homosexuality in *The Ladder*, 1956–1965," *Journal of Sex Research* 27, no. 1 (February 1990): 65–80, at 66.

13. On the DOB's representational politics and their criticism of lesbian pulp fiction, see Martin Meeker, "A Queer and Contested Medium: The Emergence of Representational Politics in the 'Golden Age' of Lesbian Paperbacks, 1955–1963," *Journal of Women's History* 17, no. 1 (Spring 2005): 165–188.

14. Gallo, *Different Daughters*. On the DOB and *The Ladder*'s antipathy for bar culture and butch women in particular, see D'Emilio, *Sexual Politics*, 106, 186. For a further discussion of the tensions and connections between those who participated in the homophile movement and those who frequented gay and lesbian bars, see Boyd, *Wide Open Town*.

15. Meeker, *Contacts Desired*, esp. chap. 2.

16. Letter to Evelyn Howe, August 24, 1963, p. 1, box 12, folder 4, LMP; emphasis in the original.

17. Letter to Barbara Gittings, September 13, 1963, box 55, folder 20, GLP.

18. Letter to Barbara Gittings, undated, c. 1964, box 55, folder 13, GLP.

19. Letter to Priscilla Cochran, April 19, 1968, p. 1, box 3, folder 10, LMP.

20. Ibid., p. 2.

21. Ibid.

22. Craig Loftin estimates that *ONE* received only 5 to 10 percent of its letters from women. See Loftin, *Letters to ONE: Gay and Lesbian Voices from the 1950s and 1960s* (Albany: State University of New York Press, 2012), 7.

23. Letter to James Schneider, October 26, 1963, p. 1, folder 11, box 90, OR. Spellings are as in the original.

24. Letter to D'Ann Carroll [Irma Wolf], July 11, 1956, folder 3, box 90, OR. The full text of this letter is also available in Loftin, *Letters to ONE*, 101–102.

25. Letter to DOB, July 20, 1956, box 11, folder 7, LMP. For this woman's correspondence with the Mattachine Society, see Letter to "Sirs," May 28, 1955, box 7, folder 19, MC; Letter to "Sirs," November 29, 1955, box 7, folder 32, MC.

26. Letter from Del Martin, October 3, 1956, box 11, folder 7, LMP.

27. Letter to DOB, March 21, 1957, p. 3, box 11, folder 7, LMP.

28. See Letter to DOB, March 21, 1957, box 11, folder 7, LMP; Undated letter to DOB, c. 1957, box 11, folder 7, LMP.

29. Letter to Hal Call, January 29, 1957, p. 2, box 7, folder 31, MC.

30. Marion Zimmer Bradley and Jody Shotwell, for example, were also in contact with multiple homophile groups.

31. Letter to Barbara Gittings and Kay Lahusen, undated, c. 1965, p. 3, box 59, folder 3, GLP.

32. Ibid.

33. Letter to Del Martin, April 8, 1958, p. 3, box 11, folder 3, LMP.

34. Letter to "Dear Sir," April 3, 1958, box 11, folder 3, LMP.

35. Letter to Del Martin, April 8, 1958, p. 2, box 11, folder 3, LMP.

36. Ibid.

37. Ibid., p. 1.

38. Letter to Del Martin, July 10, 1958, p. 2, box 11, folder 3, LMP.

39. Letter to DOB, October 17, 1960, pp. 6–7, box 8, folder 16, LMP.

40. Ibid., p. 6.

41. Letter to DOB ("To Whom it May Concern"), October 29, 1965, p. 2, box 3, folder 2, LMP.

42. Daniel Patrick Moynihan, *The Negro Family: The Case for National Action* [1965], in *The Moynihan Report and the Politics of Controversy*, ed. Lee Rainwater and William L. Yancey (Cambridge, MA: MIT Press, 1967), 43–124.

43. Deborah Goleman Wolf, *The Lesbian Community* (Berkeley: University of California Press, 1979), 57.

44. On lesbian and gay parents' concerns about losing child custody in this era, see Rivers, *Radical Relations*, 25–29.

45. Nancy Osbourne, "One Facet of Fear," *The Ladder*, June 1957, 6–7, at 6.

46. Ibid., 7.

47. Luther Allen, letter, Readers Respond, *The Ladder*, July 1957, 24–27, at 26.

48. Ibid.

49. Marion Zimmer Bradley, "Some Remarks on Marriage," *The Ladder*, July 1957, 14–16, at 14. Bradley published lesbian pulps under the names Miriam Gardner, Morgan Ives, and Lee Chapman. Later she became known for her fantasy and science-fiction books, notably *The Mists of Avalon* (New York: Ballantine, 1982).

50. Bradley, "Some Remarks," 15–16.

51. Marion Zimmer Bradley, "Marion Zimmer Bradley, Tape 1 of 1, October 17, 1988," interview by Manuela Soares, *Herstories: Audio/Visual Collections of the LHA*, accessed August 15, 2018, http://herstories.prattinfoschool.nyc/omeka/exhibits/show/daughters-of-bilitis -video-pro/item/722.

52. L. N. [Lorraine Hansberry], letter, Readers Respond, *The Ladder*, August 1957, 26–30, at 29. The "N" stands for Nemiroff, Hansberry's married name. For a further discussion of

Hansberry's letters to the DOB, see Lisbeth Lipari, "The Rhetoric of Intersectionality: Lorraine Hansberry's 1957 Letters to *The Ladder*," in *Queering Public Address: Sexualities in American Historical Discourse*, ed. Charles Morri (Columbia: University of South Carolina Press, 2007), 220–248; Gallo, *Different Daughters*, 21–23. For a discussion of Hansberry's sexuality and the restrictions placed on lesbian materials in Hansberry's collection at the Schomburg Center for Research in Black Culture, see Kevin J. Mumford, *Not Straight, Not White: Black Gay Men from the March on Washington to the AIDS Crisis* (Chapel Hill: University of North Carolina Press, 2016), 19–20; Kevin Mumford, "Opening the Restricted Box: Lorraine Hansberry's Lesbian Writing," Lorraine Hansberry: A Museum Show and Opening the Archive, OutHistory.org, accessed August 15, 2018, http://www.outhistory.org/exhibits/show/lorraine-hansberry/lesbian-writing.

53. L. N., letter, Readers Respond, 30.

54. Lorraine Hansberry to Robert Nemiroff, September n.d., 1954, p. 5, box 2, folder 1, HP.

55. Lorraine Hansberry to Robert Nemiroff, August 18, 1958, p. 2, box 2, folder 1, HP.

56. Martin and Lyon, *Lesbian/Woman*, 114. As Kevin Mumford notes, Martin and Lyon appear to have exaggerated Hansberry's involvement with the organization in an attempt to both claim her and present the DOB as more racially diverse than it was. See Mumford, *Not Straight, Not White*, 21.

57. See John D'Emilio, *Lost Prophet: The Life and Times of Bayard Rustin* (Chicago: University of Chicago Press, 2004) chap. 15; Mumford, *Not Straight, Not White*, 30–38.

58. Danielle L. McGuire, *At the Dark End of the Street: Black Women, Rape, and Resistance—A New History of the Civil Rights Movement from Rosa Parks to the Rise of Black Power* (New York: Vintage, 2011), chap. 3.

59. Darlene Clark Hine, "Rape and the Inner Lives of Black Women in the Middle West," *Signs* 14, no. 4 (Summer 1989): 912–920. Danielle McGuire traces a concomitant tradition of testimony and protest among black women regarding sexual violence in McGuire, *Dark End of the Street*.

60. For a further discussion of Hansberry's feminism and changing attitudes toward homosexuality, see Cheryl Higashida, "To Be[come] Young, Gay, and Black: Lorraine Hansberry's Existentialist Routes to Anti-colonialism," *American Quarterly* 60, no. 4 (December 2008): 899–924; Dayo Gore, *Radicalism at the Crossroads: African American Women Activists in the Cold War* (New York: New York University Press, 2011), 43–44 and 65.

61. A. C., letter, Readers Respond, *The Ladder*, July 1957, 27–28, at 27.

62. Richard Aldington, *The Love of Myrrhine and Konallis, and Other Prose Poems* (Chicago: Pascal Covici, 1926).

63. Emily Jones [Lorraine Hansberry], "Chanson du Konallis," *The Ladder*, September 1958, 8–10, 20–26. The few short stories about wives who desired women that appeared in *ONE* magazine during the 1950s similarly depicted wives who desired women as inhabiting a prison of their own making. See Georgiana Blaker, "Camouflage," *ONE*, March 1955, 35–38; Gabrielle Ganell, "And the Truth Shall Set You Free," *ONE*, November 1961, 24–27; and J. Lorna Strayer, "The Stranger," *ONE*, April–May 1956, 41–43. See also Craig Loftin, *Masked Voices: Gay Men and Lesbians in Cold War America* (Albany: State University of New York Press, 2012), chap. 8.

64. Editor's introduction to Joy O. I. Spoczynska, "The Experiment That Failed," *The Ladder*, June 1960, 7–15, at 7.

65. Editor's note to Jan Fraser, "The Other Side of the Fable," *The Ladder*, August 1960, 16.

66. Miriam Gardner [Marion Zimmer Bradley], "The House on the Borderland," *The Ladder*, May 1960, 5–6, at 5.

67. Ibid., 6.

68. Ibid.

69. J. E., letter, Readers Respond, *The Ladder*, May 1960, 26.

70. Ibid.

71. Letter to Leslie Stanton, November 5, 1960, p. 2, box 11, folder 12, LMP.

72. Ibid.

73. See, for example, Joy O. I. Spoczynska, "The Experiment That Failed," *The Ladder*, June 1960, 7–15; Jan Fraser, "The Other Side of the Fable," *The Ladder*, August 1960, 15–16; and B. H., letter, Readers Respond, *The Ladder*, November 1960, 22–23.

74. See Stein, *City of Sisterly and Brotherly Loves*, 192–193.

75. Jody Shotwell, "Letter to Meredith," *The Ladder*, August 1960, 17–18, at 18.

76. See, for example, M. K. R., letter, Readers Respond, *The Ladder*, October 1963, 26.

77. Miriam Gardner [Marion Zimmer Bradley], "Behind the Borderline," *The Ladder*, October 1960, 6–11, at 11.

78. Ibid.

79. "Why Am I a Lesbian?" *The Ladder*, June 1960, 20–23, at 23.

80. Y & A, letter, Readers Respond, *The Ladder*, August 1960, 26.

81. Editor's note below Y & A, letter, Readers Respond. On stereotypes of bisexual women in the magazine, see also C. O. Massachusetts, letter, Readers Respond, *The Ladder*, July 1964, 25–26.

82. Marion Zimmer Bradley to Barbara Gittings, February 15, 1965, box 58, folder 10, GLP.

83. "DOB Questionnaire Reveals Some Facts About Lesbians," *The Ladder*, September 1959, 4–26, at 14.

84. Ibid., 15. Kinsey's significance for the DOB's members is also evidenced by *The Ladder*'s first issue, which included a tribute to the researcher who had recently passed away. For more on this survey, see Gallo, *Different Daughters*, chap. 3.

85. Letter to DOB, October 17, 1960, p. 6, box 8, folder 16, LMP.

86. The word "lesbian" appeared on *The Ladder*'s cover for the first time in January 1964; photographs (instead of line drawings) appeared in September 1964. For more on *The Ladder*'s changing views of homosexuality, see Esterberg, "From Illness to Action"; Kristin Esterberg, "From Accommodation to Liberation: A Social Movement Analysis of Lesbians in the Homophile Movement," *Gender and Society* 8, no. 3 (September 1994): 424–443. On Gittings's activism in particular, see Kay Tobin and Randy Wicker, *The Gay Crusaders* (New York: Arno Press, 1975), 209–210; Jonathan Katz, *Gay American History: Lesbians and Gay Men in the U.S.A* (New York: Crowell, 1976), 420–433; and D'Emilio, *Sexual Politics*, 168–175.

87. Editor's note below Marilyn Barrow, letter, Readers Respond, *The Ladder*, September 1964, 25.

88. Elizabeth Tudor, "Letter to an Old Friend," *The Ladder*, April 1965, 21–23, at 21.

89. Nola, "A Christmas Dialogue," *The Ladder*, December 1964, 13–18, at 17.

90. Rose Marie of Portland [Nora], "Plea to the Silent Ones," *The Ladder*, December 1963, 11–13, at 11. More on this article and its author (whom I've called Nora) later in this chapter.

91. Marilyn Barrow, "The Very Vast Wasteland: The Celibate the Passer and the Nun," *The Ladder*, April 1964, 9–10, at 9.

92. Marilyn Barrow, letter, Readers Respond, *The Ladder*, September 1964, 25.

93. Ruth M. McGuire, "Counsellor's Corner," *The Ladder*, August 1969, 29–31.

94. Gene Damon [Barbara Grier], "Lesbian Marriage," *The Ladder*, August 1958, 12–13.

95. G. van B. [Ger van Braam], "Notes from Abroad: Isolation in Indonesia," *The Ladder*, June 1964, 9–11, at 11.

96. Florence Conrad [Jaffy], "DOB Questionnaire Reveals Some Facts About Lesbians," *The Ladder*, September 1959, 4–26. A comparison of data the DOB gathered about lesbians versus data gathered by the Mattachine Society and ONE, Inc., showed that while a smaller number of men married heterosexually, more men who did so remained married than women who did so; see Florence Conrad [Jaffy], "DOB Questionnaire Reveals Some Comparisons Between Male and Female Homosexuals," *The Ladder*, September 1960, 4–25, at 15.

97. In this way, their strategy resembled that of the Mattachine Society; see Martin Meeker, "Behind the Mask of Respectability: Reconsidering the Mattachine Society and Male Homophile Practice, 1950s and 1960s," *Journal of the History of Sexuality* 10, no. 1 (January 2001): 78–116.

98. Letter from Barbara Gittings, August 15, 1965, box 58, folder 14, GLP.

99. Letter to Cleo Glenn, January 17, 1963, p. 1, box 12, folder 2, LMP.

100. Letter to Barbara Gittings and Kay Lahusen, November 15, 1963, p. 2, box 55, folder 14, GLP.

101. Robert W. Wood, *Christ and the Homosexual; Some Observations* (New York: Vantage Press, 1960).

102. Letter to Cleo Glenn, January 17, 1963, p. 1, box 12, folder 2, LMP.

103. Letter to Barbara Gittings, April 15, 1963, pp. 1–2, box 12, folder 2, LMP.

104. This woman's *Ladder* writings, written under various pseudonyms, include: B. H., letter, Readers Respond, *The Ladder*, November 1960, 22–23; Rose Marie, "Plea to the Silent Ones"; and Mrs. B, "Living Propaganda," *The Ladder*, January 1965, 13–14.

105. Rose Marie, "Plea to the Silent Ones."

106. Letter to DOB, December 11, 1963, box 55, folder 20, GLP.

107. Letter to Barbara Gittings and Kay Lahusen, December 31, 1963, box 55, folder 14, GLP.

108. Letter to George Saslow, M.D., January 17, 1964, p. 4, box 57, folder 6, GLP.

109. Letter to Barbara Gittings and Kay Lahusen, February 22, 1964, pp. 2–3, box 57, folder 6, GLP.

110. Letter to Kay Lahusen and Barbara Gittings, June 17, 1964, p. 2, box, 57, folder 6, GLP.

111. Ibid.

112. Letter to Kay Lahusen, October 1, 1964, box 57, folder 4, GLP.

113. Mrs. B, "Living Propaganda." For a similar story, see Letter to Barbara Gittings ("Hi There"), January 25, 1963, p. 2, box 11, folder 15, LMP; Letter to Barbara Gittings and Kay Lahusen, August 15, 1963, p. 1, box 55, folder 6, GLP.

114. Bradley, "Bradley, Tape 1 of 1."

Chapter 4

1. Foster Craddock, *An Authentic Report on Lesbianism* (North Hollywood, CA: Challenge Publications, 1966), first page, unnumbered.

2. Kinsey et al., *Sexual Behavior in the Human Female*, 454.

3. Ibid., 455.

4. "DOB Questionnaire Reveals Some Comparisons," 15.

5. See Kennedy and Davis, *Boots of Leather*; Donna Penn, "The Sexualized Woman: The Lesbian, the Prostitute and the Containment of Female Sexuality in Postwar America," in Meyerowitz, *Not June Cleaver*, 358–381. For an alternative perspective, emphasizing the femme's threat, see Robert J. Corber, *Cold War Femme* (Durham, NC: Duke University Press, 2011).

6. Penn, "Sexualized Woman."

7. Moynihan, *Negro Family*.

8. Ruth Feldstein makes a related argument in *Motherhood in Black and White: Race and Sex in American Liberalism, 1930–1965* (Ithaca, NY: Cornell University Press, 2000). On "momism," see May, *Homeward Bound*, 73–74; Jennifer Terry, "'Momism' and the Making of Treasonous Homosexuals," in *"Bad" Mothers: The Politics of Blame in Twentieth-Century America*, ed. Molly Ladd-Taylor and Lauri Umansky (New York: New York University Press, 1998), 169–190; and Plant, *Mom*.

9. Johnson, *Lavender Scare*, 12.

10. Kinsey et al., *Sexual Behavior in the Human Female*, 484–485.

11. See Canaday, *Straight State*, chap. 5; Stacy Braukman, "'Nothing Else Matters but Sex': Cold War Narratives of Deviance and the Search for Lesbian Teachers in Florida, 1959–1963," *Feminist Studies* 27, no. 3 (September 2001): 553–575. There were also a few highly publicized police raids on lesbian bars in this period; see Boyd, *Wide Open Town*, chap. 2.

12. See Richard von Krafft-Ebing, *Psychopathia Sexualis: With Especial Reference to the Antipathic Sexual Instinct: A Medico-forensic Study*, trans. Franklin S. Klaf, 12th ed. (New York: Arcade, 1998), 265; Havelock Ellis, *Studies in the Psychology of Sex*, vol. 1, *Sexual Inversion* (New York: Random House, 1942), 20, 275; Magnus Hirschfeld, *The Homosexuality of Men and Women*, trans. Michael A. Lombardi-Nash (Amherst, NY: Prometheus Books, 2000), 129; Sigmund Freud, "The Psychogenesis of a Case of Female Homosexuality," *International Journal of Psycho-Analysis* 1, no. 2 (1920): 125–149; Katharine Bement Davis, *Factors in the Sex Life of Twenty-Two Hundred Women* (New York: Arno Press, 1972), 301–310; George W. Henry, *Sex Variants: A Study of Homosexual Patterns* (New York: Hoeber, 1948), 549–918.

13. Anastasia Jones, "'She's That Way': Female Same-Sex Intimacy and the Growth of Modern Sexual Categories in the U.S., 1920–1940" (PhD diss., Yale University, 2013), 23.

14. See Christina Simmons, "Companionate Marriage and the Lesbian Threat," *Frontiers* 4, no. 3 (Autumn 1979): 54–59; Maurice Chideckel, *Female Sex Perversion: The Sexually Aberrated Woman As She Is* (New York: Eugenics Publishing Company, 1938), 37.

15. Edmund Bergler's books on sexuality include: *Unhappy Marriage and Divorce: A Study of Neurotic Choice of Marriage Partners* (New York: International Universities Press, 1946); *Counterfeit-Sex: Homosexuality, Impotence, Frigidity* (New York: Grune and Stratton, 1958); *Kinsey's Myth of Female Sexuality: The Medical Facts* (New York: Grune and Stratton, 1954), which he coauthored with William Kroger; *Homosexuality: Disease or Way of Life?* (New York: Hill and Wang, 1956); and *One Thousand Homosexuals: Conspiracy of Silence, or Curing and Deglamorizing Homosexuals?* (Paterson, NJ: Pageant, 1959).

16. Terry, *American Obsession*, 310.

17. See, for example, Margaret Little, review of *Female Homosexuality: A Psychodynamic Study of Lesbianism*, by Frank Samuel Caprio, *International Journal of Psycho-Analysis* 36 (1955): 400–401; B. B. Zeitlyn, review of *Variations in Sexual Behavior*, by Frank Samuel Caprio, *International Journal of Psycho-Analysis* 39 (1958): 435.

18. Caprio's books on sexuality include: *Sexual Deviations* (Washington, DC: Linacre Press, 1950), which he coauthored with Louis Samuel London; *The Sexually Adequate Male* (New York: Citadel Press, 1952); *The Sexually Adequate Female* (New York: Citadel Press, 1953); *Female Homosexuality: A Psychodynamic Study of Lesbianism* (New York: Citadel Press, 1954); and *Variations in Sexual Behavior* (New York: Citadel Press, 1955).

19. See, for example, Therese Benedek, *Psychosexual Functions in Women* (New York: Ronald Press, 1952).

20. Helene Deutsch, *The Psychology of Women: A Psychoanalytic Interpretation*, vol. 1 (New York: Grune and Stratton, 1944–1945), 341–346.

21. Bergler, *Counterfeit-Sex*, 337.

22. Terry, *American Obsession*, chap. 9.

23. Bergler, *Counterfeit-Sex*, 337.

24. Ibid.

25. Frank Caprio, "The Story of a Lesbian," *Sexology*, October 1953, reprinted in *The Best of "Sexology: The Illustrated Magazine of Sex Science"*, ed. Craig Yoe (Philadelphia: Running Press, 2008), 232–239, at 239.

26. Caprio, "Story of a Lesbian," 236.

27. Caprio, *Female Homosexuality*, 146–147.

28. Ibid., 148.

29. Ferdinand Lundberg and Marynia F. Farnham, *Modern Woman: The Lost Sex* (New York: Harper and Bros., 1947), 11.

30. Bergler and Kroger, *Kinsey's Myth*, 143.

31. Ibid., 158.

32. Caprio, *Female Homosexuality*, 168.

33. Ibid., 10.

34. As reported in Charles W. Socarides, "Theoretical and Clinical Aspects of Overt Female Homosexuality," *Journal of the American Psychoanalytic Association* 10, no. 3 (July 1962): 579–592, at 591.

35. Ibid., 592.

36. Jess Stearn, *The Sixth Man* (Garden City, NY: Doubleday, 1961); Jess Stearn, *The Grapevine* (Garden City, NY: Doubleday, 1964).

37. Meeker, *Contacts Desired*, 140.

38. P. G., "Readers Respond," *The Ladder*, June 1964, 23.

39. Stearn, *Grapevine*, 2.

40. Ibid., 23.

41. Ibid., 323.

42. Ibid., 2.

43. Ibid., 360.

44. Ibid., 276.

45. Ibid., 370.

46. Philip Wylie, *Opus 21: Descriptive Music for the Lower Kinsey Epoch of the Atomic Age, a Concerto for a One-Man Band, Six Arias for Soap Operas, Fugues, Anthems and Barrelhouse* (New York: Rinehart, 1949).

47. Wylie, *Generation of Vipers*.

48. *Young Man with a Horn*, directed by Michael Curtiz (1950; Burbank, CA: Warner Home Video, 2005), DVD. See also Vito Russo, *The Celluloid Closet: Homosexuality in the Movies* (New York: Harper and Row, 1987), 100–102.

49. Dorothy Baker, *Young Man with a Horn* (New York: Houghton Mifflin, 1938).

50. Dorothy Baker, interview by Elisabeth Freidel, June 25, 1962, p. 68, box 13, brown package, BP.

51. On Baker's meeting with the screenwriters and producer, see Letter from Jerry Wald to Steve Trilling, November 15, 1946, volume 1467, folder 7, WBP; Undated telegram from Jerry Wald to Dorothy Baker, volume 1467, folder 7, WBP. A 1949 script outline made Amy's homosexuality clear; see Carl Foreman, Revised Outline, May 5, 1949, volume 1467, folder 4, WBP.

52. Dorothy Baker, interview by Elisabeth Freidel, June 25, 1962, p. 68, box 13, brown package, BP.

53. For censors' responses to the film, see volumes 1350 and 1255, WBP.

54. Edwin Schallert, "Trumpeter Story Lacks in Climax," *Los Angeles Times*, March 4, 1950, 10.

55. "The Screen: Two New Films on the Scene; Kirk Douglas Seen as 'Young Man with a Horn,' New Bill at Radio City Music Hall," *New York Times*, February 10, 1950, 31.

56. *Walk on the Wild Side*, directed by Edward Dmytryk (1962; Culver City, CA: Sony Pictures Home Entertainment, 2004), DVD.

57. For this discussion of *Walk on the Wild Side*, see Peter Bunzel, "Shocking Candor on the Screen, a Dilemma for the Family" *Life*, February 23, 1962, 88–94, 99. For more on this transformation of the Hollywood production code, see Russo, *Celluloid Closet*, chap. 3.

58. "British Movie on Homosexuality Denied Seal of Approval Here," *New York Times*, November 16, 1961, 45.

59. Yvonne Keller, "'Was It Right to Love Her Brother's Wife So Passionately?': Lesbian Pulp Novels and U.S. Lesbian Identity, 1950–1965," *American Quarterly* 57, no. 2 (June 2005): 385–410.

60. John William Tebbel, *Paperback Books: A Pocket History* (New York: Pocket Books, 1964); Kenneth C. Davis, *Two-Bit Culture: The Paperbacking of America* (Boston: Houghton Mifflin, 1984); and Paula Rabinowitz, *American Pulp: How Paperbacks Brought Modernism to Main Street* (Princeton, NJ: Princeton University Press, 2014). For the sales figures for *Women's Barracks*, see Susan Stryker, *Queer Pulp: Perverted Passions from the Golden Age of the Paperback* (San Francisco: Chronicle Books, 2001), 51.

61. Benjamin Morse, *The Lesbian: A Frank, Revealing Study of Women Who Turn to Their Own Sex for Love* (Derby, CT: Monarch Books, 1963).

62. Ibid., 67.

63. W. D. Sprague, *The Lesbian in Our Society* (New York: Tower Publications, 1962); capitalization for emphasis in the original. This same statistic appeared in Craddock, *Authentic Report*, 45.

64. Sprague, *Lesbian in Our Society*, 51.

65. Ehrenreich, *Hearts of Men*, chap. 4.

66. William Iversen, "Love, Death, and the Hubby Image," *Playboy*, September 1963, 92.

67. On Hugh Hefner and *Playboy* magazine's depictions of homosexuality in this period, see Carrie Pitzulo, *Bachelors and Bunnies: The Sexual Politics of Playboy* (Chicago: University

of Chicago Press, 2011), 109–117; Fraterrigo, *Playboy and the Making of the Good Life*, 40–44, 110.

68. Gene Damon [Barbara Grier] to Jaye Bell, March 11, 1963, box 2, folder 1, LMP. On Grier's relationship with a married woman, see Gene Damon [Barbara Grier], "Lesbian Marriage," *The Ladder*, August 1958, 12–13.

69. Allan Seager, *Death of Anger* (New York: Avon Book Division, 1960).

70. "Text of President Eisenhower's Message to Congress," *New York Times*, January 8, 1960, 10.

71. Davis, *More Perfect Unions*, 93.

72. Ibid., 96.

73. George Simon, *The Third Lust* (New York: Universal Publishing and Distributing, 1963), cover.

74. George Simon, *Girls Without Men* (New York: Universal Publishing and Distributing, 1964).

75. Gardner Fox, *Scandal in Suburbia* (New York: Hillman, 1960); Herb Roberts, *Love in the Suburbs* (New York: Universal Publishing and Distributing, 1963).

76. Eric Schaefer, "Pandering to the 'Goon Trade': Framing the Sexploitation Audience Through Advertising," in *Sleaze Artists: Cinema at the Margins of Taste, Style, and Politics*, ed. Jeffrey Sconce (Durham, NC: Duke University Press, 2007), 19–46; Jeffrey Sconce, "Altered Sex: Satan, Acid, and the Erotic Threshold," in *Sex Scene: Media and the Sexual Revolution*, ed. Eric Schaefer (Durham, NC: Duke University Press, 2014), 235–261, at 245.

77. Richard Yates, *Revolutionary Road* (New York: Atlantic-Little, Brown, 1961).

78. On the ways that housing policies privileged married couples, see Clayton Howard, "Building a 'Family Friendly' Metropolis: Sexuality, the State, and Postwar Housing Policy," *Journal of Urban History* 39, no. 5 (September 2013): 933–955.

79. Ann Bannon's *Women in the Shadows* (1959), for example, includes a biracial lesbian wife. For a discussion, see Julian Carter, "Gay Marriage and Pulp Fiction: Homonormativity, Disidentification and Affect in Ann Bannon's Lesbian Novels," *GLQ: A Journal of Gay and Lesbian Studies* 15, no. 4 (2009): 583–609. On the Johnson Publishing Company, see Adam Green, *Selling the Race: Culture, Community, and Black Chicago, 1940–1955* (Chicago: University of Chicago Press, 1997), chaps. 4 and 5.

80. "Strange Love," *Tan Confessions*, November 1950, 16, 63–65. See also Leisa D. Meyer, "'Strange Love': Searching for Sexual Subjectivities in Black Print Popular Culture During the 1950s," *Feminist Studies* 38, no. 3 (Fall 2012): 625–657.

81. "Why Lesbians Marry Men," *Jet*, January 1, 1953, 20–23, at 21. For similar articles, see Gladys Bentley, "I Am a Woman Again," *Ebony*, August 1952, 92–98; "Women Who Fall for Lesbians," *Jet*, February 25, 1954, 20–22.

82. "Why Lesbians Marry Men," 23.

83. Marion Zimmer Bradley, "Lesbian Stereotypes in the Commercial Novel," *The Ladder*, September 1964, 14–19, at 16.

84. Ibid; emphasis in the original.

85. Gene Damon [Barbara Grier], review of *Scandal in Suburbia*, by Gardner F. Fox, Lesbiana, *The Ladder*, September 1963, 24. For a positive review, see Gene Damon [Barbara Grier], review of *The Flesh is Willing*, by Dorcas Knight, Lesbiana, *The Ladder*, January 1964, 15.

86. Stryker, *Queer Pulp*, 61.

87. *We Walk Alone* (Greenwich, CT: Fawcett, 1955; New York: Feminist Press, 2006); citations refer to the Feminist Press edition; *We, Too, Must Love* (Greenwich, CT: Fawcett, 1958; New York: Feminist Press, 2006); citations refer to the Feminist Press edition; *Carol in a Thousand Cities* (Greenwich, CT: Fawcett, 1960); and *We Two Won't Last* (Greenwich, CT: Fawcett, 1963). All authored by Ann Aldrich [Marijane Meaker].

88. See Stephanie Foote, afterword to Aldrich [Meaker], *We, Too, Must Love*, 159–185; Martin Meeker, "A Queer and Contested Medium: The Emergence of Representational Politics in the 'Golden Age' of Lesbian Paperbacks, 1955–1963," *Journal of Women's History* 17, no. 1 (Spring 2005): 165–188.

89. Aldrich [Meaker], *We Walk Alone*, xii.

90. Ibid., 91.

91. Ibid., 139.

92. Ibid.

93. Aldrich [Meaker], *We, Too, Must Love*, 127; emphasis in the original.

94. Marijane Meaker, interview by the author, November 18, 2011.

95. For statistics, see Meeker, *Contacts Desired*, 99, 119.

96. Highsmith's estimate, as given in her afterword to Patricia Highsmith, *The Price of Salt* (New York: W. W. Norton, 2004), 261. Originally published as Claire Morgan [Patricia Highsmith], *The Price of Salt* (New York: Coward-McCann, 1952).

97. Highsmith, *Price of Salt*, 230.

98. Joan Schenkar, *The Talented Miss Highsmith: The Secret Life and Serious of Art of Patricia Highsmith* (New York: St. Martin's Press, 2009), 266. For Schenkar's discussion of Highsmith's inspiration for *The Price of Salt*, see chap. 17; on Highsmith's former lover Virginia Kent Catherwood, see 282–286.

99. Ann Bannon, *Journey to a Woman* (Greenwich, CT: Fawcett Publications, 1960; San Francisco: Cleis Press, 2003); citations refer to the Cleis edition. Valerie Taylor, *Return to Lesbos* (New York: Midwood-Tower, 1963; Tallahassee, FL: Naiad Press, 1982); citations refer to the Naiad edition.

100. Christopher S. Nealon, *Foundlings: Lesbian and Gay Historical Emotion Before Stonewall* (Durham, NC: Duke University Press, 2001), 16.

101. Suzanna Danuta Walters, "As Her Hand Crept Slowly Up Her Thigh: Ann Bannon and the Politics of Pulp," *Social Text* 23 (Autumn–Winter 1989): 83–101. See also Diane Hamer, " 'I Am a Woman': Ann Bannon and the Writing of Lesbian Identity in the 1950s," in *Lesbian and Gay Writing: An Anthology of Critical Essays*, ed. Mark Lilly (London: Macmillan, 1990), 47–75; Angela Weir and Elizabeth Wilson, "The Greyhound Bus Station in the Evolution of Lesbian Popular Culture," in *New Lesbian Criticism: Literary and Cultural Readings*, ed. Sally Munt (New York: Columbia University Press, 1992), 95–113.

102. Ann Bannon, interview by David Garland, *Spinning on Air*, WNYC Radio, November 26, 2006, accessed August 14, 2018, http://beta.wnyc.org/shows/spinning/2006/nov/26/.

103. Valerie Taylor, "Five Minority Groups in Relation to Contemporary Fiction," *The Ladder*, January 1961, 6–13, 16–22, at 9. Taylor admitted to having a lesbian affair in several interviews, including one with Studs Terkel; see Studs Terkel, "Valerie Taylor, 79: Tucson, Arizona," in *Coming of Age: The Story of Our Century by Those Who've Lived It* (New York: New Press, 1995), 309–314.

104. Jane Rule, *Desert of the Heart* (Toronto: Macmillan Canada, 1964; Tallahassee, FL: Bella Books, 2005); citations refer to the Bella edition. On Rule's work as a whole, see Marilyn R. Schuster, *Passionate Communities: Reading Lesbian Resistance in Jane Rule's Fiction* (New York: New York University Press, 1999).

105. Rule, *Desert of the Heart*, 51–52.

106. *The Killing of Sister George*, directed by Robert Aldrich (1968; Santa Monica, CA: MGM Home Entertainment, 2005), DVD. For a further discussion of the film, see Russo, *Celluloid Closet*, 170–174.

107. On the controversy surrounding the film's X rating, see Christie Milliken, "Rate It X? Hollywood Cinema and the End of the Production Code," in Schaefer, *Sex Scene*, 25–52.

108. Jill Gardiner, *From the Closet to the Screen: Women at the Gateways Club, 1945–1985* (London: Pandora, 2003), chap. 7.

109. Kelly Hankin, "Lesbian Locations: The Production of Lesbian Bar Space in *The Killing of Sister George*," *Cinema Journal* 41, no. 1 (Autumn 2001): 3–27, at 14.

110. Joyce Pierson, interview by Arden Eversmeyer, August 2, 2008, p. 16, OLP.

111. Respondent #212, interview by Terrie Lyons, p. 112, box 2, folder 212, LP.

112. Letter to Phyllis Lyon and Del Martin, November 2, 1972, p. 6, box 23, folder 9, LMP.

113. See Rabinowitz, *American Pulp*, chap. 7.

114. Letter to Valerie Taylor, ca. 1993, box 2, folder 2, VTP.

Chapter 5

1. Faderman, *Odd Girls*, 207.

2. On lesbian feminist politics, see Shane Phelan, *Identity Politics: Lesbian Feminism and the Limits of Community* (Philadelphia: Temple University Press, 1989), chap. 3; Faderman, *Odd Girls*, 216–217, 248–252; Verta Taylor and Leila Rupp, "Women's Culture and Lesbian Feminist Activism: A Reconsideration of Cultural Feminism," *Signs* 19, no. 1 (1993): 32–61.

3. On lesbian separatist ideology, see Charlotte Bunch, "Learning from Lesbian Separatism," in *Lavender Culture*, ed. Karla Jay and Allen Young (New York: Jove/HBJ, 1978), 435; Sara Lucia Hoagland and Julia Penelope, *For Lesbians Only: A Separatist Anthology* (London: Onlywomen, 1988).

4. Ambitious Amazons, untitled statement, *Lesbian Connection* 1, no. 6 (July 1975): 1–2, at 1; emphasis in the original.

5. Ibid.

6. Lynne D. Shapiro, *Write On, Woman! A Writers' and Artists' Guide to Women's Alternate Press Periodicals* (New York: Lynn D. Shapiro, 1979), 25.

7. Jeanne Córdova, "Ticket to Lesbos: Who Qualifies?," *Lesbian Tide* 7, no. 6 (May–June 1978): 19–20, at 19; capitalization in the original.

8. Sidney Abbott and Barbara J. Love, *Sappho Was a Right-On Woman: A Liberated View of Lesbianism* (1972; repr., New York: Stein and Day, 1977), 117.

9. Toby Marotta, *The Politics of Homosexuality* (Boston: Houghton Mifflin, 1981), 235.

10. On the Stonewall riots, see Martin Duberman, *Stonewall* (New York: Dutton, 1993); Stein, *Rethinking*, 79–114. In contrast to those who portray the GLF as exceptional, Emily Hobson argues that the organization was part of a long history of gay and lesbian radicalism that persisted in the 1980s; Emily K. Hobson, *Lavender and Red: Liberation and Solidarity in the Gay and Lesbian Left* (Oakland: University of California Press, 2016).

11. On the creation of these groups, see Marotta, *Politics of Homosexuality*, 237–238; Karla Jay, *Tales of the Lavender Menace: A Memoir of Liberation* (New York: Basic Books, 1999) chap. 9.

12. Susan Brownmiller, "Sisterhood Is Powerful!," *New York Times Magazine*, March 15, 1970, 23, 128–136, at 140; emphasis in the original.

13. Quoted in Marotta, *Politics of Homosexuality*, 244.

14. For examples, see Martha Shelley, "Stepin Fetchit Woman," *Come Out!*, November 14, 1969, 7; Rita Mae Brown, "Coitus Interruptus," *Rat*, February 1970, 12. On the importance of Judy Grahn's writings in fostering lesbian feminist ideology on the West Coast at this same moment, see Chelsea Del Rio, "Voicing Gay Women's Liberation: Judy Grahn and the Shaping of Lesbian Feminism," *Journal of Lesbian Studies* 19, no. 3 (2015): 357–356.

15. Radicalesbians, "The Woman-Identified Woman" (1970), reprinted in *Dear Sisters: Dispatches from the Women's Liberation Movement*, ed. Rosalyn Baxandall and Linda Gordon (New York: Basic Books, 2000), 107–109.

16. On this choice, see ibid., 107; Rosen, *World Split Open*, 167–169; Jay, *Tales of the Lavender Menace*, 141.

17. Julie Enszer has pointed out that lesbian separatist ideas emerged earlier in a publication of the Revolutionary Lesbians in Ann Arbor, Michigan; see Julie R. Enszer, " 'How to Stop Choking to Death': Rethinking Lesbian Separatism as a Vibrant Political Theory and Feminist Practice," *Journal of Lesbian Studies* 20, no. 2 (2016): 180–196.

18. Anne M. Valk, "Living a Feminist Lifestyle: The Intersection of Theory and Action in a Lesbian Feminist Collective," *Feminist Studies* 28, no. 2 (Summer 2002): 303–332, at 321. See also Anne M. Valk, *Radical Sisters: Second Wave Feminism and Black Liberation in Washington, D.C.* (Urbana: University of Illinois Press, 2008), chap. 6.

19. Rodger Streitmatter, *Unspeakable: The Rise of the Gay and Lesbian Press in America* (Boston: Faber and Faber, 1995), 159.

20. Sharon Deevey, "Such a Nice Girl," *The Furies*, January 1972, 2. For a similar story, see Coletta Reid, "Recycled Trash," *The Furies*, June/July 1972, 8.

21. Deevey, "Such a Nice Girl," 2; emphasis in the original.

22. *Passionate Politics: The Life and Work of Charlotte Bunch*, directed by Tami Gold (2011; Newburgh, NY: New Day Films, 2012), DVD.

23. See Mary Ellman, "Women's Work," *New York Review of Books*, November 1, 1973, 18–19. On the *Library Journal*, see Faderman, *Odd Girls*, 225.

24. Jill Johnston, *Lesbian Nation: The Feminist Solution* (New York: Simon and Schuster, 1973), 276.

25. Ibid., 156.

26. Ibid., 70.

27. Ibid.

28. For discussions of the political tensions at Sagaris, see Alice Echols, *Daring to Be Bad: Radical Feminism in America, 1967–1975* (Minneapolis: University of Minnesota Press, 1989), 268; Rosen, *World Split Open*, 252–260.

29. Nancy Breeze, interview by Arden Eversmeyer, January n.d., 2007, p. 13, OLP.

30. Ibid., p. 14.

31. Ibid.

32. Murphy's papers are archived at the June L. Mazer Lesbian Archive at the University of California, Los Angeles.

33. Sharon Zecha, "Herstory," *Lesbian Tide* 1, no. 6 (January 1972): 12–13, at 12. On the history of *The Lesbian Tide*, see Jeanne Córdova, *When We Were Outlaws: A Memoir of Love and Revolution* (Midway, FL: Spinsters Ink, 2011).

34. For examples, see Barbara Macciocca, "On Becoming Sensual," *Women: A Journal of Liberation* 3, no. 1 (1972): 37–38; Davelynn, "Davelynn's Story," *Women: A Journal of Liberation* 4, no. 1 (1974): 56–57; Cynthia Rich, "Reflections on Eroticism," *Sinister Wisdom* 15 (Fall 1980): 59–63; and Susan J. Wolfe and Julia Penelope Stanley, eds., *The Coming Out Stories* (Watertown, MA: Persephone Press, 1980).

35. C. J. Martin, "Diary of a Queer Housewife," in Wolfe and Stanley, *Coming Out Stories*, 56–64, at 63.

36. Melanie Kaye, untitled column, *Heresies* 1, no. 3 (Fall 1977): 42–43, at 42.

37. Combahee River Collective, "A Black Feminist Statement," in *This Bridge Called My Back: Writings by Radical Women of Color*, ed. Cherríe Moraga and Gloria Anzaldúa (1981; New York: Kitchen Table, Women of Color Press, 1983), 210–218, at 213. For more on the founding of the Combahee River Collective, see Kimberly Springer, *Living for the Revolution: Black Feminist Organizations, 1968–1980* (Durham, NC: Duke University Press, 2005), 56–61.

38. Cherríe Moraga, preface to Moraga and Anzaldúa, *This Bridge Called My Back*, xiii–xix, at xiii.

39. Barbara Smith and Beverly Smith, "Across the Kitchen Table: A Sister-to-Sister Dialogue," in Moraga and Anzaldúa, *This Bridge Called My Back*, 113–127. For examples of women of color who *did* support separatism, see Anna Lee, "A Black Separatist," in Hoagland and Penelope, *For Lesbians Only*, 83–92; Dana R. Shugar, *Separatism and Women's Community* (Lincoln: University of Nebraska Press, 1995), 48–50, 97–98; and Enszer, "How to Stop Choking," 191.

40. Pat Parker, *Child of Myself* (San Lorenzo, CA: Shameless Hussy Press, 1972), unnumbered pages. For more on Parker's poetry, see the recent special issue on her work: " 'Where Would I Be Without You': Judy Grahn and Pat Parker," ed. Cheryl Clarke and Julie R. Enszer, special issue, *Journal of Lesbian Studies* 19, no. 3 (2015).

41. Beverly Smith, "The Wedding," in *Home Girls: A Black Feminist Anthology*, ed. Barbara Smith (New Brunswick, NJ: Rutgers University Press, 2000), 164–169, at 164. Originally printed in "Conditions: Five, The Black Women's Issue," ed. Lorraine Bethel and Barbara Smith, special issue, *Conditions* (Autumn 1979).

42. Rosita Angulo Miret Libre de Marulanda, untitled article, *Azalea* 3, no. 3 (Fall 1980): 12–13. For another example, see Becky Birtha, "A Mother-Daughter Victory: An Interview," *Azalea* 3, no. 1 (Winter 1979–1980): 17–23.

43. Arlene Stein, *Sex and Sensibility: Stories of a Lesbian Generation* (Berkeley: University of California Press, 1997), 67.

44. On coming out as involving the creation of a new self, see Shane Phelan, "(Be)Coming Out: Lesbian Identity and Politics," *Signs* 18, no. 4 (Summer 1993): 765–790, at 774.

45. Abbott and Love, *Sappho Was a Right-On Woman*, 27–28.

46. Ibid., 19.

47. Carl Wittman, "Refugees from Amerika: A Gay Manifesto," in *Come Out Fighting: A Century of Essential Writing on Gay and Lesbian Liberation*, ed. Chris Bull (New York: Thunders Mouth Press/Nation Books, 2001), 69–79, at 72. Originally published in the *San Francisco Free Press* (December 22, 1969–January 7, 1970), 3–5.

48. Wittman, "Refugees from Amerika," 71.

49. Martin and Lyon, *Lesbian/Woman*, 159–160.

50. Ibid., 160; emphasis added.

51. Handwritten note (response to letter to Phyllis Lyon, May 10, 1973), May 10, 1973, p. 1, box 25, folder 3, LMP.

52. Handwritten note (stapled to letter to Phyllis Lyon, April 26, 1973), n.d., p. 1, box 24, folder 9, LMP.

53. Charlotte Bunch and Rita Mae Brown, "What Every Lesbian Should Know," in "Lesbian/Feminist Issue," special issue, *Motive* 32, no. 1 (1972): 4–8, at 7.

54. Gutter Dyke Collective, "Separatism," *Dykes and Gorgons* 1, no. 1 (May/June 1973): 16–17.

55. Heather Murray, "Free for All Lesbians: Lesbian Cultural Production and Consumption in the United States During the 1970s," *Journal of the History of Sexuality* 16, no. 2 (May 2007): 251–275.

56. On *Tribad*, see Streitmatter, *Unspeakable*, 168.

57. A. Enke, *Finding the Movement: Sexuality, Contested Space, and Feminist Activism* (Durham, NC: Duke University Press, 2007), 80–83.

58. "Conflict at East Lansing's Lesbian Center," *Lesbian Connection* 1, nos. 1 and 2 (October and December 1974): 12.

59. Kathleen Thompson, interview by A. Enke, June 31, 2004, quoted in Enke, *Finding the Movement*, 82.

60. Shelley, "Stepin Fetchit Woman," 7.

61. Steven Angelides, *A History of Bisexuality* (Chicago: University of Chicago Press, 2001), 18.

62. Michael du Plessis, "Blatantly Bisexual; or, Unthinking Queer Theory," in *RePresenting Bisexualities: Subjects and Cultures of Fluid Desire*, ed. Donald E. Hall and Maria Pramaggiore (New York: New York University Press, 1996), 19–54, at 30.

63. "In Sisterhood and Revolution, Mil. Wisc.," *Lesbian Connection* 1, no. 4 (March 1975): 23.

64. Abbott and Love, *Sappho Was a Right-On Woman*, 155.

65. For examples of early bisexual women's writing, see Debbie Willis, "Bisexuality: A Personal View," *Woman: A Journal of Liberation* 4, no. 1 (Winter 1974): 10–11; Laura Della Rosa, "The Bi-Sexual Potential," in *After You're Out: Personal Experiences of Gay Men and Lesbian Women*, ed. Karla Jay and Allen Young (New York: Link Books, 1975), 65–57; Jem, "A Bi-Sexual Offers Some Thoughts on Fences," in Jay and Young, *After You're Out*, 68–69.

66. Paula C. Rust, *Bisexuality and the Challenge to Lesbian Politics: Sex, Loyalty, and Revolution* (New York: New York University Press, 1995), chap. 6; Amber Ault, "Hegemonic Discourse in an Oppositional Community: Lesbian Feminists and Bisexuality," *Critical Sociology* 20, no. 3 (October 1994): 107–121; and Mariam Fraser, "Lose Your Face," in *The Bisexual Imaginary: Representation, Identity and Desire*, ed. Bi Academic Intervention: Phoebe Davidson, Jo Eadie, Clare Hemmings, Ann Kaloski, and Merl Storr (London: Cassell, 1997), 38–57.

67. Peter Osborne, "Gender as Performance: An Interview with Judith Butler," *Radical Philosophy* 67 (Summer 1994): 32–39.

68. This analysis is, of course, greatly influenced by Michel Foucault's "repressive hypothesis"; see Foucault, *History of Sexuality*.

69. See for example, Ruth Gibian, "Refusing Certainty: Toward a Bisexuality of Wholeness," in *Closer to Home: Bisexuality and Feminism,* ed. Elizabeth Reba Weise (Seattle, WA: Seal Press, 1992), 3–16; Brenda Marie Blasingame, "The Roots of Biophobia: Racism and Internalized Heterosexism," in Weise, *Closer to Home,* 47–53; and Robin Sweeney, "Too Butch to Be Bi (or You Can't Judge a Boy by Her Lover)," in *Bisexual Politics: Theories, Queries, and Visions,* ed. Naomi Tucker (New York: Haworth Press, 1995), 179–188.

70. As the foundational queer theorist Judith Butler has noted, "Sexual position always involves becoming haunted by what's excluded. And the more rigid the position, the greater the ghost." Osborne, "Interview with Judith Butler," 34.

71. Judy Klemesrud, "The Disciples of Sappho, Updated," *New York Times Magazine,* March 28, 1971, 38–52, at 52.

72. A Redstockings Sister, "I Am 23 a Mother and a Lesbian," *Rat,* August 9, 1970, 13, 24, at 24; reprinted in *Lesbians Speak Out,* ed. Carol, Natalie, Ellen, and Pat of Free Woman's Press (San Francisco: Free Women's Press, 1971), 57–60.

73. Ibid. For another example, see Martha Andrews, "Half Life," *Focus: A Journal for Lesbians,* August 1978, 8.

74. O and S, "Women," *Sisters,* March 1972, 5–6, at 5.

75. Heather Love, *Feeling Backward: Loss and the Politics of Queer History* (Cambridge, MA: Harvard University Press, 2007), 13, 161.

76. G., "To O and S," *Sisters,* April 1972, 27.

77. "The Furious Young Philosopher Who Got It," *Life,* September 4, 1970, 22. See also "The Liberation of Kate Millett," *Time,* August 31, 1970, 18–19.

78. Kate Millett, *Flying* (New York: Knopf, 1974), 15; Victoria Hesford, *Feeling Women's Liberation* (Durham, NC: Duke University Press, 2013), 79.

79. "Women's Lib: A Second Look," *Time,* December 14, 1970, 50.

80. On this event, see Judy Klemesrud, "The Lesbian Issue and Women's Lib," *New York Times,* December 18, 1978, 47; Echols, *Daring to Be Bad,* 219–220; and Hesford, *Feeling Women's Liberation,* chap. 2.

81. Ti-Grace Atkinson, "Lesbianism and Feminism: Justice for Women as 'Unnatural,'" in *Amazon Odyssey: The First Collection of Writings by the Political Pioneer of the Women's Movement* (New York: Link Books, 1974), 131–134, at 132.

82. Respondent #207, interview by Terrie Lyons, p. 21, box 2, folder 207, LP.

83. Ibid.

84. Respondent #121, interview by Terrie Lyons, p. 24, box 1, folder 121, LP.

85. Ibid., pp. 12–13.

86. Ibid., p. 13. On antipathy toward lesbian mothers within the lesbian community, see Rivers, *Radical Relations,* 104–108.

87. Alice Y. Hom,"Unifying Differences: Lesbian of Color Community Building in Los Angeles and New York, 1970s–1980s," (PhD diss., Claremont Graduate University, 2011), 87.

88. On lesbian battles over pornography and sadomasochism, see Phelan, *Identity Politics,* chaps. 5 and 6; Faderman, *Odd Girls,* chap. 10; Lisa Duggan and Nan D. Hunter, *Sex Wars: Sexual Dissent and Political Culture* (New York: Routledge, 1995); and Whitney Strub, "Lavender, Menaced: Lesbianism, Obscenity Law, and the Feminist Antipornography Movement," *Journal of Women's History* 22, no. 2 (Summer 2010): 83–107. On battles over the place of male children, see Rivers, *Radical Relations,* 157–165.

89. Jackie Henry [pseud.], quoted in Stein, *Sex and Sensibility*, 81.

90. Stein, *Sex and Sensibility*, 128.

91. Robin Morgan, "Lesbianism and Feminism: Synonyms or Contradictions?," *Lesbian Tide* 2, no. 10 (May/June 1973): 30–34, at 30.

92. Ibid.

93. Ibid., 33.

94. Ibid.

95. Ibid., 32; emphasis in the original. For a further discussion, see Susan Stryker, *Transgender History* (Berkeley, CA: Seal Press, 2008), 103–105; A. Finn Enke, "Collective Memory and the Transfeminist 1970s: Toward a Less Plausible History," *Transgender Studies Quarterly* 5, no. 1 (February 2018): 9–29.

96. Pat Buchanan, "The Living Contradiction," *Lesbian Tide* 2, no. 10 (May/June 1973): 6–7, at 6; emphasis added.

97. Carol De Arment, "Inept Mess," *off our backs* 3, no. 8 (May 1973): 10; emphasis in the original.

98. Millett, *Flying*, 123.

99. Ibid., 131; Hesford, *Feeling Women's Liberation*, 172.

100. Carol Kleinman, "Kate Millett—One Step Beyond Heterosexuality," *Chicago Tribune*, April 6, 1975, sec. 5, 5.

101. Larry McMurtry, " 'Flying' Low: Kate Millett's New Plane," *Washington Post*, June 10, 1964, B1, B9.

102. See, for example, Elinor Langer, "Confessing," *Ms. Magazine*, December 1974, 69–71, 108, at 71; Juliet Mitchell, "Women in Love," *New Statesman*, June 13, 1975, 781.

103. Julia Penelope Stanley, "Fear of *Flying*," *Sinister Wisdom* 1, no. 2 (Fall 1976): 52–62, at 52; Fran Moira, Mecca Reliance, and Anne Williams, "kate millett: finally, all i had was who i am," *off our backs* 4, no. 10 (October 1974): 26.

104. Ilene Barth, "Kate Millett: 'Feminists Have Changed the Intellectual Climate,' " *LI: Newsday's Magazine for Long Island*, May 8, 1977, 11, 12, 14, 29–31, at 29.

105. Jane Rule, "With All Due Respect: In Defense of All Lesbian Lifestyles," in Jay and Young, *After You're Out*, 22–26, at 23.

106. Ibid., 26. On Rule's resistance to understandings of lesbian identity as fixed and stable, see Schuster, *Passionate Communities*, 119.

107. Rich, "Compulsory Heterosexuality," 648.

108. Ibid., 654.

109. Ibid., 659.

110. Anita Cornwell, " 'I Am Black, Woman, and Poet': An Interview with Audre Lorde," in *Black Lesbian in White America* (Tallahassee, FL: Naiad Press, 1983), 37–50, at 45; emphasis in the original.

111. Ibid.

112. Audre Lorde, "Age, Race, Class and Sex: Women Redefining Difference," in *Sister Outsider: Essays and Speeches* (Trumansburg, NY: Crossing Press, 1984), 114–123, at 120.

113. Ibid., 121.

114. Alexis De Veaux, *Warrior Poet: A Biography of Audre Lorde* (New York: W. W. Norton, 2004), 72–99.

115. Donna Landry and Gerald MacLean, eds., *The Spivak Reader: Selected Works of Gayatri Chakravorty Spivak* (New York: Routledge, 1996), 214.

116. Joanna Russ, "Not For Years, But For Decades," in Wolfe and Stanley, *Coming Out Stories*, 103–118 at 111.

117. J. Lapis Springtree, interview by the author, April 10, 2014.

Chapter 6

1. Letter to Phyllis Lyon, November 13, 1972, p. 1, box 25, folder 3, LMP.

2. Letter to Del Martin and Phyllis Lyon, August 6, 1973, p. 3, box 25, folder 3, LMP.

3. Ibid.

4. Letter to Phyllis Lyon, November 13, 1972, p. 1, box 25, folder 3, LMP.

5. For examples of wives whose affairs continued to unfold in the spaces of everyday life in this period, see Respondent #112, interview by Terrie Lyons, box 1, folder 112, LP; Sue "Rainbow" Williams, interview by Arden Eversmeyer, January 23, 2007, OLP; Mare Chapman, interview by Sophie Steinberger, March 16 and 19, 2012, DLLP; and Deborah Faison, interview by Lori E. Harris, March 17, 2010, DLLP.

6. Marty Elkin, interview by Barbara Foley Morrison, March 19–20, 2013, p. 38, DLLP.

7. Respondent #205, interview by Ellen Lewin, p. 8, box 2, folder 205, LP.

8. Ibid., p. 9.

9. Faderman, *Odd Girls*, 208.

10. Anita Shreve, *Women Together, Women Alone: The Legacy of the Consciousness-Raising Movement* (New York: Viking, 1989), 198. On consciousness-raising, see also Jo Freeman, *The Politics of Women's Liberation: A Case Study of An Emerging Social Movement and Its Relation to the Policy Process* (New York: Longman, 1975), chap. 4; Rosen, *World Split Open*, 196–201.

11. Anonymous, interview by the author, December 10, 2013.

12. Bea Howard, interview by Arden Eversmeyer, March n.d., 2003, OLP.

13. Cynthia Kelley, interview by Arden Eversmeyer, October n.d., 2006, p. 11, OLP; emphasis added.

14. Kathleen C. Berkeley, *The Women's Liberation Movement in America* (Westport, CT: Greenwood Press, 1999), 75.

15. Respondent #113, interview with by Ellen Lewin, p. 14, box 1, folder 113, LP.

16. Elizabeth "Deedy" Breed, interview by Arden Eversmeyer, May 23, 2001, p. 15, OLP.

17. For a similar case, see Cynthia Kelley, interview by Arden Eversmeyer, October n.d., 2006, OLP.

18. Henrietta Bensussen, interview by author, December 17, 2013, p. 12. For a similar story, see Arden Kate, interview by Arden Eversmeyer, March 28, 2008, pp. 12–13, OLP.

19. Henrietta Bensussen, journal entry, summer 1983, pp. 2–3, author's collection.

20. On the long history of the police harassment of gay bars and the LGBT challenges to it, see D'Emilio, *Sexual Politics*, chap. 9; Chauncey, *Gay New York*; Kennedy and Davis, *Boots of Leather*; Stein, *City of Sisterly and Brotherly Loves*; Meeker, "Behind the Mask"; Boyd, *Wide Open Town*; Christina B. Hanhardt, *Safe Space: Gay Neighborhood History and the Politics of Violence* (Durham, NC: Duke University Press, 2013); and Stewart-Winter, *Queer Clout.*

21. Mare Chapman, interview by Sophie Steinberger, March 16 and 19, 2012, p. 31, DLLP.

22. Respondent #213, interview by Terrie Lyons, p. 64, box 2, folder 213, LP. For a similar account, see Respondent #212, interview by Terrie Lyons, box 2, folder 212, LP.

23. For examples, see Faderman, *Odd Girls*, 288.

24. Respondent #115, interview by Ellen Lewin, p. 21, box 1, folder 115, LP.

25. See Thorpe, "A house where queers go," 40–61.

26. Anita, interview by Rochella Thorpe, June 29, 1992, p. 4, box 2, folder 3, TF.

27. Ibid., p. 5.

28. Mistinguette Smith, interview by the author, December 22, 2013, p. 15. See also mistinguette, "cabaret," in *Does Your Mama Know? An Anthology of Black Lesbian Coming Out Stories*, ed. Lisa C. Moore (Decatur, GA: Redbone Press, 1997), 71–72.

29. On the founding of Salsa Soul Sisters, see Candice Boyce, excerpted interview, in *The Question of Equality: Lesbian and Gay Politics in America Since Stonewall*, ed. David Deitcher (New York: Scribner, 1995), 77–79; Hom, "Unifying Differences," chap. 3.

30. On the founding of Sapphire Sapphos, see Beemyn, *Queer Capital*, 207–210.

31. On the Asian Women's Group and other organizing efforts on behalf of San Francisco's lesbians, see Trinity A. Ordona, "Asian Lesbians in San Francisco: Struggles to Create a Safe Space, 1970s–1980s," in *Asian/Pacific Islander American Women: A Historical Anthology*, ed. Shirley Hune and Gail M. Nomura (New York: New York University Press, 2003), 319–334. For more on Lesbianas Unidas, see Laura M. Esquivel, "An East L.A. Warrior Who Bridged the Latina/o and the Gay Worlds," in *Queer Brown Voices: Personal Narratives of Latina/o LGBT Activism*, ed. Uriel Quesada, Letitia Gomez, and Salvador Vidal-Ortiz (Austin: University of Texas Press, 2015), 78–96; Ellen M. Gil-Gómez, "Lesbianas Unidas: Shaping Nation Through Community Activist Rhetorics," *Journal of Lesbian Studies* 20, no. 2 (2016): 197–212. On LGBT Latina/o organizing in the 1970s more broadly, see Faderman and Timmons, *Gay L.A.*, 348–350; Stein, *Rethinking*, 124–125.

32. "Alberta Ashley: A Profile by Candice (Sekou) Boyce," *Salsa Soul Sisters Gayzette*, July/August 1979, 2–3.

33. Hom, "Unifying Differences," 112.

34. Sue Fox, "After the Revolution," *Washington Blade*, June 23, 1995, 43, 45, 47, at 47.

35. Sarah E. Igo, *The Known Citizen: A History of Privacy in Modern America* (Cambridge, MA: Harvard University Press, 2018), chap. 7.

36. Murray, *Not in This Family*, chap. 2.

37. Of the *Time* articles, see Christopher Cory, "The Homosexual: Newly Visible, Newly Understood," *Time*, October 31, 1969, 56, 62, 64–66; "Four Lives in the Gay World," 62; "A Discussion: Are Homosexuals Sick?" 67. For the *Life* article, see Michael Durham, "Homosexuals in Revolt: The Year That One Liberation Movement Turned Militant," *Life*, December 31, 1971, 62–72.

38. See Abraham H. Maslow, *Toward a Psychology of Being* (New York: Van Nostrand, 1968); Carl Rogers, *On Becoming a Person: A Therapist's View of Psychotherapy* (Boston: Houghton Mifflin, 1961). On the human potential movement's role in the history of American psychology and culture, see Ellen Herman, *The Romance of American Psychology: Political Culture in the Age of Experts* (Berkeley: University of California Press, 1995), 264–275; Jessica Grogan, *Encountering America: Humanistic Psychology Sixties Culture and the Shaping of the Modern Self* (New York: Harper Perennial, 2013).

39. George R. Bach and Ronald M. Deutsch, *Pairing* (New York: Peter H. Wyden, 1970). On *Pairing*'s sales, see Ellen Ross, "'The Love Crisis': Couples Advice Books of the Late 1970s," *Signs* 6, no. 1 (Autumn 1980): 108–122, at 109.

40. Bach and Deutsch, *Pairing*, x.

41. For more on humanistic psychologists' influence on marital-advice literature, see Steven Mintz and Susan Kellogg, *Domestic Revolutions: A Social History of American Family Life* (New York: Free Press, 1988), 205–207; Davis, *More Perfect Unions*, 188–189.

42. Schutz was a particularly well-known encounter-group leader with a major media presence in the late 1960s and early 1970s; see Marion S. Goldman, *The American Soul Rush: Esalen and the Rise of Spiritual Privilege* (New York: New York University Press, 2012) 6, 36–37.

43. Jerry Gillies, *My Needs, Your Needs, Our Needs* (Garden City, NY: Doubleday, 1974), 73.

44. Bach and Deutsch, *Pairing*, 169.

45. Respondent #110, interview by Terrie Lyons, p. 14, box 1, folder 110, LP.

46. Ibid.

47. Sue "Rainbow" Williams, interview by Arden Eversmeyer, January 23, 2007, p. 10, OLP.

48. Letter to Phyllis Lyon, November 6, 1972, p. 1, box 23, folder 12, LMP. See also Respondent #112, interview by Terrie Lyons, p. 6, box 1, folder 112, LP.

49. Letter to Phyllis Lyon, November 6, 1972, p. 2, box 23, folder 12, LMP.

50. See Letter to Lesbian Liberation, September 9, 1983, p. 2, box 159, folder 15, BWHBC.

51. Elizabeth "Betsy" McConnell, interview by Arden Eversmeyer, May 9, 2009, p. 9, OLP.

52. Pat Gandy, interview by Arden Eversmeyer, January 7, 2009, p. 23, OLP. See also Respondent #304, interview by Terrie Lyons, p. 14, box 3, folder 304, LP.

53. Pat Gandy, interview by Arden Eversmeyer, January 7, 2009, p. 23, OLP.

54. See Celello, *Making Marriage Work*; Davis, *More Perfect Unions*.

55. Martha Weinman Lear, "Save the Spouses, Rather Than the Marriage," *New York Times Magazine*, August 13, 1972, 18.

56. Celello, *Making Marriage Work*, 119.

57. Beverly Todd, interview by Arden Eversmeyer, April n.d., 2001, p. 5, OLP.

58. Letter to Phyllis Lyon and Del Martin, April 25, 1973, p. 1, box 23, folder 8, LMP.

59. Letter to Del Martin and Phyllis Lyon, August 14, 1973, p. 1, box 23, folder 12, LMP.

60. Letter to Lesbian Liberation, n.d., p. 1, box 160, folder 1, BWHBC.

61. For an example of a husband who believed his wife's relationship with another woman would pass, see Deborah Faison, interview by Lori E. Harris, March 17, 2010, DLLP.

62. Letter to Phyllis Lyon and Del Martin, March 4, 1974, p. 2, box 23, folder 6, LMP.

63. Ibid.

64. See Nancy F. Cott, *Public Vows: A History of Marriage and the Nation* (Cambridge, MA: Harvard University Press, 2000), 208–209; Coontz, *Marriage, a History*, 249; Celello, *Making Marriage Work*, 126–127; and Davis, *More Perfect Unions*, 187–189.

65. Carl R. Rogers, *Becoming Partners: Marriage and Its Alternatives* (New York: Delacorte Press, 1972), 1. Other books of this genre include Megan Terry, *Couplings and Groupings* (New York: Pantheon Books, 1972); Roger W. Libby and Robert N. Whitehurst, *Renovating Marriage: Toward New Sexual Life Styles* (Danville, CA: Consensus Publishers, 1973); and Lawrence Casler, *Is Marriage Necessary?* (New York: Human Sciences Press, 1974).

66. Rogers, *Becoming Partners*, 66.

67. David Viscott, *How to Live with Another Person* (New York: Arbor House, 1974), 64.

68. Nena O'Neill and George O'Neill, *Open Marriage: A New Life Style for Couples* (New York: M. Evans, 1972). On its length of time on the best-seller list, see Margalit Fox, "Nena O'Neill, 82, an Author of 'Open Marriage' Is Dead," *New York Times*, March 26, 2006, accessed August 15, 2018, http://www.nytimes.com/2006/03/26/books/25oneill.html. On the book's national sales, see Ross, "Love Crisis," 109.

69. O'Neill and O'Neill, *Open Marriage*, 74.

70. Ibid., 259.

71. Nena O'Neill, *The Marriage Premise* (New York: M. Evans, 1977), chap. 15.

72. Rogers, *Becoming Partners*, 140.

73. Zev Wanderer and Erika Fabian, *Making Love Work: New Techniques in the Art of Staying Together* (New York: Putnam, 1979), 57.

74. Ibid.

75. For examples, see Anonymous, interview by the author, March 30, 2014; Ellen Symons, "Parallel Universes," in *From Wedded Wife to Lesbian Life: Stories of Transformation*, ed. Deborah Abbott and Ellen Farmer (1995; repr., Freedom, CA: Crossing Press, 1999), 23–26; and Phyllis Chesler, *Mothers on Trial: The Battle for Children and Custody* (New York: McGraw-Hill, 1986), 128–129.

76. Respondent #305, interview by Ellen Lewin, p. 17, box 3, folder 305, LP.

77. Letter to Phyllis Lyon and Del Martin, April 26, 1973, p. 1, box 23, folder 12, LMP.

78. One study of fifty swinging wives found that not one changed her underlying sexual preference for men after having sexual experiences with women. Joan K. Dixon, "Sexuality and Relationship Changes in Married Females Following the Commencement of Bisexual Activity," in *Two Lives to Lead: Bisexuality in Men and Women*, ed. Fritz Klein and Timothy J. Wolf (New York: Harrington Park Press, 1985), 115–133.

79. David Allyn, *Make Love, Not War: The Sexual Revolution, an Unfettered History* (Boston: Little, Brown, 2000), 254.

80. Respondent #121, interview by Terrie Lyons, p. 9, box 1, folder 121, LP.

81. Ibid.

82. Ibid., p. 10. For a similar story, see Respondent #303, interview by Terrie Lyons, pp. 20–21, box 3, folder 303, LP.

83. Respondent #121, interview with by Terrie Lyons, p. 13, box 1, folder 121, LP.

84. Ibid., p. 26.

85. Jane E. Brody, "Bisexual Life-Style Appears to Be Spreading and Not Necessarily Among 'Swingers'" *New York Times*, March 24, 1974, 57; "The New Bisexuals," *Time*, May 13, 1974, 79; and "Bisexual Chic: Anyone Goes," *Newsweek*, May 27, 1974, 90. See also Marjorie B. Garber, *Vice Versa: Bisexuality and the Eroticism of Everyday Life* (New York: Simon and Schuster, 1995), 26–27; Paula C. Rodriguez Rust, "Popular Images and the Growth of Bisexual Community and Visibility," in *Bisexuality in the United States: A Social Science Reader*, ed. Paula C. Rodriguez Rust (New York: Columbia University Press, 2000), 537–553.

86. On Barbara Walters's show, see Janet Bode, *View from Another Closet: Exploring Bisexuality in Women* (New York: Hawthorn Books, 1976), 27.

87. Barry Kohn and Alice Matusow, *Barry and Alice: Portrait of a Bisexual Marriage* (Englewood Cliffs, NJ: Prentice-Hall, 1980), 1.

88. Letter to Lesbian Liberation, May 30, 1981, p. 1, box 160, folder 5, BWHBC.

89. Letter to Lesbian Liberation, August 30, 1978, p. 1, box 159, folder 15, BWHBC.

90. Letter to Lesbian Liberation, March 22, 1981, pp. 2–3, box 160, folder 2, BWHBC.

91. Ibid.

92. By some accounts, the San Francisco–based Sexual Freedom League functioned as an early bisexual organization in the late 1960s, but it was not explicitly bisexual. Stephen Donaldson, "The Bisexual Movement's Beginnings in the 1970s: A Personal Retrospective," in Tucker, *Bisexual Politics*, 31–45.

93. Ibid., 34.

94. Ibid., 36–37.

95. Fritz Klein, *The Bisexual Option: A Concept of One Hundred Percent Intimacy* (New York: Arbor House, 1978), 122. On bisexual organizing in New York, see also Chuck Mishaan, "The Bisexual Scene in New York City," in Klein and Wolf, *Two Lives to Lead*, 223–225.

96. On the Bisexual Center in San Francisco see, Jay P. Paul, "San Francisco's Bisexual Center and the Emergence of a Bisexual Movement," in *Bisexualities: The Ideology and Practice of Sexual Contact with Both Men and Women*, ed. Erwin J. Haeberle and Rolf Gindorf (New York: Continuum, 1998), 130–139; Maggi Rubenstein and Cynthia Ann Slater, "A Profile of the San Francisco Bisexual Center," in Klein and Wolf, *Two Lives to Lead*, 227–231; and Naomi Tucker, "Bay Area Bisexual History: An Interview with David Lourea," in Tucker, *Bisexual Politics*, 47–61. On Chicago's Bi-Ways, see George Barr, "Chicago Bi-Ways: An Informal History," in Klein and Wolf, *Two Lives to Lead*, 234.

97. Amanda Udis-Kessler, "Identity/Politics: A History of the Bisexual Movement," in Tucker, *Bisexual Politics*, 17–45. See also Megan Morrison, "Bisexuality: Loving Whom We Choose," *BBWN* [later *Bi-Women*]: *Newsletter of the Boston Bisexual Women's Network* 2, no. 3 (May/June 1984): 1–2, 7; Dannielle Raymond and Liz A. Highleyman, "Brief Timeline of Bisexual Activism in the United States," in Tucker, *Bisexual Politics*, 333–337.

98. *Bi-Lines*, December 1984, p. 1, box 1, Action Bi-Women folder, Grant S. Hornston Papers, Gerber/Hart Libraries and Archive.

99. "Lani," in *Bi Lives: Bisexual Women Tell Their Stories*, ed. Kata Orndorff (Tucson, AZ: See Sharp Press, 1999), 98–112, at 100.

100. Ibid., 105.

101. On the National Bisexual Conference, see Clare Hemmings, *Bisexual Spaces: A Geography of Sexuality and Gender* (New York: Routledge, 2002), chap. 4. Ka'ahumanu is also the coeditor of Loraine Hutchins and Lani Ka'ahumanu, eds., *Bi Any Other Name: Bisexual People Speak Out* (New York: Alyson Publications, 1991).

102. Respondent #110, interview by Terrie Lyons, p. 15, box 1, folder 110, LP.

103. Ibid.

104. Philip W. Blumstein and Pepper Schwartz, "Lesbianism and Bisexuality," in *Sexual Deviance and Sexual Deviants*, ed. Erich Goode and Richard R. Troiden (New York: William Morrow, 1974), 278–295.

105. Gretchen Courage, interview with the author, May 7, 2014, p. 15.

106. Robyn Ochs, "In Memoriam," *Bi-Women: The Newsletter of the Boston Bisexual Women's Network* 5, no. 6 (October/November 1987): 3.

107. Eli Coleman, "Bisexual Women in Marriages," in Klein and Wolf, *Two Lives to Lead*, 87–99, at 87. Originally published in *Journal of Homosexuality* 11, no. 1–2 (Spring 1985): 87–100.

108. Mare Chapman, interview by Sophie Steinberger, March 16 and 19, 2012, p. 27, DLLP. See also Respondent #205, interview by Ellen Lewin, p. 8, box 2, folder 205, LP; Respondent #307, interview by Ellen Lewin, p. 13, box 3, folder 307, LP.

109. Mare Chapman, interview by Sophie Steinberger, March 16 and 19, 2012, p. 28, DLLP.

110. Carol Hoke, interview by Rochella Thorpe, February 4, 1992, TF. See also Respondent #213, interview by Terrie Lyons, p. 13, box 2, folder 213, LP.

111. O'Neill, *Marriage Premise*, 200.

112. Melanie Thernstrom, "Rethinking Matrimony," *New York Times*, December 31, 2006, accessed August 15, 2018, http://www.nytimes.com/2006/12/31/magazine/31o_neill.t .html.

113. Cott, *Public Vows*, 208.

Chapter 7

1. For details about the Mitchell's belongings, see findings of fact and conclusions of law, Mitchell v. Mitchell, No. 240665 (Cal. Super Ct., Santa Clara County, June 8, 1972), box 196, folder 9, LMP.

2. Rita A. Goldberger, "Custody Battle Continues," *Lesbian Tide* 2, no. 9 (April 1973): 3, 25, 26, at 3.

3. Sasha Gregory, "Gay Mother Wins Children's Custody," *Advocate*, July 1979, 6, 12.

4. Ibid., 6. On the letters, see Goldberger, "Custody Battle Continues."

5. For details, see Gregory, "Gay Mother Wins."

6. Ibid., 6.

7. On alimony and child support payments, see Gregory, "Gay Mother Wins," 6; "Dubious Win: Lesbian Can Keep Kids, But Loses Love Life," *Berkeley Barb*, July 14–20, 1972, 11.

8. Undated letter to Phyllis Lyon and Del Martin, p. 1, box 196, folder 9, LMP.

9. Deborah L. Rhode and Martha Minow, "Reforming the Questions, Questioning the Reforms: Feminist Perspectives on Divorce Law," in *Divorce Reform at the Crossroads*, ed. Stephen S. Sugarman and Herma Hill Kay (New Haven, CT: Yale University Press, 1991), 191–210, at 195.

10. On these changes, see Alison Lefkovitz, *Strange Bedfellows: Marriage in the Age of Women's Liberation* (Philadelphia: University of Pennsylvania Press, 2018), chap. 2.

11. On the attack on same-sex households in the 1970s including those of lesbian mothers, see Lefkovitz, *Strange Bedfellows*, chap. 6.

12. McLaughlin et al., *Changing Lives*, 60–61.

13. Andrew J. Cherlin, *Marriage, Divorce, Remarriage* (Cambridge, MA: Harvard University Press, 1992), 21–22.

14. Weiss, *To Have and To Hold*, see chap. 6.

15. Glenda Riley, *Divorce: An American Tradition* (New York: Oxford University Press, 1991) 158.

16. Lester Velie, "What's Killing Our Marriages?," *Readers Digest*, June 1973, 152–156, at 156.

17. See Riley, *Divorce*, 159.

18. See Cherlin, *Marriage, Divorce*, 52–53. On long-term trends, see also Carl N. Degler, *At Odds: Women and the Family in America from the Revolution to the Present* (Oxford: Oxford University Press, 1980).

19. On WITCH and this action, see Echols, *Daring to Be Bad*, 96–98; Rosen, *World Split Open*, 204–205.

20. Alix Kates Shulman, "A Marriage Agreement," *Up from Under* 1, no. 2 (August/September 1970): 5–8; reprinted in "Living by Contract," *Life*, April 28, 1972, 42–46B, and Alix Kates Shulman, "A Challenge to Every Marriage," *Redbook*, August 1971, 57, 138–139, 141.

21. Davis, *More Perfect Unions*, 191.

22. On the ways social workers responded to domestic violence historically, see Linda Gordon, *Heroes of Their Own Lives: The Politics and History of Family Violence, Boston, 1880–1960* (New York: Penguin Books, 1988). On domestic violence in women's divorce petitions, see, for example, Elaine Tyler May, *Great Expectations: Marriage and Divorce in Post-Victorian America* (Chicago: University of Chicago Press, 1980), 31–36.

23. Berkeley, *Women's Liberation Movement*, 69. For more on feminist struggles against domestic violence in the 1970s, see Susan Schechter, *Women and Male Violence: The Visions and Struggles of the Battered Women's Movement* (Boston: South End Press, 1982); Rosen, *World Split Open*, 181–188.

24. Doreen Brand, interview by Bea Howard, May n.d., 2003, OLP. See also Edith Daly, interview by Arden Eversmeyer, January n.d., 2004, OLP; Beverly Hickock and Doreen Brand, interview by Sharon Lutz, October 5, 1994, OHC.

25. Martha Wienman Lear, "Save the Spouses, Rather Than the Marriage," *New York Times*, 12, 13, 15, 18, 20, 24–27, at 13; emphasis in the original.

26. Barbara Ehrenreich and Deirdre English, *For Her Own Good: 150 Years of the Experts' Advice to Women* (1978; repr., Garden City, NY: Anchor Press, 1979), 297–311. For more on the human potential movement and its relationship to feminism, see Grogan, *Encountering America*, chap. 12.

27. On the complex and often contradictory messages that women's magazines presented to readers in the 1970s, see Beth L. Bailey, "She 'Can Bring Home the Bacon': Negotiating Gender in the 1970s," in *America in the Seventies*, ed. David R. Farber and Beth L. Bailey (Lawrence: University of Kansas Press, 2004), 107–129; Susan J. Douglas, *Where the Girls Are: Growing Up Female with the Mass Media* (New York: Random House, 1994), chap. 11; and Rosen, *World Split Open*, 308–314.

28. "End of a Marriage," *Good Housekeeping*, February 1974, 75, 134, 136–140, at 140.

29. For examples, see Letter to Lesbian Liberation, January 29, 1977, p. 1, box 159, folder 13, BWHBC. See also Respondent #110, interview by Terrie Lyons, p. 15, box 1, folder 110, LP.

30. Letter to "Sisters," July 17, 1979, pp. 3–4, box 23, folder 6, LMP.

31. Letter to Phyllis Lyon, May 10, 1973, p. 3, box 25, folder 3, LMP.

32. See, for example, F. Ivan Nye, "Child Adjustment in Broken and Unhappy Unbroken Homes," *Marriage and Family Living* 19, no. 4 (November 1957): 356–361; Lee G. Burchinal, "Characteristics of Adolescents from Unbroken, Broken, and Reconstituted Families," *Journal of Marriage and Family* 26, no. 1 (February 1964): 44–51. For a review of such studies, see Lynne Carol Halem, *Divorce Reform: Changing Legal and Social Perspectives* (New York: Free Press, 1980), 176–181.

33. E. Mavis Hetherington, Martha Cox, and Roger Cox, "The Aftermath of Divorce," in *Mother-Child, Father-Child Relations*, ed. J. H. Stevens Jr. and M. Matthews (Washington,

DC: National Association for the Education of Young Children, 1978), 146–176; E. Mavis Hetherington, "Divorce: A Child's Perspective," *American Psychologist* 34, no. 10 (October 1979): 851–858.

34. Susan Gettleman and Janet Markowitz, *The Courage to Divorce* (New York: Ballantine, 1974), 86–87.

35. Ben B. Lindsey and Wainwright Evans, *The Companionate Marriage* (New York: Ayer, 1927).

36. George Thorman, *Broken Homes* (New York: Public Affairs Committee, 1947), 15–20, cited in Riley, *Divorce*, 162.

37. See Katherine L. Caldwell, "Not Ozzie and Harriet: Postwar Divorce and the American Liberal Welfare State," *Law and Social Inquiry* 23, no. 1 (Winter 1998): 1–53.

38. Riley, *Divorce*, 162. For more on divorce reform in the 1960s, see Robert V. Sherwin, *Compatible Divorce* (New York: Crown Publishers, 1969); Nester C. Kohut, *Positive Divorce Reform for America* (Chicago: Association for the Advancement of Family Stability, 1969).

39. Uniform Marriage and Divorce Act, *Family Law Quarterly* 5 (1971): 205–251, at 227.

40. For a thorough and comprehensive discussion of when precisely all fifty states adopted no-fault legislation, see Denese Ashbaugh Vlosky and Pamela A. Monroe, "The Effective Dates of No-Fault Divorce Legislation in the 50 States," *Family Relations* 51, no. 4 (October 2002): 317–324. On the spread of no-fault divorce law nationally, see Lenore Weitzman and Ruth B. Dixon, "The Transformation of Legal Marriage Through No-Fault Divorce," in *Marriage and Cohabitation in Contemporary Societies: Areas of Legal, Social and Ethical Change*, ed. John M. Eekelaar and Sanford M. Katz (Toronto: Butterworths, 1979), 143–153; Halem, *Divorce Reform*; Sugarman and Kay, *Divorce Reform at the Crossroads*; and Milton C. Regan, *Family Law and the Pursuit of Intimacy* (New York: New York University Press, 1993).

41. Kenneth D. Sell, "Divorce Advertising—One Year After *Bates*," *Family Law Quarterly* 12 (Winter 1979): 275–283.

42. Ann Marevis, interview by Arden Eversmeyer, March 9, 2010, p. 7, OLP.

43. Morton M. Hunt, *The World of the Formerly Married* (New York: McGraw-Hill, 1966), 10. See also Morton M. Hunt, "Help Wanted: Divorce Counselor," *New York Times Magazine*, January 1, 1967, 15–17.

44. "The Broken Family: Divorce U.S. Style," *Newsweek*, March 12, 1973, 47–50, 55–57, at 57.

45. Mel Krantzler, *Creative Divorce: A New Opportunity for Personal Growth* (New York: M. Evans, 1973).

46. *Women's Survival Manual: A Feminist Handbook on Separation and Divorce* (Philadelphia, Women in Transition, 1972). This work was later republished as *Women in Transition: A Feminist Handbook on Separation and Divorce* (New York: Scribner, 1975).

47. Jane Wilkie, *The Divorced Woman's Handbook: An Outline for Starting the First Year Alone* (New York: William Morrow, 1980).

48. Sidney M. De Angelis, "The Complete Guide to Divorce—American Style," *New Woman*, April 1986, 132–139, at 139.

49. Janet Lathrop, interview by Hannah Pepin, April 8, 2012, p. 21, DLLP.

50. Ibid.

51. Barbara Kalish, interview by Arden Eversmeyer, January n.d., 2001, p. 12, OLP.

52. Ibid., p. 13. On Barbara's dildo business, see Barbara Kalaish [Kalish], interview by Marie Cartier, July 7, 2007, quoted in Marie Cartier, "Baby, You Are My Religion: The Emergence of 'Theeology' in Pre-Stonewall Butch-Femme/Gay Women's Bar Culture and Community" (PhD diss., Claremont Graduate University, 2010), 537–538.

53. United States National Commission on the Observance of International Women's Year, ". . . To Form a More Perfect Union . . .": Justice for American Women; Report of the National Commission on the Observance of International Women's Year (Washington, DC: Department of State, 1976), 102.

54. Lenore J. Weitzman, The Divorce Revolution: The Unexpected Social and Economic Consequences for Women and Children in America (New York: Free Press, 1985).

55. Harriet Marks-Nelson, interview by Arden Eversmeyer, January 21, 2009, p. 14, OLP.

56. Henrietta Bensussen, interview by the author, December 17, 2013, p. 15.

57. Avis-Ann Strong Parke, interview by Arden Eversmeyer, October 15, 2007, p. 52.

58. For a comprehensive discussion of the displaced homemakers' movement, see Lisa Levenstein, "'Don't Agonize, Organize!': The Displaced Homemakers Campaign and the Contested Goals of Postwar Feminism," Journal of American History 100, no. 4 (March 2014): 1114–1138.

59. Barbara Ehrenreich and Karin Stallard, "The Nouveau Poor," Ms., July–August 1982, 217–224; Karin Stallard, Barbara Ehrenreich, and Holly Sklar, Poverty in the American Dream: Women and Children First (Boston: South End Press, 1983), 6, 9. See also Margaret Cerullo and Marla Erlien, "Beyond the 'Normal Family': A Cultural Critique of Women's Poverty," in For Crying Out Loud: Women's Poverty in the United States, ed. Diane Dujon and Ann Withorn (Boston: South End Press, 1996), 87–120, at 97.

60. On the conditions under which women were granted alimony in the early twentieth century, see May, Great Expectations, 150–155.

61. On these changes in maternal preference, see Mary Ann Mason, From Father's Property to Children's Rights: The History of Child Custody in the United States (New York: Columbia University Press, 1994), chap. 4.

62. Michael Wheeler, Divided Children: A Legal Guide for Divorcing Parents (New York: W. W. Norton, 1980), 40; Dennis K. Orthner and Ken Lewis, "Evidence of Single Father Competence in Childrearing," Family Law Quarterly 13, no. 1 (Spring 1979): 27–47, at 28.

63. Doris Jonas Freed and Henry H. Foster Jr., "Divorce in the Fifty States: An Overview," Family Law Quarterly 14, no. 4 (Winter 1981): 229–237, 239, 241–284, at 263–264.

64. Nancy D. Polikoff, "Why Are Mothers Losing: A Brief Analysis of Criteria Used in Child Custody Determinations," Women's Rights Law Reporter 7, no. 3 (Spring 1982): 235–244. As Martha Fineman has argued, treating mothers and fathers "equally" in this way denied, and in fact exacerbated, inequality between them, bolstering male control over the family at a moment when it appeared to be in threat; Martha Albertson Fineman, The Illusion of Equality: The Rhetoric and Reality of Divorce Reform (Chicago: University of Chicago Press, 1991).

65. Chesler, Mothers on Trial, xiii.

66. Rivers, Radical Relations, 57.

67. Nadler v. Nadler, 255 Cal. App. 2d 523; 63 Cal. Rptr. 352 (1967).

68. Letter to Del Martin, May 14, 1981, p. 1, box 125, folder 3, LMP.

69. Ibid.

70. Respondent #112, interview by Terrie Lyons, p. 6, box 1, folder 112, LP.

71. Letter to Del Martin, June 9, 1974, p. 2, box 196, folder 7, LMP.

72. "Milwaukee County, Wisconsin Lesbian Mother Wins Custody (October 1976)," flyer, box 125, folder 13, LMP.

73. Respondent #303, interview by Terrie Lyons, p. 22, box 3, folder 303, LP.

74. Respondent #214, interview by Terrie Lyons, p. 12, box 2, folder 214, LP.

75. Chaffin v. Frye, 45 Cal. App. 3d 43; 119 Cal. Rptr. 23 (1975). For more on the Chaffin case, see Carlos A. Ball, *The Right to Be Parents: LGBT Families and the Transformation of Parenthood* (New York: New York University Press, 2012), 5–6. For case documents and news clippings, see also box 124, folders 7 and 8, LMP. For examples of other women who fought for custody against their children's grandparents, see Hunter and Polikoff, "Custody Rights," 705–711. In even rarer instances, the state could intervene directly to contest lesbian mothers' custody: see In re. Tammy F., 1 Civ. No. 32648 Cal. App. (1973). For further discussion of *In re. Tammy F.*, see R. A. Basile, "Lesbian Mothers I," *Women's Rights Law Reporter* 2, no. 2 (December 1974): 3–25, esp. 21–22.

76. Respondent #305 interview by Ellen Lewin, p. 25, box 3, folder 305, LP.

77. Gifford Guy Gibson, *By Her Own Admission: A Lesbian Mother's Fight to Keep Her Son*, with Mary Jo Risher (Garden City, NY: Doubleday, 1977), 159–160.

78. Ibid., 165.

79. See, for example, court transcript, *Nadler v. Nadler*, box 124, folder 18, LMP.

80. "Lesbian Mother Witch Hunt!," undated flyer, box 124, folder 9, LMP. See also Sharon McDonald, "Lesbian Mothers: In Court," *Lesbian Tide* 6, no. 1 (July–August 1976): 23; "Mother Framed," *Big Mama Rag* 4, no. 6 (June–July 1976): 5; and "Lesbian Mothers Win," *New Women's Times* 2, no. 9 (September 15–October 15, 1976): 8.

81. Court transcript, *Nadler v. Nadler*, pp. 22–23, box 124, folder 18, LMP.

82. Chaffin v. Frye, 45 Cal. App. 3d 43; 119 Cal. Rptr. 23 (1975). On the transformation of sodomy laws, see William N. Eskridge Jr., *Dishonorable Passions: Sodomy Laws in America, 1861–2003* (New York: Viking, 2008); Marie-Amélie George, "The Harmless Psychopath: Legal Debates Promoting the Decriminalization of Sodomy in the United States," *Journal of the History of Sexuality* 24, no. 2 (May 2015): 225–261.

83. Richman, *Courting Change*, 99.

84. For a further discussion of this sexual double standard, see Rivers, *Radical Relations*, 229n8; Chesler, *Mothers on Trial*, chap. 5.

85. "Lesbian Mothers Custody Struggle," *Leaping Lesbian* 1, no. 4 (May 1977): 11–14. See also Rivers, *Radical Relations*, 88.

86. Respondent #205, interview by Ellen Lewin, p. 11, box 2, folder 205, LP.

87. Kathy Fraze, "Grandmother Gets Children of Townends," *Akron Beacon Journal*, March 28, 1975, B3. For Townend's correspondence with Del Martin and Phyllis Lyon about her case, see box 25, folder 3, LMP.

88. Jacobson v. Jacobson, 314 N.W.2d 78 (N.D. 1981).

89. Letter to Del Martin, May 28, 1974, p. 1, box 25, folder 3, LMP.

90. Respondent #112, interview by Terrie Lyons, pp. 10, 14, box 1, folder 112, LP.

91. Donna J. Hitchens, *Lesbian Mother Litigation Manual* (San Francisco: Lesbian Mother Rights Project, 1982), 27; Ball, *Right to Be Parents*, 25.

92. Respondent #309, interview by Terrie Lyons, p. 18, box 3, folder 309, LP.

93. In re Jane B., 380 N.Y.S.2d 848 (Sup. Ct. 1976).

94. Mariana Romo-Carmona, "Una madre," in *Compañeras: Latina Lesbians*, ed. Juanita Ramos, (New York: Routledge, 1994), 185–193, at 191.

95. Ibid., 192. For more on Romo-Carmona's activist career, see Hom, "Unifying Differences," chap. 2.

96. Rivers, *Radical Relations*, 61.

97. Romo-Carmona, "Una madre," 186.

98. Joan Gibbs and Claudette Furlonge, editors' introduction to special issue, *Azalea* 3, no. 1 (Winter 1979–1980): 1.

99. Birtha, "Mother-Daughter Victory," 20.

100. Respondent #110, interview by Terrie Lyons, p. 21, box 1, folder 110, LP.

101. Letter to Lesbian Liberation, March 7, 1981, p. 1, box 160, folder 4, BWHBC.

102. Respondent #121, interview by Terrie Lyons, pp. 45–46, box 1, folder 121, LP.

103. "Lesbian Mothers Union," *Mother Lode* no. 5 (Summer 1972): 2.

104. "A Dollar a Day Keeps the Husbands Away," advertisement for LMNDF in *Lesbian Tide* 7, no. 1 (July/August 1977): 27.

105. Jen Colletta, "Rosalie Davies, 70, Lesbian Activist," *Philadelphia Gay News*, July 23, 2009, accessed August 16, 2018, http://www.epgn.com/news/obituaries/1241-3018545-rosalie -davies-70-lesbian-activist.

106. Rivers, *Radical Relations*, 86–87. For more on the history of lesbian mothers' rights groups, see Rivers, *Radical Relations*, chap. 4; Robert O. Self, *All in the Family: The Realignment of American Democracy Since the 1960s* (New York: Hill and Wang, 2012), 230–235; and Ball, *Right to Be Parents*, 36–37.

107. On the Ann Arbor group, see Rivers, *Radical Relations*, 88; for the Austin group, see child custody defense fund flyer, box 124, folder 19, LMP; for the Denver group, see letters and clippings from Ginny Yaseen's case, box 125, folder 11, LMP.

108. For more on the Risher case, see Gibson, *By Her Own Admission*; clippings in box 125, folder 2, LMP.

109. Anne J. Rowen to "Sisters and Brothers," June 15, 1981, p. 3, box 124, folder 1, LMP.

110. Untitled note, *Mom's Apple Pie*, November 1975, 4.

111. "Lesbian Mother Jeanne Jullion Lost Her Children," flyer for the March and Rally for Jobs and Justice, undated, box 124, folder 14, LMP. For more on the Jullion case, see Jeanne Jullion, *Long Way Home: The Odyssey of a Lesbian Mother and Her Children* (San Francisco: Cleis Press, 1985); clippings in box 124, folder 14, LMP.

112. Rivers, *Radical Relations*, chap. 4.

113. See, for example, Judge Ross Campbell, "Child Custody: When One Parent Is a Homosexual," *Judge's Journal* 17, no. 2 (Spring 1978): 38–41, 51–52. Judges were also unmoved, if not irritated, by lesbian mothers' rights-based claims to privacy or equal protection. Kimberly Richman has argued that well beyond the 1980s judges continued to be resistant to lesbian mothers' arguments that they had been discriminated against in child custody rulings, perceiving such appeals as attempts to secure undeserved "special rights" and to marginalize the more fundamental rights of the children in question. Richman, *Courting Change*, 97.

114. Sandy and Madeleine were the subject of newspaper articles across the country, as well as the first documentary about a lesbian family: *Sandy and Madeleine's Family*, directed

by Sherrie Farrell, John Gordon Hill, and Peter M. Bruce (San Francisco: Multi Media Resource Center, 1973), film. For newspaper clippings on the case, see box 125, folder 5, LMP.

115. Transcript of Court's oral decision, Schuster v. Schuster and Isaacson v. Isaacson, Nos. 36868–7 (Wash. Super. Ct. King County, Sept. 3 1974), p. 5, box 196, folder 10, LMP.

116. Schuster v. Schuster, 585 P.2d 130 (Wash. 1978). For a much more detailed description of the case, see Ball, *Right to Be Parents*, chap. 1.

117. E. R. Shipp, "A Lesbian Who Won Child Custody Battle," *New York Times*, September 5, 1980, B9; Jil Clark, "Activist Lesbian Mother Wins N.J. Custody Battle," *Gay Community News*, August 16, 1980, 1, 6.

118. "Major Court Decision Allows Lesbian Mother to Retain Custody," *Gay Community News*, February 3, 1979, 1, 6, at 6. On one of the earlier rulings, see "Michigan Judge Rules Lesbian Mother Unfit in Ann Arbor Custody Case," *Gaysweek*, March 13, 1978, 6. For additional clippings and Brief in Support for Leave to Appeal, see box 196, folder 8, LMP.

119. Hitchens, *Lesbian Mother Litigation Manual*, 27.

120. Marie-Amélie George, "The Custody Crucible: The Development of Scientific Authority About Gay and Lesbian Parents," *Law and History Review* 34, no. 2 (May 2016): 487–529, at 496.

121. Nancy Polikoff notes that scholars' estimates of the number of gay and lesbian custody cases vary by several million; Nancy D. Polikoff, "Raising Children: Lesbian and Gay Parents Face the Public and the Courts," in *Creating Change: Sexuality, Public Policy, and Civil Rights*, ed. John D'Emilio, William B. Turner, and Urvashi Vaid (New York: St. Martin's Press, 2000), 305–335, at 306.

122. Nancy Meany, "A Letter," *Mom's Apple Pie*, July/August 1979, 3.

123. "Mother Wins in Court, Loses to Poverty," *Mom's Apple Pie*, January 1977, 7.

124. Lisa, "About Me," *Mom's Apple Pie*, February 1979, 6.

125. Unaddressed letter (part of series of correspondence with Del Martin), January n.d., 1979, p. 6, box 25, folder 5, LMP.

126. Unaddressed letter (part of series of correspondence with Del Martin), December 1, 1978, p. 1, box 25, folder 5, LMP.

Chapter 8

1. Julius Fast and Hal Wells, *Bisexual Living* (New York: M. Evans, 1975), 26; emphasis in the original.

2. Fast and Wells, *Bisexual Living*, 7. Julius Fast, *Body Language* (New York: M. Evans, 1970). *Body Language* ranked eighth on *Publishers Weekly*'s list of best-selling nonfiction in 1970; see Michael Korda, *Making the List: A Cultural History of the American Bestseller, 1900–1999* (New York: Barnes and Noble, 2001), 153.

3. Fast and Wells, *Bisexual Living*, 29.

4. Ibid., 46.

5. Garber, *Vice Versa*, 27.

6. Enid Nemy, "The Woman Homosexual: More Assertive, Less Willing to Hide," *New York Times*, November 17, 1969, 62.

7. See "Judy Klemesrud, N.Y. Times Writer," *Chicago Tribune*, October 15, 1985, sec. 2, 7.

8. Judy Klemesrud, "The Disciples of Sappho, Updated," *New York Times Magazine*, March 28, 1971, 38, 41–42, 44, 46, 48, 50, 52, at 46, 45.

9. Marge Piercy, *Small Changes* (New York: Ballantine, 1973), 511.

10. Alix Kates Shulman, *Burning Questions* (New York: Knopf, 1978), 282.

11. Carol Anne Douglas, *To the Cleveland Station* (Tallahassee, FL: Naiad Press, 1982). Black reviewers disapproved of Douglas's troubling depiction of a white lesbian as a black lesbian's savior. See, for example, Cheryl Clarke, Jewelle L. Gomez, Evelynn Hammonds, Bonnie Johnson, and Linda Powell, "Conversations and Questions: Black Women on Black Women Writers," *Conditions: Nine* 3, no. 3 (Spring 1983): 88–137.

12. Ann Allen Shockley, *Loving Her* (Indianapolis: Bobbs-Merrill, 1974); Sheila Ortiz Taylor, *Faultline* (Tallahassee, FL: Naiad, 1982).

13. On the novel's importance for black lesbians, see Jewelle Gomez, "A Cultural Legacy Denied and Discovered: Black Lesbians in Fiction by Women," in *Homegirls: A Black Feminist Anthology*, ed. Barbara Smith (New York: Kitchen Table, Women of Color Press, 1983), 110–123; Alice Walker, review of *Loving Her*, by Ann Allen Shockley, *Ms.*, April 1975, 120–124.

14. On the novel's challenge to black nationalist politics, see Alycee J. Lane, foreword to *Loving Her*, by Ann Allen Shockley (1974; Boston: Northeastern University Press, 1997), v–xvi; Madhu Dubey, *Black Women Novelists and the Nationalist Aesthetic* (Bloomington: Indiana University Press, 1994), 152–153.

15. Maythee Rojas, "Shaking Up *La Familia*: The Chican@ Nation and Lesbian Mother-hood in Sheila Ortiz Taylor's *Faultline*," *Women's Studies* 45, no. 2 (2016): 142–161.

16. The literature on *The Color Purple*—both the novel and Steven Spielberg's film adaptation of it (which I have not discussed in this chapter as Celie and Shug's sexual relationship is all but erased)—is vast. For descriptions of the controversy it inspired (particularly the film, but the novel as well) due to its negative representations of black men, see: E. R. Shipp, "Blacks in Heated Debate over *The Color Purple*," *New York Times*, January 27, 1986, A13; Jacqueline Bobo, "Sifting Through the Controversy: Reading *The Color Purple*," *Callaloo* 12, no. 39 (Spring 1989): 332–342; and Cheryl B. Butler, "*The Color Purple* Controversy: Black Woman Spectatorship," *Wide Angle* 13, no. 3–4 (1991): 62–69.

17. For Walker's ideas about the term "lesbian" and her preferred term, "womanist," see Alice Walker, review of *Gifts of Power: The Writings of Rebecca Jackson (1795–1871), Black Visionary, Shaker Eldress*, ed. Jean McMahon Humez, *Black Scholar* 12, no. 5 (September/October 1981): 64–67, at 67. On black lesbian feminists' mixed reactions to Walker's decision not to use the word "lesbian," see Clarke et al., "Conversations and Questions," 121–124.

18. Walker, *Color Purple*, 220.

19. Ibid.

20. bell hooks, "Reading and Resistance: *The Color Purple*," in *Alice Walker: Critical Perspectives Past and Present*, ed. Henry Louis Gates Jr. and K. A. Appiah (New York: Amistad, 1993), 284–295.

21. Joanne S. Frye, *Living Stories, Telling Lives: Women and the Novel in Contemporary Experience* (Ann Arbor: University of Michigan Press, 1986); Gayle S. Greene, *Changing the Story: Feminist Fiction and the Tradition* (Bloomington: Indiana University Pres, 1991); Lisa Marie Hogeland, *Feminism and Its Fictions: The Consciousness-Raising Novel and the Women's Liberation Movement* (Philadelphia: University of Pennsylvania Press, 1998); and Jane F. Gerhard, *Desiring Revolution: Second-Wave Feminism and the Rewriting of American Sexual Thought, 1920 to1982* (New York: Columbia University Press, 2001), chap. 4.

22. Zimmerman, *Safe Sea of Women*, 20–21; emphasis in the original.

23. Christine Holmlund, "When Is a Lesbian Not a Lesbian? The Lesbian Continuum and the Mainstream Femme Film," *Camera Obscura* 9, no. 25–26 (January–May 1991): 144–180.

24. For feminist film scholarly critiques, see, for example, Chris Straayer, "The Hypothetical Lesbian Heroine," *Jump Cut*, 35 (April 1990), 50–57; Mandy Merck, "'Lianna' and the Lesbians of Art Cinema," in *Films for Women*, ed. Charlotte Brunsdon (London: British Film Institute, 1986), 166–175; and Cindy Patton, "The Cum Shot: 3 Takes on Lesbian and Gay Sexuality," *Out/Look* 1, no. 3 (Fall 1988): 72–22.

25. For positive reviews of *Lianna* in the feminist and gay press, see, for example, Carrie Thorn, "*Lianna* Comes Out in the Movies," *WomaNews*, 4 no. 3 (March 1983): 14; "Review: *Lianna*," *Gay Community News*, February 19, 1983, 7, 9. On lesbian demand for copies of these films in VHS format, see, "Desert Hearts Video, Naiad Diversifies!," *Feminist Bookstore News* 9, no. 1 (September/October 1986): 59.

26. B. Ruby Rich, "Desert Heat," *Village Voice*, April 8, 1986, 72–73.

27. Denise Kulp, "Whatever's for Us: Lesbians in Popular Culture," *off our backs* 16, no. 6 (June 1986): 24–25.

28. Shelley Samuels, interview by the author, January 3, 2014.

29. David Lynne, *The Bisexual Woman: A Timely Examination of Lesbians Trapped in Conventional Marriages* (New York: Midwood, 1967).

30. Roger Blake, *The Bi-Sexual Female* (Cleveland, OH: Ambassador Books, 1968), 1. "Frenched" was a slag term for oral sex, commonly used in the 1960s.

31. For a survey of the field of "alternative lifestyles," including literature on swinging and other marital alternatives, see Roger H. Rubin, "Alternative Lifestyles Revisited, or Whatever Happened to Swingers, Group Marriages, and Communes?," *Journal of Family Issues* 22, no. 6 (September 2001): 711–726. For emblematic edited collections on marital alternatives, see Joann S. DeLora and Jack R. DeLora, eds., *Intimate Life Styles: Marriage and Its Alternatives* (Pacific Palisades, CA: Goodyear, 1972); James R. Smith and Lynn G. Smith, eds., *Beyond Monogamy: Recent Studies of Sexual Alternatives in Marriage* (Baltimore: Johns Hopkins University Press, 1974).

32. James W. Ramey, "Emerging Patterns of Behavior in Marriage: Deviations or Innovations?," *Journal of Sex Research* 8, no. 1 (February 1972): 6–30, at 14.

33. George C. O'Neill and Nena O'Neill, "Patterns in Group Sexual Activity," *Journal of Sex Research* 6, no. 2 (May 1970): 101–112.

34. Charles Palson and Rebecca Palson, "Swinging in Wedlock," *Society* 9, no. 4 (February 1972): 28–37, at 30.

35. For research describing such behavior as "homosexual," see Palson and Palson, "Swinging in Wedlock"; Charles A. Varni, "An Exploratory Study of Spouse Swapping," in Smith and Smith, *Beyond Monogamy*, 246–259.

36. Ramey, "Emerging Patterns," 15.

37. O'Neill and O'Neill, "Patterns in Group Sexual Activity," 107.

38. Ibid., 108.

39. Ramey, "Emerging Patterns," 15.

40. Carolyn Symonds, "Sexual Mate-Swapping: Violation of Norms and Reconciliation of Guilt," in *Studies in the Psychology of Sex*, ed. James M. Henslin (New York: Appleton-Century-Crofts, 1971), 81–109, 96–97.

41. Gilbert D. Bartell, *Group Sex: A Scientist's Eyewitness Report on the American Way of Swinging* (New York: Peter H. Wyden, 1971), 151.

42. Ibid., 152–153.

43. Interestingly, Bartell included this statistic in an earlier article but not in his book; see Gilbert Bartell, "Group Sex Among the Mid-Americans," *Journal of Sex Research* 6, no. 2 (May 1970): 113–130, at 128.

44. Bartell, *Group Sex*, 154.

45. Brian G. Gilmartin, *The Gilmartin Report* (Secaucus, NJ: Citadel Press, 1978), 262.

46. Ibid.

47. See, for example, ibid., 265; emphasis added.

48. Ibid., 264.

49. Paul Rubenstein and Herbert Margolis, *The Groupsex Tapes* (New York: David McKay, 1971), 50.

50. Ibid., 51.

51. Richard Warren Lewis, "The Swingers," *Playboy*, April 1969, 149–150, 216–228, at 221.

52. "The American Way of Swinging," *Time*, February 1971, 51; Enid Nemy, "Group Sex: Is It 'Life Art' or a Sign That Something Is Wrong?," *New York Times*, May 10, 1971, 38; Bill Hazlett, "Swinging: Exactly What Is It? Who Takes Part? Why?" *Los Angeles Times*, May 16, 1971, OC1, 8, 9; and "Group Sex," *Newsweek*, June 21, 1971, 89–89.

53. Michael Tolkin, "Sex with the Proper Swinger," *Village Voice*, November 28, 1977, 1, 27–30, at 29.

54. Jane Margold, "Bisexuality: The Newest Sex-Style," *Cosmopolitan*, June 21, 1974, 189–192, at 189.

55. Ibid., 190.

56. Ibid., 192.

57. Ibid., 190.

58. Korda, *Making the List*, 159. On Robbins's career, see Andrew Wilson, *Harold Robbins: The Man Who Invented Sex* (London: Bloomsbury, 2007).

59. Harold Robbins, *The Lonely Lady* (New York: Simon and Schuster, 1976), 416.

60. Korda, *Making the List*, 160.

61. Erica Jong, *How to Save Your Own Life* (New York: Holt, Rinehart and Winston, 1977), 154.

62. Ibid., 152.

63. Ibid., 149.

64. On these changes and the rise of "porno chic" in the 1970s, see D'Emilio and Freedman, *Intimate Matters*, 327–328; Whitney Strub, *Perversion for Profit: The Politics of Pornography and the Rise of the New Right* (New York: Columbia University Press, 2010), chap. 5; and Carolyn Bronstein and Whitney Strub, eds., *Porno Chic and the Sex Wars: American Sexual Representation in the 1970s* (Amherst: University of Massachusetts Press, 2016).

65. *Sin in the Suburbs*, directed by Joseph Sarno (1964; Seattle, WA: Something Weird Video, 2004), DVD. See Heather Butler, "What Do You Call a Lesbian with Long Fingers? The Development of Lesbian and Dyke Pornography," in *Porn Studies*, ed. Linda Williams (Durham, NC: Duke University Press, 2004), 167–197.

66. *The Lickerish Quartet*, directed by Radley Metzger (1970; New York: First Run Features, 2005), DVD. *Score*, directed by Radley Metzger (1972; New York: First Run Features, 1999), DVD.

67. Butler, "Lesbian with Long Fingers," 174; *The Private Afternoons of Pamela Mann*, directed by Henry Paris [Radley Metzger] (1974; United States: VideoXpix, 2011), DVD.

68. *Just the Two of Us*, directed by Barbara Peeters and Jacque Deerson (1975; New Almaden, CA: Wolfe Video, 2007), DVD. On Barbara Peeters's career and activism in the film industry, see Maya Montañez Smukler, *Liberating Hollywood: Women Directors and the Feminist Reform of 1970s American Cinema* (New Brunswick, NJ: Rutgers University Press, 2018).

69. Jane E. Brody, "Bisexual Life-Style Appears to Be Spreading and Not Necessarily Among 'Swingers,'" *New York Times*, March 24, 1974, 57.

70. "The New Bisexuals," *Time*, May 13, 1974, 79.

71. Jurate Kazickas, "Bisexuality: A Phase or an Alternative Lifestyle?," *Daytona Beach Morning Journal*, April 12, 1974, 7a.

72. Ann Landers, "Bisexual Wife Has the Problem, but He Needs Further Counseling," *Star-News*, September 23, 1975, 6.

73. Ann Landers, "Bisexual Wife Shares Her Side of the Story," *Times Daily*, December 27, 1979, 9.

74. Judy Klemesrud, "Underground Book Brings Fame to a Lesbian Author," *New York Times*, September 26, 1977, L38.

75. Rita Mae Brown, *Rubyfruit Jungle* (Plainfield, VT: Daughters, Inc., 1973), 173.

76. Mary Gordon, *Final Payments* (New York: Random House, 1978), 239–240.

77. Jane DeLynn, *Some Do* (New York: MacMillan,1978), 137, 174.

78. Ibid., 341.

79. Jo Eadie has argued that bisexual women are often portrayed in film as socially disruptive in some sense; Jo Eadie, "'That's Why She Is Bisexual': Contexts for Bisexual Visibility," in Bi Academic Intervention, *Bisexual Imaginary*, 142–160, at 155.

80. On bisexual film characters as victims of violence, see Wayne M. Bryant, *Bisexual Characters in Film: From Anaïs to Zee* (New York: Haworth Press, 2009), chap. 6.

81. *Doctors' Wives*, directed by M. J. Frankovitch (1971; Culver City, CA: Sony Pictures Home Entertainment, 2010), DVD.

82. *They Only Kill Their Masters*, directed by James Goldstone (1972; Burbank, CA: Warner Home Video, 2009), DVD.

83. *Lenny*, directed by Bob Fosse (1974; Santa Monica, CA: MGM Home Entertainment, 2002), DVD.

84. Roger Ebert, review of *Lenny*, directed by Bob Fosse, RogerEbert.com, date unknown, accessed August 16, 2018, http://www.rogerebert.com/reviews/lenny-1974.

85. *Manhattan*, directed by Woody Allen (1979; Santa Monica, CA: MGM Home Entertainment, 2000), DVD. Interestingly, *Manhattan* did serve as a cultural touchstone for at least one man whose wife left him for a new lesbian life. See Shelley Samuels, interview by the author, January 3, 2014.

86. Margaret Mead, "Bisexuality: What's It All About?," *Redbook*, January 1975, 29, 31, at 29.

87. Ibid., 31.

88. Pepper Schwartz and Philip Blumstein, "Bisexuals: Where Love Speaks Louder Than Labels," *Ms.*, November 1976, 80–81. See also Philip W. Blumstein and Pepper Schwartz, "Bisexuality in Women," *Archives of Sexual Behavior* 5, no. 2 (March 1976): 171–181.

89. Bode, *View from Another Closet*, 33.

90. Charlotte Wolff, *Bisexuality: A Study* (1977; repr., London: Quartet Books, 1979), 109. On the significance of Wolff's work, see Toni Brennan and Peter Hegarty, "Charlotte Wolff's Contribution to Bisexual History and to (Sexuality) Theory and Research: A Reappraisal for Queer Times," *Journal of the History of Sexuality* 21, no. 1 (January 2012): 141–161.

91. Klein, *Bisexual Option.*

92. Bode, *View from Another Closet*, 125; on the bisexual women's rap group see 28.

93. Ibid., 96.

94. Orlando, "Bisexuality: A Choice Not an Echo?," *Ms.*, October 1978, 60–62, 70–72, 75, at 75.

95. Elissa M., "The Path to Bisexuality: A Story," *BBWN* [later *Bi-Women*]: *The Newsletter of the Boston Bisexual Women's Network* 2, no. 6 (November–December 1984): 1–2, 7–8, at 7.

96. Ibid., 8.

97. Natalie Bacon, "Who Am I?," *Bi-Women: The Newsletter of the Boston Bisexual Women's Network* 5, no. 1 (February/March, 1987): 1–2; reprinted from *Bi-Lines*, November 1986.

98. Jay Ziskin and Mae Ziskin, *The Extra-Marital Sex Contract* (Los Angeles: Nash, 1973), 167–168.

99. Douglas, *To the Cleveland Station*, 7.

100. Clare Hemmings, "Bisexual Theoretical Perspectives: Emergent and Contingent Relationships," in Bi Academic Intervention, *Bisexual Imaginary*, 14–37, at 30.

Epilogue

1. Elizabeth Gilbert, *Eat, Pray, Love: One Woman's Search for Everything Across Italy, India and Indonesia* (New York: Viking, 2006); Glennon Doyle Melton, *Love Warrior* (New York: Flatiron, 2016); the author is now known as Glennon Doyle.

2. Elizabeth Gilbert, "ME & RAYYA," Facebook, September 7, 2016, accessed March 13, 2017, https://www.facebook.com/GilbertLiz/posts/1107564732658974:0.

3. Glennon Doyle Melton, "Love Wins Part One," Facebook, November 13, 2016, accessed March 13, 2017, https://www.facebook.com/glennondoylemelton/posts/101547038 03624710:0.

4. Alexandra Topping, " 'Love Is Always Complicated': Elizabeth Gilbert and the Rise of Later-in-Life Lesbians," *Guardian*, September 9, 2016, accessed September 9, 2018, https://www.theguardian.com/world/2016/sep/09/love-is-always-complicated-elizabeth-gilbert-and-the-rise-of-later-in-life-lesbians.

5. Dr. Jennelle, "Why Elizabeth Gilbert and I Are the Worst Lesbians Ever—Answer: Because We're Not Lesbians," *Dr. Jennelle* (blog), undated, accessed September 9, 2018, http://www.drjennelle.com/worst-lesbians-ever/.

6. Ibid.

7. Celebrities commonly listed alongside Gilbert and Melton for their sexual fluidity include Cynthia Nixon and Portia de Rossi.

8. Lisa M. Diamond, *Sexual Fluidity: Understanding Women's Love and Desire*, (Cambridge, MA: Harvard University Press, 2008).

9. Katie Heaney, "Is Sexual Fluidity Actually on the Rise?" *Cosmopolitan*, March 27, 2017, accessed September 9, 2018, https://www.cosmopolitan.com/sex-love/a9156810/sexual -fluidity-what-to-know/.

10. Susie Orbach, "Why Elizabeth Gilbert's Story of Love and Illness Finds an Echo with So Many of Us," *Guardian*, September 9, 2016, accessed September 9, 2018, https://www.theguardian.com/commentisfree/2016/sep/09/eat-pray-love-sex-elizabeth-gilbert.

11. Barbee J. Cassingham and Sally M. O'Neil, *And Then I Met This Woman: Previously Married Women's Journeys into Lesbian Relationships* (Racine, WI: Mother Courage Press, 1993). The book was reprinted in an expanded and revised edition: Barbee J. Cassingham and Sally M. O'Neil, *And Then I Met This Woman: Previously Married Women's Journeys into Lesbian Relationships* (Freeland, WA: Soaring Eagle, 1999).

12. Abbott and Farmer, *From Wedded Wife to Lesbian Life.*

13. Carren Strock, *Married Women Who Love Women* (Los Angeles, CA: Alyson Books, 1998). Citations are from Carren Strock, *Married Women Who Love Women* (New York: Routledge, 2008). Other, related publications do not focus specifically on married women but include a significant number of formerly or still married women's stories. See Robin McCoy, *Late Bloomers: Awakening to Lesbianism After Forty* (San Jose, CA: Writers Club, 2000); Candace Walsh and Laura Andre, eds., *Dear John, I Love Jane: Women Write About Leaving Men for Women* (Berkeley, CA: Seal Press, 2010).

14. "Wives Who Confess They Are Gay," *The Oprah Winfrey Show*, aired October 2, 2006, on ABC. See also Courtney Nelson, "Oprah Examines the Coming Out Process for Married Women," After Ellen, October 3, 2006, accessed September 9, 2016, https://www.afterellen.com/tv/4175-oprah-examines-the-coming-out-process-for-married-women.

15. For biographical details about Fleischer, see Joanne Fleisher, *Living Two Lives: Married to a Man and in Love with a Woman* (Los Angeles: Alyson Books, 2005), xvi-xvii; Joanne Fleisher, "Married to a Man and in Love with a Woman," *Huffington Post*, February 2, 2012, accessed March 21, 2017, http://www.huffingtonpost.com/joanne-fleisher/joanne-fleisher_b_2367892.html.

16. Cassingham and O'Neil, *And Then I Met This Woman*, 216.

17. For a critique of Diamond's book, see Jane Ward, *Not Gay: Sex Between Straight White Men* (New York: New York University Press, 2015), 12–21. Though the term "queer" might be a more appealing label for such women, this word figures significantly only in Walsh and Andre, *Dear John*, which is geared toward a younger audience and consists of the stories of Gen Xers rather than their parents or grandparents. See, for example, Lisa M. Diamond, foreword to Walsh and Andre, *Dear John*, 7–10, at 10.

18. Fleisher, *Living Two Lives*, 138.

19. Ibid. For similar examples, see Cassingham and O'Neil, *And Then I Met This Woman*, 1–8, 57–68; Abbott and Farmer, *From Wedded Wife to Lesbian Life*, 85–90.

20. Strock, *Married Women Who Love Women*,147.

21. JoAnn Loulan, foreword to Fleisher, *Living Two Lives*, xi–xiv, at xiv.

22. Cassingham and O'Neil, *And Then I Met This Woman*, 234.

23. Strock, *Married Women Who Love Women*, 229.

24. "Common Abbreviations," Ask Joanne, December 14, 2010, accessed March 14, 2017, https://askjoanne.forums.net/thread/18/common-abbreviations. See also Walsh and Andre, *Dear John*, 13.

25. As historian Judith M. Bennett writes in describing this "patriarchal equilibrium," "There has been much change in women's lives, but little transformation in women's status in relation to men." Judith M. Bennett, *History Matters: Patriarchy and the Challenge of Feminism* (Philadelphia: University of Pennsylvania Press, 2006), 79.

26. Abigail Geiger and Kim Parker, "For Women's History Month, a Look at Gender Gains—and Gaps—in the U.S.," Pew Research Center, March 15, 2018, accessed September 6, 2018, http://www.pewresearch.org/fact-tank/2018/03/15/for-womens-history-month-a-look-at-gender-gains-and-gaps-in-the-u-s/.

27. On lesbian mothers' continued custody struggles, see Ball, *Right to Be Parents*, 57; Nancy D. Polikoff, "Custody Rights of Lesbian and Gay Parents Redux: The Irrelevance of Constitutional Principles," *UCLA Law Review Discourse* 60 (2013): 226–239.

28. Sharon Otterman, "When Living Your Truth Can Mean Losing Your Children," *New York Times*, May 25, 2018, accessed August 24, 2018, https://www.nytimes.com/2018/05/25/nyregion/orthodox-jewish-divorce-custody-ny.html.

29. Tattercoats, comment on "Indecision," Ask Joanne, October 26, 2016, accessed August 24, 2018, https://askjoanne.forums.net/thread/5319/indecision.

30. Grrrl, comment on "Needing Advice," Ask Joanne, December 9, 2016, accessed August 24, 2018, https://askjoanne.forums.net/thread/5355/needing-advice.

31. Christine Florky, interview by the author, December 18, 2013; Mary Davidson, interview by the author, December 18, 2013.

32. Pam Folts, interview by the author, January 17, 2014.

33. J. Lapis Springtree, interview by the author, April 10, 2014. See also, Leah, interview by the author, January 7, 2014; Anonymous, interview by the author, October 23, 2015.

34. For political critiques of the self-help industry, particularly as it relates to feminist issues, see Susan Faludi, *Backlash: The Undeclared War Against American Women* (New York: Crown, 1991), chap. 12; Elayne Rapping, *The Culture of Recovery: Making Sense of the Self-Help Movement in Women's Lives* (Boston: Beacon Press, 1996); and Dana L. Cloud, *Control and Consolation in American Culture and Politics: Rhetoric of Therapy* (Thousand Oaks, CA: SAGE Publications, 1998).

INDEX

ACKNOWLEDGMENTS

For years I have dreamt about the end of this project, and the moment when I would sit down and thank the many people and institutions who made it possible. It is strange and wonderful to finally be able to do that now. This project began a decade ago in the History Department at New York University. It would not exist without Linda Gordon's generous guidance and support. Linda is not only a tremendous scholar, but also a kind and thoughtful mentor. I am deeply grateful to her for inspiring this project and encouraging me to find my voice. Michele Mitchell, Andrew Needham, John D'Emilio, and Steven Mintz all provided feedback that proved integral as I set about writing the book. I cannot imagine making it through the lonely years of writing without the support and encouragement of my fellow "nerd club" members Melissa Milewski, Lilly Tuttle, Peter Wirzbicki, Natalie Blum-Ross, and Dylan Yeats. I am so thankful to have had them all as colleagues and friends so early on.

Critical funding from many institutions has helped to make this book possible. I received support from a MacCracken Fellowship from the Graduate School of Arts and Sciences at New York University; an Andrew W. Mellon Dissertation Fellowship in the Humanities from New York University's History Department; a Phil Zwickler Memorial Research Grant from the Human Sexuality Collection at Cornell University; a Travel-to-Collections award from the Sophia Smith Collection at Smith College; and a Dissertation Fellowship in Women's Studies from the Woodrow Wilson Foundation. Additional funding enabled me to develop the book: a Mary Lily Research Grant from the Sallie Bingham Center for Women's History and Culture at Duke University; a Faculty Seed Grant from the Institute for Research on Women and Gender at the University of Michigan; and a Humanities Research Award from the College of Liberal Arts at the University of Texas at Austin.

I was tremendously lucky to have been awarded a postdoctoral fellowship in the Society of Fellows at the University of Michigan. This project benefited immensely from the support I received there. My team of formal and informal mentors—Dena Goodman, Nadine Hubbs, Sara McClelland, and Valerie Traub—provided invaluable professional guidance and key insights that helped to deepen my thinking about marriage and women's same-sex desires. I thank them for advocating for me and for this project. Regina Morantz-Sanchez generously read my manuscript and pushed me to broaden my claims. Matthew Lassiter read and commented on my entire body of work and challenged me to think more about the role of the state in this story. Many other scholars at Michigan generously shared their time and expertise with me as I revised this project: Kathleen Canning, Elizabeth Cole, David Halperin, Donald Lopez, and Scott Spector. Thank you also to postdoctoral fellows Sarah Loebman, Jennifer Nelson, Martha Sprigge, and Damon Young for their critical feedback, friendship, and encouragement.

I feel so thankful to have found a home in the wonderfully supportive American Studies Department at the University of Texas at Austin. My colleagues in American studies, history, women's and gender studies, and LGBTQ studies have helped to nurture my career, and they have enriched this project in countless ways. Thank you in particular to Ann Cvetkovich, Janet Davis, Laurie Green, Courtney Handman, Susan Heinzelman, Steven Hoelscher, Randolph Lewis, Lisa Moore, and Sam Vong for their support and mentorship.

Many other people have helped me with this project by sharing knowledge and resources, asking hard questions, and encouraging me along the way. Thank you to Sujay Pandit, Einav Rabinovitch-Fox, Whitney Strub, Stephen Vider, and Cookie Woolner. I am also grateful to those who organized and participated in workshops and conference panels where I shared early drafts of this work. Opportunities to present at the American Historical Association, the Center for LGBTQ Studies at the City University of New York Graduate Center, and the Yale Research Initiative on the History of Sexualities improved this book immeasurably.

I have benefited from invaluable assistance at many stages in researching this project. To begin with, I am indebted to the many women whose stories are captured in this book. I am grateful to them for taking the time to speak with me or other scholars, and for sharing their very personal histories and experiences. Thank you to the archivists at the Human Sexuality Collection at Cornell University Library, the ONE National Gay and

Lesbian Archives at the University of Southern California Libraries, the Schlesinger Library at the Radcliffe Institute, the New York Public Library, and the Lesbian Herstory Archives. Thank you in particular to Nichole Calero and Amy Hague at the Sophia Smith Collection, and Patricia Delara and Rebekah Kim at the GLBT Historical Society. Sidney Schubarth, Callum Goulet, and Kathryn Martinez painstakingly transcribed oral history interviews for me, and Emma Maniere served as a research assistant in a pinch on more than one occasion. She also generously read and provided feedback on a draft of the book.

I am also thankful for the opportunity I've had to work with the University of Pennsylvania Press. Bob Lockhart and Margot Canaday saw promise in this project at a very early stage. They supported and guided me through the years-long process of revision and editing. The Press's two outside reviewers, who later identified themselves as Heather Murray and Rebecca Davis, provided invaluable insights and key critiques, which helped me to sharpen and clarify my arguments and prose. Thank you also to Gwen Burda and Lily Palladino for their hard work and patience in copyediting the manuscript.

Portions of this book appeared earlier in print. An earlier version of Chapter 4 appeared in *Gender and History* 24, no. 2 (August 2012): 475–501. Parts of Chapters 2 and 6 appeared in the *Journal of Social History* 46, no. 1 (Fall 2012): 1–22.

My friends and family have been tireless supporters through the ups and downs of writing and research. Thank you to the many friends who provided housing, transport, food, and fun on research trips to Ithaca, Boston, Northampton, and Los Angeles. Gill Frank has engaged with this project since the beginning, providing feedback and guidance at every stage. I am grateful for his continued mentorship and friendship. Elizabeth Lee has been a constant writing companion, cheerleader, therapist, and editor throughout graduate school and ever since. I am so thankful for her daily chats, her wisdom, and her ability to see the positive in every possible situation. My parents, Burt and Pam Gutterman, have encouraged my career at every turn. Thank you to my mom especially, for her help with childcare on research trips, at conferences, and during the final writing push. And I can't imagine making it through the last year of revisions without the daily help and support of my mother-in-law, Connie Jang. Thank you also to my sisters, Morgan Gutterman and Caryn Constantinides, and to my brother-in-law, Leslie Constantinides, for keeping me grounded, pushing me forward, and making me smile. Caryn also designed the beautiful cover art.

My greatest thanks go to my partner, Patty Jang, who read every draft of every chapter of this book dozens of times and never complained. She has enabled this book in so many ways, providing research assistance, tech support, a critical eye, and emotional encouragement. While I sat endlessly in front of my computer in the decade it has taken me to finish this project, she did everything else needed to make our family life possible, from caring for our children to organizing cross-country moves. Thank you as well to our amazing kids, Audra and Jay. They have done nothing at all to speed along this book's progress, but they have done roughly ten million things to make me laugh. I love them more than I can say.